Poetry Los Angeles

Poetry Los Angeles

READING THE ESSENTIAL POEMS OF THE CITY

Laurence Goldstein

Ann Arbor
The University of Michigan Press

Published in the United States of America by
The University of Michigan Press
Manufactured in the United States of America
♾ Printed on acid-free paper

2017 2016 2015 2014 4 3 2 1

A CIP catalog record for this book is available from the British Library.
ISBN 978-0-472-07224-8 (cloth : alk. paper)
ISBN 978-0-472-05224-0 (paper : alk. paper)
ISBN 978-0-472-12041-3 (e-book)

To my wife
Nancy Goldstein
And in memory of my parents
Cecil Goldstein and Helen Goldstein

Let us imagine, for example, a landscape whose combined vastness and definitiveness—whose united beauty, magnificence and *strangeness,* shall convey the idea of care, or culture, or superintendence on the part of beings superior, yet akin to humanity—then the sentiment of *interest* is preserved, while the art intervolved is made to assume the air of an intermediate or secondary nature—a nature which is not God, nor an emanation from God, but which still is nature in the sense of the handiwork of the angels that hover between man and God.

EDGAR ALLAN POE, "THE DOMAIN OF ARNHEIM"

City of angles, saxes, jukes. Of singles, sex, and jewels.
Of the Lost and Jealous. The Angelless. L./Aliens.
Shangri-L.A. El Lay Grande. The LA-byrinth, sick of tryin',
With centers everywhere, like Pascal's God, in plazas and pavilions,
Minimalls for drive-bys, drive-ups, minimaulings,
Carjackings, gangbangings, gaudy private compounds . . .
"Uh-huh, this is Lozengeles," as my polyglot,
My exiled, suave, intensely hoarse Iraqi friend observes.
What are the limits of its mesh and mess?

STEPHEN YENSER, "LOS ANGELES FRACTALS"

Contents

Preface

In his picaresque narrative of 1982, *Californians: Searching for the Golden State,* the distinguished novelist James D. Houston wrote the following: "Los Angeles is a region of the mind, still fed by all the legends we know so well, by all the movies still filmed here, and the countless novels set here—Hollywood novels, detective and police novels, decadence and drug novels, Malibu novels, family sagas—and by all the songs."[1] As with so many evocations of the city's crazy-quilt identity, I found something missing in this catalogue when I read *Californians* upon publication. It's the same element missing in virtually every writer's list of cultural products giving character and imagery to Los Angeles. There is no reference, here or elsewhere in Houston's book, to poetry.

The neglect of poetry has become a too-familiar topic in contemporary literary criticism, even as hard data confirm rising support for the lyric medium. But verse has been more than marginalized in the discourse of Los Angeles. There has seemed to exist in this country a conspiracy of silence, as if the media obsession with other literary and art forms in Southern California has intentionally suppressed the once-privileged Orphic voice. Of course, no conspiracy exists. Houston did not take orders from some Pynchon-like secret society devoted to erasing poetry from the public imagination. But he confirmed my suspicion that overlooking poems about Los Angeles had become a reflexive habit of modern publishing, widespread among literary critics, editors of anthologies, historians and sociologists, and even some poets. I made notes in response to Houston's book, thinking that my professional grievance might lead someday to an essay, or at least an op-ed column for the *Los Angeles Times*. Taking offense is one mother of invention, and I credit the seed planted by Houston's disregard for starting me on the long quest that ended in this book-length study of poems about Los Angeles.

In 1982 I was searching for a challenging book topic, having published a few years earlier a scholarly work titled *Ruins and Empire: The Evolution of a Theme in Augustan and Romantic Literature*. In that study of how writers in all genres had engaged the topic of decayed monuments and spoiled natural landscapes, I surveyed a series of texts beginning with Edmund Spenser's and John Dyer's laments upon the ruins of Rome, proceeding to William Wordsworth's anxiety that his beloved Lake District was falling victim to greedy developers and rapacious politicians, and ending with Thomas Cole's recognition in his poetry and paintings that the course, and negative consequences, of empire had established themselves in America as permanent facts of national consciousness. Always interested in the poetry of place, I surprised myself by entering so deeply into a subject so melancholy. Someday, I promised myself, I would turn my attention to a cheerful topic more in keeping with my upbringing and temperament. Little did I suspect that the dystopian vision of decline and disaster I studied in *Ruins and Empire* would recur so prominently in the literature of Southern California.

As the reader will guess, I was raised in Los Angeles, or more specifically in Culver City, an enclave of the metropolis. One doesn't think of one's hometown as anything special while growing up there; it's just the place you live till either high school or college graduation sets you free. After earning a B.A. from UCLA in 1965 I left California for graduate study at Brown University and then a teaching job at the University of Michigan. I underwent the exile's fate of becoming increasingly fascinated by the place I had left behind, realizing as I absorbed more of the general cultural fixation on Los Angeles that in fact I *had* lived in a locale of enormous significance for the past, present, and future history of the U.S. and the world. I visited often, spending summers and sabbaticals, and reading as much California literature as I could. I began to keep a folder of poems about the city, and to teach some of the contents in introductory poetry courses and ultimately in a seminar titled "The Literature of Los Angeles." As the folder got larger and larger I despaired of writing about the general topic with the continuity and depth readers had a right to expect from such a project. I postponed composition while I studied the standard critical texts on the phenomenology and literature of cities, such as (in order of publication) Kevin Lynch's *The Image of the City*, David R. Weimer's *The City as Metaphor*, Monroe K. Spears's *Dionysus in the City*, Raymond Williams's *The Country and the City*, Burton

Pike's *The Image of the City in Modern Literature,* John H. Johnston's *The Poet and the City,* William Chapman Sharpe's *Unreal Cities,* Richard Lehan's *The City in Literature,* and Robert Alter's *Imagined Cities.* I took inspiration from case studies of American poets' involvement with the urban milieu, such as Michael Davidson's *The San Francisco Renaissance: Poetics and Community at Mid-Century,* Peter Davison's *The Fading Smile: Poets in Boston from Robert Frost to Robert Lowell to Sylvia Plath,* and David Lehman's *The Last Avant-Garde: The Making of the New York School of Poets.*

I couldn't help but notice, however, that the genre of city poetry was devolving into a lesser status in literary criticism and theory beginning in the 1980s. Modern poets had exuberantly documented their residence in or visits to cities for about a hundred years, roughly from 1857, the publication date of Charles Baudelaire's *Les Fleurs du mal* [Flowers of Evil], to the early 1960s, which welcomed the *Lunch Poems* of Frank O'Hara, *Life Studies* and *For the Union Dead* by Robert Lowell, Allen Ginsberg's two masterpieces *Howl* and *Kaddish,* and Galway Kinnell's rhapsodic evocation of the Lower East Side of Manhattan, "The Avenue Bearing the Initial of Christ into the New World." During this century the High Modernists and their heirs had defined their careers by long poems or sequences focused on the urban landscape, both in celebration and in denigration. Of course poets will continue to write poems about cities till the end of time. But the Matter of the Modern Metropolis seemed fated to lose energy and cachet no less than the Matter of Rome. The change could be measured in the way masterpieces of fiction that focused on cities, like Thomas Mann's *Death in Venice,* Andrey Bely's *Petersburg,* James Joyce's *Dubliners* and *Ulysses,* Virginia Woolf's *Mrs. Dalloway,* and John Dos Passos's *Manhattan Transfer,* had yielded the canonical center to more enigmatic and fantastical (or "magical") fiction like Samuel Beckett's *The Unnameable,* Gabriel García Márquez's *One Hundred Years of Solitude,* Vladimir Nabokov's *Pale Fire,* Toni Morrison's *Beloved,* Maxine Hong Kingston's *The Woman Warrior,* Alice Munro's *The Progress of Love,* . . . and parodic texts like Donald Barthelme's *City Life* and Italo Calvino's *Invisible Cities.*

In fiction and poetry, the fundamentally realist tradition of sustained attention to urban forms and deep immersion in questions of their meaning and effect on citizens was giving way to a different aesthetic, though one originating in the abstract constructions of modernist texts themselves. Early on, I took note of Fredric Jameson's wistful remark that new media and new habits of consumption had left readers

> with that pure and random play of signifiers which we call postmodernism, and which no longer produces monumental works of the modernist type, but ceaselessly reshuffles the fragments of preexistent texts, the building blocks of older cultural and social production, in some new and heightened bricolage: metabooks which cannibalize other books, metatexts which collate bits of other texts.[2]

So far as poetry was concerned, the experimental turn leaned ever more decisively toward disjunctive and anti-lyric forms with a minimum of sustained meditation about the textures of place and the complex reciprocal dynamics of personal engagements with urban locations. Ron Silliman argued that "non-referential" and "autonomous" language should be the common pursuit of poets and critics alike; he suggests that the principal feature of Paris is that the word "Paris" has five letters, just like "Ghana," "China," and "Spain."[3] Contemporary poets were directed to make language and textuality the central content of their post-structuralist or Conceptualist innovations. Cultural Studies absorbed some of these avant-garde strategies. Descriptions and histories of innovative work as "palimpsests" or "compost poems" (in phrases popularized by Jed Rasula),[4] or as radical reworkings of traditional forms of mimesis, appealed to me, for a while, as useful models for contemporary scholarship. After *Ruins and Empire* I published a book about the semiotics of the flying machine from Leonardo da Vinci to J. G. Ballard, and then another about the networking or sequencing of American poems, decade by decade, that responded to the cinema. At the same time, I kept filling that folder with poems about Los Angeles. I kept teaching classes about the literature of place. I edited a literary anthology, *Writing Ann Arbor,* to further educate myself in the conventions and components of urbanism.

And finally, I decided that it was time to scrutinize at length the verse composed about the American city I found most compelling. Los Angeles is "a region of the mind," as James D. Houston declared. I was not even sure how much actual territory I should claim under that name. Should I confine myself to poems located in the City of Los Angeles, and the County of Los Angeles, or scoop into my basket of readings the whole region between Santa Barbara and Orange County? Death Valley, Palm Springs, Disneyland, even Las Vegas and Tijuana, are insistent presences in poems more or less about Los Angeles, just as Cape Cod and resorts in Maine find their way into poems "about" Boston. And the so-called Inland Empire of cities, towns, and deserts east and south of Los Angeles, in San Bernardino and Riverside counties, had begun to show up in the poems of refugees from expensive coastal communities. "The Brain - is wider than the Sky -," Emily Dickinson wrote, and in the same way a "region of the mind" extends beyond city limits on a map. In any case, I'm less interested in accounting for how locales are identified in Frommer's and Fodor's guidebooks than I am in describing how poets let their imaginations roam freely and figuratively across boundaries into proximate domains readers can actually visit.

This book engages the question, Why do readers—especially editors, anthologists, and literary critics, but also essayists and fiction writers as intellectually curious as Houston—not show more interest in poems about Los Angeles? One answer: Because scholars of contemporary literature have not sufficiently defined what the essential poems about Los Angeles look like, what features they share, and what they contribute to our sense of the city's spatial being. Readers need a working anthology of worthy poems as a database accompanied by substantial commentary on those poems that establish the consanguinity of high-quality verse responses to this particular urban terrain. Such an anthology-plus would create a gallery exhibition making L.A. more real, less confusingly disjoined and decentered, as defining forms, voices, and themes come into relief by means of the revealed associations between key poems. Such poems make their contents meaningful by answering back both to the vague stereotypes fostered by the media James D. Houston enumerates *and* to academic critiques of representational poetry. *Poetry Los Angeles* intends to offer such guidance in order to make Los Angeles and its hard-working poets more visible in the canonical literature of place.

Two questions about the project persisted as I began work. First, the aforementioned hostility of vanguardist critics and poets to the traditional lyric's convention of a first-person speaker seeking to depict with steady gaze and pictorial verisimilitude the appearance and affect of a particular site. This type of often anecdotal lyric, so runs the complaint, emerges from a culture of egotism that militates against creative thinking about identity, political and literary repression, and the radical contingencies of everyday experience. The argument continues: the rhetorical strategies and manners of stylization in the personal lyric have become too familiar, too reportorial, too photographic in their efforts at mimesis, to usefully identify the changes that time and technology have wreaked upon our contemporary modes of perception and contemplation of places and objects. For poetry to advance, it must break down the routine formulas of exchange between the sovereign self and the all-too-static location being observed. In this postmodern aesthetic, "placelessness" has become a descriptive term not of some enfeebling psychological condition but of language's triumph over the world's spatial manifestations and boundaries. Though skeptical of such skepticism, I have kept these propositions in mind as I framed my interpretations of poems about an urban entity notorious for being elusive of definition.

Second, I had to acknowledge the long-standing complaint that Los Angeles was a place unworthy of poetic treatment. The evidence for this claim lay in the failure to produce major poetry about L.A. Bill Mohr, in his study of the small-press, independent bookstores, and poetry communities in the city, *Hold-Outs: The Los Angeles Poetry Renaissance 1948–1992*, cites some typical expressions of this sense of a missing *chef d'oeuvre*. "There are no masterpieces here, no great artificers, just intensities of immanence and becoming-minor," Julian Murphet remarks. Clayton Eshleman is quoted from an interview: "Los Angeles poets want to be known as a school in order to increase their visibility, to have an identity larger than any one of them could possibly have individually. . . . There is no Los Angeles poetry. Los Angeles is a suitcase city."[5] These are daunting assertions I will address at some length in the chapters that follow. They are oppositional arguments that enable me to engage more precisely and comprehensively the broad subject of how poets conjure a complex city into imaginative form.

As I spoke about this project-in-process, timidly at first but with growing confidence, my colleagues and friends provided encouragement. Most of them had only sampled Los Angeles briefly in their lives, and felt confused by all the conditions inhospitable to our conventional notions of what a city is. Perhaps this book would bring some order to that strange constellation of names on the map spreading across "the Southern California continuum," as James D. Houston calls it. My students—occasionally a precocious poet, a grandchild of a movie star, an aspiring fashion designer turning her attention from New York to Los Angeles just before graduation—clearly enjoyed our immersion in poems so welcoming of extended classroom exegesis. An essay on Los Angeles poetry I wrote for Dana Gioia and Scott Timberg's collection *The Misread City: New Literary Los Angeles* attracted attention and queries if there was more to come. So I have completed this labor of love, this sentimental journey, this first-ever critical study of remarkable poems about the city that has marked me since birth.

When I asked friends and fellow scholars—and fellow poets as well, for I have been publishing poems set in Los Angeles for decades—if they could name one or two of their favorite poems about the city, they usually responded with some version of "I'll get back to you." I understand this response very well, for I know that recent poems of place tend to receive less attention and devotion, with a few famous exceptions, than poems of mentality, of social and political protest, of radical linguistic experiment, of family conflicts, of body and sexuality, and of psychological dysfunction. (These are elements that commonly appear in topographical poems, of course.) But there has been a countervailing tendency in this era of environmentalism and accelerating urbanization to honor poems that use actual sites either as significant backdrops or fundamental figures of presence nourishing to the poet and reader. Poets diminish themselves, their art, and their social responsibility, I intend to argue, if they abandon the two-thousand-year-old practice of engaging the city with clarity and complex imaginative rhetoric. Los Angeles offers places unlike those of other cities in their ambiguities and their relevance to our moment in history. In this book I wish to pay tribute to the poems, not (solely) to the places, for those poems have the potential to change our thinking about more than a single region. They map not only locations but the modes of consciousness and verbal invention that interact with and discern patterns of cultural behavior in any global metropolis. They constitute, in Guy Davenport's fine phrase, a geography of the imagination.

That geography, or "psychogeography," to borrow a term from Guy Debord,[6] is constituted in large part of the "legends" James D. Houston alludes to in the passage above. And those legends are not just local; they derive from literary texts and traditions that need to be noticed and included in analyses of complex poems about this specific city. As Houston makes clear, the legends draw from all the media that nourish the sensibility of poets who try to make sense of Los Angeles, in part or as a whole. I have welcomed into my text quotations from and allusions to these predecessor texts, including social texts that drive the spirit of inquiry into sites as famous as Hollywood, Watts, and Venice or Malibu. I have tried to position or situate my chosen texts among cognate poems, and fiction and films, of the American and European past in order to spotlight the cross-fertilization of artistic forms. With all the taste and judgment I could muster I have chosen from my folder some forty poems I reprint in full, and numerous excerpts from other poems, but that folder is stuffed with other intricately designed examples I regretfully leave behind. And I am well aware that the folder itself is only a partial gathering of the hundreds of thousands of poems about the city that so far go unconsidered.

I need to underscore one fundamental point about this book. This is not a study of Los Angeles *poets*, many of whom have published high-quality work on a variety of topics. This is a study of *poems* about Los Angeles, whether by local authors or visitors. Some of my favorite Los Angeles poets find no place in this book, or only brief mention, because no single poem of theirs fit the requirements described in this preface and the ensuing introduction.

One further cautionary note. The self-reference in this preface, and more sparingly throughout the book, derives from my conviction that my own life history and sensibility are essential to the telling of this story. Whenever the word "essential" is used in contemporary criticism there are bound to be complaints about privileging a bygone mode of thinking. I justify calling the poems reprinted in this book "essential" because they have proven fundamental and necessary to my understanding of how the poetic imagination works upon settings familiar to me. In this preface I have referred to such poems as "worthy" and "high-quality." Taken together they form a critical mass that elevates each and all to a standard of achievement that deserves prolonged attention in a literary marketplace in which the single poem, however well-wrought, tends to vanish overnight. I have tested these poems on many readers, students and faculty alike. I exhibit them in these essayistic pages with confidence in my judgment and the certain expectation of contrary opinions.

I take heart from the willingness of friends, during the last two years especially, to read the manuscript and offer useful corrections. Advice from those who know Los Angeles well, and equally from those who know it principally through other media, has been invaluable in shaping my study of poems essential to a full comprehension of Southern California culture. In the acknowledgments at the back of the book I thank them for their generous help.

Four important notes. In a poem titled "Los Angeles," Leonard S. Bernstein observes that "visitors say 'San Francisco,' / But settle for 'L.A.'"[7] To avoid monotony I use both "Los Angeles" and "L.A." in this book, trying in most cases to suit the usage to the presiding tone of formality or its opposite.

Short paragraphs within parentheses occupy a status halfway between a stage in the continuity of the discourse and a footnote. Rather like an insert in a cinematic text, they highlight or extend or digress upon an immediately preceding passage.

I have borrowed the title *Poetry Los Angeles* from a 68-page anthology of the same title released by Villiers Publications in England in 1958. This forum for the work of eighteen poets connected to the *California Quarterly* and *Coastlines* group of authors contains no commentary and has never been reprinted. (In fact, only two poems in the anthology present Los Angeles explicitly as their subject matter.) I see my book as a fulfillment of the hopes invested in this early effort at securing serious attention to Los Angeles poets.

Wayne Thiebaud's painting *Urban Freeways*, which graces the cover of this book, is best described as "an abstracted concept of freeways," as by Karen Tsujimoto in her study, *Wayne Thiebaud* (University of Washington Press, 1985), 134. Tsujimoto affirms that the painting's true subject is not a specific city but "the baroque maze of shapes that snake, curl, and cut across the canvas." Adapted from Thiebaud's memories and sketches of Los Angeles and San Francisco, *Urban Freeways* serves as a charming representation of Los Angeles's preeminent iconic structure.

Introduction

"Everything's been Los Angelized," complained Thomas McGrath in his personal record of wartime and postwar America, *Letter to an Imaginary Friend* (1962).[1] Readers of his book-length poem in every part of the United States did not require a gloss for this outraged statement, especially if they knew that McGrath, a North Dakota native, considered himself a proletarian forerunner and exemplar of the counterculture taking shape in the 1950s along the West Coast. In the twenty-first century we may need reminding precisely what McGrath intended by that nasty epithet. Had Los Angeles truly become the twentieth-century agent of commercial, political, and consciousness-altering forces that would harrow the world ever afterward? Did he mean that this one amorphous city at the edge of the continent reigned absolute and irresistible, having eclipsed the coherent America of patriotic textbooks, speeches, and poems? Whatever he meant to say, his alarm awakens us to the central issues informing almost all of the significant poems written about Los Angeles in McGrath's lifetime and following his death in 1990.

Los Angeles, renowned for its social history of prosperity and corruption, was easily stigmatized as the metropole of a new kind of evil empire, extending its values and lifestyle by means of Hollywood movies, television, Top 40 radio, and other popular culture. Los Angeles made a narcissistic fantasy of the so-called California Dream, ran the charge, and reinvented itself continually as a site of ostentatious privilege in an enviable place on the map that drew millions of people from regions where life was harsher.

Waves of immigrants who poured into Los Angeles before, during, and after World War II might have protested that, if truth be told, everything back home was insufficiently Los Angelized. But prophets seldom look on the bright side. In *Letter to an Imaginary Friend* McGrath chose to steer his verse to the dark side of what he called "the vast dream foundries and mythical money go-downs / Of the city of death." (118).

For decades before McGrath published his magnum opus in 1962, amplified in 1970 and thereafter, poets had pondered how best to represent Los Angeles to a world already being transfigured, if not converted, by the gospel, consumer products, and fantasies of the Golden State. If, like McGrath, lyric poets considered the city as a bellwether in the "entropy of the failing system" (50), they tended to leave the subject alone, for systemic problems are best described by novelists and sociologists. And there was no lack of both, after the Great Depression impoverished so much of America and made coastal cities shine more tantalizingly, and deceptively, as pockets of opportunity. The exodus of the peasant class from the Dust Bowl toward California in John Steinbeck's *The Grapes of Wrath* is an epic treatment of this theme. How much the Joad family wanted to be Los Angelized, to be reborn at the frontier of history, rather than foundering in their Midwestern wasteland! And how much Los Angeles poets would have liked to write a volume of lyrics with the range and profundity of Steinbeck's novel, or the moral and verbal complexity of Nathanael West's novel *The Day of the Locust,* also published in 1939.

But poets had no first-rate poetry about Los Angeles to draw upon as models, and the city was a source of confusion to poets who visited for a spell, to script a movie or dry out in the desert sun. No Hart Crane or Federico García Lorca or Vladimir Mayakovsky had arisen to hymn the sublime architecture and ascendant spirit of a local monument, as they did the Brooklyn Bridge. No Carl Sandburg or Gwendolyn Brooks had walked the streets of the city—it was too spread-out!—as they did the downtown and neighborhoods of Chicago. San Francisco had a renaissance thanks to the high-energy immigrants who appreciated the European character of the hills and harbors, and the willed community spirit of those who made this compact city their spiritual home. Writers like Robinson Jeffers, Kenneth Rexroth, and the Beats cultivated the landscapes of northern California, not always with good grace, and made them beacons for the rebellious generation that took seriously McGrath's critique of conditions south of Big Sur. But the city blessed by its founders in 1781 with the toponym El Pueblo de

Nuestra Señora la Reina de los Angeles de Porciúncula, so ambitious in its city planning and so eager to be admired and even loved, seemed to repel skilled poets whose expertise was regional scenery and local character types. Even those who resided in its precincts preferred to write mainly about some patch of land elsewhere, anywhere but L.A. A kind of pathology took hold among poets, a sense of inferiority compared to the screenwriters and later the television writers and songwriters, and ultimately the webmasters, who commanded rewards of money and status while polishing the image of their adopted homestead at frontier's end—though they too were often unhappy and alienated from the sources of power and joy in the city.

The suspicion grew that Los Angeles was not quite amenable to, or worthy of, sustained treatment by modern poets. And the same was true of the local readership, for, as Whitman wrote, "Great poetry needs great audiences." Lacking the same deference to cultural tradition one finds on the East Coast, and the same patience for the complexities of literary texts, Los Angeles became stigmatized across the nation as a subliterate society. Randall Jarrell, who had spent some of his childhood in the city, wrote in a letter of 1954 from Laguna Beach, "This is certainly an uncultivated part of the World—you get the impression that the inhabitants, at breakfast, spell out *Little Nancy* with their fingers and their reading for the day is done."[2] That is snob wit, but the regional bias in American literature was a settled matter of discourse, so taken for granted that writers in the East and Midwest barely acknowledged "the other coast," as they called it, as more than an exotic appendage, a pulp outlier to the great tradition of letters passed down by New England and New York writers, and even Southern writers (as William Faulkner, Robert Penn Warren, Eudora Welty, and Flannery O'Connor burnished their growing reputations), during the twentieth century. Poetry, especially, seemed to lack the rewards that would attract talented young writers to stake their claim anywhere between Death Valley and the beach. Or if they did settle, like, say, Ann Stanford, writing splendid poems *in* Los Angeles, they (she) avoided Los Angeles as a subject almost entirely. Stanford wrote principally *about* ornamental gardens, the Mediterranean, and the classical Greek myths. To do otherwise would have seemed . . . provincial.

Estelle Gershgoren Novak presents a different view in her anthology and commentary, *Poets of the Non-Existent City: Los Angeles in the McCarthy Era* (2002), which argues for a vital community of poets, literary magazines, public readings, and house parties full of song, recitation, and polemics. Embittered by the House Un-American Activities Committee, the McCarthy hearings, and other inquisitions that led to the firing of some poets (including Thomas McGrath) from local jobs in education and filmmaking, these poets bent their talents toward a literature of protest, of social and political resistance. "Los Angeles poetry took root in the city and became its literary and social conscience," Novak asserts.[3] Bertolt Brecht's dour poems about Hollywood stand out as one example, along with McGrath's disappointed commentaries about the inability of people in Los Angeles to recognize the evil being committed before their eyes—McGrath refers to "LosAngeles AsiaMinor of the intellect" (111) and mimics Julius Caesar's memoirs: "All Los Angeles / America / is divided into three parts" named "muggery, buggery, and thuggery" (114). Novak insists that despite, or because of, the acrimony polluting the airwaves and newspapers of Southern California, remarkable poets following the lead of Brecht and McGrath fused elements of surrealism, social realism, and the pungent diction of modernist practice to form a movement, not just a coterie, that remains unjustly neglected by scholars and common readers.

However, one cannot help noticing that Novak's long introductory essay, and the anthology that follows, reveal that the specific regional details of the cityscape of Los Angeles and its cosmopolitan community are the content of very few noteworthy poems. Rather, the poets compose with the half-concealed assumption that readers either will not care to hear about the city, or that it is not worthy of being scrutinized with the sustained attention expended by city poets of the past, from Ovid and Juvenal down to Lola Ridge, Langston Hughes, and Kenneth Fearing. Very few of the poems in the anthology describe actual locations, and those poems are usually more routine than the poems hurling thunderbolts at the universal evils of the time. The manifestos of journals like *The California Quarterly* and *Coastlines* demanded that poets write about what they saw around them, but note the emphasis, and slippage, in this sample editorial statement by Gene Frumkin from *Coastlines*: "As a literary magazine, our first duty is toward the things of the world, for without these there is no literature, no art—just desolation. Among these things are the timeless human problems, public and private. We must try to see them honestly, from the inside, in the material we publish and in our own commentaries."[4]

In this passage a process of abstraction occurs by which the author glances at the physical "things of the world" but proceeds immediately to the "timeless human problems," presumably love, death, justice, nature, and faith. What gets neglected in such a process is the unique contribution of *place* or milieu to the final product. Don't "things of the world" occupy space in a unique physical setting? Aren't "actualities," to use the honorific word that concludes Marianne Moore's tribute to the Brooklyn Bridge in the poem "Granite and Steel," worth dwelling upon and exemplifying in such a manifesto? Lost in the rush toward transcendent, necessarily general, social and psychological concerns is the primary setting, the *locus*, of the moral drama being enacted in the consciousness of the poems' speakers. For poets who cherish the native grounds of their testimony, the eclipse of locality—its landmarks, icons, residents, and savory idioms—as informing material of the poems cannot help but diminish the originality, urgency, and persuasiveness of their witness. If the city is "non-existent" in the sense Novak emphasizes—that the rest of the country hardly noticed Los Angeles as a crucible of poetic culture—it arguably still is non-existent, or nearly so, to a large portion of readers nationwide. That the sceneless quality of immediately postwar verse has given way to a prolonged and passionate attention to scenes on the ground during the last half-century has been little noted in recent commentary.

Poems of place have always been part of an environmental imagination central to the literary tradition. Readers of verse naturally take pleasure in the way poets chart their changes of consciousness in the process of confronting a field of vision both unique and shared, whether rural or urban. In *A Writer's America: Landscape in Literature*, Alfred Kazin, speaking of Emerson, Thoreau, Whitman, Dickinson, Hawthorne, Faulkner, Bellow, and Ellison, praises how "the enduring sense of place such writers created fills American writing with the sight and fury of a hundred different American settlements."[5] It was the richly described landscapes, Kazin notes, that astonished D. H. Lawrence when he read the American classics and reported on them in a seminal book of literary criticism, *Studies in Classic American Literature* (1923). Kazin locates no poet to praise in his section on Los Angeles, which he devotes to Nathanael West, Raymond Chandler, Norman Mailer, and Joan Didion. His neglect of Los Angeles poetry, in a book published in 1988, confirms Novak's suspicion that the city's poems are invisible, a non-entity in the literature of the region.

II

The purpose of this book is to make recent poems about the city of Los Angeles visible just as they make their subject matter visible, and audible, and tangible. Studies of poems about cities tend to be author-specific: Baudelaire on Paris, Whitman on New York, Cavafy on Alexandria. (For London there seems to be no one dominant career, no poetry version of Dickens or Woolf. London is best apprehended by means of anthology.[6]) Perhaps the problem, as Brecht and McGrath tentatively diagnosed, has always been that very early in its history Los Angeles had been typed as a place that repels subtle and profound scrutiny, first by the onslaught of propaganda for the pagan pleasures of its "sun-kissed" groves and beaches—Southern Pacific Railroad advertised California as "The Climatic Capitol of the World: The Land of Sunshine, Fruit and Flowers"—and swiftly thereafter as a dark, Dostoevskian world of depravity and crime. Poets who set their intelligence to crafting first-rate poems about Los Angeles locations knew in their bones how profoundly their own imagination had been saturated by all the clichés, all the pop and pulp mythology, all the worn-out stereotypes invested in the city even before the first decent poem about milieus like Hollywood, Santa Monica, or downtown found its way into print. How poets have surrendered to local mythologies, promoted by leading industries and persistent audience demand, or resisted them in search of some authentic, existential spirit of place, is the major topic undertaken by this book.

Poetry in English about the eastern United States appeared very shortly after the first European footsteps on the continent; the South and Midwest also became significant subjects as the Romantic spirit migrated to the New World where it inspired poets like William Cullen Bryant and Walt Whitman to look westward for material in their grand prophecies of the nation's irresistible destiny. Except for some verse about the Gold Rush and cowboy life of the Golden State, more for the voice than the eye, nothing much worth reprinting appears about California until the first decades of the twentieth century, when Robinson Jeffers and a few other literary figures began to mine the territory for landscapes and states of mind of interest to poetry readers in the English-speaking world. Some commentators credit pioneers of California verse such as Bret Harte, Joaquin Miller (known as "Byron of the Sierras"), Ina Coolbrith, Helen Hoyt (and her anthology of 1932, *California Poets*), George Sterling, and Edwin Markham, but none of their poems garnered significant esteem in the postwar era.[7]

I would identify as the earliest poem about Southern California worth close examination, the primal text of the entire tradition I study in this volume, Karl Shapiro's "Hollywood" (see page 65), part of his ever-intriguing first volume *Person, Place and Thing*, published in 1942. As I note later, Shapiro borrows some of his imagery from Nathanael West's seminal novel of the Hollywood locale, *The Day of the Locust*. These two works that first influenced my understanding of the dynamics of literature about Los Angeles were written by Jewish moralists who found the cityscape provocative in its complex iconography and its insistent contradictions, and eminently worthy of serious literary treatment. (I would add Budd Schulberg's novel *What Makes Sammy Run?* [1941] as an enticement of the same era.) For West and Shapiro, Hollywood was an exotic, fantastical realm, a new culture in a nation still ambivalent about its boundaries and goals. "O can we understand it?" Shapiro declaims with tongue in cheek. His implied answer is Probably Not, because Hollywood could not present itself to his hasty survey as a definable place; it seemed to him little more than a fun-house assemblage of facades nourished for profit by the movie studios. Hollywood was not worth his time, especially since it was only a transit stop on his way to the Pacific Theater of Operations. A poet did not have to speculate whether the subject possessed sufficient meaningfulness when he was dumped by a transport ship onto the sands of New Guinea.

In fact, the answer to Shapiro's question is Yes, we can understand Hollywood and Los Angeles—the former became a synecdoche for the latter—if we first comprehend the waxy mass of assumptions, attitudes, ideologies, and resentments that have always been formulated in place of a precise topographical description. Shapiro's poem is a pastiche of misreadings of the city, including Vachel Lindsay's hopeful comparisons in *The Art of the Moving Picture* (1914) of Los Angeles to Florence as sites of renaissance splendor. (Lindsay hints that Jerusalem might be an apt analogy as well.) Yes, Hollywood might emerge as a "possible proud Florence," Shapiro asserts in the closure of his touristy piece, but only if you think of Dante's fallen city as filled with the same "parasites," "quacks," and "morons" Shapiro discerns in his brief walking tour of Hollywood Boulevard. Likewise, West puts into the mouth of his most deluded characters the imagery of "paradise," as when Mrs. Loomis, stage mother of the child performer Adore, utters this kind of language:

> "I've been here since Mr. Loomis passed on six years ago. I'm an old settler."
>
> "You like it then?" Tod asked.
>
> "Like California?" She laughed at the idea that anyone might not like it. Why, it's a paradise on earth!" (138)

In that last sentence West is filching James M. Cain's conclusion to a 1933 essay on the city: "[Los Angeles] is going to be a paradise on earth."[8] Cain would see matters differently when he composed his hardboiled fiction, including *The Postman Always Rings Twice*, *Double Indemnity*, and *Mildred Pierce*, later in the decade. But his essay, titled "Paradise," endorsed the prevailing cliché for Southern California. Serious poets writing about Los Angeles had to answer back to Lindsay, Cain, and Mrs. Loomis, and in sterner, smarter tones than Shapiro's.

By "answer back" I mean that every poet inevitably has buried deep in his or her consciousness secondhand images of Los Angeles, some prefabricated sense of place they share with citizens within and beyond the city limits. Poets along with the general population were prepossessed by the folklore purveyed by the media. And that folklore was necessarily incoherent and contradictory, for it was generated by strangers to the land. The imperative of national journalism in the early and middle decades of the twentieth century was to ridicule the city for precisely that incoherence, as expressed in its presumed frivolity and wackiness. *Life* magazine ran a photo essay in its 21 November 1938 issue titled "Cuckooland" ("Screwy California" in the issue's table of contents) that caricatured the spirit of place by featuring faddists, nudists, eccentric hermits, evangelists, and pet-lovers who bury their dogs in expensive coffins, as if they formed the majority of the population. Nathanael West, and the authors of earlier Hollywood novels such as *Spider Boy* (Carl Van Vechten, 1928) and *Queer People* (Carroll and Garrett Graham, 1930), presented the same congeries of lunatics. Who were most likely to flock to what *Life* called an "absolutely screwy" place if not birds of a feather?

To the readers of such satire, the society of spectacle set amidst the sunny beaches and orange groves pretty much defined the city and by extension the city's poets. Were they or were they not living in a pagan place commonly described as "paradise"? And later in the twentieth century, the question became inverted. Was Los Angeles as menacing as *noir* depictions of Hollywood and South Central insisted? Was Los Angeles "Hell Lite" as Carol Muske-Dukes jokingly averred in a retrospective on poetic visions of the city?[9] Poets needed to code their re-creations of local sensibility and local sites with an informed and individualized response to mass media formulas and clichés. Poets had the responsibility, but rarely the talent, to lend the "non-existent city" revelatory detail and meaningfulness. Like native informants giving information to explorers and anthropologists, poets needed to articulate the city's parts in order to construct together a more authentic place from locations they knew intimately. If they could do that, they could triumph over the false reports of sojourners who had no birthright or long-time acquaintance to author the script and draw the maps of the poets' own "unreal city."

I borrow the term "unreal city" from T. S. Eliot's *The Waste Land* where it appears twice, and then a third time in an auditory chime in the concluding section:

> What is the city over the mountains
> Cracks and reforms and bursts in the violet air
> Falling towers
> Jerusalem Athens Alexandria
> Vienna London
> Unreal

The phrase has had an unusual success, even for Eliot. In a footnote to its first appearance Eliot credits Baudelaire's poem "Les Sept Vieillards" (The Seven Old Men) as the source of the coinage. In that work, the speaker is struck with a hallucination when confronting a strange old man in the Paris streets: he imagines seven men of the exact appearance passing as apparitions before him. Baudelaire does not use a locution like "Unreal," but the word would certainly apply exactly as it did in its first English usage, by Shakespeare in *Macbeth* when the guilty new monarch screams at the ghost of his friend Banquo, whose death he has ordered: "Hence, horrible shadow! Unreal mockery, hence!" (III.4). Ghosts and delusions are genuinely unreal. But can a city be called unreal? Can all cities be unreal, as Eliot's lines above suggest?

Los Angeles, more than any city in America, has suffered that designation repeatedly, not just from *Life* magazine and satirists who mass-produced Hollywood novels to satisfy a large reading public's desire for scandal about movie people, but also from journalists and memoirists almost from the city's founding. Edmund Wilson, a quintessential New York intellectual, lampooned the city in his travelogue of the 1930s, *American Jitters*: "Sunkist Caliphonia, here I come! and the brown papier-mâché hills where every prospect appeases and the goofs hang like ripe fruit."[10] Norman Mailer offers a compendium of all the clichés in his classic essay on John F. Kennedy's visit to the city for the 1960 Democratic National Convention: "it is all open, promiscuous, borrowed, half-bought, a city without iron, eschewing wood, a kingdom of stucco, the playground for mass men—one has the feeling it was built by television sets giving orders to men."[11] The sense of history is as thin and wobbly as the architecture, he goes on to argue, as does William Irwin Thompson in the first chapter of *At the Edge of History*, titled "Looking for History in Los Angeles," and Joan Didion in her occasional essays collected in *Slouching Towards Bethlehem*, *The White Album*, *Where I Was From*, and *After Henry*. The city, as Mailer writes, is "pretty-pretty" but it lacks the solidity of the great eastern cities. It's unrooted, jerry-built, a timeless city of surfaces and dreams rather than substantial and enduring structures. Munchkin-land, as Woody Allen calls it in *Annie Hall*. La La Land. "City of Dreadful Joy." Nadaland. Toytown. Psycholand. Lost Angels. Smogville. The Big Orange. "A Gobi of suburbs"; A. M. Homes, writing in 2002, declares that L.A. is "perhaps the most surreal place in America."[12] One could compile insults, if that's what they are, for several pages. Los Angeles poets harboring the belief that they lived in a *real* city had their work cut out for them. Slowly, under the pressure of literary example, they formed strategies of resistance to the hostile (or affectionate) charges that accused them of being foggy ghosts in their own lotus land.

(Kevin Starr, the preeminent historian of the state of California, remarks in a much-quoted passage about the California version of the American Dream that "Los Angeles sprung from a Platonic conception of itself, the Great Gatsby of American cities."[13] This epithet has had a significant influence on the literature of the city. As a judgment on the citizens of a growing metropolis it suggests that there is something both fraudulent and fascinating about the successful personalities enshrined in the city's mythic history of itself.)

Poems about Los Angeles have an attitude, no doubt about it. But this rhetorical edge is hardly unique to the West Coast. In this book I take as axiomatic Linda Gregerson's assertion that "poetry, like public speaking, has a suasive agenda. . . . [the poem] always also seeks to convince, or coerce, or seduce a reader; it is never disinterested, never pure; it has designs on the one who listens or reads."[14] Poems often affect a pose of judicious neutrality, of universality, of speculative disinterestedness. But especially in urban poetry, because the city offers a spectacle of swift social change and visual provocations, we are made to notice the pressing agenda as the strophes develop their artful designs of persuasion and resistance.

III

How does such resistance work? The poet who knows Los Angeles well must take care to clear the ground of debased images before proceeding to witness lucidly what is in fact before her eyes. I'll use a poem by Suzanne Lummis to show how the deconstruction of demeaning tropes works on the page.

Suzanne Lummis

SHANGRI-LA

> In New York they think all of California is like L.A. And they think everyone in L.A. has a maid. And they don't believe you if you try to tell them.
>
> *RADIO TALK SHOW CALLER*

It's true, here we are all blonde,
even in the dark, on Mondays
or in slow traffic.

Even in our off-guard moments,
startled by a passer-by,
we are young.

Here we are all privileged,
even in our sleep. At night
the maids hover like sweetly

tranquilized angels over
the glazed or enameled surface
of things, purring *clean clean* . . .

It's all true. We girls sip lemon-lime through a straw,
make love, Revlon our nails.
We take our long sleek legs out for a walk,
let them catch light.

When someone snaps, "Get real!"
it hurts us, real pain like we've seen
in the news. So we throw beach robes
over our tans, and cruise down the boulevard
tossing Lifesavers into our mouths,
car radios singing *am*.

New York, is it true
that in the rest of the world it is winter?

Our state is a mosaic of blue pools,
even the Mojave, and the palm trees
line up straight to the Sierra Nevadas,
and the surf comes down slow like
delirious laundry, even near Fresno.

New York, is it true that great cold
makes the bones ache as if broken?

We're sorry we can't be reached
by plane or bus, sorry one can't pull
even the tiniest thing out of a dream.
We're like the landscape inside
a plastic dome filled with water.

But turn us over, then upright.
See?
No snow falls.[15]

—⬩—

After almost a century of resentful critiques of Los Angeles, one would think that the bromide requiring least revision, because most transparent, most banal, is that hoariest of identifications, Southern California as "The Land of Sunshine." But Suzanne Lummis has this label branded into her consciousness by way of inheritance. Her grandfather was Charles Fletcher Lummis (1859–1928), one of the region's most devoted and eminent boosters during the formative years of its development. As the founder and editor of *Land of Sunshine* (after 1902, *Out West*), a magazine that, along with its long-lasting rivals *Sunset* and *Touring Topics* (later *Westways*), essentially created the popular image of the Southwest in general and Southern California in particular, Lummis popularized what became the stereotype of L.A. as a golden land, an Arcadia full of the fruits of the earth flourishing year round. David Fine underlines this point:

> . . . it was the oranges that got most of the attention. Boosting the region was clearly the editorial priority. The early issues are filled with celebrations of the sunshine, citrus crops, and health benefits that Southern California offered. In his monthly column "In the Lion's Den," Lummis ranted euphorically about the God-given natural wealth of the region.[16]

Lummis popularized Los Angeles specifically as "the new Eden of the Saxon home-seeker," a desirable destination for the "refined, intelligent class" with roots in the European world.[17] A hundred years later, Lummis's familial descendant can be expected to be ambivalent about her heritage. The special character of this subtropical region, cultivated and glorified during the twentieth century as a figure of Eden, often recurs in Suzanne Lummis's poems where it is submitted to a variety of ironic and defensive treatments.

Los Angeles inevitably got tagged with the name "Shangri-La" after the tremendous success of *Lost Horizon*, James Hilton's novel of 1933 and Frank Capra's film adaptation of 1937. In this decade of the Depression and the sense of an inevitable swiftly oncoming world war, the fantasy of an asylum *somewhere* in the world was appealing to the entire civilized community. Hilton and Capra set their narratives in a secret, nearly inaccessible valley in the Himalayas, and gave it the memorable name that has become a synonym for paradise. This utopian world boasted a perfect climate, bountiful nature, and, most important, a contented and healthy population that seemingly did not age but flourished in full strength in a blissful state just short of immortality. Also, an enlightened government maintained harmonious order by its humane policies. "You seem a very fortunate community, and most hospitable to strangers," remarks the protagonist, Glory Conway, in the novel. Capra's sets were visually delectable, all of them constructed in Los Angeles or on nearby ranches. As with the Emerald City of Oz, in another film of the late 1930s, Hollywood itself, and its environs, emerged in the public imagination as the type of Shangri-La, the enchanting Fountain of Youth offering, in Hilton's words, "a world of incomparable refinements" and "utter freedom from worldly cares."[18]

In the twenty-first century, as memories of the novel and film grow more diffuse and melt into oversimplification, it's necessary to recall that Shangri-La is also presented as a rather tiresome place where the absence of challenges, including aging, reduces the many decades of vigorous physical health to a long plateau of monotonous geniality emptied of ambition, bracing conflict, and high achievement. One of the (female) natives longs to escape from this "captivating" world, along with three of the travelers who have been abducted and brought to the valley by airplane. The narrative proceeds to have it both ways, like Lummis's poem. Conway allows himself to be persuaded to flee the sheltered oasis, but after years of wandering in the fallen world he returns to Shangri-La, acknowledging its superior claims on his wayward spirit.

In Lummis's poem the title alerts the knowledgeable reader that some form of irony, and ambiguity, lies ahead. After the epigraph inflates the thematic balloon for inevitable popping, the poem slides into a dramatic monologue recited by a smug persona who has no intention of abandoning the demi-paradise of Los Angeles. (The unseen auditor for whom the speaker performs her theatrical speech is the populace of New York City.) The artistry and pleasure of the poem reside in its invitation to laugh at the send-up of Charles Fletcher Lummis's sentiments but also hear the defiant claiming of them by a longtime resident of the city who clearly enjoys the amenities she also unconsciously burlesques. "Here we are all privileged," she intones in a Paris Hilton kind of voice, tinged with a bit of pity for the reader/audience, and rubbing it in with an insouciant wit likely to provoke, even enrage, the hapless New Yorkers, victims of temperatures presumably hovering at zero outside.

(Contrast the double-voiced rhetoric of Lummis's speaker with the single-minded boosterism of Frank Sinatra's "L.A. Is My Lady," or even more so, Randy Newman's popular anthem, "I Love L.A." "Hate New York City / It's cold and it's damp," the song begins and concludes by repeating in joyful voice that L.A. enjoys one fine sunny day after another. It's possible to enjoy this feel-good lyric while still appreciating how clearly it exemplifies the difference between an invigoratingly complex poem and a bland cocktail of clichés.)

Published in 1999, "Shangri-La" knows perfectly well that it's preposterous to claim, "we are all blonde. . . . we are young. . . . Here we are all privileged." Lummis has constructed a figure capable of making native and non-native readers equally uncomfortable. Former New Yorker Nathanael West invented the seventeen-year-old Faye Greener as a Hollywood nymph who in her best moments is the gorgeous, self-composed idol, or fetish, of her surrounding community. She is a first cousin to Lummis's speaker, who likewise puts herself on display and vamps the reader by assuming the pose of an alluring agent of public relations. (That is, she advertises the charms of Los Angeles no less than her creator's ancestor.) Her first words to the reader are assurances that she is blonde, that is, white. To be white is already to be "privileged" but the reader knows that her good fortune has been called into question by decades of local history preceding 1999. Her "sleek legs" are tanned, but not so much so that she can be mistaken for a black or brown person. Once she and her friends were the fantasy symbol of the city as a whole, and still she is autonomous, part of a cohort of Saxon princesses like herself. A happy occupant of the youth culture synonymous with Los Angeles since the 1950s, she lives in an affluent bubble, too easily popped, and is pained when "someone snaps 'Get real!'"

When the note of reality enters, the poem changes direction and tone. The final five stanzas, beginning halfway through, summon the cold of winter that harrows most of her readers. The tone becomes taunting, teasing. "New York, is it true . . . ?" begins two stanzas in a prosecutorial voice, hinting that the neglect of Los Angeles may be a result of envy not taste. The implied bubble of detachment from worldly woe ("We're sorry we can't be reached / by plane or bus") is now reified as "a plastic dome filled with water." The speaker and her ilk, archetypes of teen culture, are preserved from aging, from Faustian ambition, even from the seasonal chill that enters the bones of her cross-country rivals. "No snow falls" is her final thrice-accented statement. The reader might respond "So what?" in the voice of Glory Conway in *Lost Horizon*. Life is more complex and fascinating than the spoiled girl of the poem can imagine. True, but from her perspective, beside a swimming pool under the palm trees at some glamorous hotel like the "Pink Palace" (Beverly Hills Hotel), cruising the boulevard in a luxury car, this is the good life, and all the more fulfilling because others are jealous of it, prohibited from it, condemned to fantasize about becoming Los Angelized in her style rather than their own. Charles Fletcher Lummis would recognize these charmed girls as his endangered legacy.

And indeed, the poem contains an iconography of concrete details that constitute the romanticized image of West Los Angeles. Each of the opening tercets ticks off one familiar media cliché: *blonde, young, privileged, clean clean*. And the quatrain that follows loads the poem with further features belonging to the world of advertising and video: the sensual pleasures of tropical drinks, of sex, of fashion, of painting one's nails ("Revlon" makes a melodious transitive verb), and most compelling of all, the exhibitionism of showing off their long sleek legs in the abundant warm light. This is the same delectable light that has drawn so many migrants to the city, but few so fortunate as the speaker and her kindred. City poems often complain about the teeming, swarming nature of the stinking crowds on the sidewalks and in other public spaces, as in William Wordsworth's shocked encounter in London with "That huge, fermenting mass of human-kind" and Charles Baudelaire's epithet "Fourmillante cité, cité pleine de rêves" [Spawning city, city full of dreams].[19] But Lummis's hedonistic coven of Angelenos are fortune's favorites. They don't have to walk through the crowded downtown streets, they "cruise down the boulevard" in a city where driving has replaced promenading as a sign of privilege for the upper classes. No doubt they show off their legs in bistros or country club patios; they stroll down Rodeo Drive or through Century City, pausing to savor expensive new commodities in the tony boutiques of Beverly Hills. They are not like the worn-out prostitutes and crones in a Baudelaire poem, but models of glamour.[20]

After the defensive taunt about winter in New York, there's more site-specific iconography: *blue pools, palm trees*, and *surf*. All the liquidity and pastoral foliage adds to the insistent seduction of the reader. In Linda Gregerson's terms, the speaker is one of those rhetors, no less than Shakespeare in his sonnets, whose discourse "simultaneously enact[s] and discredit[s] a rhetorical proposition they appear to be invested in."[21] If the chaos and anonymity of city life repels many poets who fear the snares of urbanity, this speaker feels triumphantly at home in her milieu. She and her fraternal sisters are not wary of the outdoors, thanks to the "angels" who keep watch over them (one thinks of the sylphs serving Belinda in Alexander Pope's *The Rape of the Lock*). When the following stanza snaps us back to the fallen world, hard plosives roughen the monosyllabic texture of the speaker's cruel raillery:

New York, is it true that great cold
makes the bones ache as if broken?

One wants to step into the poem and shake some sense into this mocking princess. But doing so would only secure her triumph over our envious selves shivering on the cold hillside. Yes, the speaker is also a descendant of La Belle Dame Sans Merci, as in Keats's disconsolate ballad. "No snow falls" deliberately echoes "No birds sing."

The best poems about Los Angeles keep the reader off balance, as this one does. They challenge us, no less when they are comic, to sort out our fundamental subconscious attitudes toward the city, whether or not we are personally acquainted with its sights and sounds. For the poem to do its disenchanting work, readers must see through the blithe rhetoric of spokespeople like this deluded creature. The city she lives in is unreal in obvious ways, but it is also substantially real, as anyone with personal experience of the upscale setting will testify. Such poems tend to speak for a recognizable population in contradistinction to citizens of more or less fortunate parts of the nation. Just as the Watts riot, and the Rodney King riots, do not trouble the fortunate "we" of Lummis's poem, because South Central is as remote from Beverly Hills and Bel-Air as is Manhattan, Kansas, or Manhattan, New York, so each major experience of reality in the diverse sections of the city has a different voice, different values. Perhaps the one attitude that links most poems about L.A. is the fervent desire, bred in the movie capital, to appear extraordinary, to demand attention for some bold expression of personality. If the casual narcissism of Lummis's speaker seems now to echo the rhetoric of all citizens in a Facebook and YouTube culture, then Los Angeles is probably going to take the blame for having made self-obsession and self-glorification so contagious. Very few people in the wealthy precincts of the basin, canyons, and palisades have ever queried, with Emily Dickinson, "I'm Nobody! Who are you?" The poems in *Poetry Los Angeles* more often than not assert claims of uniqueness and satisfaction with the gusto of a Hollywood agent. But the gusto has a core of self-undermining ridicule audible to the trained reader. "Thank goodness for poetry, the great cliché buster," Suzanne Lummis has written.[22]

Claims of uniqueness would be improbable without the unusual topographical features of the city. Not that the poets meditating on a discrete sector agree on its identity—far from it. Because there are multiple discriminations necessary when laying out and remarking upon the many first-rate poems about the city, it has seemed necessary to organize this book according to geography. So often in poetry, the speaker is located . . . nowhere exactly, an isolated voice ruminating on the state of things in general. As I've suggested, this is an aspect of too much self-conscious poetry written "about" Los Angeles by authors seeking a topic worthy of their attention. Lummis's poem about the rich girls of West L.A. driving around in a cloud of unknowing titillates us like the best examples of comic verse. It is only one of many intriguing poems with the intention of revealing something rarely articulated in poetic form about the soul of the city. Daring poems like this one are the subject of my analysis.

IV

Poetry Los Angeles is organized as a sequence of readings of worthy poems, almost all of them neglected in standard anthologies and literary essays by distinguished critics. Books of close readings in which the author scrutinizes remarkable poems with something in common, illuminating their distinctive and often hidden qualities by juxtaposing each with the larger group, have always been a favored mode of literary commentary. I came under the sway of this methodology early in my career after I read Paul Carroll's *The Poem in Its Skin* (1968), which performed, chapter by chapter, close readings of single poems by young poets like John Ashbery, Isabella Gardner, Allen Ginsberg, Frank O'Hara, and James Wright. Another inspiring model of this enabling structure was Thomas R. Edwards's *Imagination and Power: A Study of Poetry on Public Themes* (1971), which provided a chronological series of interpretive readings of political poems from Marlowe and Shakespeare on to Auden, Eliot, Yeats, and Lowell. More recent texts as different as Helen Vendler's *Dickinson: Selected Poems and Commentaries*, Camille Paglia's *Break, Blow, Burn*, and (extending the practice to single volumes) John Lowney's *History, Memory, and the Literary Left: Modern American Poetry 1935–1968*, do more than provide exegesis, however. They are not just "reader's guides" designed as glosses to aid quick consumption of difficult poems. They provide historical, literary, and biographical contexts to set each poem in a constellation of other texts. I undertook such a project with my volume of 1994, *The American Poet at the Movies: A Critical History*, which told the story of American poets' responses to the film medium by focusing on one key poem in each chapter, each poem from a different decade of the twentieth century. I did each poem the courtesy of studying form and content, and constructing a genealogy that helped to explain the poem's otherwise mysterious success. I considered my selection of poems, each printed in full, to be a miniature version of an anthology, though most of the study consisted of commentary. Jason Shinder later published, with my assistance, a full anthology, *Lights, Camera, Poetry! American Movie Poems: The First Hundred Years* (1996).

In thinking about writing a book like this one, I took seriously John H. Johnston's distinction between the Virgilian eclogue, in which the far-off city is little more than an accumulation of vices, a perpetual and ever-growing hazard for farmers and shepherds, and the topographical mode, in which the poet "views the metropolis not merely in terms of its internal social norms and variations but in terms of its natural situation and surroundings, in terms of its physical fabric, its essential character."[23] In this fundamental distinction I recognized the germ of what might be called the prose version and the verse version of Los Angeles. Fiction writers seized upon the pastoral mode, paradoxical as it may sound, in their creation of *noir* narratives that emphasized the loss of innocence and virtue in the predatory atmosphere of L.A. Nathanael West founded this genre by writing the seminal version of the Hollywood novel; Raymond Chandler, Chester Himes, and James M. Cain took the corruption and violence further into the diverse districts of the city. It hardly needs demonstrating that *noir* fiction, whether by Dorothy B. Hughes, Ross Macdonald, Joan Didion, Michael Tolkin, James Ellroy, Bret Easton Ellis, Michael Connelly, Walter Mosley, Jonathan Kellerman, Bruce Wagner, or hundreds of others, have stamped upon Los Angeles a bleak reputation, in film as in fiction, in popular song as in film, that intensifies in effect as the decades pass.

Poets are free from the commercial pressures of producing narratives adhering to *noir* formulas, which is *of course* not to say that their work does not investigate the darkest parts of the urban psyche and the urban space. For the most part, however, the best poems about Los Angeles are topographical; they locate themselves in neighborhoods that mandate certain perspectives and challenges, certain ways of representing landscape and the figures moving in the landscape. Many of the finest poems about Los Angeles are written by tourists, by travelers, by temporary residents who register their sense of place and then move elsewhere. Most poets treated in this book anchor their fact-based poems in a historical place and time, with explicit references to objects, public sites, and matching human figures, that establish the emotional *feel* and visual *texture* of a locale the reader could witness firsthand. The result, on the whole, is a poetry that reassures readers by its fresh mixture of the familiar and unfamiliar. The daring language of such poems, most often a mix of vernacular and elevated modes of speech, secures a place in the reader's imagination. It's as if these contemporary poets have committed themselves to making sure that there will be a fair amount of *there there,* in contrast to Gertrude Stein's famous assertion about Oakland, further to the north, that "there is no there there." In David Barber's splendid poem "Funicular," one sees and feels the real and metaphorical activity of Angels Flight, at the base of Bunker Hill, "With all that jouncing, the cable's shivery tension / Coming up through the soles of your feet." Josephine Miles praises the Romeo and Juliet enacters on a float in the Rose Bowl Parade; Tom Disch adopts a barker's voice to advertise the city of the dead in "In Defense of Forest Lawn"; Ann Stanford (in a rare poem about the cityscape) remembers the Union Station of her youth; in "The San Gabriels" and "The Sierras" Martha Ronk expresses awe for the mountain chains surrounding the city: "How many ages to make them / how sharp the intake of breath at altitudes greater than / the irregular outline of a saw bringing down pines." These people and places get impressed on the memory and further nourish the constructive power of the personal and public imagination, as well as the vivid presence of the setting.[24] Such poems remind us to gaze at actualities in our surroundings and define ourselves in part by our engagement with the environment.

According to Norman M. Klein's influential text, *The History of Forgetting: Los Angeles and the Erasure of Memory* (1997), places impose on their viewers a "phantom limb" or "imago" effect. The experience of any distinctly articulated milieu is likely to leave memory traces that the mind turns into a "social imaginary" that may or may not resemble the memories of others but which becomes compelling, even obsessive, and leads to the desire to reproduce the effects in reverie, in conversation, in written or visual discourse. These representations, in their turn, leave memory traces on readers/viewers who have no immediate experience of the place but introject their informant's vision of the past. Klein argues that in order for something to be remembered, something else must be forgotten—specifically, the original image that gets covered over by a "scar" of representation. If, through the forces of urban renewal, an old neighborhood is erased in favor of a new one, or if a familiar landscape is radically re-formed, it may be that the truth of the originals passes into myth or disappears from memory entirely, until some artwork reintroduces them, if only for the period of time it takes to watch a scene in a film or hear a song or read a landscape poem. Klein does not discuss poetry, but his theoretical construct serves our reading experience of numerous first-rate poems about the city.

V

To illustrate Klein's thesis, and my interpretive methodology in this book, I'll comment on a poem that enacts some of the dynamic strategies of cultural memory and artistic representation when evoking a well-known site, Chavez Ravine, a hillside community linked to a now-vanished district of downtown Los Angeles called Sonora Town.

James Harms

THE DODGERS, 1958

There were no peacocks on the lawns. No angels in the palm trees.

The ravine was filled with a litter of houses, most of them tar paper
and cinder block, though here and there a lucky terra cotta roof rose
  above an accident
of bougainvillea, an arbor beyond a blue wall.

Down the hill in the middle distance: Chinatown, City Hall.
The children chased an old tire with a stick
as if pursuing an unattainable cliché.

A front porch rotted beneath *abuela*, the Chevys parked on the grass.
There were no peacocks on the lawns. No angels.

The young men in dusty fedoras (John Fante, Bukowski, the recent
Hollywood arrivals looking for work) crossed easily at the lights,
dodging out of habit the ghosts of streetcars on Wilshire Boulevard.

While in Brooklyn, trolleys rang down to silence, replaced by subways,
  fleets of taxis.

As always, the money drifted toward the ocean, to Pacific Palisades,
Malibu.

And so O'Malley looked elsewhere: the cheap real estate east of town,
Mt. Washington, the Monterey Hills.

Then he moved the Mexicans out of Chavez Ravine
to make room for a home team.[25]

—•—

As with Suzanne Lummis's poem, this one turns on the contrast, and conflict, between New York and Los Angeles. The move by the Brooklyn Dodgers to Los Angeles in 1958 is the most controversial transfer in the history of baseball; it changed profoundly and forever the life of citizens in the two metropolises, and even today can rouse powerful passions when people on either end of the deal confront each other. Let me insert a personal anecdote here. In 1984 Norman Mailer came to the University of Michigan to deliver the Hopwood Lecture and I was appointed to the airport detail. I picked up Mailer at the Detroit terminal and drove him into Ann Arbor. We chatted companionably about literary matters during the hour's drive, but when I mentioned that I grew up in L.A. he grew sullen. After a brief silence he said that he had never recovered from the trauma of having his hometown team move to the West Coast and still resented people from the city that had dispossessed Brooklyn fans of their beloved Dodgers.

Harms takes care to tamp down the significance of the move as it impacted a small community, the Mexican American residents of the Chavez Ravine site where some 1,000 families were removed by eminent domain and a new stadium erected. "There were no peacocks on the lawns. No angels in the palm trees," he begins, using a full stanza format for the two sentences printed out as one emphatic line. Don't worry, he seems to say to the reader, I'm not going to make this a sentimental, guilt-inducing elegy, I'm not going to mythologize the lost Hispanic world on the hillside as some exotic peacock- and angel-haunted landscape in the manner of Wallace Stevens. The second stanza shifts toward the rhetorical mode of social realism, cataloguing the commonplace low-cost structures that would eventually succumb to bulldozers. As if writing a prospect poem in the premodern style, Harms tells us that "Down the hill in the middle distance" lay Chinatown and City Hall—that is, the Civic Center. "Chinatown" contains a special resonance now, thanks to the Roman Polanski/Robert Towne film, a narrative of memory and forgetting with a morally ambiguous plot that tells us how Greater Los Angeles muscled its way into a deal that allowed it to import the water it needed to expand and how it mortgaged its soul in doing so.

Thanks to its free-verse structure, each long line spooling out an abundance of information to settle in the mind before extending the description further, the poem establishes a rapport between the reader and the cityscape of the past, the lost world of Mexican American settlement. Then it nods further backward in homage to two of the city's most famous, and mutually admiring, writers, John Fante and Charles Bukowski, imagining them coming to the city, "dodging . . . the ghosts of streetcars." The verb calls attention to the fact that the Dodgers got their name because the team and their fans had to dodge the Brooklyn streetcars to get to the stadium. Though streetcars had disappeared in Los Angeles by 1958 the name persisted, ensuring that the team would in its essence always represent Brooklyn as well as L.A. Local myth has it that the trolley tracks for the Big Red Cars were uprooted by the machinations of automobile companies that didn't want competition from public transportation. This story-line, enshrined in the popular film *Who Framed Roger Rabbit?*, fits the poem's narrative of dispossession and amnesia, but recent scholarship has challenged it in many details.[26] For readers aware that the trolley tracks were laid by unskilled immigrants imported from Mexico by the Pacific Electric Railway, the juxtaposition of site references achieves an additional thematic depth. Then a flashback within the flashback that is the entire poem gives us a glimpse of radical change in Brooklyn, a one-line elegy. (One could insert a memory of Marianne Moore, who wrote feelingly about her idolized Dodgers.) Then the subject position pivots swiftly to the west side of Los Angeles, the ideal spot for a baseball stadium thanks to the presence of wealthy patrons who would appreciate a short ride to the game. But no, the high cost of real estate forbids a ballpark. So just as suddenly back to the downtown area, as Walter O'Malley settles on the Chavez Ravine site, and just like the lordly Noah Cross in *Chinatown*, he effects the radical change in the city's fortune. The original settlement of 300-plus acres, already slated for urban renewal before 1958, disappears by fiat.

In *Notes from Underground*, Dostoevsky's protagonist asserts, "There are intentional and unintentional cities."[27] Saint Petersburg, the novel's setting, is an intentional city, raised according to plan beginning in 1703 by Peter the Great. Los Angeles has the reputation of being unintentional, sprawling into suburban and unincorporated spaces with little administrative design. Yet this poem (like *Chinatown*) asserts the opposite, that corporations and titans of finance made the city what they willed, in despite of human obstacles. The poem pronounces no didactic judgment on O'Malley, however, nor is the dusty ravine glamorized. By 1958 it was just a downscale, ramshackle neighborhood of a kind that often falls victim to decisions made by developers and city planners. The existence of Dodger Stadium has brought joy to millions of people since 1962, the team's first season in the new facility after several years of play in the Coliseum, and the poem lets the reader assess whether it was or was not an outrage to swap a shantytown for an amenity on the scale of the National League ballpark. Like Lummis's poem, this one keeps us off balance as we find our stock response to assign blame checked by the other side of the argument about progress and change. The speaker of this documentary-style poem is not introspective, nor is he polemical. He is more of a camera eye than an authorial presence with a tragic consciousness or an axe to grind. He declares things as they are, and will not proffer more than a hint of social critique. In resisting the lure of liberal pieties he chooses the more complex role of public historian.

By contrast, Michael Connelly protests the city's shady deal with O'Malley in his novel *Echo Park*, and James Ellroy does the same in his novel *White Jazz*. Connelly's detective, Harry Bosch, recalls as he investigates a crime in the area how "the city moved all the people out and bulldozed the bungalows and shacks they had called home. . . . To Bosch it seemed that as far back as he could remember in L.A. the fix was always in."[28] Bosch quotes a song from Ry Cooder's CD, *Chavez Ravine*, in which a worker wielding a bulldozer on the doomed community of Mexicans repeatedly absolves himself, intoning as a refrain the song title, "It's Just Work for Me," summoning the same emotional distancing that informs Harms's poem. In another cut in the CD, "3rd Base, Dodger Stadium," the speaker professes that "I'm a baseball fan, too" as he traces the memories of shacks and trees and happy settlers where the bases now stand. In this lament, the shiny white bases come to sound like the Stations of the Cross.[29]

Unlike Lummis's poem Harms's takes pleasure in naming specific locales in the city, on the assumption that readers like to see familiar names show up in the white field of the page. Harms's poem is relentlessly descriptive and disjointed, directing our eye like a tour guide. The shifting tableaux are anchored or supplemented by famous place names—Chinatown, Wilshire Boulevard, Pacific Palisades, Malibu—as well as districts many Angelenos may not be able to locate: Mt. Washington, Monterey Hills. What these discrete places have in common, the poem suggests in its closure, is a "home team." The Dodgers are both a real and conceptual hub that inspires feelings of relatedness and community. More than City Hall, the stadium is the true downtown, the genuine *agora*. No historical event, the poem suggests, occurs in some neighborhood fictive as Shangri-La. If "The Dodgers, 1958" features a collage of seemingly dissociated planes in Cubist fashion, it also presents a coherent chronological structure verifiable in the public records. Most poems set in the city acquire their resonance, their aura, from the sense of actuality endowed by locations we can re-cognize as the poem's meditation or narrative takes form. And the poem itself becomes the scar of representation, for all its neutral, conciliatory tone. For the duration of reading this account of what has been forgotten, the reader is compelled to remember.

In *Landscape and Power* W. J. T. Mitchell begins by asserting, "The aim of this book is to change 'landscape' from a noun to a verb." "Landscape" already is a verb, but Mitchell refers to the *genre* of landscape representation, arguing that woods, rivers, and mountains exist in great artworks not (just) as depicted objects but as a discourse, a "vast network of cultural codes."[30] The same may be said of the cityscape as rendered, for example, by Lummis and Harms above and by other poets throughout this book. Poets may or may not focus intently on tall buildings, beachfront architecture, freeways, etc., but they necessarily, because they have suasive intentions, contextualize and process the significance of what they reclaim and render in language. They are always dramatizing, always interpreting, and to do so they must call upon the models of rhetoric with which they are most familiar, whether poems or some other discourse. They make their gestures of resistance and remembering "essential" when they succeed in articulating a vision of the city that compels assent or at least engagement in their readers. That is what "power" is. And that is the basis of my choices of reprinted poems in this volume.

From this point forward I will present chapters that collect and comment on poems gathered together (for the most part) by areas, locations, defined spatial categories. Each place is a site of contention in which the individual poet not only takes advantage of customary associations but challenges perspectives claiming a privileged meaning. Such independence of mind and treatment is par for the course in poems about cities or rural areas. If one lines up all the published poems about Brooklyn Bridge, or Broadway, or the bohemian/ethnic East Side of Manhattan, there is an astonishing range of disputed claims for the literal or symbolic qualities of each New York landmark. The same is true for the New England country scenes depicted in zillions of lyric poems from the nineteenth and twentieth centuries. (Robert Frost alone provides a dazzling array of topographical sites with differing valuations.) Los Angeles seems even more inchoate as a literary place, and its poets more uncertain, because there is no consensus on which poems deserve a place at the center in the canon of texts about the city. And, to our great benefit, new poems keep appearing to persuade us of new valuations.

What we do know is that, because there can be no single, standard, privileged representation of an actual location, by a poet or any other writer, the variety of rhetorical strategies in constructing versions of a site or a city is infinite. The poet's motive for representation, for tweaking the usual associations of place, may be anger, or irony, or wonder, or the pressures of personal anecdote, but the net effect is one of refreshing readers' perceptions about a familiar spot in the atlas. In turn, those fresh ways of thinking about place, of imagining it into life as if it were a classic narrative of improved landscape as fantastical as Poe's Domain of Arnheim, contribute to the forces of renewal, both literary and social, that preserve what is valuable in the urban landscape and condemn what is demeaning and corrupt. The passage from Stephen Yenser that I use as an epigraph to this book (along with one from "The Domain of Arnheim") provides abundant wordplay to make sense of the name and nature of Los Angeles. As with Poe's angel-designed earthly paradise, Yenser's "mesh and mess" changes form and meaning with each glimpse. To render landscape in language that creates a new awareness of order and disorder, energy and entropy, is to revitalize the sense of community. It is the ambition of all poets reinterpreting a great city to effect this new vision by producing poems of lasting value.

There is no "major" poem anywhere near as foundational to the public's image of Los Angeles as the masterpieces of fiction that still define the region. Thomas McGrath could have written such a poem, perhaps, some extended and particularized vision of the city as resonant and complex as the canonical lyrics of Old World urban settings. But so far Los Angeles is a city inclusive of poems rather than a city half-created by poems. I offer this book as a path into the wilderness, a path in search of the signposts and landmarks that will help construct a comprehensive road map of the tradition.

ONE

The Pacific Ocean of the Poets

It's hard / to address water
—BRENDA HILLMAN[1]

Sun-drenched site of summertime revels. Beautiful young bodies silhouetted against foaming surf. Children building sand castles. Palm trees and seabirds framed in the rising and setting sun. Moonlight shimmering on the high tide. So much of Southern California's powerful allure has consisted of indelible visual images derived from tourist brochures, magazine layouts, movies, television, and Internet video. Poets have contributed very little to this iconography. Throughout history poets have planted in our consciousness compelling language for the Atlantic Ocean, the Mediterranean and Caribbean seas, the Mississippi and Nile rivers, Italy's Lake Como and Kashmir's Dal Lake. But modern poets have fallen short of evoking in memorable language the unique features of the sea-edge from Santa Barbara down to Baja California, and the complex culture of coastal municipalities. Or they have written poems deserving of public appreciation and failed to make a connection.

The lyrics that resound in the minds and hearts of American citizens derive entirely from popular songs, such as The Beach Boys' "Surfin' USA" and "Surfer Girl," Jan and Dean's "Surf City," The Mamas and the Papas' "California Dreamin'," The Four Preps' "26 Miles," about Catalina Island, Van Morrison's "Venice USA," Patti Smith's "Redondo Beach," and George Strait's "Marina del Rey." Since the early twentieth century, songwriters have usurped the elite poet's self-appointed task of mapping, describing, and dramatizing the far western boundary of the American continent, the far eastern edge of the Pacific Rim, with unforgettable metaphors, witty wordplay, and home truths.

Whose fault is this? The answer to that question is not a simple one.

I

The Pacific Ocean entered the Western imagination via memoirs by explorers, traders, captains and seamen of vessels plying from port to port. Centuries after Balboa made his amazing discovery of the Pacific in 1513, Hernán Cortés, Juan Rodríguez Cabrillo, Francis Drake, and many others followed with reports about the California coastline. Richard Henry Dana Jr.'s personal history, *Two Years before the Mast* (1840), and two memory fictions by Herman Melville, *Typee* (1846) and *Omoo* (1847), provided exotic story lines and characters while registering protests against commercial exploitation of regions like the Pacific Islands. Poets did not contribute to this construction of the offshore history, not even hardy and popular types like Joaquin Miller, Robert Service, and George Sterling, who preferred as subject matter the rugged prospector camps and raffish saloons in the western part of the continent. Nor did genteel nineteenth-century poets seek to engage the Pacific coast, except as picturesque tableaux in the manner of the *Plein Air* painters whose work, often quite lovely, adhered to the restrictive formulas of premodern taste.

Walt Whitman wanted to plant the first American flag on the Pacific shore. The "Western Sea," as he called it in "Starting from Paumanok," loomed in his imagination as the significant terminus of the Open Road, but the road the settlers trod in his hymnal "Song of the Pioneers" led to a place he could not precisely imagine. In his bombastic lyric "Facing West from California Shores," written without having experienced the actual terrain, Whitman conjures not a real place but a mythic staging area for travel from maternal origin through mortality and back to the cosmic womb. He calls the Pacific shore a "land of migrations" where one embarks as a figurative child and navigates around the world in a westerly life-cycle that terminates in the original site. These two manifest destinies, the personal and the national or imperial, become mystically intertwined in his visionary book *Leaves of Grass*. Whitman wrote with some specificity about landscape in "Song of the Redwood-Tree" set in the Yosemite and Mendocino mountains and forests. But he could not have prophesied what we now call Manhattan

Beach or Newport Beach except symbolically, as one vast shoreline from which a voyager might sail and sometime in his or her future run onto the sands of the "spice islands" and other stepping-stones back through the lost childhood to the cosmic embrace. "The ocean, the symbolic site of California's endings, is also . . . the place of beginnings," David Fine remarks in a commentary on Carolyn See's novel *Golden Days*, which ends with a nuclear attack on Los Angeles, but moves its few survivors down to Topanga State Beach for a redemptive ceremony of rebirth.[2]

Whitman's impulse and his example persist. The Pacific shore is an attractive location for poets not only because it provides beauty and sport but because it signifies the possibility of transfiguration, of ecstasy, of radical change of personality and lifestyle. David Orr writes that "the beach . . . is an area that lends itself to discussions of in-betweenness, hybridity, and unstable identities."[3] One might employ another of Whitman's texts, the Preface to *Leaves of Grass*, which claims, "The United States themselves are essentially the greatest poem," in order to assert that the Pacific Ocean and its shoreline communities constitute one of the most perfect lyric poems imaginable, its water and sea-edge imagery always available for symbolic use. Mel Weisburd, editor of the poetry journal *Coastlines* during the 1950s, drives the boundary of land and ocean in "Along the Coast," reminding himself that "earth's surface is mostly water / and unconscious, to be farmed only by poetry."[4] Gail Wronsky published in 2000 a tribute in the style of the Good Gray Poet, "Tonight, Walt Whitman, the Pacific." Intended for recitation at a public occasion, the tenth anniversary of the American Oceans Campaign, it glorifies the Pacific as it addresses Whitman:

> we'll celebrate the salt spray dashing on the rocks in Venice;
> we'll celebrate the winds piping and screeching through the sea caves in
> Malibu;
> we'll celebrate the absence of oil drilling off the glittering coast of the
> Pacific Palisades . . .[5]

And so forth. What matters in such poems is not the quality of the verse but their function as placeholders for the genuine bards of the beach who will render this marine landscape knowledgeably, with felt passion and persuasive rhetoric. In order for the Pacific to be entirely a liminal place made sacred by Whitman's zealous nationalism, there must be language capable of attaching this far western frontier to other locations he and his disciples—

Hart Crane, William Carlos Williams, Carl Sandburg, Vachel Lindsay, Muriel Rukeyser, Allen Ginsberg—established in the canon. Whitman showed how the coastline can be assimilated into the city proper, if the poet's imaginative dredging is extensive enough. The East River is no Pacific Ocean, but "Crossing Brooklyn Ferry" demonstrates how intimately water and meditation are wedded, in Melville's phrase. Without some such memorable articulation of the Pacific and its enthralling hold upon the imagination of Americans, the whole of the city's literature falls short of bringing the "Western Sea" into the consciousness of readers who seek inspiration from the poetic tradition beginning with Homer. The place can never quite be Greater Los Angeles without a masterpiece or two to anchor and delineate the spiritual value system and natural ecosystem of the coastline.

The California poet who by consensus *owns* the Pacific Ocean is Robinson Jeffers. He gazed at it day after day for decades from Hawk Tower atop a granite house he and his wife built with their own hands above Carmel Bay. Though he is the epitome of the *northern* California temperament, we must appreciate his mystique of the ocean and coastal community so that southland depictions come into proper focus by contrast. In fact, Jeffers spent some ten years of his youth in Southern California, including two years of matriculation at Occidental College. His first book, *Flagons and Apples*, was printed in Los Angeles by the Grafton Press in 1912 and contains a few poems set in Hermosa and Redondo beaches. By the time he published his second book, *Californians* (1916), however, he had fixed his imagination exclusively on the region of Big Sur and Mill Valley. Los Angeles and its environs became the portion of reality he deliberately repressed. Later in life he tellingly remarked at a poetry reading: "Now perhaps it is time for some California scenery. You must understand that this is not Southern California; there are no orange-groves and no oil-wells, but high mountains rising steep from the ocean, pasturing a few cattle and many deer."[6] Jeffers had forgotten that the southern part of the state has mountains and beaches as well.

How Jeffers describes his surroundings exerted a profound effect on writers who followed in his prodigious wake. He begins with the all-important fact that unlike the Atlantic Ocean, which unites the Old World and the New but also represents a gulf of separation between them, the Pacific is too vast to be a figure of extension and connection; rather, it represents what Derek Walcott calls a "mythopoetic coast," as much an allegorical resource as a body of water.[7] The Pacific did not offer, like the Atlantic, an easy passage to a parental and ancestral civilization; for the white-skinned pioneers it was an alternative to civilization, an escape from civilization, perennially wild and thrilling to the imagination. It served writers of Jeffers's generation as the dependable *nunc stans* of local geography, the unchanging and static form distinct from an ever-evolving cultural community. While many aspiring American authors migrated east just before and just after the Great War of 1914–18, settling in future-oriented cities like Paris and London or points even more eastern along the Mediterranean, Jeffers made his singular way down the coast from Washington to California, all the time writing apprentice lyrics and narrative poems he confessedly modeled after Wordsworth, Rossetti, and Yeats.

Jeffers offers the best précis of his worldview in a retrospective essay included in his volume *Selected Poetry* (1938). When he first came upon the Carmel coast,

> I could see people living—amid magnificent unspoiled scenery—essentially as they did in the Idyls or the Sagas, or in Homer's Ithaca. Here was life purged of its ephemeral accretions. Men were riding after cattle, or plowing the headland, hovered by white sea-gulls, as they have done for thousands of years, and will for thousands of years to come. Here was contemporary life that was also permanent life; and not shut from the modern world but conscious of it and related to it; capable of expressing its spirit, but unencumbered by the mass of poetically irrelevant details and complexities that make a civilization.[8]

To construct a language commensurate with this primitivist, nostalgic vision, Jeffers turned to the toolbox of bardic figures and attitudes. His narratives of people caught up in the grandeur of life belonging to an agricultural and seacoast society demanded a diction adapted from Sophocles and Euripides rather than the slangy dialogue that his contemporary, Eugene O'Neill, crafted for his rowdy seafarers. Jeffers's model of versification remained the long free-verse lines of Whitman and the hexameters of Homer. The scenery is often a dark place, clouded over or cast in twilight shadows. "Civilization" as defined affirmatively by progressive writers of his era is largely absent from his visionary lyrics. He provides pictorial vistas of the ocean akin to the sublimity of Romantic models in both poetry and painting. J. M. W. Turner and Winslow Homer inspired him, not the incitements of Cubism. Often the poem lifts our eyes from water, sand, and rock to the pelicans, herons, or golden eagles flying above the waves scouting for prey:

Fresh as the air, salt as the foam, play birds in the bright wind, fly
falcons
Forgetting the oak and the pinewood, come gulls
From the Carmel sands and the sands at the river-mouth, from Lobos
and out of the limitless
Power of the mass of the sea, for a poem
Needs multitude, multitudes of thoughts, all fierce, all flesh-eaters,
musically clamorous
Bright hawks that hover and dart headlong, and ungainly
Gray hungers fledged with desire of transgression, salt slimed beaks,
from the sharp
Rock-shores of the world and the secret waters.[9]

Jeffers insists that his fluent poem "needs multitude," and his eye turns deliberately away from the few human beings lounging in a wild landscape dominated by natural creatures and forces. It is mesmerizing, incantatory poetry, complex in syntax (the above passage is a single sentence), and elevated in diction, the perfect expression of a solitude-loving neo-romantic who seeks union with the profoundest natural forces of the world.

But it was utterly useless as inspiration for the poets and songwriters who passed their time in Southern California. How strange it was in the late 1950s, as I sat on the sands of Venice Beach watching the volleyball games and overhearing the low idioms of my peers, to think of Jeffers some three hundred miles north writing the prophetic poems later collected in *The Beginning and the End* (1963) a year after his death, and how strange it must have been for him to overhear from radios on the Carmel and Big Sur beaches the blithe lyrics of The Beach Boys as he composed his last tragic testament.

Whitman and Jeffers have this in common: they recognize that the liminal property of the shoreline enforces a captivity of the spirit akin to the womb's and the grave's. Serious verse about the beach, about the Ocean, will always be atavistic, retrospective, apocalyptic. The journey *toward* the beach, or *onto* the beach, will always have an ecstatic fatality of purpose. Put another way, the Dionysian union of man and nature experienced by beachgoers is evoked as a death of the self, a surrender to overwhelming and ultimately anti-human cosmic forces. For this reason, the Apollonian poet in Southern California will always be tempted to travel in the opposite direction, *away from* the paganism of spent youth and the seductions of profound spiritual transformation, toward places marked as civilized where poetry will be valued more than self-erasing immersion in the beckoning surf. The world of rapturous enchantment belongs to the operatic north, where Jeffers's descendants like William Everson (Brother Antoninus), Gary Snyder, Kenneth Rexroth, and Czeslaw Milosz cultivated the austere yet satisfying natural religion of their forerunner in Carmel. In the south of California, few beachgoers or weekend sailors on their pleasure crafts welcomed a critique of "ephemeral accretions" or a devotional attitude toward the gulls and stormy surf at the water's edge.

Mark Jarman

THE SUPREMES

In Ball's Market after surfing till noon,
we stand in wet trunks, shivering
as icing dissolves off our sweet rolls
inside the heat-blued counter oven,
when they appear on his portable TV,
riding a float of chiffon as frothy
as the peeling curl of a wave.
The parade m.c. talks up their hits
and their new houses outside of Detroit
and old Ball clicks his tongue.
Gloved up to their elbows, their hands raised
toward us palm out, they sing,
"Stop! In the Name of Love" and don't stop
but slip into the lower foreground.

Every day of a summer can turn,
from one moment, into a single day.
I saw Diana Ross in her first film
play a brief scene by the Pacific—
and that was the summer it brought back.
Mornings we paddled out, the waves
would be little more than embellishments:
lathework and spun glass,

gray-green with cold, but flawless.
When the sun burned through the light fog,
they would warm and swell,
wind-scaled and ragged,
and radios up and down the beach
would burst on with her voice.

She must remember that summer
somewhat differently, and so must the two
who sang with her in long matching gowns,
standing a step back on her left and right,
as the camera tracked them
into our eyes in Ball's Market.
But what could we know, tanned white boys,
wiping sugar and salt from our mouths
and leaning forward to feel their song?
Not much, except to feel it
ravel us up like a wave
in the silk of white water,
simply, sweetly, repeatedly,
and just as quickly let go.

We didn't stop either, which is how
we vanished, too, parting like spray—
Ball's Market, my friends and I.
Dredgers ruined the waves,
those continuous dawn perfections,
and Ball sold high to the high rises
cresting over them. His flight out of L. A.,
heading for Vegas, would have banked
above the wavering lines of surf.
He may have seen them. I have,
leaving again for points north and east,
glancing down as the plane turns.
From that height they still look frail and frozen,
full of simple sweetness and repetition.[10]

—•—

Mark Jarman, an admirer of Jeffers, offers one of the most complex responses to the archetypes established by his spiritual father to the north. His poem "The Supremes," from *Far and Away* (1985), finds the speaker at a moment of migration, headed for "points north and east" in defiance of the customary westward movement across the continent in memoirs and fictions about Los Angeles. In fact, there are two migrations in the final strophe: Ball, the owner of a beachside market, has "sold high to the high rises" and is hand-carrying the profits to Las Vegas. Ball and the speaker leave behind them a scene of transformations, a melancholy version of the "new life" represented by the modern city as contrasted with the sweetness of the surf the "tanned white boys" experienced in their teen rituals of surfing and beachcombing. That Ball's Market gives way to condos is a small occasion for mourning, but that "Dredgers ruined the waves"! What seemed so elemental, so fundamentally unchangeable, are wrenched into social time as some radical alteration—perhaps a marina, or rock jetties making the waves more hospitable to family bathers—tames the ocean and eviscerates the speaker's memory of ecstatic surfing.

Jarman, born in 1952, spent significant portions of his life in Southern California, but his biography is remarkable for his many academic interludes as student and professor, chiefly in Santa Cruz, Iowa City, and Evansville, before accepting a long-term appointment as Professor of English at Vanderbilt University beginning in 1983. A partisan of the neo-narrative movement, he has authored many lyrics like "The Supremes" that relate a story apparently autobiographical, raising the vexed question of whether the emotion summoned by the meditative and narrative elements should be ascribed to an invented persona or to the author. Like and unlike the manifestly invented speaker of Suzanne Lummis's "Shangri-La," the narrator of Jarman's poem traces the exemplary experience of an "I" and a generational "we." Would the poem lose significant power if we read it as impersonal, as a sequence of memories and emotions related to the author by a friend but not undergone by Jarman himself? Would a reading of the poem that distances its contents from the status of personal testament render the particularity, the seemingly reportorial detail, a shade less compelling? As the first lyric to be studied in this book that presents these questions, "The Supremes" will help us to identify the range of rhetorical possibilities available to the lyric poet confronting a landscape he or she ostensibly wishes to re-create from memory as a paradigm of Southern California experience.

"The Supremes" derives some of its persuasive strategies from tradition. It makes claims for the power of the ocean in line with Whitman's and Jeffers's depictions. But it situates the commercial landscape of the beach within the recognizable territory of urban malaise. The elegiac tone of the conclusion recalls for us other city poems that end on a downbeat of plangent recollection: Robert Lowell's "For the Union Dead"; James Merrill's "18 West 11th Street"; and C. K. Williams's memoirs of home repair and social breakdown, "Bread" and "Tar." Thanks to the setting of "The Supremes," Jarman pursues a complex emotional train of thought akin to those canonical lyrics of the postwar world, with their unrelieved gloom and high-pitched crescendos of despair.

The story line of "The Supremes" is complicated by the central trope of the poem: a comparison of the waves to the singing of The Supremes, a Motown girl group whose hit tunes filled the airwaves during the 1960s and 1970s. The group appears in the opening lines as televised images, and their voices, which most readers will hear in their heads as the poem proceeds, "ravel us up like a wave / in the silk of white water" so that song and surf fuse into a mystical harmony that is the essence (and finally, the limitation) of adolescence. Eden had its divine music, its transcendent melodies, according to Robert Frost in "Never Again Would Bird Song Be the Same," and we can still hear them in the songs that birds learned from Eve and mimicked down through the generations. The ocean, too, has its transfiguring soundtrack, and for the speaker it is recollected, perpetually accessible, in the voice of Diana Ross and her two co-performers. The third strophe stays with them in a complex set of perceptions: the source image is generated in Detroit, then transmitted to the TV set in Ball's Market, and then through the speaker's nostalgic association of song and surf to readers who relive their own past thanks to the poem's meaningful allusiveness.

What is crucial in this apotheosis of an African American singing group anchored in Detroit is that the music is not generated by The Beach Boys, Dick Dale, Jan and Dean, or any of the other white lyricists of the beach subculture. The siren songs of The Supremes, as figures of an alternative and distinctly "other" culture, figuratively lure the speaker away from the plenitude and romance of the Pacific. And the language of the poem, as with all of Jarman's work, rejects the debased slang of beach songs and beach movies; nothing is "bitchin'" and no "hoods," "greasers," "surf bums," "hot doggers," or "Big Kahunas" populate the verbal beachscape. The poem actively resists the clichés of popular culture in formulating a personal testament of considerable linguistic gravity.

History provides another turn, another nuance of meaning, when we consider that Motown Records moved all its operations to Los Angeles in 1972, a migration that contributed to the physical devastation of Detroit commonly signified by the race riots there in 1967. The movement west by Motown Records is most often ascribed to Diana Ross's ambition to star in romantic movies, one of which is recalled by Jarman's speaker in the second strophe. The film—presumably *Lady Sings the Blues* (1972)—implicates Hollywood in the melancholy plot of West Coast seduction of the young. This artful subtext poses a critique of greedy commercialism already established in the subplot of Ball's defection from the beach, and it anticipates the speaker's own irresistible desire to go forward, not stop and linger, despite his felt knowledge of what he is giving up.

"Stop! In the Name of Love" is a song directed toward the singer's boyfriend, who is paying court to another woman. It is the furthest thing from a cultural statement, yet Jarman makes it into one by connecting it to the rupture of his supposed state of innocence, his blissful baptism in the surf. For the sake of his innocence, in the very name of it, he inwardly breathes a prayer that time have a stop as he dwells in reverie on the unruined seascape belonging to his teen memories. But the waves, time's repetitive markers, did not stop, cannot stop even in the nostalgic scene he re-creates in the civilized artifact of his poem.

"We didn't stop either, which is how / we vanished, too, parting like spray . . . ." The beach is a site of leave-takings, even for those who remain in the city and revisit less and less frequently their old haunts up and down the coast as they age and change. The poet has the power to stop time, to stop it in the name of love. At the heart of a fundamentally discursive poem, Jarman places a lyric passage meant to eternize the moment, personal to the poet in a way readers can only approximate by sympathy.

> Mornings we paddled out, the waves
> would be little more than embellishments:
> lathework and spun glass,
> gray-green with cold, but flawless.
> When the sun burned through the light fog,
> they would warm and swell,
> wind-scaled and ragged,
> and radios up and down the beach
> would burst on with her voice.

The sonic architecture of such a passage puts to shame the crude effects of pop lyrics. Repetition of the "g," "w," and "a" sounds, not in a fixed pattern but in the open phrasing held intact by the basic four-beat line, accentuates the brief rhythmic moments of concentrated tension, as in the spondaic phrases like "spun glass," "light fog," "wind-scaled," "burst on." The layering of images line by line, like the brushstrokes of lacquer applied to a perfect glass vessel, suspends the reader in a kind of trance akin to the rapture of bobbing in the waves. "The poet's love for the facts of the landscape is expressed through phrasing," Jarman remarks in an essay.[11] In order to sustain its vision of experience, the poem's prosody must convey a visual and auditory sense of constant pleasure in the waves and wind, in the privileged textual moment of immersion. The diction and rhythm perform at a level superior to the vernacular, and the imagery possesses that sheen associated with photographic and cinematic enhancement of the Pacific light. The final words of each line, especially, highlight the chief stimuli in the experience of swimming.

Jarman does not conjure just one spot of time, one epiphany, but a period of time, a succession of summer days, as indicated by the conditional "would" verb construction. "Embellishments" is a word that catches the eye, for we are aware that the poet is embellishing the visceral memory by the decorative gestures of his word choices. The waves are compared not only to the silken sounds of The Supremes but to a kind of "flawless" glass ornamented with facets and colors to please the connoisseur. The process of creation and re-creation is made manifest to readers by the addition of tidal effects, observed and felt—the "swell" especially is replicated in the basic iambic rhythm. And just as we settle into the waves/lines of this ecstatic experience, the interruptions of radios break the spell. We are back in time, albeit an idyllic time; we can date it by measuring how far we are in our present day from that enchanted summer, that Golden Age.

"Supreme" means "superior to all others." Applied to a singing group, the word is an example of hyperbole, exaggeration. Applied to an epoch in one's life, it may be an assertion that certain experiences—say, recurrent adolescent ones—remain as the fountainhead of life thereafter. On these spots of time depends the sense of power that drives and sustains one through life. Jane Tompkins calls attention to the way writers about the West tend to prefer "the fully saturated moment" to more discursive lyric and narrative tableaux. "The frontier is a way of imagining the self in a boundary situation—a place that will put you to some kind of ultimate test." Such moments, and their anecdotal frames, convey "something purer and more authentic, more intense, more real."[12] These supreme experiences occur in surfing, the iconic sport at the end of the frontier. Dorothy Barresi in "Surfing as Meditation" does not hesitate to associate surfing with baptism into the timeless experience of the sacred and, more than that, with the ecstatic letting go that belongs to a vision of otherworldly redemption, what she calls "*apocalypso millennium*":

> In the one true theocracy,
> only he who prays himself black & blue will be saved, sucked,
> embodied,
> all the way to Zuma Beach and beyond
> in one glorious undertow of spirit over choice,
> because there is no choice—
> if it's true.[13]

In the supreme experience of surfing one enacts, or reenacts, the primal swim through amniotic fluid, as well as early mystical experiences of Wordsworthian "clouds of glory" repeated in imagination as an exalted rite of body and spirit alike. In the line after the passage above, the seabirds caw at the human child, "Fuck the body!" The pleasure of giving one's body to the waves in exchange for transfiguration of the spirit heightens the trauma of leaving the ocean home for the afterlife of mature rewards that pleasure the mind and chasten the soul.

In his essay "Looking for History in Los Angeles" William Irwin Thompson describes "the rich fantasy life of the L.A. man" and explains his own migration away from the city as an effort to ground himself by reclaiming an ancestral connection in the Old World: "My own adolescent fantasy of the real thing was Ireland. Ireland was green, while Los Angeles was desert."[14] When he visits Ireland he receives an "awakening slap in the face," not least from discovering that Ireland had too much history, too much of the burden of time and not enough of the grand green contours of open space. At the edge of the edge of history, at the continent's rim, west of Watts, where Thompson is awakened by another salutary slap in the face, lay the supreme site, if Jarman can be believed. The public beach, with its congregation of semi-nude bodies in all shapes, colors, and postures, is the alpha point of being for those who were nurtured by it.

"The Supremes" is remarkable for its shifting point of view, from far away to close up, from the social to the tactile, from time past to time present. Freud argued that memories of early life do not emerge in our later life as exact replicas, as pristine copies. They are created in the guise of invented images and narratives. The images are essential because only what is knowable, palpable, linguistic, can articulate the argument about transcendence without disappearing into a reflex nostalgia for unity of being. When Jarman casts his last backward glance after several revisitations of the beach, the remembered scene is blunted, the language moderated. The waves are "frail and frozen, / full of simple sweetness and repetition." The diction belongs to the value-free recollection of soda and burgers on the sand, not of ecstasy and transcendence. These are lines that expose the perils of nostalgia. Nature in the form of water's body becomes "simple," and perhaps a bit boring, a bit monotonous and forbiddingly chilly. The poet, having enchanted himself with reveries of temporal satisfaction, disenchants himself in order to keep moving as an adult toward the next civilized space.

As in romance narrative, the beach plays the role of a Bower of Bliss, a passage of time coincident with the onset of adolescent sexuality, including the low-grade sensualism of The Supremes. In fact, The Supremes are part of the problem. Diana Ross becomes a figure of La Belle Dame Sans Merci, the siren of sweet sounds that militate against growing older, growing up, finding one's niche in the history of civilization as poet and citizen. Like Eden, the ocean ejects its happy lovers east into a harsher, historical world of grown-up experience, perhaps via the Santa Monica Freeway, past the high-rise offices and Skid Row slums of downtown, and then to challenging "points east and north."

Jarman qualifies as a former resident, and his quarrel with the Pacific beach is softened by sentiment. He does not speak in the poem as a remote observer, like Whitman and Jeffers, but as an active participant in the life changes he documents. Not a fisherman or dockworker, nor a real-estate speculator like Ball, he takes on himself the role of an elegist of his own bodily shape-shifting from surfer to poet-professor in the elite institutions of American culture. Now it is his poetry that offers "embellishments" formerly attributed to the waves and melodies of his lost youth. The poem charts the interaction of surfaces and depths in the retrospective mode. The speaker demonstrates his understanding that he is condemned to be a tourist in the terrain of his own life history. His time as a surfer fades into the glamour of a historical epoch falsely represented in popular culture by the formulas of *Baywatch* and the beach party movies. In the second stanza he identifies his adolescence as "one day," the singular experience of timelessness that belongs, as with so many aspirations in Los Angeles, to a poet's unrecoverable past.

II

The most trenchant representations of the city have often been by tourists, emigrants, and vagrants passing through. Their critiques have tended to complain about the surfaces of everyday life in Los Angeles, conveniently so since the superficial is as far as most tourists can see into everyday life. Indeed, L.A. has always proffered its surfaces ostentatiously for judgment. The deep imagery and thematic complexity that Wordsworth finds in the Lake District, or Elizabeth Bishop in Brazil, Florida, and Nova Scotia, tend to be neglected in poetry about L.A., and more often than not in its fiction. When Wordsworth confessed in his autobiographical poem *The Prelude* that his imagination could not penetrate into the inner soul of the city of London:

> Oh, blank confusion! true epitome
> Of what the mighty City is herself,
> To thousands upon thousands of her sons,
> Living amid the same perpetual whirl
> Of trivial objects, melted and reduced
> To one identity, by differences
> That have no law, no meaning, and no end— (VII.722–28)

he testified to the subjugation of the poet's eye to what glitters but is not gold. The challenge for visiting poets has always been the invention of language answerable to the half-hidden presences in the briefly glimpsed landscape. When such tourists visit the Pacific coastline, their radar is likely to register one thing at once: that the "beach scene" is not the hedonistic delight advertised in the media, nor the salubrious alternative to a commercial civilization recommended by the likes of Jarman and Jeffers. The writer's disappointed response to false advertising by means of heightened rhetorical gestures is civilization's dependable weapon against fraud: satire.

Derek Walcott

SUMMER ELEGIES II

Nothing hurts as much as the word "California,"
the wincing light of Los Angeles. In unfinished Venice
a fresco interrupted in its prophecy looks phonier
than what it promised: gondolas, palazzos, its own Bridge of Sighs.
It fades under its graffiti, a transferred paradise.

Sharper than the smell of eucalyptus is the ammonia
of the beach's comfort stations, mist sprayed the air.
My heart could contain the Pacific then, now it is only a-
nother grey waste, with soiled breakers in the flare
of a summer sunset, radios and barbecues. So, here

too the carousel revolves its rusty horizon, lonelier
than an abandoned carnival where the carved white horses
creak to a stop, and the freaks move their paraphernalia
to another beach: Malibu, San Francisco, Santa Barbara.

We recited the names of the avenues, La Cienega,
Pico; I understood the false fronts, the fake Spanish façades,
the dusty brooms of the palms; I was eager
to make a clean sweep, to find the poetry in roof-wide ads

for the latest release, the billboards plugging Sony, a
new way to live, ours, we were sure, a second-best bet, a Hertz
or an Avis; now so many songs have California
in them, and the H in Hollywood hurts.

I hadn't thought to make light of this: the light of
Los Angeles. I meant it painting the hillside pines.
I meant it, lying under the cool sheets, but it was only the right of
any ruin to burst into flowers briefly, strange flowers, fresh vines.

There's sometimes more pain in a pop song than all of Cambodia,
and that's the trouble, the heart puts love above it
all, any other pain—Chernobyl, a mass murder—
the world's slow stain is there; we cannot remove it.

The irony of it, Cynthia, is that we can never own a-
nother heart. I must smile, or die, hence this lightness.
Hence this fake chic, these stanza windows like a posh boutique
in a semitropical desert. Shall I stop the jokes and speak
for the soul? Soul, was she not your fair and final brightness?

Didn't your bodies fit perfectly? Bone to bone, a
miracle of calibration and metre, didn't the shape
of lips, and the small well under her throat,
rhyme easily as my hand fitting under her damp nape?
She fitted the ribs of my body like a boat.

Shoot the end of this now. Let the last line
be an empty lot after work. West Venice changes its gels
for the fade. We become, said Borges, books when we are dying.
I died and did not become any book in the city of angels.[15]

—•—

Derek Walcott moves beyond satire to sarcasm in the second of his "Summer Elegies" in *The Arkansas Testament* (1987). Awarded the Nobel Prize for Literature in 1992, Walcott is most famous for his poems located in the Windward Antilles, especially St. Lucia where he was raised and which he employs as his Ithaca in the epic *Omeros*. But he is also a drifter, a cosmopolitan, a *flâneur*, a "fortunate traveler" in the (sarcastic) words of one of his book titles, who reports in his dispatch-like poems the status of his spiritual condition as he wanders through diverse regions of the world. In some places he is reverent, remembering their glories; in others like Venice West (an alternative name for California's Venice), he is satirical, lampooning the pretension of the borrowed name and the degraded landscape, "grey waste, with soiled breakers in the flare / of a summer sunset, radios and barbecues." When he rhapsodizes about seaside places in the Caribbean and Africa, as in *Omeros*, he provides close-up descriptions of the fishermen and shopkeepers, the markets and ceremonies, that sanctify the land- and seascape. But in Venice Walcott adopts the standard-issue critique of the West Coast, and he deploys a variety of rhetorical devices to demean the sites that yearn to be invested with value.

The rhyme scheme cavorts in a buffoonish manner, like a stand-up comedian turning and twisting his patter to extract some laughs from a tough audience. "California" is made to rhyme with "phonier" in the opening stanza, and the deprecatory rhyme continues throughout the poem: ammonia, paraphernalia, La Cienega, down to "[billboards plugging a] Sony, a / new way to live." And then inspiration wanes, the "a" gambit at the end of scattered lines grows tiresome, and the rhyme peters out. Other feminine rhymes supporting the creaky architecture of chiming syllables—"above it . . . remove it" and so forth—deliberately call attention to Walcott's condescension.

The burlesque of rhyme consorts well with the risible objects he chronicles as he visits the ruined glamour of a site once known as "The Coney Island of the Pacific," but better known as "The Slum by the Sea" when I spent my summer days there in the 1950s and '60s. I gloried in the famous light of early morning, but for Walcott the modifier for that light is "wincing," a transferred epithet that suggests the discomfort of beachgoers who stare into the sun or (turning to the West) into the glare rising from the waves, but also implies the sun's discomfort with the sordid scene it lights up in city and sea-edge alike. The unfinished fresco in the poem's first stanza condenses the entire history of the second-tier Venice. Amusement piers had crowded the Venice shoreline for several decades, culminating in the erection of Pacific Ocean Park (POP) in 1958. But that property on the border of Venice and Santa Monica, the site of a carousel of beautifully carved horses, deteriorated badly in the ensuing decades. In the third stanza of Walcott's elegy "the carousel revolves its rusty horizon" while the "freaks" (presumably the countercultural druggies) move to beaches further north.

Written in the decade before Venice Beach's revival as a retro amusement area best known for its eccentric transients, homeless campers, and vendors; for Gold's Gym at Muscle Beach; and for its rollerblading paths along Ocean Front Walk on a paved track through the field of sand, Walcott's poem notices in a montage of images not only the ruined carousel but "the false fronts, the fake Spanish facades" of the old villas and hotels; even the palm trees are "dusty" with the detritus of time. Again, the contrast to the vitality and piety of the beach scenes in *Omeros* is striking. The last line of that grand narrative, "When he left the beach the sea was still going on," affirms that the humble fisherman Achille will have a world of plenty to count on; but in this elegy located at the edge of history, Walcott leaves no live creature behind, nothing like the mackerel, snappers, octopus, and sea-fans that await Achille, or the sublime vistas that await Walcott the fortunate traveler as he turns his steps toward more authentic destinations.

Authentic, let us be clear on this point, because historical. Walcott knows the complex history of the West Indies, and thus by metaphorical extension the history of the Ocean. "The Sea Is History" is the title of one poem in which he asserts the superior knowledge of what lies behind and beyond the coastal town, the simple fishing village:

> Where are your memories, your battles, martyrs?
> Where is your tribal memory? Sirs,
> in that gray vault. The sea. The sea
> has locked them up. The sea is History.[16]

Looking at the sea from the vantage of St. Lucia he divines the explorers' galleons, the slave ships, the cargo boats, the colonial wars, the generations of fishing and trade, and other events re-created in his imagination by history books and local legend, so that the waves function as a library of events and images. Venice has a history of sorts, and the coastal sites along the Pacific even more so, but Walcott determinedly ignores it, when he does not lampoon it. He has no need even to lift his gaze to the Pacific, except to note the "soiled waves," as blank a vista as the phony replica of a great city, and as unworthy of an elevated language of description.

Walcott acknowledges that his caustic poem mimics the "fake chic" and contrived preening of his surroundings. "There's sometimes more pain in a pop song than all of Cambodia," he sighs, and then abandons the offensive aphorism for some off-key language of romance before giving up the effort to make lyric material of the unworthy landscape. Note the final stanza:

> Shoot the end of this now. Let the last line
> be an empty lot after work. West Venice changes its gels
> for the fade. We become, said Borges, books when we are dying.
> I died and did not become any book in the city of angels.

The poem offers both cinquains (in the general sense of the term) and quatrains, and this concluding ABAB stanza is the best in the poem. The self-reminder of the opening ("Shoot the end of this now") makes the parallel of Venice West and Hollywood explicit, as the poet urges himself to direct the terminal scene of his wobbly and extensive pan around the beach town. He conceives the "last line" as the "empty [studio] lot" that precedes and follows the "work" of creation. "Gels" is an especially nice touch. A gel is a colored sheet placed in front of a light source as a filter. It enhances the affect of the scene being filmed, an illusion appropriate to the deluded occupants who imagine themselves living among not only extraordinary light and color but "angels." "Gels" is a thematic rhyme with "city of angels": L.A. requires an optic gloss to make itself glamorous. One might say that Walcott applies an aural gloss to his verse by making extensive use of the liquid "l" and the fricative "s," as in phrases like "I hadn't thought to make light of this: the light of / Los Angeles." Jorge Luis Borges is an acknowledged master of illusions and especially of the way books gather into themselves the human life they outlive. "I died and did not become any book" is a self-pitying flourish, worthy of Lord Byron's melancholy Childe Harold, who travels to a glorious European city named Venice in order to declare himself "a ruin amidst ruins."[17] Walcott adopts Byron's melodramatic tone for the sake of a memorable punch line. Venice West is no Venice, no Ithaca, no St. Lucia. Walcott cannot and will not become its bard, though he leaves behind a faux elegy to entertain his future admirers, none of them (he asserts) living in Los Angeles.

Walcott patterns his failed romance with Venice by making use of "Cynthia" as the muse or spirit of place. This is the Cynthia of Sextus Propertius who likewise confessed defeat in the presence of an unworthy mistress. Ezra Pound hovers in the background of Walcott's sour take on the city, both for his translations of Propertius and the skewed, satirical quatrains of "Hugh Selwyn Mauberly." ("All things are a flowing, / Sage Heracleitus says; / But a tawdry cheapness / Shall outlast our days.") Pound had praised Propertius for his colloquial speech, gaudy imagery, and what we might now call creolized shifts in linguistic registers; "he is tying blue ribbons in Horace's and Virgil's respective tails, by the *tone* in which he uses his erudition," Pound wrote in a letter to May Sinclair.[18] For Walcott, Venice West is an occasion for mirth, an unworthy butt of his condescension. The sculpted quatrains and neo-classical attitude suit him, as they did Pound, for he has written in this poem some of the most piquant lines about the jumped-up beach town of any poet. It is not just snobbery but a keen nose that notices that "the ammonia / of the beach's comfort stations" is more pungent than the scent of sea spray that delights Jeffers and Jarman. Yet, he does not notice the actual spray; he does not advance toward the waves to authenticate his churlish claim. The poem sounds like the product of a single day spent walking or riding around the area, all the time spent in germinating laugh lines rather than discovering some unexpected beauty or accounting for the decadent glamour that drew him in the first place. He makes his deferential bow to Pound and Propertius, but in this comedy of language he more resembles the poet Crispin of Wallace Stevens's mock epic of a failed sea voyage, "The Comedian as the Letter C." In Walcott's mockery, and self-mockery, the Pacific does not rear its stately whitecaps, nor the beachgoers present their proletarian charm for his inspection. On the checklist of Walcott's global travels, this body of water and its patrons rate scarcely one star.

One would not know from Walcott's scornful treatment that Venice was the principal center of poetic activity in Los Angeles during the three decades following World War II. It borrowed its identity not from Italy but from Greenwich Village and North Beach, and advertised its bohemian spirit as one site of Beat Generation art and literature. Lawrence Lipton published a best-selling work of journalism, *The Holy Barbarians* (1959), documenting the poetry wars as seen from a beachfront perspective. Bill Mohr has called attention to the work of poets and editors in Venice, especially Stuart Perkoff and Bruce Boyd, who made the Venice West Expresso Café a tourist site and the center of a community of writers. Mohr asserts that Perkoff's sequence "Feasts of Death, Feasts of Love" is a central text of Los Angeles poetry, in part because it is so resonant a statement of Jewish anguish following the revelation of the Holocaust. Mohr notes as well that one of Perkoff's best late poems, "In Pound's Last Years in Venice, Italy," can be read as a memoir of Perkoff's own experience in Venice, California. John Thomas, another prolific poet and habitué of the Café, arrived in Los Angeles after visiting Pound in Venice.[19] Walcott's implied placement of Pound as a ghostly presence in the Beat hangout on the beach works as part of the mystique of modernist poetry, not just a snobbish joke.

Worth noting as part of the Matter of Venice is the title poem of Lipton's volume of 1976, "Bruno in Venice West." The comparison of the European and American Venices implicit in Walcott's poem is foregrounded in Lipton's 221-line fantasia, in five-line stanzas plus one tagline, that features an imaginary encounter between the poet and the Italian philosopher, mathematician, and scientist Giordano Bruno (1548–1600) during a reenacted Renaissance fair in the streets of California's Venice. The thematic architecture of the poem is shaky, especially when one considers that Bruno spent very little time in Venice, and that he was persecuted by the Inquisition, imprisoned for seven years, and burned at the stake by Church fiat, not in Venice but in Rome. Lipton wants his readers to think of the HUAC, the McCarthy hearings, and right-wing persecution of freethinking intellectuals, as well as the technological terrors unleashed on the world by the popes of the U.S. and the Soviet empires. But downscale and funky Venice could not be a worse choice to evoke the dominions of the Kremlin and the Pentagon. Lipton's critique of the two Venices and his protest against the "thermodynamically" irresistible Bomb, both very promising threads in the poem's argument, tend to work at cross-purposes and create confusion for the reader.

However, what is interesting for our purposes are the sketches of the seaside setting enabled by the scaffolding, precarious as it is. The poet is walking beside Bruno as a guide to the inferno of sinful signs on every side:

This, Bruno, is the Grand Canal,
swamp scum, litter; that's old Michael
toting a six-pack to his rented room,
the window shades are drawn on Teena
and her lesbian lover, tears will flow—

O Sappho of the golden eyes—this door
conceals a love of three; those eyes
in the window, broken mirrors in an empty
room; rags and ashes, old newspapers, doors
rot on their hinges, and the old go mad . . .[20]

In the manner of T. S. Eliot's use of Boston and London in "The Love Song of J. Alfred Prufrock," "Preludes," and *The Waste Land*, and Venice in his anti-Semitic travesty of the Continental romance lyric, "Burbank with a Baedeker: Bleistein with a Cigar," Lipton moves back and forth across time to establish a synchronic resemblance of Venice and "Venice West." Venice had always been associated with the secretive, erotic, and perverse, a connection Thomas Mann and Henry James exploited in their novellas *Death in*

Venice and *The Aspern Papers*, respectively. In the twentieth century Venice had become a decayed city living off the splendor of its past, one reason the Venice West of Walcott and Lipton resonates ironically (they are both like and unlike) with its namesake. Bruno is the archetype of the despised and persecuted figure of creative intelligence, but his chances of redeeming the secondhand society are nil because he cannot thrive in the degenerate environment of the resort town founded by the developer Abbot Kinney in 1905:

> Kinney's dream
> of gondolas and gondoliers, his
> picture postcard Venice, chicken wire
>
> And Pittsburg Pipe and Iron, the columns
> plaster, peeling now, the Grand Canal
> fouled up with oil, the derricks taller
> than windmills, we too, O merchant prince
> live on to see the dregs and ravelings—
>
> Tall steel and glass, high windows,
> greed piled high on pride . . . (3)

Lipton's enjambment and sound devices keep the verse from dullness, and he provides snapshots of the place with reportorial vigor, but he lacks Walcott's sardonic wit in his phrasing, as well as the cumulative historical vision of masters like Pound, Eliot, and Lipton's acknowledged mentor Kenneth Rexroth. Venice West is no Pisa, no London, no New York City, and Lipton's effort to aggrandize it by inviting the ghost of Bruno to tour its shabby properties and its polluted canals makes his commendable ambitions fall short of success. But the poem remains prophetic for its historicist treatment of this often derided resort town on the edge of the city, now spruced up by the presence of Marina del Rey's amenities and likely to be transformed by Google's steps to develop Venice West as a simulacrum of Silicon Valley to the north. Like Naples, a neighborhood of Long Beach with more impressive canals but the same risible aspirations for status, Venice West falls short of even the "hyperreality" Umberto Eco describes in his book of searches for the "absolute fake," a travelogue of places, many of them in California, that mimic authentic Old World sites of historical importance.[21] Unlike the other Venice, the seat of a great empire for several centuries, the western version was obviously not ready for the prime-time role assigned to it in this intriguing but off-balance poem.

III

It's questionable whether Los Angeles in general, or the southern coast in particular, will ever receive the kind of homage that Robinson Jeffers pays to the early twentieth-century seascapes of northern California. As Jeffers feared, a deliberately minor poetry of complaint succeeded the oracular, high Romantic mode that characterized late nineteenth-century poetry, vulnerable to satire but monumental in its grandiose forms and imagery. Where are the heroic gestures of a Byron, Swinburne, or Whitman in contemporary poetry? It may be that in the postmodern period poets suffer from the lack of ambition to make those gestures. Yet if there is any place in the state or nation worthy of the archaic models of poetry, surely it would be the mythopoetic coast. Several texts departing from the now-suspect lyric mode have engaged the Pacific Ocean as experienced by Southern Californians, each with an ambitious social agenda and an experimental format.

One widely admired example is the 190-page work *The California Poem* (2004) by Eleni Sikelianos. This sprawling text is a topographical and geographical anatomy, in which a significant portion of the totality of the territorial and cultural structure of California is re-presented and analyzed by the poet in discrete passages of lyrical, discursive, and scientific description. Sikelianos's acknowledged sources are William Blake's treatment of the figure of Albion in *The Four Zoas* and *Jerusalem*, Whitman's self-conceived American in *Leaves of Grass*, William Carlos Williams's giant protagonist in *Paterson*, and bits and pieces of literary, historical, scientific, and cinematic material woven into her grand design. In a review of the volume Karla Kelsey nominates H.D. as a predecessor, if only on the basis of gender.[22] If modern epics like *Trilogy* and *The Cantos* nourish the poem formally, Sikelianos eschews the labored historical allusions that insist on holding up every aspect of contemporary life for comparison with historical precedents. If anything, she makes a joke of allusion as a literary device. Lana Turner and Marlon Brando are named as local deities, thanks to their appearance in seminal films about the southern and northern California terrain: *The Postman Always Rings Twice* and *The Wild One*, respectively.

More than any other literary predecessor, John Steinbeck presides over her vision of California. Sikelianos grew up in northern California and identifies with the Great Central Valley and the Monterey coast more than with any feature of the southern region. When she glances briefly here and there at the northern seaside neighborhoods she sees them as versions of Tortilla Flat and Cannery Row, and she borrows liberally from *The Log of the Sea of Cortez* for data about the marine ecosystem in the Gulf of California. That late twentieth-century Southern California communities resist the kind of Romantic evocations of Steinbeck's 1930s locations compels her to keep well clear of sites like Venice West and Santa Monica, which are too vulnerable to Walcott's kind of satirical treatment and less amenable to the sentimental and nostalgic glorification of Steinbeck and William Saroyan, or, for that matter, the visions of Los Angeles's and Long Beach's bohemian coastal spots by John Fante and his latter-day disciple Charles Bukowski.

The presiding locale of *The California Poem* is the Pacific Ocean, which is so often analogized to a sea of grass or wheat that the borderline of water and land becomes usefully eroded. "The sea / is a meadow of ripe saltwater," she remarks characteristically.[23] The figure of the Pacific serves her purposes because, granting distinctions of marine life, the ocean is continuous and ontologically identical from top to bottom of the state's coastline. Though Robinson Jeffers is unnamed in the poem he is a nourishing influence on the rapturous vision of the Pacific and its special appeal as the defining feature of the State of California and of "Eleni's" personal experience of its peculiar mystique: "Who // *cares* about the sea? // I do // because the sea / makes us land-like but think // sea-like" (56). The structure of the poem, she suggests, is patterned on the tides and waves running up and down the coast, with all their eddies and fitful alternations of calm and storm. And the ocean becomes an inescapable figure of Death toward the end of the poem. "Undertow. Riptide. A current pulls your feet toward open sea" (180), she says of the "drag and purpose" of the element inimical to human settlement. The tiny fauna of the earlier sections of the poem give way to the great white shark. In a footnote for a later section she queries herself, "Why did I watch *Jaws* three times in a row then go swimming at midnight? This changed the way I felt about the ocean later" (191).

The tone of homage in the poem arises from its taxonomic status as a first cousin to the georgic, a classical form that since the time of Virgil has set itself to distinguishing false from true values in land use and cultivation. A georgic tends to be synoptic as well as analytic, assembling data from a vast area of rural (and afterward, urban) territory. A georgic is didactic, moralistic, and full of stories and anecdotes to supplement the descriptive passages. The so-called modernist epic, of which *Paterson* and Charles Olson's *The Maximus Poems* are the canonical examples, mandates a sequence of discrete scenes and local circumstances, each submitted to inspection, so that the grounds of praise and blame become lucidly articulated. The patterns will require constant rereading, just as physical exploration of land and sea cannot be completed in a single voyage or trek. The rewards and discoveries are ample if the poet has sufficient command of the linguistic range to represent significant portions of the whole field. Sikelianos has successfully fulfilled this obligation—and it's possible that the poem will continue growing as the years pass.

References to films cited above may threaten to inform her imaginative understanding of the southern Pacific spaces, but Sikelianos fights back against her moviegoing habit. She does not, like Walcott, travel to a specific site like Venice, or Hollywood, and describe it at length stanza by stanza, but she displays a nervous tendency to be distracted by the presence of a damaged civilization in the south:

> its industrial wastelands, its Crips
> & Bloods, the
> ACTION! CAMERA! and fully-armed cactus. Each studio is a
>   nation-
> state of its own under the cloudless blue
> neon & the bright
> stucco Draco
> of sun
> of tile (17)

—•—

>   . . . obloquies on
> L.A., evil
> smog-choked city
> to the South, like black witchcraft
> practiced next door, a rotten

pot (*olla podrida*), of those cities
historically lousy with devils (60)

—•—

Where are we?
Bad Water.
What city are we in?
In tinder-dry CA
When the French came, they called it
            Les Anges, but before that we called it
Los Angeles de los Stinking Devils (*diables puants*),
    Bahia de los Fumos (94)

—•—

To the south, my beaches have been given over
to oil-
drilling companies, cargo
wharves, factory-built
blackness by the sea, squatting
buildings, black smoke
up to the edge of the water, concrete
haunches jumbled

and built blackness right into the water—
a huge city lurking in absence of light lies
under the waves
as they roll—roll *evil* (108)

And so on. When she summons Dante in a dream and imagines him walking in the inferno of "deserts turned to great cities" (104), we don't have to wonder what urban site she has in mind.[24]

Set against this cumulative vision of degradation, the sea remains "my hedon eden" (16). For all its susceptibility to devastation from industrial and real-estate development, California was once an eden entire, she claims, and she marshals euphoric language to celebrate "the infancy of the world" (22) carried down to her by folktales and the direct observation by historians and scientists of the remaining beauty of complex systems of life. The formal structure of *The California Poem* is a collage of timelines, lists of extinct or threatened species, photographs, meditative hymns and girlish anecdotes, joking passages (as when she concludes a survey of evolution by pointing to Jayne Mansfield as a final product), prose passages, graphic designs to enhance her didactic lessons, and occasional diary entries. Lineation is very free in the manner of collage work by Williams, Olson, and Gary Snyder. Occasionally the poem is opaque in expression, a challenge to readers to devote more time to making sense of it. Recurrent passages on the Pacific are more than a leitmotif; they act as impressionistic devotions to the principal feature of the landscape she seeks to preserve from destruction. Some of these passages insist on making the sea a trope of language, of lines of poetry. The verse arrangement has both a "free" and "fractal" quality in the sense defined by Alice Fulton in an oft-reprinted essay. "In the largest terms," Fulton remarks, "the search for a style is the search for a language that does justice to our knowledge of how the world works."[25] The capacious frames of reference throughout Sikelianos's poem, drawing especially upon the languages of science, necessitate a constant reciprocal dynamic between the material and verbal worlds, the rhetoric anchored in what natural science and social science have to tell us and what languages they choose to do so.

The ocean is a *perennial* occupant of her imagination, and her proximity to it in memory belies her distance from it during the years of composition. For all its reportorial devotion to fact, to materials both natural and handmade, the poem is visionary, an embodiment of consciousness structured as an unstable, hybrid assemblage of data in a diversity of dialects and registers. By such a structure, Sikelianos aims to express her suspicion of the personal lyric as a means of comprehending the fundamental identity of an entity as complicated as California. Though she enjoys stepping forward occasionally in her own name and voice, she signals to readers and to other poets that the truth of the matter lies in the assembling of fragments, just as the *bricoleur* or *sammler* puts each part of his or her collection into a privileged niche. The emotion we come to expect in a personal lyric by Jeffers, Jarman, or Walcott is muted, critiqued, by the presence in a poem on this scale of so much factual data.

Making the presence of the Pacific Ocean more compelling to poets is the fact that Los Angeles, a semi-arid area, depends on an abundance of fresh water for its prosperous lifestyle. As the population of Los Angeles County swells beyond the ten million of 2012, the sense of there being water up and down the coast but scarcely enough to drink (or nourish the lawn or the farm) increasingly haunts the literature of the city. If Los Angeles were truly fortunate it would have a lordly river coursing through the heart and extended lineaments of the city, brimming with fresh nourishment straight from the Sierra Nevada mountain range and pleasuring the citizenry with its abundant wildlife and recreational venues. The archetype of rivers is a central one for all poetry, beginning with the four rivers branching from one in the Garden of Eden. The analogy with Eden is ever-present in urban poetry as well. In poems about New York, Chicago, New Orleans, and of course London, Paris, and Rome, the river that runs through the city often serves as a thematic focus for the poet's meditations on matters of community identity and destiny.

But poets cannot make much use of the Los Angeles River, a fifty-one-mile waterway beginning in the Santa Susana Mountains looming over the San Fernando Valley and flowing south to its mouth in Long Beach. Los Angeles does not have another significant river system; the Los Angeles Aqueduct had been constructed in 1913 as an alternative source, bringing water from the Owens River to much of the farmland in the San Fernando Valley. The Los Angeles River was confined by the U.S. Army Corps of Engineers in a concrete channel with sloped sides after a powerful flood devastated the area in 1938 and led to calls for flood control. Before and since that time the Colorado River and nearby lakes have made up the city's deficit in available freshwater by means of aqueducts and reservoirs. "Without the resources of the Colorado River, there would be no modern Southern California," Kevin Starr remarks. "The Colorado is the vital waterway of the region, 'the Mississippi of the Far West.'"[26] The concrete replacing the Los Angeles River's natural bed and free-flowing course provides a painful symbol of technological repression of natural forces in a coastal city renowned for its hedonic enjoyment of water. Poets want to marvel at the local river environment as poets elsewhere exploit the mythic and imagistic richness of the East River and the Hudson, the Mississippi, the Thames, the Seine, the Tiber, the Rhine.

How would a contemporary poet persuade readers of the unnatural, the *intolerable*, condition of the imprisoned river, in ecological terms and also as an impediment to promotion of the city as an authentically natural paradise? What poetic form makes perfect sense, and what suasive content? One sustained effort to re-conceptualize the river is Lewis MacAdams's sequence of lyrics *The River: Books One, Two, Three* (2009). Unlike Williams's

Paterson, which provides the epigraph and the informing prosody, *The River* is a polemic of fierce and unrelenting ecological advocacy. Its purpose is to awaken a neglectful public to atrocities perpetrated by the U.S. Army Corps of Engineers and commercial forces, which have degraded the once-vibrant waterway. "I am as fanatical as a mullah and twice as obsessed," MacAdams proclaims.[27] "Today the river is a toxic waste, / They have to haul the mud out of its mouth / in eighteen-wheelers" (I.26). And again, "I feel poisoned, scourged, / a citizen of a penal colony. / I set out to be a hero and / a legend, and ended up a lobbyist" (2.19). Alternating with these fulminations are lyrics of joyful personal engagement while traversing the few miles of "oasis" or public access stretches of the river. Some of these lyrics achieve graceful effects that artfully complement the passages of protest. The reader feels, and understands, the harsh denunciations because the real pleasures are articulated plainly and seductively.

Here is a sample of *The River*, in full, from Book Two.

Lewis MacAdams

TO ARTESIA

I think of the river
the way it reads in the
Sam Shepard story,
Cruising Paradise—
a "huge concrete serpent,"
a "dumping ground for murder victims."
I think of the river beside a freeway off-ramp as
roller-bladers, bent into it,
spandexed buttocks rotating,
roll downstream. I think
of William Mulholland's
"gentle limpid stream"
coursing from a Pharoah's [*sic*] forehead
or from the brow of a Rhine-maiden,
green-eyed and coffee-colored,
a bracelet of drowned children
wrapped around her wrist, descending

from the mountains east of Irwindale
into the *jardin des rocas*. The river
is a rigorous mistress,
but when you tickle her
with your deeds, you can hear laughter
from beneath her concrete corset. (2.29)

—•—

The title sounds as if the poem is addressed to a Greek goddess, but in fact the origin is the Latin word *Artesium* from the Artois province in France. Presumably it was there that an ancient spring or aquifer existed, buried over by an impermeable layer of rock that needed to be bored through to reach the natural well beneath. The poem presents the act of ridding the water source of its imprisoning "concrete corset" as a moral obligation derived in part from ancient practices and ancient myth. The poem's strategy is to shame the reader by insisting on the river's need to be rescued from the ogres of flood control. For this task MacAdams mobilizes voices and cultural/historical references to expose the scandalous state of an unjustly inhibited force of nature.

To "think of the river" as a modernist poet is to defer respectfully to a skein of intertextual sources, beginning with a phrase from Sam Shepard, whose play *True West* is arguably the most complex drama about Los Angeles in the modern repertoire. Immediately afterward is an empathetic evocation of colorfully adorned roller-bladers coursing down the concrete waterway like skaters over ice in the depths of winter. (Many readers will recall the car chase down the river's concrete bed in the film *Terminator 2: Judgment Day*.) Glamorous figures of the Pharaoh on the Nile and a Rhine maiden flow from William Mulholland's fond epithet for the river he sought to supplement by siphoning water from the Owens River, damaging the Owens Valley in the process. To write devotedly in this condensed and graceful manner, as a Renaissance lover would to a mistress, is to entice even from the corseted waterway, uncomfortable in her concrete garment, the laughter, perhaps in the form of lilting music, that poets have always heard from imaginary figures of erotic enchantment swimming beside them as they walked a river's edge. A poem that asks to be recited at public or private occasions, "To Artesia" serves a ceremonial purpose in the revival of natural religion in the city.

What kind of religion? The reference to Pharaoh links the poet's reverence with historical and specifically biblical sources. According to Kevin Starr, it was the Colorado River that was customarily compared to the Nile in the promotional literature of the late nineteenth and early twentieth centuries, with Imperial Valley serving as the Egyptian Delta presided over by the all-powerful figure of the man-god Pharaoh. As the prophetic narrative of America took form, and different regions of the U.S. came into typological association with biblical places and persons, the redemptive power of the Nile got transferred from one American river to another to flaunt the new nation's kinship with Middle Eastern regions cherished or condemned in biblical and other archaic texts. The Colorado received the homage given to the Mississippi, and thence to lesser rivers like the Los Angeles River. MacAdams probably has in mind Langston Hughes's poem "The Negro Speaks of Rivers," with its image of the Nile and pyramids as glorious and inspiring figures deserving of wonder and piety. A poem that connects Pharaoh with William Mulholland desires to recall for readers what's at stake in the public's dispossession of the Los Angeles River by the administrative masters of water and power.

The shame induced in readers for their de facto refusal to join the poet's organization, Friends of the Los Angeles River, belongs to the remorse of several generations who have watched massive operations of renovation and radical change in the city. MacAdams chooses to make his willed identity as a river poet enviable, using a notebook style in his book to chronicle the vivifying occasions of pleasure—e.g., the glimpses of heron, wild river roses, and red-wing blackbirds—available to the common reader. But righteous indignation continually calls him back to a sterner tone. He corrects himself after admiring how the pelicans dive for fish near Long Beach: "It doesn't pay to be / merely pictorial. / Pelicans, you must be / the agents of your / *own* survival" (I.7). Robinson Jeffers had proceeded on the same assumption, as he invested moral value in the hawks, herons, egrets, and pelicans on the northern coast. Gary Snyder, who blurbs the book as a heterogeneous delight, "awash with backwaters and broken concrete, bird and fish knowledge, hydrology and community hearings," presides as a major influence. MacAdams incorporates river poems by George Turberville and D. H. Lawrence into his ongoing project as further testimony to the ways a free-flowing river could provide gratification and civic-mindedness in a technologized urban space like Los Angeles.

IV

The Los Angeles River is the most haunting absence in the ecosystem of natural forms, but it has attracted little attention from poets compared to the massive presence of the ocean into which it flows. The Pacific Ocean remains the grand epitome of the watery world, and its coastal centers of population gather all the motifs we are accustomed to finding in appreciative poems about great rivers and lakes. To the extent that poets feature the ocean as a site of sunbathing and splashing around, not of fishing or trade or spiritual contemplation, the Pacific is trivialized, demystified and robbed of its dignity. Rivers link the working community together in canonical poems about cities. As in *The Waste Land*, *The Maximus Poems*, and any number of poems by Whitman, trades define the cityscape and the spiritual vitality of the society. Los Angeles poetry lacks this grandeur of conception, if only because poets have turned their gaze away from the fisher-kings and the labor community spreading from the docks and wharves into the inner city. In this way, as in others, the Pacific Ocean remains the largest untapped resource for working poets in the United States.

I can best introduce the most recent significant text responding to the absence of ecological consciousness by citing a distinguished author who places the dilemma directly before us. Charles Wright is a major American poet who has profoundly enhanced our understanding of places amenable to his imaginative sympathy, such as Virginia, Appalachia, and Italy. A short-time resident of Southern California, he found himself less confident in trying to generate authentic speech about the coast. Wright confesses doubt in "California Dreaming" about his credentials when faced with the enormity of the Pacific waters glimpsed from Laguna:

> [Some nights] . . .
> I sit outside in the gold lamé of the moon
> as the town sleeps and the country sleeps
> Like flung confetti around me,
> And wonder just what in the hell I'm doing out here
> So many thousands of miles away from what I know best.
> And what I know best
> has nothing to do with Point Conception
> And Avalon and the long erasure of ocean
> Out there where the landscape ends.[28]

"What I know best" remains the issue. Wright speaks for the sense of futility in re-creating the dazzling complexity of historical and ahistorical presence represented by the Pacific Ocean and its beachfront. His posture in this passage is unromantic, its satirical barb turned inward upon himself rather than outward upon beach properties as in Walcott's jocular elegy. But poets like Sikelianos, and Brenda Hillman in her books *Cascadia* (2001) and *Practical Water* (2009), have created angles of vision on the ocean different than the conventional subjective and hortatory one that Wright finds himself unable to perform. In writing encyclopedic poems, Sikelianos and Hillman have sacrificed the pleasures provided by short topographical lyrics about the Pacific with a well-defined speaker and a dramatic or anecdotal structure—lyrics abundantly present in volumes like Jarman's *Far and Away* and James Harms's *Modern Ocean* and *The Joy Addict*. But their instinct to satisfy readers' patience and intellectual curiosity with plentiful data and contemporary political issues may emerge as the chief resource for poets in the twenty-first century who seek mimetic form commensurate with the plenitude of the Pacific.

The most recent landmark of this topographical ambition is Susan Suntree's *Sacred Sites: The Secret History of Southern California* (2010), a poem of 265 pages, presented in 8.5 by 11 inch format, based on extensive geological, archeological, and ethnographic research. Gary Snyder refers to *Secret Sites* as an "epic" in his Foreword; he might have compared it to religious and philosophical texts whose narratives are not of heroic feats of arms but are philosophical accounts of natural evolution, as in Lucretius's investigation into the nature of things, or another long chronicle of elder time that, like Suntree's, opens with the resonant phrase, "In the beginning."

Written in the free-verse style of field composition, this text offers itself as both an archaic and modernist scripture for a scientific era, in which "dark energy" shapes the ephemeral and permanent natural entities—the oceans, fields, mountains, and rivers—that flash across the reader's eyes in dissociated leaps. The virtual absence of a self-referential speaker, even one as modest as Sikelianos, makes this bardic chronicle sound more postmodern—informational, data-rich, a better fit for a generation seeking alternatives to the poetics of personal reference. Los Angeles is scarcely glimpsed in the unfolding pageant beginning with chemical life in the cosmos. By page 100 the story has advanced only to the end of the Ice Age, one million B.C., with some flash-forwards that warn that prehistoric land-forms and Ur-life are fated to devolve toward a future status as mere real estate:

In Southern California, summer rain stops falling.

Plants and animals move uphill and back down,
die off, reshape, reappear.
Stressed by altering sea levels and the cycling cold,
they scatter from one niche to another
quilting a splendid (still famous) diversity.

(Southern California boosters will one day brag:
ski among pines in the morning
lunch among oaks in the afternoon
stroll through beach dunes after dinner.
Buy it!)[29]

These asides recall Sikelianos's witty tonal shifts. *Sacred Sites* makes demands on the lyric-reader's patience and taste, but for those who seek the prose virtues of historicity and thematic range, the poem offers an experience of textuality comparable to the tradition of long-form American poetry and ecologically minded prose beginning in the early days of the Republic and reaching a crescendo in *Leaves of Grass*. When "That old seabed the Los Angeles Basin" rises from underwater to host "the First People," the ancestors of the region, the poem becomes a forum for Native American creation myths, a genre of stories familiar to readers of world literature. Overall, the poem is a sustained and detailed history of the land that becomes Southern California; Land and Water are the heroic figures that precede and accompany the indigenous people and cultures of the region. When these founders in turn give way to the "White People," "Los Angeles enters Western history" (243). The ensuing narrative of the death of native tribes from diseases introduced by whites and the dispossession of their territories as an effect of missionary and military conquest, argues that already in the sixteenth century Los Angeles had taken on *noir* dimensions as a port of call fated to turn its back on the vital natural presences that shape its heritage and its ambiguous future.

Suntree points out that Los Angeles is a place where residents find whale bones and shark bones buried under their lawns; where scientists at the La Brea Tar Pits excavate in nearby backyards millions of fossil fragments from the periods of extinction when the whole region was a great ocean; where buildings and sidewalks are made of concrete containing bits and pieces of ammonite shells and magma dredged from earth and sea. Prehistory dwells in and under the urban landscape, for those with visionary aptitude to apprehend it and literary skill to describe the city as fundamentally vulnerable to the chthonic forces of energy pushing constantly against the 740 miles of the San Andreas Fault. Likewise, the ancient era persists in the faces of blood descendants of vanished peoples like the Tong-va, Gabrielinos, and the Chumash, and in their extinct languages as well, which resurface in the relatively few surviving names they coined for places and trees.

Mike Davis has argued that "the general tendency in Los Angeles to destroy memory, to scorch the earth of any recollection," must be offset by "the conservation of memory," a cultural task historically undertaken by poetry.[30] The Pacific Ocean, once the occupier of the southland, continues to yield up its lore, both as the subject of stories and the former terrain of the city's geographical identity. "The sea is history," Derek Walcott asserted. Is it also future history, and if so, in what purified form will it manifest its power and glory? In Los Angeles, the city's origins and history are fundamentally joined to the destinies of Land and Ocean, our fundamental figures for the Sublime.

TWO

Hollywood, "Here" and Everywhere

> I looked toward the movie, the common dream,
> The he and she in close-ups, nearer than life,
> And I accepted such things as they seem . . .
>
> —DELMORE SCHWARTZ, "METRO-GOLDWYN-MAYER"[1]

I

If we claim that the "district"—its official designation—of Hollywood is the heart and soul of Los Angeles, the cynosure of every gaze around the world, especially at Oscar time, we immediately run up against the chief paradox that attaches to city and district alike. Simply stated, Hollywood is hardly a *place*. It is more an idea of a place, a fantasy of a place, a wish-fulfillment of a place, a geographical neighborhood belonging to the social imaginary. If you walk the streets of Hollywood you do not find a Main Street economy that serves and cherishes the ongoing busyness and perpetual change of a traditional social community. You find, rather, what Umberto Eco designates as a "hyperreality," a realm of signs pointing most often to some previously flourishing and now extinct or diminished form of existence. Tourists from all over the world saunter reverentially down the Walk of Fame on Hollywood Boulevard and take pictures of the terrazzo-and-brass stars embedded in concrete, each blazoning the name of a figure from Hollywood's past. An occasional crowd alerts you to the site of stars for Marilyn Monroe, James Dean, Elvis Presley. Memorabilia shops sell posters and stills of familiar film scenes and beloved actors; restaurants are usually retro in menu and furnishings; advertising for studio theme parks—of which Universal Studios Hollywood is the dominant amusement center—promise thrilling rides like *Back to the Future* and *Jurassic Park* as well as haunted houses like the creepy residence of Norman Bates from *Psycho*. Theaters of renowned lineage—Grauman's Chinese, The Egyptian, El Capitan—do exhibit new films, though increasingly they serve as cinémathèques for institutions such as UCLA, the Los Angeles County Museum of Art, and Turner Classic Movies, more interested in recycling the classics. But even the new films tend to be remakes, sequels and prequels, or pastiches easily summarized in pitchman lingo as derivative mash-ups: "*No Way Out* meets *Jagged Edge* with a twist from *The Searchers*" is the travesty invented by Michael Tolkin in his novel *The Player*.[2] On every block, in every office, the ghosts of Hollywood past are the most ubiquitous and compelling presences.

Karl Shapiro

HOLLYWOOD

Farthest from any war, unique in time
Like Athens or Baghdad, this city lies
Between dry purple mountains and the sea.
The air is clear and famous, every day
Bright as a postcard, bringing bungalows
        And sights. The broad nights advertise
For love and music and astronomy.

Heart of a continent, the hearts converge
On open boulevards where palms are nursed
With flare-pots like a grove, on villa roads
Where castles cultivated like a style
Breed fabulous metaphors in foreign stone,
        And on enormous movie lots
Where history repeats its vivid blunders.

Alice and Cinderella are most real.
Here may the tourist, quite sincere at last,
Rest from his dream of travels. All is new,
No ruins claim his awe, and permanence,

Despised like customs, fails at every turn.
        Here where the eccentric thrives,
Laughter and love are leading industries.

Luck is another. Here the bodyguard,
The parasite, the scholar are well paid,
The quack erects his alabaster office,
The moron and the genius are enshrined,
And the mystic makes a fortune quietly;
        Here all superlatives come true
And beauty is marketed like a basic food.

O can we understand it? Is it ours,
A crude whim of a beginning people,
A private orgy in a secluded spot?
Or alien like the word *harem*, or true
Like hideous Pittsburgh or depraved Atlanta?
        Is adolescence just as vile
As this its architecture and its talk?

Or are they parvenus, like boys and girls?
Or ours and happy, cleverest of all?
Yes. Yes. Though glamorous to the ignorant
This is the simplest city, a new school.
What is more nearly ours? If soul can mean
        The civilization of the brain,
This is a soul, a possible proud Florence.[3]

—•—

This is not the Hollywood Karl Shapiro glimpsed on a brief layover as he prepared for deployment in the Pacific theater of the 1941–45 war. In fact, Shapiro spent only a single day in the city before boarding a bus to San Francisco and transport to war-torn islands in the former East Indies. His description of Los Angeles fills only a paragraph in the first volume of his autobiography, and it is entirely composed of satirical remarks about the "somewhat nightmarish" architecture.[4] Like so many others in *Person, Place and Thing* (1942), this poem has the feel of a reportorial dispatch in the manner of W. H. Auden writing from Iceland or China. The brisk iambic pentameter stanzas assemble memorable phrases and sentences designed to be quoted in books like this one. Though he consciously sought to produce snapshots full of local color, Shapiro remarks on this early period of his writing that *idiom* not accuracy was his constant concern.

Stanza 1. Geographically, Shapiro is probably correct in positioning Hollywood as equidistant from the Japanese and European conflicts. He delineates a charmed place, a Shangri-La aloof from the miseries of violence elsewhere. Bertolt Brecht, writing in the same wartime years, remarked in his journal on the sensation of being fortunately shipwrecked in Los Angeles: "i feel as if i had been exiled from our era, this is tahiti in the form of a big city."[5] This privileged and exotic location allows Shapiro to compare Hollywood to classical Athens and the Baghdad of previous millennia. (A nice irony for the readers of 1990–2014 and onward.) Likewise, the praise of the clear air will bring a grim smile to the reader's lips. Smog had not yet settled on the area, rendering "astronomy" a problematic occupation in the basin and foothills. The word "sights" is a blemish; he could not resist the chime of "Bright . . . sights . . . nights." Presumably he refers to *vistas* one sees on the up-to-the-moment postcards of the early 1940s, eventually to be superseded by the nostalgic postcards of the present day featuring replicas of those same early 1940s cards.

Stanza 2. Shapiro gets down to the labor of accurate description; but it's a hopeless task because he notices very little worth putting into a poem. Of course there are palm trees on the "open boulevards," but he didn't need to witness these iconic figures firsthand to inform us of their existence. He fills in the scene by borrowing the terms of engagement from Nathanael West's *The Day of the Locust*: castles, fabulous metaphors in foreign stone, and the enormous movie lots that occupy several chapters of West's novel, beginning with Chapter One. "History repeats its vivid blunders" derives from Chapter Eighteen, in which the filming of the charge up Mont St. Jean during the Battle of Waterloo fails because not enough struts were used to support the movie mountain, just as Napoleon was unaware that a ditch below the mountain had secretly been dug to bring down his cavalry. Shapiro borrowed West's brilliant rhetorical stroke as a way of paying homage to the first great writer to envision Hollywood as a place entirely dominated by signs blazoning the inauthentic and hyperreal.

Stanzas 3 and 4. Shapiro learns from his first two stanzas how to frame his third, demi-prescient stanza. "Alice and Cinderella are most real." He gets it half-right. Yes, Hollywood carried the reputation of being both Wonderland and what Walt Disney would later incorporate as Fantasyland in the city of Anaheim; Shapiro is reporting on a realm flourishing in a Golden Age constructed both before and after the year of his visit. The 1939–41 period is often cited by film historians as the apex of studio moviemaking in America, presenting a series of masterpieces and high-level genre films testifying to the mature skills of an army of technicians and artists. But he notes truly in the next stanza that eccentrics thrive, and implicitly have preeminent status and power in Hollywood's "leading industries." Notice how positive his attitude is when he identifies "Laughter and love" (how awkward, naming "love" once again in the stanza's closing line, as in the closing line of stanza 1) as the essence of film. He has donned rose-colored glasses to look at this enchanted site, and framed language on the run to match the propaganda of Hollywood itself. An accidental tourist, he has not witnessed "ruins," but only because he is looking at buildings rather than into the spirit of place. On this point Brecht diverges from Shapiro's reflexive wonderment. In his poem sequence "Hollywood Elegies," the exile from Nazi Germany spotted the desperation behind the "heaven" of palm trees and orange juice stands alike: "The angels of Los Angeles / Are tired out with smiling."[6] The air Brecht breathes is not clear but toxic with oil fumes from local wells, and, he adds metaphorically, from the choking overabundance of celluloid. His own fortunes threatened by the situation in Europe, he senses a city in decline in the charmed manufacture of make-believe history.

Stanzas 5 and 6. Shapiro's inspirational homily concludes, "If soul can mean / The civilization of the brain, / This is a soul, a possible, proud Florence." True to what is sometimes called a city of one-liners, Shapiro's aphoristic closure stamps an identity on Hollywood in the time-tested promotional manner. Vachel Lindsay had made the same claim in his enthusiastic monograph of 1915, *The Art of the Moving Picture,* in which he opined that films would become the chief manifestation of religious feeling in the twentieth century and that directors would take the place of priests and prophets in the public imagination. However hard fiction-writers like Nathanael West, Budd Schulberg, Raymond Chandler, James M. Cain, and Horace McCoy hammered away at the duplicity, corruption, and quotidian cruelty of the tycoons of the dream factory, poets preferred to laud the place as a type of paradise. "O can we understand it?" he asks and the answer comes in the concluding stanza: "Yes. Yes." We can understand it because it nourishes the moviegoers' desire for perfect happiness. (Shapiro intuits that "A private orgy in a secluded spot" would satisfy that desire for most voyeurs in the theaters.) Hollywood was promoted as the Athens or Florence of America precisely because it served as a metaphor for the brash modernist technology that would enthrall body and soul alike.

"This is a soul, a possible proud Florence." Of all the millions of verse lines devoted to Southern California, this encomium remains the most memorable and pungent, the one most likely to cause an inward gasp of shock from the reader. The deviations from the iambic disturb the text no less than the bold content. "This" certainly receives a heavy accent, referring emphatically back to the poem's title; yet "is" seems no less important a word in the line because it re-presents the countercultural assertion running through all of the stanzas. The dactylic word "possible" tempers the assertion somewhat, if only in its falling rhythm, but the modest adjective runs up against the monosyllabic "proud." The strong stress on that word calls for a trochee in order to perform a graceful rhythmic conclusion, and here Shapiro had an abundance of options. "Broadway" would seem to be the preferred choice, the entertainment capital of a metropolis commonly compared to Los Angeles. "Boston," "London," and "Paris" must have contended in Shapiro's mind during composition before he set down his apt choice.

Even though the word "possible" makes the claim conditional, the fact that this line closes the poem puts into the reader's mind in the most dynamic way an association of studio products with some of the greatest artworks in human history. For readers in the second decade of the twenty-first century a lifetime of cultural critique has been dominated by the discourse of popular media signified most ubiquitously by the movies. Texts by Hortense Powdermaker, Walter Benjamin, Theodor Adorno, Max Horkheimer, Dwight Macdonald, Daniel J. Boorstin, Neil Postman, Neal Gabler, and a succession of writers for journals like *Partisan Review*, *Critical Inquiry*, and *Representations* have deplored what Rita Barnard calls "the kitsch-space of Hollywood" as well as Hollywood films for their banalities, their simplifications, their routine realism and ridiculous fantasy alike.[7] "Hollywood" became a byword for the degradation of the artistic spirit in their lexicon. "The characteristic aim of modern art, to be *unacceptable* to its audience, inversely states the unacceptability to the artist of the very presence of an audience—audience in the modern sense, an assembly of voyeuristic spectators," Susan Sontag remarked in *Styles of Radical Will* (1969).[8] Hollywood and great art are placed in opposition by Sontag, who grew up in Van Nuys and fled Los Angeles to study and settle in eastern

American cities. The studios did not disdain an audience, needless to say, any more than did Giotto, Leonardo da Vinci, Michelangelo, or Raphael. Shapiro framed his comparison shrewdly, for "London" and "Paris" had by 1942 taken on the mantle of modernity, of the abstract, of a poetics too elite for the author of *Person, Place and Thing* and polemical books of literary criticism like *In Defense of Ignorance*.

Vachel Lindsay, in the first notable American poem about the movies, "Mae Marsh, Motion Picture Actress" (1915), established the terms by which most future writers would appraise the new medium and its host city:

> She is Madonna in an art
> As wild and young as her sweet eyes:
> A frail dew flower from this hot lamp
> That is today's divine surprise.

For Lindsay, Mae Marsh is a divinity endowed with charismatic and cultural power by "today's divine surprise," the movie projector. In the sixteenth chapter of his nonfiction book, *The Art of the Moving Picture*, Lindsay asserted that the holy city of America had changed from Boston to Los Angeles, and that dream goddesses like Mae Marsh, Mary Pickford, Blanche Sweet, and Lillian Gish were the madonnas of a new religion. Their nativity as divinized icons of a specular culture would always occur in Los Angeles, the New Jerusalem in Lindsay's evangelical cosmology, but their presence would extend to every theater—that is, every new church—in the newly wired world. Erotic and spiritual in the same body, each angelic figure presided "here" and "here" and "here" in Shapiro's emphatic beats.

(In fact, Lindsay became disillusioned throughout the 1920s by what he saw as the increasing depravity of behavior on the screen, with his favored virginal types giving way to vamps, sirens, and seductresses. By the time Shapiro wrote his ode to the frontier city, Hollywood had already left behind not only the madonnas of the early silents but the love goddesses—Jean Harlow, Mae West, Clara Bow, Gloria Swanson—of the late 1920s and 1930s.)

These actresses, and their male counterparts, are among the ruins of time Shapiro neglects to notice in his rubbernecking jaunt down Hollywood Boulevard. "No ruins claim his awe," he says of the fortunate traveler through the landscape he also, paradoxically, compares to the damaged cities of the classical world. One might argue that nostalgia for early cinema history was premature in 1942, but that anything still standing in Hollywood from the early 1940s can now be claimed as either a heritage site (Farmers Market, Hollywood Roosevelt Hotel, Grauman's Chinese Theater) or a ruin. Exhibit A is the Hollywood sign that is probably the city's chief "sign" in the semiotic or symbolic sense. In his poem "Summer Elegies," already discussed, Derek Walcott remarks that "the H in Hollywood hurts" and then half-apologizes for further darkening the light on the hillsides. But he never articulates just why that letter, also signifying Heaven or Hell, brings him pain equal to the squalid inauthenticity of Venice West. Is it because he could not bear to live in a fantasy locale where, as Shapiro writes, "Alice and Cinderella are most real"? For these two poets the effects of prolonged immersion in a dreamlike Hollywood was a speculative matter, not a viable option. They had never known the actual Hollywood, only the images promoted in the mass media. It was a different matter for Randall Jarrell (born 1914), an exact contemporary of Karl Shapiro (born 1913), whose book *The Lost World* revisited a Hollywood he had experienced happily, in the flesh, during the years 1926–27.

In the title sequence of poems from this elegiac volume of 1965, Jarrell repopulates his enchanted playground not only with his grandparents and friends but with the Metro-Goldwyn-Mayer lion, Tawny, who performed in *Tarzan* and roared briefly at the beginning of every MGM film. The three poems of the sequence titled "The Lost World," and the volume's final and most plangent lyric, "Thinking of the Lost World," are like nothing else in American poetry. For these memorials Jarrell suspends his customary superior tone and modernist angle of regard on experience in favor of a full-throated sentimental immersion into the movie-charged atmosphere of the American locality he came to think of as most real. For readers who had admired his increasingly sophisticated poems and essays, and his academic novel *Pictures from an Institution*, during the 1940s and 1950s, these limpid (but complexly rhymed) lyrics, often in a child's voice, revealed much about Jarrell's approach to topographical poetry. Wordsworth and Proust are commonly cited as his models, and of course they are, but the placement of Hollywood at the center of his retrospective narrative moves the poems well away from the rural landscapes of Windermere and Illiers-Combray. So successful is Jarrell's re-creation of the movie capital during the silent era that no poet of equal skill and reputation has tried to rival his achievement.

Not that Jarrell spends much time peering at streets or noticing strangers—or, like Shapiro, trying to summon the spirit of place in neat aphorisms. Children's apprehension of place does not occur by way of sustained scrutiny of features in sites they visit or occupy. Their perceptions are gathered on the fly and left in the mind to be revised, revalued, and amplified in later life. What the child Jarrell noticed of his surroundings was haphazard, incidental, and often related to his everyday reading and moviegoing as part of a complex gestalt he later tried to reproduce in poems like "A Street Off Sunset." Reminded as an adult living in Greensboro, North Carolina, by the odor from a Vicks VapoRub Ointment factory, of a Hollywood-based home where he was anointed with Vicks at bedtime and of his happy hours in a tree house on a eucalyptus tree, he indulges by means of time travel in a reverie of his younger self's joyful spell in the earthly paradise:

> My lifetime
> Got rid of, I sit in a dark blue sedan
> Beside my great-grandmother, in Hollywood.
> We pass a windmill, a pink sphinx, an Allbran
> Billboard; thinking of Salâmmbo, Robin Hood,
> The old prospector with his flapjack in the air,
> I sit with my hands folded: I am good.[9]

The windmill is immediately recognizable as the ostentatious icon in front of the Dutch-themed bakery-restaurant Van de Kamp's franchised around the city. Photos of it can be found in *California Crazy & Beyond: Roadside Vernacular Architecture*, which also displays an image of the "pink sphinx" as the office of Sphinx Realty Company at 537 North Fairfax Avenue. (Entrance was through a door in the statue's neck.) Pancake houses abounded in the area, and we can trust Jarrell's memory of one nearby diner with an outdoor sign or statue of a prospector rustling up his breakfast. The important aspect of that particular memory is that it appears in the same participial phrase as Robin Hood and Salammbô as subjects for the adolescent's "thinking" while he sits in polite silence inside a car. (He refers certainly to silent movie versions of those two fictions, though presumably the precocious child could have taken Flaubert's version of the latter in stride.)[10] Most significant, the conclusion "I am good" derives from the mix of places and texts, as if the mere remembering of so much charming imagery represented a spiritual state of precocious virtue.

We are invited to suppose that even if the speaker had remained in Los Angeles after 1927 he would have cherished these bits and pieces of memory as signs of his well-being. He would have been the ambassador of this imperial capital of romance, carrying everywhere his messages of good cheer in the form of poems. But in "Thinking of the Lost World," separated from the triptych "The Lost World" by seventeen other poems with no special relation to these memoirs of Hollywood, Jarrell revisits not just his childhood in Hollywood but his commentary on it earlier in the volume. Growing up is not so catastrophic, he seems to affirm. Dumas's novel *Twenty Years After,* when re-read thirty-five years later, "Is as good as ever . . . Except that it is unbelievable." Probably the same is true of A. Conan Doyle's novel *The Lost World.* The initial Proustian impulse to reconsider his past centered on his memory of seeing props of a dinosaur and pterodactyl from the silent film adaptation of Doyle's romance of prehistory. That film of 1925 was exactly contemporary with Jarrell's year-long residence in Hollywood. Encrypted in his sequence of poems is the mordant joke that he has grown up to become the mad scientist Professor Challenger who brings back to the civilized world these archaic beasts who escape captivity and alarm the city of London. Ingratiating as his poem is, it is also an aggrieved relic of irrecoverable lost time.

What cannot stay the same is the actual Hollywood of Jarrell's tenacious memory. Its deterioration as a physical site matches his own aging skin, all too noticeable in the rearview mirror as he drives through the territory:

> Back in Los Angeles, we missed
> Los Angeles. The sunshine of the Land
> Of Sunshine is a gray mist now, the atmosphere
> Of some factory planet: when you stand and look
> You see a block or two, and your eyes water.
> The orange groves are all cut down . . . My bow
> Is lost, all my arrows are lost or broken,
> My knife is sunk in the eucalyptus tree
> Too far for even Pop to get it out,
> And the tree's sawed down. It and the stair-sticks
> And the planks of the tree house are all firewood
> Burned long ago; its gray smoke smells of Vicks.

Smog becomes the all-pervasive sign of ruined time, the gray smoke of degenerative change that has cancelled out the beloved artifacts of the speaker's early life. His tremolo of lament is conventional, even clichéd, as the clearly adult voice of the first lines descends to the elementary diction and syntax of the child's voice. This is one of Jarrell's signature passages in which the tears of things, the Virgilian *lacrimae rerum*, rise from the page with the penetrative power of Vicks. The city once exerted its romantic spell, and now it becomes a modern *topos* for forms of the classical elegy.

The Lost World poems are objects of pathos, naked in expression, but always artfully dressed in the poses of confessional rhetoric. The name Sunset Boulevard, for example, merely a place-name early in the sequence, insists by the third poem on its metaphorical associations:

> Into the blue wonderland
> Of Hollywood, the sun sinks, past the eucalyptus,
> The sphinx, the windmill, and I watch and read and
> Hold my story tight.

Nothing is more conventional in the elegy than trying to wrest enlightenment from the fading light of day; Jarrell concludes this haunting group of poems with a final happy anecdote, immediately following the lines above, in which his grandfather comes home from work and calms the boy's fears about a narrative he has read in *Amazing Stories* about a mad scientist plotting to destroy the world. In the manner of nostalgic reverie, the content of Jarrell's anecdotes change their tone often during the four poems. They are suffused with tender if rueful emotion. We are fortunate to have this unique collection of lyrics from a poet of such complex sensibility about a period of history beclouded in popular culture with the smog of melodrama. Poems evoking the state of innocence, including its primal terrors, offer resistance to what are often formulaic fables full of violence and corruption designed for a ready-made market of casual readers. As texts that belong to the matrix of visions of early Hollywood shared by Lindsay, West, and Shapiro, such texts form a solid core of complex representation in which celebration and critique of the city mingle for mixed emotional effects.

Poems both enchanted and disenchanted by Hollywood will be examined later in this chapter. First, let's turn to a poem with a generous outlook that revalues some of the themes outlined above: Robert Hass's "Old Movie with the Sound Turned Off" from *Time and Materials*, one of the most honored volumes of American poetry of the first decade of the twenty-first century.

Robert Hass

OLD MOVIE WITH THE SOUND TURNED OFF

The hatcheck girl wears a gown that glows;
The cigarette girl in the black fishnet stockings
And a skirt of black, gauzy, bunched-up tulle
That bobs above the pert muffin of her bottom—
She must be twenty-two—would look like a dancer
In Degas except for the tray of cigarettes that rests
Against her—*tummy* might have been the decade's word,
And the thin black strap which binds it to her neck
And makes the whiteness of her skin seem swan's-down
White. Some quality in the film stock that they used
Made everything so shiny that the films could not
Not make the whole world look like lingerie, like
Phosphorescent milk with winking shadows in it.
All over the world the working poor put down their coins,
Poured into theaters on Friday nights. The manager raffled—
"Raffled off," we used to say in San Rafael in my postwar
Childhood into which the custom had persisted—
Sets of dishes in the intermission of the double feature—
Of the kind they called Fiestaware. And now
The gangster has come in, surrounded by an entourage
Of prize fighters and character actors, all in tuxedo
And black overcoats—except for him. His coat is camel
(Was it the material or the color?—my mind wanders
To earth-colored villages in Samara or Afghanistan).
He is also wearing a white scarf which seems to shimmer
As he takes it off, after he takes off the gray fedora
And hands it to the hatcheck girl. The singer,
In a gown of black taffeta that throws off light
In starbursts, wears black gloves to her elbows
And as she sings, you sense she is afraid.
Not only have I seen this film before—the singer
Shoots the gangster just when he thinks he's been delivered

From a nemesis involving his brother, the district attorney,
And a rival mob—I know the grandson of the cigarette girl,
Who became a screenwriter and was blackballed later
Because she raised money for the Spanish Civil War.
Or at least that's the story as I remember it, so that,
When the gangster is clutching his wounded gut
And delivering a last soundless quip and his scarf
Is still looking like the linen in Heaven, I realize
That it is for them a working day and that the dead
Will rise uncorrupted and change into flannel slacks,
Hawaiian shirts; the women will put on summer smocks
Made from the material superior dish towels are made of
Now, and they'll all drive up to Malibu for drinks.
All the dead actors were pretty in their day. Why
Am I watching this movie? you may ask. Well, my beloved,
Down the hall, is probably laboring over a poem
And is not to be disturbed. And look! I have rediscovered
The sweetness and the immortality of art. The actress
Wrote under a pseudonym, died, I think, of cancer of the lungs.
So many of them did. Far better for me to be doing this
(A last lurid patch of fog out of which the phrase "The End"
Comes swimming; the music I can't hear surging now
Like fate) than reading with actual attention my field guides
Which inform me that the flower of the incense cedar
I saw this morning by the creek is "unisexual, solitary, and terminal."[11]

—•—

The situation of the poem demands that we hear the ruminative tone—equable, bemused, self-correcting, easily distracted—as the actual voice of the author. And indeed some of the details line up precisely with what Hass has told us of his life in other poems and essays. But it is not fundamentally a self-regarding poem; it adverts the reader's attention at all times to what the speaker, idling at home in northern California, regards from beginning to end: the 1930s Hollywood film running soundlessly on the TV in his room. Released from a banality of dialogue we can infer from the described banality of plot and character, the speaker is liberated into the romance of visuals, the play of surfaces, that dazzle the viewer in a good silent film. The

Hollywood studio and the mechanics of film production are ever-present in the catalogue of images, from the hatcheck girl's gown in the first line down to the gauzy fog that ends the film and (almost) the poem. In precisely the religious sense Vachel Lindsay outlined in *The Art of the Moving Picture*, wherever there is film there is Hollywood, the virtual Jerusalem of all cinematic experience. Any motion picture is a manifestation of the sacred spirit emanating from the easily mocked streets and buildings scattered across Hollywood Boulevard from Fairfax to Vine.

Is that last statement defensible? When we read a poem about the movies, or about a single movie, we expect a stimulus-and-response structure in which the speaker responds to the film in a manner that enhances our understanding of both film and viewer. Such interactive poems are like movie reviews; the very word "review," a second seeing that adjusts or amplifies the effect of the first impression, calls attention to the dynamics of the spectatorial experience. If we read a fine poem like Robert Duncan's "Ingmar Bergman's SEVENTH SEAL" we take pleasure from Duncan's informed interpretation of the film's medieval narrative: he even mimics the postures he would take if he were one or more of the characters. But we don't think about the film's origins in a studio in Sweden. Or if we read Richard Howard's pastiche of George Meredith reviewing the film *Woman of the Year*, the status of the film as a Hollywood product drawing upon conventions of the genre hammered out in production rooms and rehearsed by famous actors is not brought into play, though of course the artifice of both the film and poem are stage-front.[12] But in "Old Movie with the Sound Turned Off" the presence of Hollywood is an essential part of the diegesis, the "telling" of the narrated situation in the unnamed film full of shadows.

"Presence" is itself a conflicted term which has achieved great success in modern cultural theory, derived from its use in Walter Benjamin's 1930s essay "The Work of Art in the Age of Mechanical Reproduction."[13] Hass shows how the power of poetry depends upon the way authors complicate the simple "condition of being present," which is the basic definition of the word. The chief presence of this poem is the speaking voice of the author. If a film were made of this poem an actor would be hired to impersonate this voice and the persona who utters it. But nothing we would see on the screen would summon the essential location, which is northern California but is also southern California. The subordinate and spectral "presence" in the poem is the old movie, which is both present in the speaker's purview and also an artifact of 1930s Hollywood—a fact to which the speaker constantly calls attention. (The television monitor is also an enabling presence.) To the extent that the speaker seeks to enter into the industrial origins of the film, he must describe into being, into presence, the shiny black-and-white objects that intermittently catch his eye. By its effects he comes to know more, and tell more, about Hollywood, about the essential creative magic of the studio. Hollywood is not a subject of the film, though Los Angeles may be. The closest he comes to imagining a location for the actors who fascinate him is Malibu. Yet Malibu is not described in the poem because its association with the film world is taken for granted as part of "the neighborhood of one of superior especially royal rank," to cite another definition of presence.

The aura of Malibu Beach is essential to the poem's narrative. As a colony of Hollywood, attached by the umbilical cord of Highway One, it has accumulated literary associations ever since the 1930s, when James M. Cain called it "the finest beach ever created by God" and F. Scott Fitzgerald, who shared a beach house there with Sheilah Graham from April to November 1938, imagined Monroe Stahr building a grander version of such a beach house for his beloved Kathleen in *The Love of the Last Tycoon*. Malibu became the anti-Venice, the glamour capital and regal court of the southern California seacoast. When Hass places his actors in this romantic spot, probably at the Malibu Inn, he manifests the union of fortunate people and paradisal place that Cain imagined as the essence of Los Angeles's self-creation as a movie mecca, a West Coast Shangri-La. The actresses Cain names "blend in with the seascape, being in much the same key; they too are dazzling, a little wearisome, and more than a little unreal, that suggestion of having stepped out of somebody's fever dream that goes with the Pacific Ocean and no other ocean."[14]

A useful analogy is Karl Shapiro's poem "Buick," also from *Person, Place and Thing*. A Buick encountered anywhere in the world, including a poem, announces its status as a glamorous industrial product and its origin as a factory in Michigan, at least in the early 1940s. When the speaker sees the car, perhaps in a showroom, and takes it for a ride, he summons, in galloping anapests appropriate to the speed and ostentatious styling, the car's passage into being: "how alien you are from the booming belts of your birth and the smoke / Where you turned on the stinging lathes of Detroit and Lansing at night . . ." If the word "Hollywood" has any meaning beyond its limited geographical one, it lies in the way its presence is stamped into the manifested life of its creations even as they travel to sites anywhere in the world.

Hass cuts from the evocative black-and-white images, and the agency of celluloid that preserves the radiant glow of the two commanding colors, to his memory of the theaters in San Rafael and thereabouts where the Fiestaware was doled out in a secular rite of communion. He transits quickly back to the film, in which the white scarf "seems to shimmer" and the black taffeta "throws off light / In starbursts." And suddenly the speaker loses consciousness of the film, or rather, the film's enveloping atmosphere gathers into his consciousness the extended presence of the actress as a real person:

> I know the grandson of the cigarette girl,
> Who became a screenwriter and was blackballed later
> Because she raised money for the Spanish Civil War.
> Or at least that's the story as I remember it. . . .

What's important here is not whether Robert Hass actually did know the grandson, or for that matter, whether this is a movie he really saw on TV or just made up of whole (glittering white) cloth, but the rhetorical tactic of affirming that he has a connection to a figure otherwise lost to the unreality of the spirit world. She is a ghost from the past—a past that is not romanticized—but her fate *is* glamorized by her association with the heroic struggle of the Republican cause in the Spanish Civil War, enshrined in many Hollywood films, most memorably in the adaptation of Hemingway's novel *For Whom the Bell Tolls*. Donald Hall, in *The Movie that Changed My Life*, credits *The Last Train from Madrid* (1937) as awakening in him a moral conscience that nourished his poetry ever afterward. Pictorially, the war only survives, or mainly survives, in photographs and films. Hass has complicated the reader's response to Hollywood by singling out at least one idealistic member of the acting fraternity and contrasting her with the sordid reality of reactionary politics following upon a heroic era of resistance to fascism in the 1930s.

So far so good. The poem is artfully constructed in a manner as close to blank verse as possible. Blank verse is well within the comfort zone of most readers, hallowed as it is by Shakespeare, Milton, Wordsworth, Frost. The poet's voice is that of Everyman and the intended audience is Everyfan. But "Old Movie . . ." has one more turn to make. The speaker, prompted by his unexpected recognition of the historicity of the cigarette girl, follows the actors into their post-shooting revelry. They drive up Highway One, once known as [Theodore] Roosevelt Highway, and intermittently as Pacific Coast Highway, which links Santa Monica and Malibu Beach with Hass's residence far to the north. Now he is the filmmaker, and the poem becomes the narrative agency that frames the imagined, extra-cinematic scene in the same kind of vivid close-ups as the old movie itself:

> I realize
> That it is for them a working day and that the dead
> Will rise uncorrupted and change into flannel slacks,
> Hawaiian shirts; the women will put on summer smocks
> Made from the material superior dish towels are made of
> Now, and they'll all drive up to Malibu for drinks.
> All the dead actors were pretty in their day.

Wherever the actors are, is part of the phantom empire of Hollywood. We are accustomed to novels that take us to far-flung locations to describe Hollywood off-site: Robert Stone's *Children of Light,* Irwin Shaw's *Two Weeks in Another Town,* or closer to home base, the desert location shooting in Joan Didion's *Play It As It Lays.* There is no drawing of lines around the circumference of Hollywood's presence. The actors are dead "Now," that unassuming but vital word, given an emphatic accent by its placement as the initial word in the line, no more in evidence than the "summer smocks" and "Hawaiian shirts." But the film has been preserved, part of "the sweetness and the immortality of art." The tone of praise is not camp or mocking. It is beyond judgment, like the "flower of the incense cedar" which shares the speaker's image field with the old movie. Indeed, it is "Far better for me to be doing this" (watching the film) than consulting his field guide. Art trumps Nature. The contest is not even close.

Though the volume in which this poem appeared was widely reviewed and the book was awarded important prizes, this poem received almost no commentary in the reviews. It seems to me a masterful performance in the excursive mode, one long strophe to accommodate the turns and counter-turns, the distractions and digressions, that belong to the genre of the soliloquy or reverie-poem. The grace notes in the quotation above are characteristic. One meandering sentence of six lines is followed by a one-line aphorism. The wit involved in changing tone from "the dead / Will rise uncorrupted" to "and change into flannel slacks" is more than joking, for the corrupt figures in the gangster movie, after their round of camaraderie in Malibu, are now dead and deserve a nod of homage in that last line. "Slacks" and "smocks" make a comic end rhyme, to be sure, and the choice of "superior" for the dish towels is a verbal acknowledgment to the reader that it's OK to have some fun even in the midst of mournful remembrance. Poetic elegies for minor actors, such as Robert Polito's for Barbara Payton and Tom Neal, Alexander Theroux's for Thelma Ritter, and Los Angeles poet Michael C. Ford's for Deanna Durbin and Dorothy Dandridge, usually flash a half-smile at the reader.[15] Aren't these the conventions we notice in B movies from the 1930s, the wink Hollywood directs at the audience sitting through another formula film from the dream factory while waiting for the Fiestaware to be raffled off?

Would a visit to Hollywood Boulevard "here" and "now" bring us closer to the essential "Hollywood" than a long lingering gaze at the pretty dead actors on the screen? It is vital to the movie industry that the answer to that question be "No." It is not reality that satisfies us but hyperreality, not actual history but the imaginative "tone of time," as Wordsworth calls it. Tourists traverse the Walk of Fame to visit the shrines of the Golden Age and indulge in the *frisson* of retracing the steps of the glorious dead. Hass's poem de-creates the physical Hollywood and re-creates it in the indelible presences on the TV screen, and the fantasy of resurrection in Malibu. And how much better it is to let the poet make up words for those old movies, where the lighting is almost certainly superior to the dialogue.

II

Wanda Coleman

LOS ANGELES NOCTURNE

Eternity ends where Hollywood begins

to be THERE is to scarf and strangle
on those cool thick lids and hot brown eyes
is to possess the unpossessible/fever and cure
is to ignite those cold stars over Avalon
(like stumblers through long-unpaved hearts
looking for the back entrance to love)
is to set them in a dreamscape of asphalt & desire
a sea of tight ambition & loose thighs

southerly off Graham, streetlamps wave like raffia
when earth quakes. nightprowlers
cruise jungle to jungle, anxious to score the light

no reservations tonight. it's a dress-down affair

stilettos like high-pitched hopes heard
stabbing down sidewalks while
behind slammed doors the Molochs tally
ill-gotten dreams and low-hung coupes take
stops doin' the South Central Roll

the unreachable unbreachable unteachables
hands shoved so deep into pockets
they can feel the next world

remember the Parisian Room
remember the California Club
remember Memory Lane

Normandie zigs where Jefferson zags
(you too can touch it. as much
as you want
you too can taste it. as much
as you want

there is everything to feel. there. throbbings
in your palms like my heart)

Eternity ends where Hollywood begins[16]

—•—

The location of "Hollywood," then, is measured not by longitude and latitude but by the emotional distance of the speaker and reader from the images Hollywood manufactures. Hollywood is as close as your TV or computer monitor, where the texture of old movies, their sexual glamour and the presence of the very *look* of the past, secure the attention in a media trance. If you live in Los Angeles, or nearby, the alpha source of all your fantasies seems achingly close to the touch. Wanda Coleman, for example, who made her home for years in South Central L.A. and spent a considerable amount of time in the entertainment industry, has expressed better than any poet the tormenting appeal, and inherent corruption, of Hollywood, as a place, as a lifestyle, and as a form of consciousness. Her career ambition as a prolific poet, the author of some fifteen books of verse and fiction, is to amalgamate the public images of Hollywood and the reviled 'hood so that the stereotype of the "jungle" of African American life is extended to the degenerate district nestled in the foothills. Hollywood has assisted her in this task by painting itself *noir* and welcoming authors, of both pulp and quality fiction, who have followed suit. It is in this sense that "Eternity ends where Hollywood begins." Hollywood is the fallen city, the City of Destruction and Vanity Fair rolled into one, the sign of the fallen mortal. In "Los Angeles Nocturne" Coleman redefines Hollywood from the perspective of South Central, its urban sibling. She has coined the term "hollywatts" in her poems to make this vital connection.

A musical nocturne is defined as "a dreamy, pensive composition for the piano." Chopin's twenty-one nocturnes and the opening of Beethoven's "Moonlight Sonata" are the most famous examples. As a "night-piece" the nocturne encourages loosely structured melody and romantic shadings of sound. Maurice Ravel and Claude Debussy are renowned for their undramatic, impressionistic, free-flowing nocturnes. Poets have favored the genre since the eighteenth century, when the cult of melancholy and moonlight, the vogue of forests, graveyards, and ruins as subjects, and the general onset of Romanticism throughout Europe, led to a new kind of lyric, marked by a rhetoric of emotion and streams of consciousness. Poets struck the pose of a *flâneur*, a solitary wanderer, often at twilight, engendering reveries that proceeded capriciously, associatively, randomly, as stimuli from within and without impinged on their sensibility. In some cases the poet's eyes were wide open to social conditions, even as they strolled in a wooded glen, and more so when they walked the mean streets of London and Paris.

As musical organization becomes more dominant in a lyric poem, an increased opacity results. Coleman's stream of hermetic images and associations mimics the "dreamscape of asphalt and desire" she apprehends in the all-too-human world signified by Hollywood, where Eternity is not welcome, hardly even conceivable. She registers the "nightprowlers" who "cruise jungle to jungle" and exercise their predatory skills. The dreamscape of the poem is the field of fantasy generated by those who hope to make it big in the metropole. In a pithy kenning, Coleman describes the scene as "a sea of tight ambition & loose thighs." Licentiousness and prostitution are the tropes for social and professional exchange in this poem and many of Coleman's other downbeat takes on the city in *Ostinato Vamps* (2003) from which this poem is taken. The flow of corruption south from Hollywood matches the influx of dreamers into Hollywood, just as the distribution of movies from Movie Central colonizes the world in a culture of fantasy. The poem relentlessly focuses on the whores of Babylon:

> no reservations tonight. it's a dress-down affair
>
> stilettos like high-pitched hopes heard
> stabbing down sidewalks while
> behind slammed doors the Molochs tally
> ill-gotten dreams and low-hung coupes take
> stops doin' the South Central Roll

Where, in Los Angeles, are we? Hollywood, downtown, Compton? We follow the Hollywood and Harbor freeways on a north-south arc that defines the territory of "Moloch." (Normandie Boulevard "zigs" parallel to the Harbor Freeway; the intersection of Normandie and Florence was the center of the Rodney King riots.) The allusion directs us to Allen Ginsberg's metaphorical figure for the depraved consciousness of the city in "Howl" more than to the biblical reference, though of course that ancient antagonist is relevant to Coleman's purpose as it was to Ginsberg's. The Molochs of her poem "tally / ill-gotten dreams" rather than the usual "ill-gotten gains." These Molochs are the producers, the financiers, the studio system as a whole that grinds ambition not so much into commodities as into status exchangeable for sexual favors and upward social mobility, as in the formula of Hollywood novels. It's the recognizable Weimar low-life underworld recreated in Hollywood as the glitzy nightclub, the gambling den, the exclusive restaurant. When an offstage voice whispers in italics, *remember the California Club*, it is speaking of a private social club in downtown, established in 1887 and forbidden to blacks, Jews, and women until 1987. The poem also asks us to *remember the Parisian Room*, an elegant French restaurant in West Hollywood. And finally, *remember Memory Lane* probably refers to an actual antique emporium in West Hollywood, but more generally and emblematically to the perpetual recollection and appropriation of local history that make the nocturnal ghosts of the city—the people, places, and things—accessible to the sentimental voyeur/dreamer. This is not Eternity, this is the time-bound world where the past usurps the present, where "there is everything to feel. there." The warehouses of dreams "there" on Memory Lane are inexhaustible: "you too can touch it. as much / as you want."

Hass's poem has a plot to it, constantly answering for the reader likely questions, such as, "Why / Am I watching this movie?" The answer brings in the speaker's "beloved" as yet another significant presence. But Coleman's poem constantly deflects the queries we might put to it. It is a poem full of absences rather than presences. Its continuity is emotional, even mystical, in the *Symboliste* tradition. Each line proceeds toward an absence of punctuation. The fricative "s" sounds that proliferate are often made into harsh "st" sounds ("strangle," "stars," "stumblers," "stilettos," "stabbing") and other plosive formations like "ignite the cold stars over Avalon." "Avalon" is the port city of Santa Catalina Island, twenty-six miles across the sea as The Four Preps advertised it in a popular song. It was Nat King Cole who crooned, "I found my love in Avalon beside the bay." But Avalon is also a portion of Eternity in the Arthurian myth, the afterlife awaiting the warrior's soul. Avalon is "the next world" that begins when we retract our grasping hands from the temptations of fleshly touch. Avalon is not "THERE," typeset in small caps to distinguish it from Eternity, the cold stars above Avalon. A passage through Hollywood, by contrast, is the "jungle to jungle" through which revenants wander at night like ravenous beasts. And quickly, like a piano piece of Satie, the melodious poem ends where it began, framed by a resonant line about the beginning and the end.

(Is there a happier scenario of nocturnal Hollywood featuring an African American and a nightclub? Try Rita Dove's "Hattie McDaniel Arrives at the Coconut Grove," a poem not without its reminder of racism, for in this swank ballroom "no black face has ever showed itself / except above a serving tray." Armed with an Oscar, this new celebrity enters to triumphant applause.[17])

The poetic nocturne defies the rational organization of urban design as much as it defies the rational coherence of aesthetic discourse. Robert Alter, speaking of nineteenth-century fiction about cities, identifies "phantasmagoria" as the fundamental property of the urban novel. In remarks that apply perfectly well to poems like Coleman's, he writes,

> Phantasmagoria is the exact antithesis of the guidebook representation of the city, in which everything can be mapped out, ordered as a social, architectural, and topographical system. In the solvent of phantasmagoria everything is seen as constant disorienting flux, and the lines of division between perception and hallucination, waking and dreaming, blur.[18]

Coleman's "directions" (southerly off Graham, north along Normandie after Jefferson) do not aspire to the exactitude of Nathanael West's and Raymond Chandler's precise mapping of the city. In *The Little Sister* the detective Philip Marlowe finds himself constantly circling back to Hollywood as the source of corruption that nevertheless fascinates him. Marlowe explains: "Real cities have . . . some individual bony structure under the muck. Los Angeles has Hollywood—and hates it. It ought to consider itself damn lucky. Without Hollywood it would be a mail-order city."[19] Coleman finds herself attracted constantly to Hollywood as well, especially to the neon-lit nightside of the district. It releases in her a melisma, a chant or litany that is the theme song, or plainsong, of the city's romantic understructure. The same kind of ghostly presences apprehended in the headlights of a car on the freeway appear in Gary Snyder's poem "Night Song of the Los Angeles Basin," and add to the "churn and roil," "tangle and tumble" of the city's social tumult, its perpetual power plays.[20] (Likewise the dusky characters of James Ellroy's stories in *Hollywood Nocturne*, 1994.) The oddity of some of Coleman's locutions, and the indeterminacy of those "throbbings" in the poem's closure, arise from the phantasmagoria of a city constituted of surreal images.

For so many writers, including songwriters, Los Angeles is a "city of night," a repeated phrase in the song "L.A. Woman" as sung by Jim Morrison on The Doors' 1971 album of that title. "Are you a lucky little lady in the city of light / Or just another lost angel?" he asks a woman, presumably a prostitute, in the "midnight alleys" just before he chants the refrain "city of night" numerous times, and screams the line "Motel, Money, Murder, Madness." John Rechy had used *City of Night* as the title for a best-selling novel of 1963 about the world of male hustlers in Los Angeles, and after Rechy and Morrison came Bruce Springsteen's song of that title in an album of 2010.

Springsteen's song is both an homage to and critique of Morrison: "Some people wanna die young and gloriously / But Taxi Cab driver, well that ain't me." Wanda Coleman's versatile voice in a spoken-arts album she shares with Michèlle T. Clinton, *Black/Angeles* (1988), makes an effective pairing with Morrison's throbbing blues song about a nocturnal date with his alter ego and *femme fatale*. In "How Not To Die Young" Coleman impersonates a rule-giver who knows the hazards of life in the big city. "Dying young is the worst possible way. . . . Try not to die young," she implores, too late to help Jim Morrison, who performed the role of the fallen angel and died of a heroin overdose in 1971 at the age of twenty-seven.[21]

III

Nostalgia can and does enlarge the sensibility of the one who imagines the past back into life. It endorses the good effects of making room in one's consciousness for the powerful memories, not all of them comforting, that define and distinguish the present-day memoirist among his or her peers. Ghosts are good, one might proclaim in the spirit of Hass's poem about the romance of old movies or Jarrell's fond evocation of the land of heart's desire. The opposite is also true. Ghosts of the Hollywood past can be as troubling, and murderous, as they are in the film *Sunset Boulevard*, Hollywood's classic self-portrait of the succubus that dwells in the present-day realms of the past, ready to strike out if her desire to possess us is thwarted or resisted. Norma Desmond's murder of the young screenwriter Joe Gillis, his stumbling fall into her swimming pool, and his mordant voice-over re-creation of his fatal last year, is melodramatic enough to disguise the allegory being played out before our eyes. Joe is a fictive character and he is also each of us in the audience watching this cautionary tale with a measure of *Schadenfreude*.

It is one thing, then, to warn, and titillate, us about vice, or sin, the appetitive nature of a district filled to overflowing with excesses of prostitution, gambling, blackmail, and thievery. Wanda Coleman issues such warnings in many poems complaining of exploitation and injustice. But *evil* is something different. Hollywood has received its share of blame for evil actions, including murder; indeed, the *echt-noir* tradition depends on homicide to fill out its vision of Hollywood's iniquity. That the evil is committed so often by strangers to Hollywood is hardly a mitigation, since Hollywood, like Los

Angeles as a whole, is constituted mainly of strangers who have come from elsewhere to take advantage. Often the killers are victims of some *femme fatale* who signifies the dream of Hollywood success, as in *The Day of the Locust* where Homer Simpson, a retiree from Waynesville, Iowa, is driven to murder by the twin emblems of Hollywood, Faye Greener and the boy performer Adore Loomis. *I Should Have Stayed Home* is the title of a "sensational" Hollywood novel by Horace McCoy and the signature complaint of his protagonist who is driven to killing by his girlfriend. Likewise, the title of McCoy's *They Shoot Horses, Don't They?* offers the befuddled rationale of the young male vagrant who has shot his partner, at her request, in a beachtown dance marathon after their futile dreams of success in the Depression era movie capital turn into dust.

These are stories of good people made bad by the pressures of psychic impulses and social conditions upon their feeble moral sense. Raymond Chandler created characters as selfish and possessive as Norma Desmond. His *femmes fatales* are remorseless killers of anyone who stands in their way. It's usually not dreams of success that fuel them, though there are exceptions like the sinister Velma in *Farewell, My Lovely*. The most malevolent type is represented by Dolores Gonzalez in *The Little Sister*, a pretend Mexican who has migrated from Cleveland along with a criminal gang eager to enlarge its power and wealth by taking control of the lives of Hollywood people, especially the actress Mavis Weld, who hides behind her screen name and almost fools the detective Philip Marlowe into thinking her guilty of a couple of murders. But the murders are committed by Mavis's brother Orrin Quest and by Dolores (from *dolor*, the psychological and spiritual condition of pain) who has seduced Orrin to become her agent of destruction. The toxic and predatory Dolores can stand as the worst of the worst elements in Hollywood. She would annihilate the world to get her revenge on the gangster, Steelgrave, who abandoned her and took up with movie-star Mavis instead.

In the real world of Hollywood, this figure is a convenient fiction generated by the male panic of authors like Chandler. Poets have been less inclined to buy into the *femme fatale* convention than to find their inspiration in the pantheon of actors who have inspired, if not always reverence of the Vachel Lindsay type, then some kind of respectful admiration. The movie-star poem is an ever-growing genre in contemporary literature, an act of appreciation that puts a positive spin on the presence of glamour in our everyday lives. But there is an alternative to the public devotion to Hollywood, whether it originates in a foreign theater or in the locality of the district.

Here it is not the female but the male who is foregrounded in a true history of crime that regards males as chief felons.

Let's take as a working example the case of Charles Manson, a scary figure in the annals of true crime. Manson gravitated to Hollywood not to write or act or produce, but to succeed in the recording industry that had settled into the movie colony as the next big thing. Becoming a songwriter or performer—an instrumentalist, a vocalist—has become canonized in American sound film as a prerogative of younger generations on the make. After *The Jazz Singer* (1927), the screen had filled with exuberant fresh faces jamming gleefully in order to load the Broadway and Hollywood stages with dreamers who work hard and deserve their inevitable success. Manson, a disgruntled drifter, imagined himself as an avatar of the celebrities who made the Horatio Alger route look easy. How much work does it take to write some songs and find someone to record them? David Wojahn tells the tale in abbreviated form in #16 of the poem sequence "Mystery Train," about the history of music in America.

David Wojahn

HISTORY BEING MADE: MELCHER PRODUCTION STUDIOS, LOS ANGELES, 1968

In the control booth, Doris Day's son,
                                        Terry Melcher,
Barking commands to the engineer and drummer.

They've been here half the night—three dozen takes
Of a song entitled
                    "Beastmaster 666."

The singer mumbles through his schizy *chanson*,
Terry's latest find, one Charlie Manson,

An acid burnout stand-in for Rasputin,
Who has some trouble carrying a tune,

But Terry says he's got

"a certain something,
A spirit so wise and deep it's humbling,

You dig?"
But the engineer looks skeptical,
And putters with the knobs of the control panel

As Terry speed-raps on. "Man, it's *history* being made!
In a year his name will be
a household word."[22]

—•—

It is a principle of documentary filmmaking that the director must capture "the essential story of the location." If one writes about Hollywood from a sidelong perspective, without the complicity of the eager fan in the construction of star-presence, one might well settle on Charles Manson as a fitting symbol of the culture of fantasy that had hardened into a brutal, drug-ridden, and ultimately murderous inferno. Diana Trilling has written, in an essay on Marilyn Monroe, that Hollywood is "a madness in our culture."[23] Who, at the frenzied height of the 1960s counterculture, embodied that madness more authentically than Manson? With no talent to speak of, he was free to invent himself as a Satanic outcast, the lone wolf equivalent of figures of organized crime like Bugsy Siegel, Mickey Cohen, and "Noah Cross" (of *Chinatown*), featured in hit movies influenced by the Manson killings.

Wojahn's poem is a tiny piece of the narrative. Many rock singers fashion themselves as outlaws in the underworld, as strutting rebels defined entirely by their id. They scowl for the camera, they hurl imprecations at an Establishment that they are covertly wooing and cooperating with in order to enhance their charismatic power. Manson was no different; he approached someone far down in the power structure but with connections based on his family name. The poem's first line identifies him as "Doris Day's son"; that family relation is his minimal but not inconsequential lever of influence in the entertainment industry. Terry Melcher is "barking commands" like the top dog he is in the recording studio, where one of those presumably threatening anthems is being tried out: "Beastmaster 666." The Great Beast was a terrifying figure in Yeats's "The Second Coming," reanimated by the horrors of the Great War, the Russian Revolution, and the Irish Troubles; but for Melcher's and Manson's generation it is merely a verbal prop, the sign of a hostile attitude marketable to a bored and rebellious counterculture. And the writer/singer is clearly a no-talent with a mumbling style of delivery, not that voice control is going to be very important to his singing career. It's his *look* that's important; he's photogenic, he's apparently sincere in his "schizy" disposition.

Wojahn has sketched out a dramatic scene with fine economy and lyric grace; one can imagine the piece as a music video starring the likes of Axl Rose or Trent Reznor. But he settles for a truncated closure: first, the forced irony of Melcher's praise of Manson as a wise spirit, and then the double dollop of irony in the final tercet: "As Terry speed-raps on. 'Man, it's *history* being made? / In a year his name will be / a household word.'" *Little does he know*, we are expected to mutter as readers familiar with the whole truth. The rhyme of Manson and *chanson* is another bit of hyper-ironizing. The poem presents the tip of the iceberg, and that's better than nothing. But Wojahn shirks the poet's heavier lifting, the articulation of a cultural critique following upon the insight that the murder of a pregnant Sharon Tate (and others) under grotesque circumstances, on the night of 9 August 1969—an act of sacrilege that is often cited as the genuine closure of the 1960s—has its origins in the failure of an untalented songwriter to audition for the big score. The italicized word "*history*" is indeed the clue to the essential story of the location, but there are deeper, more scandalous historical currents than Wojahn has articulated. Something like the recording session described in the poem probably occurred at 10050 Cielo Drive, where Melcher shared a house with his girlfriend, Candice Bergen, and that is also the house that Manson and his family later visited on that fateful night, prepared to inflict some form of revenge on Melcher for having spurned Manson's appeal for help in becoming a star. But the house had in the interim been leased to Roman Polanski and Sharon Tate.

It's worth noting that songwriters untouched by Manson's brand of psychotic cruelty keep current the theme of the wandering minstrel settling in L.A. The seminal lyric is The Eagles' "Hotel California" from 1977. The album cover features the posh Beverly Hills Hotel. One of the songwriters remarks that the song is about "the seamy underbelly of L.A.—the flip side of fame and failure, love and money."[24] Tyler Hilton's hit song of 2010, "Sunset Blvd," assumes the familiarity of the listener with the conventions of the genre. "So a boy went to the city of the smarter and the faster," it begins, and later addresses the singer's girl, "Baby, walk with me on Sunset Boulevard / We'll watch this devil city fall apart / From the top of this town we could see the dreams come crashing down. . . . We'll catch the late parade of broken hearts / Cause we were lost here from the start." What started in the 1930s as prophecy, the pushback against boosterism, has now hardened into cliché. No city in America seems to cultivate the self-pitying "boulevard of broken dreams" motif so persistently as Hollywood/Los Angeles.

Frederick Seidel

1968

A football spirals through the oyster glow
Of dawn dope and fog in L.A.'s
Bel Air, punted perfectly. The foot
That punted it is absolutely stoned.

A rising starlet leans her head against the tire
Of a replica Cord,
A bonfire of red hair out of
Focus in the fog. Serenading her,
A boy plucks "God Bless America" from a guitar.
Vascular spasm has made the boy's hands blue,
Even after hours of opium.

Fifty or so of the original
Four hundred
At the fundraiser,
Robert Kennedy for President, the remnants, lie
Exposed as snails around the swimming pool, stretched
Out on the paths, and in the gardens, and the drive.
Many dreams their famous bodies have filled.

The host, a rock superstar, has
A huge cake of opium,
Which he refers to as "King Kong,"
And which he serves on a silver salver

Under a glass bell to his close friends,
So called,
Which means all mankind apparently,
Except the fuzz,
Sticky as tar, the color of coffee,
A quarter of a million dollars going up in smoke.

This is Paradise painted
On the inside of an eggshell
With the light outside showing through,
Subtropical trees and flowers and lawns,
Clammy as albumen in the fog,
And smelling of fog. Backlit
and diffuse, the murdered
Voityck Frokowski, Abigail Folger and Sharon Tate
Sit together without faces.

This is the future.
Their future is the future. The future
Has been born,
The present is the afterbirth,
These bloodshot and blue acres of flowerbeds and stars.
Robert Kennedy will be killed.
It is '68, the campaign year—
And the beginning of a new day.

People are waiting.
When the chauffeur-bodyguard arrives
For work and walks
Into the ballroom, now recording studio, herds
Of breasts turn round, it seems in silence,
Like cattle turning to face a sound.
Like cattle lined up to face the dawn.
Shining eyes seeing all or nothing,
In the silence.

A stranger, and wearing a suit,
Has to be John the Baptist,

At least, come
To say someone else is coming.
He hikes up his shoulder holster
Self-consciously, meeting their gaze.
That is as sensitive as the future gets.[25]

—•—

Frederick Seidel is an unlikely candidate for the role of Jeremiah or Ezekiel, though he continues the tradition of Jewish moralistic writing about this most Jewish of communities. Unlikely because his work seems so firmly grounded in New York City and points north and east (i.e., Europe, Asia). As a retrospect on the excesses of the counterculture, Seidel's poem "1968" belongs with James Merrill's widely admired lyric "18 West 11th Street," with its mordant epigraph:

a house in Manhattan,
our home until I was five, carelessly exploded by the
'Weathermen'—young, bomb-making activists—in 1970

Seidel transfers his gaze westward in order to suggest how the violence belonging to the heart of darkness in Los Angeles frames the continent's cultural transformation. Social critic Carey McWiliams noted in several books the susceptibility of Los Angeles to Satanic temptation: "When so many people have nothing meaningful to do with their time, nothing real with which to occupy their minds, they indulge in fantasy, in silly daydreams, in perversions, and, occasionally, in monstrous crimes."[26] In fact, the recourse to murderous violence was not occasional but steady and growing from the 1920s forward. Poets had eschewed this sordid material, for a while, in favor of political commentary in the manner of Thomas McGrath's *Letter to an Imaginary Friend* and Henri Coulette's *War of the Secret Agents*, but the 1960s stripped their decorum bare. The 1950s "Los Angelized" them.

"1968," the opening poem in Seidel's landmark collection *Sunrise* (1980), presents a sour look at Hollywood and points west in keeping with Seidel's aesthetics of scorn and disgust, his theater of cruelty. "I like writing disagreeable poems," he remarks in an interview, "or certainly don't mind if a poem strikes someone as unpleasant. It is possible to offend people still, and my poems not infrequently do. One way to do it is to write beautifully what people don't want to hear."[27]

Images of narcotics dominate the first section of the poem. It hardly needs demonstrating that drugs moved to center stage in the social world of Hollywood during the 1960s; I refer the reader to Peter Biskind's muckraking history of the period, *Easy Riders, Raging Bulls: How the Sex-Drugs-and-Rock-'n'-Roll Generation Saved Hollywood* (1998). It's salutary to recall that Nathanael West had recorded the popularity of marijuana thirty years earlier, as in Faye Greener's song delivered while under the influence:

"Dreamed about a reefer five feet long
Not too mild and not too strong,
You'll be high, but not for long,
If you're a viper—a vi-paah."

—•—

"I'm the queen of everything,
Gotta be high before I can swing,
Light a tea and let it be,
If you're a viper—a vi-paah."

In "1968" another kind of party takes place, after a fundraiser for Robert Kennedy preceding his swing through California during the Democratic primary election, culminating in his assassination in Los Angeles by Sirhan Sirhan. The party in Bel Air features "A huge cake of opium" as its centerpiece, described at length in the fourth stanza. The fog coming in off the coastal waters intermingles with the foggy-minded hijinks of the partygoers, including a "rising starlet" whose "bonfire of red hair" goes out of focus in the twin fogs. The poem adds the fog of dreams to its catalogue of distortions; the Bel Air party degenerates from a spirited rally for liberal policies into the hazy fantasies of audiences drugged by the sexual promises of starlets and matinee idols alike, just as Faye Greener's male admirers fall into dazed yearnings for her body as she gyrates before them.

"1968" seems to partake of the invitation to loosen up and savor the discrete sensations, as offered in a dissociated skein of images. The speaker reports on the scene in terse sentences full of pointed menace. Each stanza, each image, is a *fleur du mal* that grows in the reader's imagination as the thematic connections of one to another become apparent. The reader is placed in a peculiar location to view the scenery unfolding in the poem, inside an eggshell painted with fantasies of "Paradise." On one level these are visions of the "artificial paradise" Baudelaire castigated in his prose meditation on drugs; on another level the paradise is specifically West Hollywood, breeding a surreal consciousness. The images have no hook to them unless the reader perceives his or her own secret and shameful desires being enacted in the Bel Air estate. The luxurious Cord is a fine touch, and even better that it's a "replica Cord," a false version of glamour; it's an expensive ornament for the surrounding buzz of post-coital and drug-induced exhaustion and bliss. The phantasmagoria reaches a high point in the penultimate stanza thanks to a memorable metonym: the "herds / Of breasts" that turn toward the "chauffeur-bodyguard" who enters a recording studio, formerly a ballroom, no doubt followed by the celebrity figure he is chauffeuring. It's a dream come true for the bovine creatures, the "cattle" who await the star presence, and for the fortunate glamour boy himself.

But as with Baudelaire's demystifying of the wish-fantasy state in favor of harsh reality, the poem discredits the fog of dreams imprinted on the eggshell. Following the reference to "Paradise" is a scene more arresting than the "blue acres of flowerbeds and stars" stretching out before the drug-takers like strawberry fields forever:

> the murdered
> Voityck Frokowski, Abigail Folger and Sharon Tate
> Sit together without faces.

This is the "Et in Arcadia Ego" moment of the poem, the skull at the bottom of the canvas in classical painting reproving the hedonism of the main characters sporting at a picnic or dalliance. These wealthy socialites, victims-to-be, are still living during the party, as is Robert Kennedy who is speeding toward the jubilant victory celebration at the Ambassador Hotel on Wilshire Boulevard. Robert Kennedy was assassinated on 5 June 1968 and the Manson murders occurred on 9 August 1969, in a canyon above Beverly Hills. The doomed creatures named in the poem are the future, and the future is owned by evil assassins who cannot tolerate the good fortune of others. Robert Kennedy's murder, then, is given symbolic power by the poet, whose presence in the poem as a witness becomes increasingly apparent. In another poem, "The New Frontier," Seidel ruminates nostalgically on the paradise of East Coast privilege: "to wake up in the blond / Hush and gauze of that Hyannis sunrise. / Bliss was it / In that dawn to be alive // With our Kool as breakfast, / Make-do pioneers."[28] The quotation of Wordsworth's famous phrase about being young at the inception of the French Revolution calls attention to this assertion as a specifically *Romantic* attitude, transplanted from Paris to Hyannis to Los Angeles, following the trajectory of celebrity-worship and egalitarian politics to its terminus when Robert Kennedy—"Shy, compassionate and fierce / Like a figure out of Yeats"—is exposed to a cruel and very American gospel: "*The gun is mightier than the word.*" Wild West violence, one of Hollywood's favorite scenarios, catches up first with the gallant knight Robert Kennedy (having erased his older brother in Dallas) and then with exemplary figures of the New West at the home of Roman Polanski and his pregnant wife.

In the last stanza of "1968" we find out the identity of the personage being escorted by the chauffeur-bodyguard into the pleasure dome with all its eager breasts. The passage is ambiguous, and highly suggestive. The body of the poem tells us who the future is bringing to Hollywood: Sirhan Sirhan, Charles Manson, and other hallucinated agents of the apocalypse. "Beastmaster 666" in Wojahn's formulation. He will not look like a dragon or demon but like a messianic icon who brings not peace but a sword; he will be well-dressed, armed and dangerous. He will partake of the style and attitude of those who await him; he will be one of them in spirit. He is the emblematic face of the generation that brings to the box office, and to the Top 40 playlist, horrific images of violence: *Easy Rider, Bonnie and Clyde, Jaws, The Godfather, Raging Bull, Taxi Driver, Apocalypse Now.* "That is as sensitive as the future gets."

And of course *Chinatown*, the film that turns the narrative history of Los Angeles in a circle back to the crimes of the late 1930s. Viewers of Roman Polanski's film, from its appearance in 1974 onward, know what the future of the city will be, and what the future of the nation will be: World War II, the Cold War, Vietnam, Watergate, and, for the director, the murder of his wife and unborn child. For Sharon Tate and her jocund friends, sharing high spirits at her estate, "Their future is the future. The future / Has been born. / The present is the afterbirth." The decade that begins with the triumphant victory of John F. Kennedy, speeds up in retrospect to his assassination by Lee Harvey Oswald, and then to the self-murder of Marilyn Monroe, and the murders of Martin Luther King Jr., Robert F. Kennedy, and Malcolm X in 1968. Polanski and his screenwriter Robert Towne propose Noah Cross as the evil master who terminates the life of his daughter, Evelyn Mulwray, a murder that will haunt the private eye Jake Gittes and presumably the city of Los Angeles ever afterward. Seidel's poem is a kindred document of Cross's paradigmatic act. "1968" is the afterbirth of some vision akin to Yeats's prophecy of the "rough beast" slouching toward Bethlehem to be born. A "stranger" to Hollywood, though he wrote a few screenplays, Seidel presents a claim for having articulated the essential story of the location. His poem takes the fatalism of the *noir* tradition literally and reaches a different conclusion about the fall from Paradise that is the alpha story of Western culture.

Seidel's moody, imagistic poem belongs to the nocturnal and intensely cinematic world of Los Angeles more than to the milieu of Boston and New York. If he lived in L.A. Seidel would be the voice of its mania and its desperation, as he is New York's oracular and modernist spokesman. Pauline Kael, in remarks about the film of Clifford Odets's play *The Big Knife*, one of Hollywood's signature self-portraits, describes its effect in this way: "It's paced too fast and pitched too high, immorality is attacked with almost obscene relish, the knife turns into a buzz saw. Maybe because of all these faults of taste, you can't take your eyes off it."[29] Seidel's poem likewise takes a melodramatic and voyeuristic delight in the excesses of Bel Air, but moviegoers will appreciate its tone and structure subliminally, and recognize its fatalism as an authentic expression of the decade's *Zeitgeist*. As with so many lyric renditions of the city, you can't take your eyes off it.

IV

When Thomas McGrath titled his volume of collected poems *The Movie at the End of the World* he intended to rebuke the coastal city that (to his mind) had come to symbolize the moral corruption of the entire United States. McGrath upheld frontier values based on an appreciation for the fundamental presences of reality. "Supposing he already knows the facts of life and the class struggle, the poet has nothing to learn from the city," McGrath remarked in a letter. Of his fellow poets he wrote, "We believe that poverty is real, that work is real, that joy and anguish and revolution are real."[30] To his mind, the *unreal* city appeared in movies, wherein, like the shadows in Plato's cave, false forms of the authentic misrepresented the basic values of a vital culture. Delmore Schwartz, as in the epigraph to this chapter, confessed to the seductive ease of lapsing into the "common dream" purveyed by Hollywood. For McGrath, the function of the poet lay in the unmasking of all ideological untruths like those propagated by the HUAC and the dream factory alike. In Hollywood, according to Karl Shapiro, "Alice and Cinderella are most real." That was the problem, for poets and for citizens. Wonderland is a false paradise, susceptible to perversion by opportunists, profiteers, assassins. Poets would never lose their love of the movies, their wonder at the spectacles inside the eggshell paradise of movie palaces. But Hollywood remained a city under suspicion. "This is the simplest city," Shapiro exulted, and then decamped for the bloody beaches of wartime Asia. Not so simple, later poets demurred. And not so innocent as the fairy tale of success, of triumph over evil, of enduring love—the heart of the American Dream—trumpeted in Hollywood's unceasing propaganda.

THREE

How Good, or Bad, Is Charles Bukowski's Poetry?

I

Charles Baxter wrote the following description of a visit to France in 2001: "Having been invited to Paris for an award, I was being interviewed by a French journalist about American and French writing, particularly poetry. The journalist asked me what I thought of the current American poetry scene, and I made some dutiful comments about a few of the leading figures and the battles between representational/linear and post-avant/nonlinear poets. 'Ah,' the journalist said. 'Here in France we all assume that American poets are making an effort to work their way out from under the giant shadow, the giant influence of Charles Bukowski.'"[1]

Whenever I mentioned to someone that I was preparing a book-length study of poems about Los Angeles, the inevitable comeback was, "Are you going to write about Bukowski?" It is a fair question because Henry Charles Bukowski, by the time of his death from leukemia in 1994, had become the celebrity face of Los Angeles poetry. His many books published by Black Sparrow Press, City Lights Books, and other small presses had reached a circulation in the millions, placing him among the best-selling poets of his generation. "Fame became of him," as Archibald MacLeish wrote of Hemingway.[2] Bukowski scripted an autobiographical film (*Barfly*, 1987), directed by Barbet Schroeder, in which Mickey Rourke portrayed the poet and Faye

Dunaway took the role of a lovelorn girlfriend; it won over many critics and viewers with its raffish charm. An earlier film starring Ben Gazarra as the poet, *Tales of Ordinary Madness* (1981), drew from Bukowski's fiction, as did another movie of 1987, *Crazy Love*. Taylor Hackford assembled a feature-length documentary homage back in 1973, and Barbet Schroeder fashioned a four-hour video of interviews with the poet, released in the mid-1980s as *The Charles Bukowski Tapes*.

Posthumously, Bukowski continues to haunt the city streets and bars. In 2003 John Dullaghan's documentary *Bukowski: Born Into This* brought him back to life, with cameo testimonies from Bono, Sean Penn, Harry Dean Stanton, and Tom Waits. *Factotum*, Bent Hamer's film adaptation of Bukowski's novel, appeared in 2005 starring Matt Dillon as the poet and Lilli Taylor as his long-suffering squeeze. In 2010, in New York City, Ute Lemper performed songs adapted from his poems in an evening titled "The Bukowski Project," which the *New York Times* reviewer described as "obviously a platform for a larger theatrical version."[3] In 2011, Company XIV in Brooklyn mounted a dance performance titled "Lover. Muse. Mockingbird. Whore." entirely devoted to Bukowski's poems about women. In 2012 a stage production titled "B.S.: Bukowski.Sondheim" fusing the lyrics and music of Bukowski and Stephen Sondheim opened in a Long Beach playhouse. Biographies and memoirs abound, as well as literary studies. In Los Angeles, and no doubt elsewhere, one can still spot bumper stickers proclaiming "I'd Rather Be Reading Bukowski." Using the transparent name Henry Chinaski for the "I" character in his poems and fiction, Bukowski succeeded in creating a persona beloved by a large portion of the literate public, even by those who never read more than one of his sixty-six (and counting) books. Bukowski himself recorded in his diary-like verse the stir of attention his "earthy / and grubby" poems aroused, as well as the idolatrous reception he prophesied as a likely afterlife.[4]

It would not be true to say that Bukowski's status has been the subject of persistent arguments among scholars of modern poetry. In the realm of mainstream and academic criticism he scarcely exists except as a code word for the kind of artless poet who attracts groupies—in his time the alter ego, or alter id, of equally famous Rod McKuen. When I traveled to Providence, Rhode Island, in 1965, for my first year in graduate school, infatuated with Bukowski's gorgeously designed volume *It Catches My Heart in Its Hands* (1963) and ready to defend it and, as time passed, his intriguing second volume *The Days Run Away Like Wild Horses Over the Hills* (1969), against what I correctly assumed would be vehement New England advocates for Robert Lowell and Richard Wilbur, I failed to stir the slightest interest in his work, and the same was true five years later when I began teaching at the University of Michigan. The one enthusiast I encountered in Ann Arbor was a German exchange student who told me that Germany was aflame with passion for Bukowski's writing. But none of the books of literary criticism I read then, or (for the most part) afterward, paid any attention to this cultural phenomenon. Not until *The Norton Anthology of Postmodern American Poetry* (1994), edited by Paul Hoover, did I see him represented in an "Establishment" anthology, and there, with only five brief lyrics, as an obligatory token figure to critique the highbrow (or "highfalutin" to use the favored word of Bukowski's followers) academic elite. His readership, however, was and is vast, devoted, and global, as Baxter's anecdote suggests. It seemed to be, for decades, largely underground, and in effect cultish, but in the way of celebrity reputations it has accumulated enormous numbers and recently some serious attention from critics who normally disdain verse of such artless character.

Bukowski proclaimed his devotion to the city of Los Angeles in no uncertain terms. In an interview with *London Magazine* in 1974 he remarked, "You live in a town all your life, and you get to know every street corner. You've got the layout of the whole land. You have a picture of where you are . . . Since I was raised in L.A., I've always had the geographical and spiritual feeling of being here. I've had time to learn this city. I can't see any other place than L.A."[5] In *Notes of a Dirty Old Man* he proclaims Los Angeles the greatest city in the universe. These are unusual claims for Los Angeles, which is so often characterized by its citizens, and especially by the East Coast literati, as a fascinating but sprawling urban space of subordinate interest to readers of serious literature. In one sense, Bukowski's embrace of the city and its bohemian life confirms some of the oft-repeated misgivings about decadence on the West Coast, for he betrays in deliberately provocative assertions what might be called an adult slacker mentality toward his stimulating environment. "I find life fairly uninteresting," he confessed in an interview, and added, "To see nobody, to do nothing. It's very fulfilling to me."[6] Of course such statements are dandyist poses rather than accurate self-portraits. But it counts for something that he felt the need to strike such poses.

Because Bukowski writes constantly, obsessively, about his life in the Los Angeles area—principally about Hollywood, downtown, and (after 1979)

San Pedro—one might assume from a distance that he has described the city throughout his thousands of poems with the kind of loving attention Wordsworth devotes to the Lake District or Gwendolyn Brooks to South Side Chicago. The case is not so simple as that, however. In most of his poems the city is scarcely visible beyond the self-reflecting scrim of his own presence. He trains a close-up lens on the existence of whatever is interacting with the "I" of the poems—a pronoun Bukowski must have flogged more often than any poet in history. The city venues—the racetracks, the diners and bars, the hospitals, the libraries, the workplaces—tend to recede into the distance as scarcely discernible backdrops. Though he will occasionally surprise the reader with quick vivid sketches of a site, he is for the most part one of those native informants more concerned with self than place. Unlike Campbell McGrath in *Spring Comes to Chicago* or Richard Blanco in *City of a Hundred Fires* (on Havana and Miami), city poets extraordinaire, Bukowski remains satisfied with a bare minimum of descriptive information and interpretation. And that seems to be the way his readers like it.

I will discuss three poems, which catch the poet venturing out of his rooming house or apartment, away from the sites in his immediate neighborhood. There are two locations that Bukowski writes about industriously. One is the workplace, most often the United States Post Office where he served, beginning in 1958, first as a mail carrier and later as a sorter at the Terminal Annex. Russell Harrison asserts that "Bukowski has written more poems depicting work and the American working class experience than any other major American poet, more, perhaps, than *any* American poet."[7] Harrison has examined these poems with some care and I won't repeat his readings here. The other location is the racetrack, be it Hollywood Park or Santa Anita, or tracks south of the city like Del Mar or Agua Caliente in Tijuana. "I've seen 70,000 horse races," he remarks in a late poem.[8] I have chosen to focus on poems and places little noticed in commentary on Bukowski.

II

TO HELL WITH ROBERT SCHUMANN

I finished my drink and went back
upstairs to hear the second half—
another piano concerto, and

2 are too many and
I couldn't make it out
having lost my program so
I left the place and drove 21 blocks
South and East
to where 2 flyweights
a Jap and a Mexican were
going at it. the
Mexican butted the Jap and
the Jap bled from a cut
above the eye
but only fought harder
he was grasshopper slim with
very thin arms but
hit very hard. it went all ten and
the Jap got the verdict. another
ten followed. I drank a lot of
beer
kept leaving to piss and
when I came back one time it
was over: k.o.,
and I walked out to my car and
since I was downtown I
drove to where I worked in the
daylight
to see if maybe the place looked less
painful and
I looked through the window and
thought I saw Ralph the stockboy in
there
crawling around on his hands and his
knees. he was an odd one and
the secretaries were afraid of him
and I thought I should call the
police
but then I thought
I don't care if he raids the
place or sets it on

fire. I got back into my car
and took the freeway back to my
apartment.

I drank a couple glasses of scotch,
set the clock for 6:30
ate a vitamin
thought about a whore in Glendale
checked the ball scores
pissed again
turned out the lights
got into bed (alone)
didn't pray
thought of places like Japan and
Central Avenue
thought about the dead and
the famous
thought about dying
while the Thames went along without
me and the girls walked up and down the
sidewalks without me
and then I thought I wouldn't mind
so much
and went to sleep and
slept good.

—•—

One could argue that "To Hell with Robert Schumann," from *The Days Run Away Like Wild Horses Over the Hills,* is not only a quintessential Bukowski poem but a quintessential Los Angeles poem. Most obviously it is a poem about driving from one neighborhood to another in the vast paved archipelago that is L.A. If the characteristic poem of the modernist movement is the testimony of an urban pedestrian registering the swift movement of motorcars, buses, trains, riverboats, firetrucks, and "the apparition of these faces in the crowd" across his field of vision, the L.A. poem puts the speaker in the driver's seat and makes him or her the camera eye, the tour guide, as the phanopoeia of city scenes come and go in vivid moments of mobile perception. It's difficult to imagine W. B. Yeats, Ezra Pound, T. S. Eliot, or Marianne Moore behind the wheel, foot on the accelerator, and much more difficult to think of what sort of poems they would have constructed from that perspective. William Carlos Williams, more than any other modernist, forged an association of short lines with the speed of perception and the speed of activity in a world characterized by moving vehicles, airplanes, cinema, telegrams, newspaper and radio bulletins, parades, and the frenzy of sports. "How shall I be a mirror to this modernity?" he famously asked in one of his earliest poems.[9] He would fill poems with mobile images, was one strategy. In "The Young Housewife" he drives by a fetching female in her négligée and compares her "to a fallen leaf"; he then makes the power of his automobile an agent for his vindictive libidinal energies as he drives over the dried leaves that metaphorically include this latest blossom beyond his grasp. By the time Bukowski began writing, such an ostentatious foregrounding of the automobile-as-symbol began to look archaic. Bukowski makes it clear in all his work that he does not consider the car an archetype of modernity; it is the inescapable necessity of everyday life in Los Angeles.

Bukowski almost always writes in short lines, sometimes just one or two words a line all the way down the page. "That's what comes of paying poets by the line or the page," as the joke had it. Whatever the reason, poems like "To Hell with Robert Schumann" communicate a visceral and cinematic experience that keeps the reader's eyes and mind unsteady. Verse had always been defined, humorously, as rows of words that never reach the right margin of the page. (Not until free verse came into being, anyway.) The empty space that surrounds the print and represents a visual mark of its incompletion, its truncation line by line, forms an element of page layout that readers now increasingly and consciously notice at the periphery of their vision. It is a principle of visual design that blank space acts as an arrow pointing to whatever is not blank space, heightening the presence, the aura, of the black words, in the case of verse. In an essay entitled "The Arrogance of Poetry," Mark Halliday puts the matter memorably:

> The unfilled part of a poem's page is the ornamental garden surrounding the castle of superior meaning. A poem says, "I can drape myself in white space like a mink coat. I stand apart from the mundane tide of utilitarian utterance. I create and require a respectful silence around me."[10]

In Bukowski's poem the reader hurtles through the sequence of sensations from start to finish; the white space confines and captivates the attention toward the montage of forms and sounds that rush by before, during, and after the experience of driving. In an interview Bukowski described Whitman warily as a "pretty good" poet. "His energy kept things moving," he conceded. "But I get a little sleepy reading those long lines."[11] The antidote for weariness with long lines is *very* short lines, a verse form perfectly suited to the attention deficit he assumed that his readers shared with himself. The skinny poem is a fundamental expression of modernist aesthetics. It is the most radical response to the demands of prose discourse replicated both in pentameter and Whitman's format of long lines. Like other verse forms it offers opportunities and limitations. So far as content is concerned, Bukowski insistently, ostentatiously, avoids the kind of complex syntax, diction, and thematic nuance we associate with short-line masters like Robert Creeley, James Schuyler, and Kay Ryan.

The first sentence of "To Hell with Robert Schumann" spreads over eleven lines. Like the second long strophe, this one begins with alcohol. Readers of Bukowski don't have to be reminded that drinking is the writer's principal preoccupation, the defining trope of his existential condition. He is an old-fashioned tosspot; Falstaffian celebrations of cups of sack abound. Here he is drinking during the intermission between live performances of two piano concertos by Robert Schumann. If we come to Bukowski's poetry with a prejudice based on his notoriously down-market aesthetics we are continually surprised by his affection for European classical composers: Bach and Beethoven especially, and also Borodin, Brahms, Bruckner, Mahler, Mozart, Shostakovich, Sibelius, and others cited in the poems. (Interestingly, given the charges of Germanophile anti-Semitism directed at him, he rarely mentions Wagner.) The art-music of choice for his generation was jazz and blues, the sound of modernity. Among other virtues, jazz seemed to offer permission to poets to syncopate their verses in ways that owed little to the iambic. Logic and the *Zeitgeist* insist that a poet like Bukowski would defer to jazz as a means of trashing the so-called genteel tradition of pre–twentieth century verse. "Just put me down as saying that the poetry of the centuries is shit," he told an interviewer. "It's shameful."[12] But he reports in many places that he loved to listen to classical music on the radio and at the occasional concert, a reactionary tendency that puts him in elite company among postwar American poets.

The poem finds him impatient with Schumann or the pianist or both; "2 are too many" he complains, offering the unpersuasive reason that he couldn't identify the music because he had lost the program. So he "drove 21 blocks" to see "a Jap and a Mexican" punch it out in what is certainly the performative antithesis of a Schumann concerto. (Most likely his destination is the Olympic Auditorium on Grand Street.) In crossing the town south and east he crosses a boundary of taste, of lifestyle, from high culture to low. The complex harmonies of melodic construction collapse into the visceral pleasures of watching two figures from elsewhere on the Pacific Rim brawl with each other, described with some relish. "I drank a lot of / beer" he writes, giving the last word a line of its own. Is this just a bad line-break or does he want all that white space pointing like an arrow toward the all-important noun that signals his self-pleasuring and self-punishing addiction on earth? Awkward line-breaks are the most obvious sign, along with lowercase letters at the beginning of sentences, of an anti-tradition poetics in Bukowski's verse. No poet of note in the twentieth century is so reckless about lineation, so wedded to the deliberately slapdash poetics of what is often called "chopped prose."

On one of his bathroom breaks—and yes, we note that the word "piss" was uncommon in poetry before the 1970s—he misses the climax of the fight, just as his drinking interrupted his enjoyment of Schumann. Bukowski often reports on failed resolutions during his spectatorial and erotic experiences. In any case, he walks to his car and drives to the site of his daytime job with the unpersuasive excuse that he wants to see if the place looks "less painful." If the reader is hoping for an episode of special resonance, perhaps this is it, here at the center of the poem. He sees a fellow worker, or thinks he sees him, but it's unclear to him what Ralph is doing. "I thought I should call the / police" but he confesses that he couldn't care less if Ralph steals from or sets the place on fire. (Bukowski always expresses sympathy for disgruntled workers.) He doesn't encourage us to become involved in the moral decision he's made; he immediately gets back in his car and takes the freeway to his apartment.

Emily Dickinson declared that she "saw New Englandly," meaning not that she focused on locations in the topographical manner of Thoreau or Hawthorne or William Cullen Bryant, but that her vision of things and people was informed by the spirit of place, be it Puritan, Transcendental, or otherwise. Bukowski is demonstrating for us in this poem how he sees Los

Angelesly. We're not informed where he hears the concert, where he stops to see the fight, what his place of work looked like, what he saw and felt on the freeway drive, or even where his apartment was and how the neighborhood appeared to him that night. This poem like most of his others is ego-driven, self-absorbed, a record of his humdrum activities. It has what we would now identify as a blog-like structure, the aimless verbal meandering of an egotist with time on his hands and an obliging keyboard. Bukowski de-dramatizes his experience, flattens its affect, disowns any obligation to discover the profundity other poets labor to construct in searching out the deep meaning of their encounters with precisely apprehended locations. The city is incidental in both senses of the word, the source of incidents and beside the main point. Disconnection and alienation are the dominant motifs of much Los Angeles poetry, along with a subjectivity that strains with infrequent success to make contact with the outer world. The temptation to write superficial poems about one's sense of estrangement from complex modes of being is not limited to poets in L.A., of course, but L.A. can be a welcoming milieu for the poet who wants to improvise as many as seven or eight poems at one sitting, as Bukowski claimed was his practice. In his poems Bukowski quotes admirers as telling him they love his work because it's "easy to understand," and he embraces the privileges granted him by civic approval on those terms.[13] Critics would say that his verse is, deliberately, as commodified as the city, full of the ubiquitous tinsel of superficial images. And they would be mainly correct.

The last strophe seems designed to respond to their implied critiques. Not by moving deeper into the psyche or the city, but by extending the randomness and shallowness of his experience until it impresses us either by its spareness or by the cumulative interest of the mundane. He drinks some scotch, he sets the clock, he swallows a vitamin, he thinks about a whore in Glendale (the specificity is a gesture of sincerity), he checks the ball scores, pisses again, turns out the lights, gets into bed. By this time the exasperated reader accustomed to the hard-won artifice of first-rate poetry is certainly dumbfounded at the determined banality of the poem. Can it be that this dull litany of trivialities is precisely what admirers enjoy in Bukowski's verse, the rote thinginess, the refusal to articulate the previously unapprehended textures of everyday life?

But the poem takes a lyrical turn. The (entire) line "didn't pray" catches the attention as a musical note that alters the mood to one more pensive.

No god or heaven for this sinner, apparently. He thinks of places like Japan (origin of one of the boxers) and "Central Avenue" perhaps in proximity to the Mexican fighter's home. We think for a moment about the multicultural demography of L.A., the most varied in the country when the poem was written. And then his reverie turns to the dead and famous, a familiar topic in Bukowski's work. And then ("and then and then": it's impossible not to fall into the paratactic mode while writing about Bukowski) the chronicle rises to a lyrical passage: "while the Thames went along without / me and the girls walked up and down the / sidewalks without me." Here he finds himself becoming "poetic," perhaps thinking of Edmund Spenser's marriage song "Prothalamion" about the Thames and its beautiful maidens, adapted by T. S. Eliot in *The Waste Land* as an ironic critique of the "unreal city" of twentieth-century London. But Bukowski characteristically chooses to evade contact with a perilously profound subject: "And then I thought I wouldn't mind / so much," he tells himself, truly or not, a radical truncation of meditations on death that grow more and more frequent in his verse after the 1970s. He falls asleep and "slept good" he writes in defiance of correct grammar, a last flippant disowning of his status as Poet, master of language.

So we return to fundamental questions: (1) how good is this poem? and (2) how good a poem about Los Angeles is it? In arguing that the two questions cannot, in poems like this one, be separated, I have subjected "To Hell with Robert Schumann" to a summary report that will seem to many readers *much* overextended. Bukowski very rarely writes a poem that demands the kind of alert attention and sustained analysis we give to canonical poems in the modern anthology. His vocabulary is simplistic, his rhythms prosaic, his powers of figurative language intermittent. (The Japanese fighter is "grasshopper slim"; that's all the metaphorical invention we get.) Bukowski is the extreme case that shadows every theorist, beginning with Wordsworth and including Whitman and William Carlos Williams, who insists that the language of poetry should not differ fundamentally from the language of common men. An author who wrote a lot of prose before he segued into verse, Bukowski denounced the "lacy bullshit" of poets who favored nuance in lineation, ambiguity and elegance in phrasing.[14] Like Mark Twain who characterized himself as an "American Vandal" in *The Innocents Abroad,* he is a vulgarian in more ways than one, laying siege to the mandarin tradition. Are his advocates, his zealous fans, vulgarians as well? Do they say, like Frank O'Hara in the poem "My Heart," "I want to be / at least as alive as the vulgar"?

Let's take a look at the word "vulgarity" and see how it helps us engage this poem whose title warns non-vulgarians away at the outset. "Vulgarity" is defined in the *Oxford English Dictionary* as "the state or quality of being ordinary or commonplace," and the favored language of vulgarians is a vocabulary "in general or common use." The attribution of "coarseness" clings to the definition in most of its cited usages, as in William Hazlitt's remark "They vulgarize and degrade whatever is . . . sacred to the mind" or Wyndham Lewis's regret for "the popularization and vulgarizing of art" that engenders second-rate forms of the genuine article. "Tis easy to astonish . . . The vulgar mass," Byron remarks in another quotation. The definitions and citations provoke accusations of class snobbery aimed at poets who practice the "golden" or "high" style, or even the common vernacular, versus the "low" or "leaden" style. Especially in America there has always been an abiding suspicion of those who do not write in the vulgate. Whitman eagerly embraced the image of "one of the roughs" lifting his "barbaric yawp" over the rooftops and disdained Tennyson as a parlor poet unacquainted with the hurly-burly locutions of life on the street. The division of American writers into Paleface and Redskin camps by postwar critics loyal to the proletarian literature they associated with progressive politics forms the background for the populist taste that celebrates Bukowski as a working-class bard. Likewise the division of humanity into the "square" and the "hip" during the period of Beat eminence brought cultural pressure on intellectuals and artists, especially in the avant-garde. Bukowski's novels such as *Ham on Rye, Post Office, Factotum,* and *Women* furthered his identification with the demotic conventions associated with craftsmen like Mark Twain, Jack London, and Henry Miller, to cite fiction writers fond of the state of California.

Bukowski does not wander the world, in body or mind, as his predecessors did. He remains fixed in place. Yet we don't hear the variety of dialects and speech patterns one would overhear traveling in those and other districts. Bukowski has a poor ear for the speech of others, except for the banter of his companions and sexual partners, and even there he tends to translate everything they say into his own unflinching lexicon. "Brittle" is an adjective he uses approvingly for Hemingway's prose, and the language of his poems is intensely brittle, "having hardness and rigidity but little tensile strength" (*OED*). There is little effort to endow his casual contacts with flexibility of character or surprising variations of speech, which would require some backstory and some complex probing into their sensibility. His preferred diction is the banal. The word "banal" originally meant "common to all," and perhaps that's the point: What's wrong with sounding like everyone else? Bukowski safely chooses vocabulary that is common to all, "easy to understand," rather than listening for the unique, eccentric, inventive idioms belonging to individuals in other communities. Nathanael West, F. Scott Fitzgerald, Norman Mailer, and Chester Himes heard the variety of idioms loud and clear when they came to Los Angeles, and in their fiction they entertained readers with the Yiddish-inflected speech along with other ethnic idioms mashed up and always audible on the streets of the city. Wherever he goes in Los Angeles, however, Bukowski hears the speech of people who sound just like him, and he reports even their slang in a lexicon that seldom strays from the comfort zone common to his likely readers.

In an essay, Derek Walcott makes the point that Robert Frost mimics the eccentric verbal habits that set his New England characters, and himself, apart from other regional poets who adhere to the common stock of words and phrases, coarse and otherwise, handed down and around from writer to writer as a form of "poetic diction."[15] (I derive the terms from Wordsworth's "Preface" to the *Lyrical Ballads.*) Bukowski may get applause because he doesn't embrace the linguistic and syntactical sophistication of Walcott, or James Merrill or Amy Clampitt or Richard Howard, or for that matter, William Carlos Williams. He may seem the soul of a former frontier city that prides itself on democratic contempt for the belle-lettristic style of the highfalutin East; but he does not actually sound like the masses who live in that city. What he gives us is not the vulgarity of the streets, which would deliver a complex charge of verbal energy, but a defiant vulgarity of self-regard.

III

Perhaps these weighty judgments derive from too small a database? I gladly turn to another poem. I follow Bukowski's example in putting the title into lowercase.

beach trip

the strong men
the muscle men
there they sit
down at the beach

cocoa tans
with the weights
scattered about them
untouched

they sit as the
waves go in and
out

they sit as the
stock market
makes and breaks
men and families

they sit while
one punch of a button
could turn their
turkeynecks to
black and shriveled
matchsticks

they sit while
suicides in green rooms
trade it in for space

they sit while former
Miss Americas
weep before wrinkled
mirrors

they sit
they sit with less
life-flow than apes
and my woman stops and
looks at them:
"oooh oooh oooh," she
says.

I walk off with
my woman as the waves
go in and out.

"there's something wrong
with them," she said, "what
is it?"

"their love only runs in
one direction."

the seagulls whirl and
the sea runs in and out

and we left them
back there
wasting themselves
time
this moment
the seagulls
the sea
the sand.

—•—

"beach trip" is the penultimate poem in *Love Is a Dog from Hell* (1977), a book mainly about Bukowski's sex life. In the 307 pages of this anatomy of scatology—or, to be generous, this cornucopia of the erotic and romantic—a poem like this one catches the eye. In a book so much about the body, "beach trip" focuses on bodies that make a spectacle of themselves. It could be set anywhere on the shoreline but who can doubt that it is Muscle Beach that the poet is visiting? For years people would come to the site, first in Santa Monica and then in Venice Beach, to watch the muscle builders lift weights, exhibit their sculpted torsos, and engage in macho horseplay. But here the weightlifters merely sit idle and catch the poet's attention because of their immobility. The world is in motion everywhere but here, and he pauses to register that fact and think about it a little.

With so much physical power at their command they "sit as the / waves go in and / out." These unusual figures seem essentially dead, fixed in their identity as "strong men," and transfixed by the poet's baleful stare. The plainness of phrasing to describe them has a kind of epitaph-like quality, as on a tombstone. We can tell that the poet is inspired by the sight because he resorts to metaphor: turkeynecks, matchsticks, the "space" acquired by suicides when they trade in their body for whatever emptiness awaits them, the "wrinkled" mirrors reflecting the wrinkled former Miss Americas. Each of these little stanzas informs us of the eventual subjugation of supposedly powerful men, and of beauty queens, to Time's power to deform their faces and bodies. The weightlifters are disfigured and subhuman creatures, "with less / life-flow than apes." The poet's "woman" misses the point he has been silently making to himself: she squeals with admiration at the muscles, oblivious to the way the more sensitive speaker has been diminishing them in his imagination for his yet unwritten poem. But she catches on. "There's something wrong / with them," she says and asks what. He replies "their love only runs in / one direction." Who is he to talk? the reader asks, having read 300 pages of self-admiring verse. But perhaps now, in the book's closure, he awakens to a higher reality than the meat self he favors up to this point.

Unlike "To Hell with Robert Schumann" this poem is static and its repetitions are those of linguistic phrasing, not of quotidian activities like driving, drinking, and pissing. In a city devoted so much to bodily glamour, the waves teach their melancholy lesson to those vain about their appearance or performance. When Bukowski condemns the weightlifters for "wasting themselves" he is expressing a remorse repeated *sotto voce* in his idylls of visiting the racetrack, drinking and smoking addictively, engaging in bar fights, watching TV, and his couplings with women. If the muscle men recall the inert British beach bum who turns a deep cocoa in the sun at Santa Monica Beach in Gavin Lambert's short story "Nukuhiva!", Bukowski performs Lambert's own cautionary role as witness to human breakdown at the sandy edge of history.[16] There's no escape from the stock market, or nuclear danger, or most of life's afflictions, including ennui. There's only the moment of writing the poem and making a record of having noticed, in W. H. Auden's words, that Time is "indifferent in a week / To a beautiful physique." Especially if it has been made beautiful by the self-aggrandizing ritual of pumping iron.

So, is "beach trip" a good poem or a bad one? First, Bukowski gets points for selecting for commentary a scene and a cast of statuary figures commonly overlooked by poets. In the few occasions poets have engaged the subject—e.g., Charles Edward Eaton's "The Weight Lifter" and Harold Norse's "Mr. Venice Beach"[17]—they tend to load the poem with filigree and sarcasm. Bukowski awkwardly tries to find a moral perspective when he encounters the bodybuilders. The waves go in and out, the stock market goes up and down, the world could be nuked at the press of a button: these are banal observations, useful only if we take them as artful critiques of the way the "I" is killing time as well, and Bukowski doesn't seem to be thinking along that self-critical track. The series of stanzas beginning "He sits" is no doubt meant to mimic the monotony of a lifestyle less interesting to the poet than steady drinking, or steady typing. He does express with some force and frankness his distaste for a life devoted to self-sculpting, but he misses the chance to dramatize the jealousy he of the famously beer-bellied physique no doubt undergoes at the sight of such well-formed bodies. Rather than analyze a potentially complex encounter, he retreats into a moralistic stance that discovers nothing, though it suggests the outlines of a superior unwritten poem.

What would such a poem look like? Of course one cannot fault Bukowski for failing to foresee that a local bodybuilder named Arnold Schwarzenegger would achieve celebrity status around the world, for becoming Mr. Universe at the age of twenty, for making a series of blockbuster movies, and not least, for winning two elections to become governor of California in 2003 and 2006. His ascent to media and political power derived from his manifestation of muscular self-fashioning and raised questions about the nexus of performance, narcissism, sexism, arrogant masculinity, and ambition that became central topics for body theorists of the 1980s and 1990s especially. Bukowski only dimly perceived the potential of bodybuilders he encountered to represent such cultural paradigms. He did not appreciate the range of symbolic possibilities because he was intent on simplistically bending his poem back toward himself, as he always does. He thinks too little about how Los Angeles and California in general might seize upon and fetishize the bodybuilder as a figure of cultural and political dominance.

The seagulls, the sea, the sand . . . the closing repetitions are an evasion, not a summary revelation. The images, the landscape, the language, are mainly commonplace. An index of the poem's carelessness is the change from "she says" to "she said" and the pointless reiteration of "runs" and "in and out" within a few lines. It's a promising draft that a conscientious poet might have improved into an exceptional poem. But what were the odds that Bukowski would labor over a revision, even if a friend were generous enough to vet this weak version? The poem lies halfway between good and bad, the half-hearted product of swift composition.

IV

At his poetry readings, in Los Angeles or at colleges mainly in the West, Bukowski's most avidly received work, by all reports, were his lengthy poems about sexual tussling with women, often whores, whom he picked up in bars or who presented themselves to him for experiences of the kind he loved to record. These are monotonous and voyeuristic poems, tedious and artless, for the most part, and often "gratuitously offensive" in the words of his admiring biographer Howard Sounes.[18] His most accomplished poems are written according to what Russell Harrison calls "an aesthetic of the little event."[19] A stimulus and a response. An insight following an experience. "born again," from Bukowski's posthumous volume *The Flash of Lightning Behind the Mountain* (2004) is a good example.

born again

this special place of ourselves
sometimes explodes in our
faces.
I got a flat on the freeway yesterday,
changed the right rear wheel on the
shoulder,
the big rigs storming by,
slamming the sky
against my head and
body.
it felt like I was clinging to the
edge of the earth,
30 minutes late for the first
post.

but strangely, something
about the experience
was very much like emerging reluctantly

a second time
from my
mother's womb.[20]

—•—

A strophe of fourteen lines is followed by one of six. Something about the dynamics of the structure suggests sonnet form, emphasized by the strong volta preceding the conjunction "but" that extends and amplifies the narrative of the first strophe. What is "this special place" he refers to in the opening line? It's unusual for Bukowski to begin with a puzzle. As readers we hold the phrase in suspension as we move into the body of the poem. In the midst of driving the freeway, on his way to the racetrack, he finds himself in peril. The car breaks down. In a volume so obsessed with aging and death it's hard not to see the action as metaphorical, the more so if we glance at an earlier poem in the volume, "speed," in which the speaker, "65 years old," races on the Pasadena Freeway against a young hot-rodder who drives faster because more indifferent to death. In "born again" the speaker undergoes a disorienting experience of terrifying force as the big rigs slam the sky against his head and body as he tries to change the tire. He finds himself in the extremity of transformation, clinging to the "edge of the earth." "The edge is what I have," writes Theodore Roethke in "In a Dark Time" and continues:

A man goes far to find out what he is—
Death of the self in a long, tearless night,
All natural shapes blazing unnatural light.

"Which I is *I*?" he asks. "A fallen man, I climb out of my fear." These abstract formulations are masterful, the work of a major poet. Bukowski is not capable of generalizing in language this rich. But he does recognize that the flat tire and the passing of the big rigs have given him a glimpse of the changed condition, "the special place of ourselves," that Roethke evokes with such resonance.

And so the closure of the poem proposes the metaphor that best suits his experience of the newly stripped-away soul. The phrase "emerging reluctantly," drawn out in the longest line of the poem, is especially telling, for it posits two selves in coexistence at this "special" moment: the man who faces imminent death and the naked reborn consciousness that takes form timidly as an afterlife. The "mother's womb" is a figure for material nature but it is acknowledged as the origin of the spirit, including the spirit of poetry. One feels Bukowski actively climbing out of his fear, in Roethke's words. Rather than writing a poem about this experience in his usual careless way, Bukowski turns the lyric into a deeper, more realized psychological place. Would that he had written more poems in this concentrated and visionary mode!

Bukowski's obituary in the *Los Angeles Times* for 10 March 1994 was headlined "Charles Bukowski Dies: Poet of L.A.'s Low-Life." Headlines are not literary criticism but in this case the subhead does make a useful point. For Bukowski Los Angeles did not exist as a congeries of sites, of locations, of the mystique and atmosphere of places. It inhered in the raffish characters he encountered day by day. His memory poems about New Orleans, Philadelphia, Atlanta, and other way stations in his adult experience present the same types of Skid Row "low-life" he rediscovered in L.A. In his book on Bukowski, Gay Brewer remarks, "For all of Chinaski's proclaimed distaste for the city and crowds, the persistent implication in Bukowski's work is that an urban landscape and its odd and damned occupants are necessary for his work."[21] The gallery of human types who move through his poems constitute the city, which otherwise was incidental to his self-referential poetics, though on occasion vividly displayed.

At the risk of writing literary commentary Bukowski and his admirers would disdain, I suggest that his popularity has much to do with the "shock" that Walter Benjamin discerned in Baudelaire's encounters with passing figures in the Paris streets, and that Georg Simmel described in his classic text "The Metropolis and Mental Life." The *flâneur* ventures into the mean streets of the big city, by foot or by automobile, and tests the stability of his ego by the novelty of his confrontations with strange people, places, and things. Bukowski seems to be a *flâneur*; he meets many people in his constant voyages out to the metropolis. But his poems seldom convey that half-mystical shock or that seizure of his imagination by the fantastic; more often they de-dramatize incidents by means of thematic repetition, slack form, and low-key everyday diction. His poetry eschews the sense of wonder, which Bukowski considered a Romantic affectation. His fey attitude is ingratiating, companionable, gemütlich. Many readers love his poems because they are "cool" and rarely probe the terror and passion of urban life as in nineteenth- and twentieth-century classics. They anesthetize like the alcohol that fills them. As the examples above suggest, they could be read, for the most part, as talismans against the troubling forces of time and death. Bukowski's manic compositional history argues for a kind of inner terror, a need for distraction and recognition, that elevates his best work above the merely commonplace.

Also, Bukowski trades on the compassion of readers for the sad autobiographical story impressed into his fiction and poetry. Even for authors, so often wounded in early life, the brutal treatment by his father during childhood, the psychological and physical pain of his face disfigured by boils, and his dismal work history made him seem a scapegoat for the world's cruelty. Driven to set down the unvarnished facts of (his) life, he made contact with readers impatient with artifice and suspicious of what seemed the arts of embellishment and disguise. Los Angeles proved to be the ideal location for immediate and ongoing self-fashioning. In a city of dispossessed strangers, and especially in his chosen community of castaways and rebels, Bukowski thrived as the hero of his own obsessively recorded story. One reads in his admirers' praise of him this fan-like devotion and emotional gratitude for Bukowski's candid and inspirational modeling of his life in spite of afflictions.

As for his fiction, Dostoevsky, Hamsun, Hemingway, Céline, and Fante were his avowed models of literary excellence. Though he referred admiringly to Robinson Jeffers he seems to have derived from his fellow Californian mainly a fatalistic philosophy, not an appreciation for landscape or an understanding of free verse technique. Bukowski tries the reader's patience, no question about it. He remarked in one poem, "if I have to write one hundred bad poems to get one good / one / I don't feel that I'm wasting my time."[22] He made a career decision to publish the hundred bad poems along with the good one, and his executors have passed into print everything he left behind. Perhaps he didn't know or care which were the bad and which the good. He wastes our time, if we read him in bulk, but he composed some poems—how many? a dozen? two or three dozen?—that readers of well-wrought poetry are fortunate to possess. They add their light to the city, and we should be grateful they exist.

FOUR

On the Freeway: Moving Fast and Standing Still

Mobility outweighs monumentality.

—REYNER BANHAM[1]

And who knows more about traffic
Than a Los Angeles poet, anyway?

—ELOISE KLEIN HEALY[2]

I

It hardly needs demonstrating that the network of freeways, beginning modestly with the Arroyo Seco Parkway in 1940 and spreading like the proverbial spider web, is the dominant single landmark of Greater Los Angeles. Surface and aerial photos of the freeways have come to signify the city as much as the Eiffel Tower does Paris, or the Colosseum Rome. The notoriety began in earnest after the world's first four-level ("stack") interchange—of the Pasadena, Santa Ana, Hollywood, and Harbor freeways—opened in 1953. Perhaps the second most famous scene in all of the city's literature (the premier place goes to the riot on Hollywood Boulevard in *The Day of the Locust*) is that of Maria Wyeth fearlessly changing lanes from the Harbor to the Hollywood freeways in Chapter 1 of Joan Didion's novel of 1970, *Play It As It Lays*. Maria makes "a diagonal move across four lanes of traffic. On the afternoon she finally did it without once braking or once losing the beat on the radio she was exhilarated, and that night slept dreamlessly." Didion elaborates on this apparently autobiographical moment in an essay in *The White Album* (1979):

> Actual participation requires a total surrender, a concentration so intense as to seem a kind of narcosis, a rapture-of-the-freeway. The mind goes clean. The rhythm takes over. A distortion of time occurs, the same distortion that characterizes the instant before an accident.[3]

As the first major city built in America after the invention of the automobile, Los Angeles grew willy-nilly as an archipelago of communities strung out across hundreds of miles. Essentially, an Interstate complex of highways was introjected into the urban design, and into the consciousness of every citizen, so that the identity of the city took shape alongside the network of roadways articulated and complicated in intricate spatial patterns. Navigating the straightaways, overpasses and underpasses, contours, and on/off-ramps of the freeway became an initiation rite, leisure pastime, and occupational necessity for residents and tourists alike. The freeways are the phenomena most memorably felt in the pulse of everyday life, whether as a mystical thrill in the manner of Didion's heroine, or as a perilous and unglamorous obstacle in the process of getting from one local place to another.

Readers of poetry will think of one other textual locus from the early 1970s to set beside Didion's passages. In Frank Bidart's poem "California Plush," part of his impressive first volume *Golden State* (1973), this native of Bakersfield looks homeward after settling on the eastern seaboard. He begins his reverie with an evocation of the sublimity of Southern California in the manner of Mark Jarman re-creating in "The Supremes" the rapture of surfing:

> The only thing I miss about Los Angeles
>
> is the Hollywood Freeway at midnight, windows down and
> radio blaring
> bearing right into the center of the city, the Capitol Tower
> on the right, and beyond it, Hollywood Boulevard
> blazing
>
> —pimps, surplus stores, footprints of the stars
>
> —descending through the city
> fast as the law would allow

through the lights, then rising to the stack
out of the city
to the stack where lanes are stacked six deep

and you on top; the air
now clean; for a moment weightless

without memories, or
need for a past.

The sweet amnesia of life in the fast lane unburdened by selfhood, released from the coils of Time, is evoked paradoxically by memories of specific objects in the cityscape of Hollywood before ascending to the egress, "out of the city" and back to the dry plains of the Central Valley further north. The Capitol Records Tower, constructed to resemble a stack of vinyl records on a turntable, corresponds like a perfect rhyme with the stack of freeway lanes, a chime that runs in the visual memory of northbound drivers forever. The fact is, Bidart acknowledges in the next passage, "the need for the past // is so much at the center of my life" that he felt compelled to escape California altogether and connect with the cultural life of the East, as with Jarman's flight from the seductive sources of bodily transport in the beach cities.[4]

The way in which the freeway works upon the psyche in Los Angeles has a cultural history that is so complex it would take more than one chapter, or one volume, to unfold. The whole story of transportation and road building since the earliest civilizations comes into play. (Chariots on Roman roads, sailing vessels following their maps on every body of water, railway cars pulled by the locomotive Walt Whitman hymned as "Type of the Modern—emblem of motion and power."[5]) When I taught a course at the University of Michigan in "The Literature of Auto-mobility" I considered how far back to begin the narrative of vehicle and road, and which premodern textual sources would best illuminate my chief examples of the twentieth-century literature of car and driver. I chose two nineteenth-century works worth summoning here as a context for the poems I want to examine. One is by the English essayist Thomas De Quincey, perhaps the most fascinating writer most readers of canonical literature neglect. *The English Mail Coach* (1849) is divided into two parts, each focused on the topic of "velocity," which De Quincey presciently takes to be the ominous and compelling subject of the future: "The Glory of Motion" and "The Vision of Sudden Death." Walt Whitman's long poem "Song of the Open Road" likewise celebrates movement across vast distances as a goal in itself, the rapture of living like a rolling stone.

The English Mail Coach deserves special attention because it is written, like everything by De Quincey, with a heightened lyricism, what he called "impassioned prose," in imitation of the Romantic poets he most admired, Wordsworth and Coleridge. Forging a high-decibel language commensurate with the dynamism of the subject matter was from the outset the chief task of the bards of locomotion. Here is a passage that exudes the essence of transcendental passion as it effects a shift of cultural value from older forms of transport to the ineffable tandem of coach and horses:

> On this system the world was not *magna loquimur*, as upon railways, but *vivimus*. Yes, "*magna vivimus*"; we do not make verbal ostentation of our grandeurs, we realize our grandeurs in act, and in the very experience of life. The vital experience of the glad animal sensibilities made doubts impossible on the question of our speed; we heard our speed, we saw it, we felt it as a thrilling; and this speed was not the product of blind insensate agencies, that had no sympathy to give, but was incarnated in the fiery eyeballs of the noblest amongst brutes, in his dilated nostril, spasmodic muscles, and thunder-beating hoofs.[6]

When horsepower was transferred to the machine, it lost none of the "grandeurs" De Quincey endows upon it; indeed, the automobile became the fundamental agency of transport, in both meanings of the word, in modern America and throughout the world. De Quincey lays out all the conventions of a new mythology of speed in "The Glory of Motion," and then turns to the downside of velocity-as-a-form-of-divinity in "The Vision of Sudden Death." This long, protracted vignette of the near collision of the massive mail coach and its brace of four horses with "a frail, reedy gig" and one horse is a piece of rhetoric that anticipates all the fictional and poetic representations of the car crash in texts to come. (De Quincey's diptych is duplicated by Karl Shapiro in his matching poems "Buick" and "Auto Wreck.") The rush of the night mail coach from London to Manchester and Glasgow becomes a dreamscape of magical flight down a wide empty road, a scene of modern technology bursting into the wilderness of unresisting nature. It would be hard to find a narrative that more perfectly enacts in its vertiginous sentences and evocative diction the subjective apprehension of both abnormal speed and the calamity of collision. All subsequent critical attention in the literature of automobility to "the motorist's eye" as organizing principle derives from De Quincey's self-reflexive experiment in point of view.

"Song of the Open Road" (1856) likewise lays down conventions that inform the poetry to come. Whitman's version of auto-mobility is literal and limited: he is infatuated by the experience of pedestrian movement for its own sake. For one thing, as a walker in the city he gains an intense if fleeting relationship with its surfaces:

> You flagg'd walks of the cities! you strong curbs at the edges!
> You ferries! you planks and posts of wharves! you timber-lined sides!
>   you distant ships!
> You rows of houses! you window-pierc'd facades! you roofs!

And so forth for many lines. Implied in his hyperkinetic catalogue structure is the perfect bliss of moving horizontally from object to object, image to image, addressing each visual figure for a split second, and then hastening to another more quickly than one could in real life. The reader's sensation of being overwhelmed by ocular data enhances the pleasure of the text, as fresh experience multiplies by leaps and bounds. Whitman takes on the role of ultimate *flâneur* hurrying by the fronts of houses, the docks full of ships, and other actualities, always celebrating the superficial "facades" he gathers within the circumference of his ever-expanding sensibility and enumerates in his exclamatory long-line free verse. He extols the lifestyle of the solitary wanderer accumulating perceptions in the same random order present to him as he walks by, but in sequences beyond the capacity for logical ordering. As De Quincey emphasizes the living, creaturely nature of the source of his locomotion, so Whitman personifies the thoroughfare; he does not feel it strange to establish a dialogue with the passageway of his desire:

> O highway I travel, do you say to me *Do not leave me?*
> Do you say *Venture not—if you leave me you are lost?*
> Do you say *I am already prepared, I am well-beaten and undenied,*
>   *adhere to me?*

O public road, I say back I am not afraid to leave you, yet I love you,
You express me better than I can express myself,
You shall be more to me than my poem.

There is probably no poet bending his imagination to the subject of freeways that is not aware of Whitman's religious zealotry and enthusiastic style in regard to the open road, which he performs in texts like "Starting from Paumanok," "Salut au Monde," and "Pioneers, O Pioneers." The "public road" is the outward manifestation of his linguistic movement, line by line, but emphatically of "more" value than poetry itself—an affirmation of life over art, though the two worlds fuse in poems like "Song of the Open Road." If Whitman is less cognizant than De Quincey of the dangers of uninhibited experience on the road, he more successfully puts the subject of solitary locomotion through the city on the agenda of twentieth-century modernism. How he would have loved the automobile! And the engineering marvel of the freeways connecting place to place, people to people, in the city of Los Angeles, which was hardly more than a village when Whitman died in 1892.

(Also in 1892, Charlotte Perkins Gilman published her canonical short story "The Yellow Wallpaper," about a New England woman suffering from "nervous depression" who imagines that a "strange, provoking, formless sort of figure" is crawling behind the surfaces of her bedroom. Forty years later Gilman had moved to Pasadena and was writing joyful poems about her liberation as a woman driving on the Grapevine, the proto-freeway running between San Joaquin Valley and the Los Angeles basin.)[7]

There is one more text I want to set in place before turning to some contemporary poems about the freeway system: Reyner Banham's classic work of urban sociology, *Los Angeles: The Architecture of Four Ecologies* (1971). Banham grew up in England, and first came to Los Angeles in 1965 to participate in a symposium at UCLA. Like many British-educated fiction writers before him (Cedric Belfrage, Raymond Chandler, Aldous Huxley, Christopher Isherwood, Evelyn Waugh, Gavin Lambert), Banham was astonished by the new culture he beheld and which he wished to define before it changed into something less potent in visual appearance and democratic promise. His praise of the unorthodox "ecologies" of Los Angeles helped to fix its riverine forms in the imagination of the world and no doubt contributed both to a new wave of immigrants and to the discursive literature, including poetry, that adapted its insights and mimicked its hyperbolical tone. Banham wrote favorably of the beach communities, the foothills (e.g., Hollywood), and the communities south of downtown; but his chief interest was the marvel of "Autopia," as he called the network of freeways that connected the sprawling city and endowed so much of the population with the daily joyfulness of driving at high speed.

Banham's achievement is to crystallize the psychogeography of his predecessors. At one point he refers to a freeway as a "carriageway," an archaic Britishism in the manner of De Quincey, and throughout his book he praises the network of highways for inducing "a state of heightened awareness that some locals find mystical" in the oracular spirit of Whitman. "The Los Angeles freeways become a special way of being alive," he asserts in the same passage.[8] Writing at a time when the freeways were blessedly burdened by millions fewer cars than they now are, he rejoices in the Brownian motion of so much heavy and handsomely customized metal circulating over so much roadway with so much convenience toward far-flung destinations. He does lament the loss of the Big Red Cars, the much-loved interurban transport of the Pacific Electric Railway with its 1,164 miles of track, uprooted in the 1950s. And he briefly acknowledges the malign conditions of smog, high-speed crashes, and traffic jams. But his misgivings fade in volume as his prose eloquently reaches again and again for the highest notes of rapture. "The Los Angeles freeway system is indeed one of the greater works of Man" is his thesis from beginning to end of his influential book.[9]

Banham's study of the built environment in Los Angeles appeared one year after Didion's novel and the two have been cited in tandem ever since to represent the high point of car culture and freeway worship in what Banham calls "the super-city." But Didion's description of Maria Wyeth's lane-changing as she negotiates the perilous transition from one freeway to another is ironic given the novel's plot. Maria seeks the mind-blowing distraction of an adrenaline rush because her life has become so empty of value and affect. A film actress whose career depends entirely on her director-husband's success, and the mother of a brain-damaged daughter, Maria's manic driving represents an emotional escape from her depressed existence akin to her addiction to drugs and casual adulterous sex. One of her trips, north on the Ventura Freeway, has taken her to an abortionist in Encino, an experience that blights her subsequent life. Likewise, the rush of speed Clay enjoys as he drives the freeway in Bret Easton Ellis's novel *Less than Zero* (1985) clearly serves him as nothing more than another toxic drug dangerous to himself and other drivers. Banham does not consider how the freeway can serve this kind of dystopian vision, nor does he foresee the kind of gridlock, and its psychic consequences, that now dominate all discourse about the freeways. (See the film *Falling Down* [1993] for a vivid visual illustration.) One can read the comic situation in the film *L .A. Story* (1991), in which a freeway sign flashes goofy inspirational messages to Steve Martin, as a satire on Banham's boosterism. Indeed, the clash of stereotypes and subversive images depicting auto-mobility in fiction and film from 1971 to the present provides useful genre memories for the persistent binary of poetry on the subject, ecstatic and melancholy by turns.

II

Eloise Klein Healy

THIS DARKNIGHT SPEED

Sometimes I feel about love
like driving places at darknight speed
with the radio on
doing what that saxophone
was barking in the bar:
"better yet, better yet, better get in a car!"

Sometimes I forget
simple words like rapture
for this animal joy,
this sense of being up to speed
and merging from a ramp,
knowing the driver in the mirror
is already adjusting to meet me
and wants it to go smooth,
wants me to have my turn,
not break acceleration
or miss a beat,

wants to meet and make a dance of it
at such a speed,
if you can imagine,
at such a speed that eyes tear from wind
blowing music out the windows.

I always believe
I could start pacing with somebody
on a long highway,
playing all the fast songs
and looking at the truck stops
for that one car

because sometimes I'm lonely
or I need to feel alive
or I just like being on the road in a car,
in a marvelous, monstrous killer-machine
that fills a human body crazy high
on landscape flying by the windows—
just a blur, just a shot of speed.

I always believe
I could get myself in somebody's eyes
wide and interstate-steady,
just flat out speeding along
and scanning the road ahead,
wanting to drive
like that
forever

and if I could keep it up,
god, if I could keep that up

I'd go absolutely right straight crazy to heaven[10]

—•—

The gospel of the glory of motion is best illustrated by Los Angeles poet Eloise Klein Healy's pumped-up lyric, "This Darknight Speed." Healy, who became the city's first Poet Laureate in 2012, forged a wholesome identity in other poems as a pedestrian in neighborhoods like Echo Park and the downtown streets filled with multicultural delicacies for sale such as fish tacos and shrimp burritos. Shopping and tasting puts her in mind of Whitman strolling and shopping in Manhattan, the muse of Healy's lyric imagination: "No wonder I love this city, song of myself."[11] But "This Darknight Speed" is no reassuring walk through the Capital of the Third World, as Los Angeles is sometimes called; it is a fantasia of "animal joy" experienced on the freeway, as her sense of self expands to include the "monstrous killer-machine" for which she has become the directive will. In her new synthetic identity as both androgyne and cyborg, she undergoes an enhanced erotic appetite. She imagines the driver visible to her in the rearview mirror as she merges from an on-ramp as a dance partner and sexual lover. Already intoxicated from drinking at a bar, she records an extraordinary moment in which normal reverie passes into a speed-induced trance, a nocturnal eruption of passion for the presentness of that "*magna vivimus*" summoned by De Quincey.

The poem takes the form of a simile or analogy. "Love" is the first term, or rather *feeling* about love, which is then compared to driving, and the two energy fields become unified as the lyric pulls out all the stops in its insistence that the ecstasy of driving is not only like sexual consummation, it is better than sex. She is summoning *the* rapture, like that of the prophet Elijah, who is gathered immediately into Heaven riding a chariot of fire enveloped in a whirlwind. The city itself disappears in the darkness, but the darkness is arguably the favored visage of the city when one enters the on-ramp. Especially in the earlier decade when the poem was composed, nighttime driving on the freeway was an experience of extreme mobility, with almost no resistance to the highest level of velocity on the speedometer. The poem has a fairytale dimension, like the fables of magic carpets or Romantic texts indulging supernatural fleetness as in Shelley's "The Witch of Atlas." More important for our purposes is the poem's congruence with other descriptions of ecstasy in Los Angeles surroundings: in the anti–self-consciousness of surfing, or the "Paradise" of drugs and cinema.

Another example of the same rhapsodic sentiment is Wanda Coleman's poem of 1983, "On Speed." The speaker drives under the long-distance spell of a lover who has ended their relationship, and whom she desires to repossess by the force of her heavy foot on the pedal. She pushes the car to its limit as she cycles through the freeway system, pumped up with erotic velocity:

> i hit the underpass, merge, w/traffic
> on on on
> the 405, San Diego's freeway south
> circle sharp, down to the right then up over
> the rise his eyes Moraga, Sunset beyond the hills
> and on on on
> the junction of the 405 to the 10 east again
> on Santa Monica's freeway to the 101, Hollywood ahead
> the radio shrieks
>
> i am made of steel
> and have 4 wheel drive
>
> love is 85 miles per hour[12]

The sense of acceleration increases as the signposts of measured verse disappear in the growing excitement: punctuation vanishes; capital letters at the beginning of each line, even the pronoun "I," shrink to lowercase; information takes on the air of telegraphic style. A flashback/insert like "his eyes" fuels the reckless speed as she hurtles down the straightaway of the 405, her abandon a sign of her romantic enchantment.

If Los Angeles is commonly signified by images of leisure, of deceleration and relaxation in keeping with the Bower of Bliss motif, its modernist undersoul remains an iconography of acceleration, updated from "the storm-flight of these maniacal horses" De Quincey hymned in his fugue-poem of the mail coach. In many freeway poems the music throbbing on the car radio matches the roar of the engine and the loud hectic sound of tires on the road. That is, the sound that accompanies the ecstatic pleasure of speed is technologized as part of the hybrid identity of car and driver. All the associative leaps and cinematic shifts of register that became standard practice for the generations of poets after 1940 were forged in the automobile factories and tested on the highways of the modern city, Los Angeles most of all. Much more than fiction, poetry responded to the cultural conditions impressed on verbal art by the technology of motion.

Speed fulfills fundamental desires for transfigured being, as Healy and Coleman show, but/and sheer velocity is antisocial to the core. Coleman's speaker is constantly "monitoring the rear view for the highway patrol." In popular songs about the freeway the speeding automobile is almost always shadowed by "Big John Law," as in Jan and Dean's "Freeway Flyer": "The fastest cars around, there ain't no doubt / Are those big black & white jobs that really move out / On the Hollywood Freeway flyin' past / Writin' up hot shoes drivin' too fast." Likewise Guy Clark sings in "L.A. Freeway": "If I can just get off of this LA freeway / Without getting killed or caught / I'd be down that road in a cloud of smoke / For some land that I ain't bought bought bought." Are you pushing your speedometer up to get a rush, get away, or get caught? Are you headed toward heaven or toward a new life that is just a simulacrum of the old life, in a suburban house you haven't bought? The moral conflicts that beset the solitary soul in Los Angeles, where life is so often temporary and transitional, reach a crisis point when one enters the on-ramp and the question of destination looms like a pileup or emergency site.

"Speed kills" runs the familiar warning sign on highways. But Speed, imagined as a demon lover with a moniker to match, heightens the libido just short of ecstasy, leaving only a little psychic room to turn the wheel, watch for obstacles in the road. Healy's poem proceeds in brief syntactical units, one to a line, rising in emotional force as the reader hurtles toward a climactic rush of pleasure:

> I'd go absolutely right straight crazy to heaven

There is no final period to close the last, strongly stressed line, just the empty space that signifies fulfillment beyond the ending. This hedonistic manifesto could not be written about San Francisco or Portland. It belongs to the frontier city most deeply imbued with edgy fantasies of mobile liberation from habits of moral constraint.

In "Song of Aeterna 27 over Los Angeles," James Schevill satirizes the depiction of thrill-seeking in songs and poems about the freeway. He prefaces the poem with an explanatory epigraph: "Aeterna 27, the new face cream that eliminates wrinkles and makes you eternally 27 – A BILLBOARD SIGN." Here is the whole poem:

Racing on freeways over Los Angeles
In lanes of poured, white liberty
I see the sails of billboards flare
Through smog the golden letters
AETERNA 27

In the smoggy, rear-view mirror,
My sagging lines of 40 fade,
I sail homeward in my fancy
A Flying Dutchman to my wrinkle-free girl
AETERNA 27[13]

The wit of this sardonic poem lies in its juxtaposition of two versions of the American Dream: the stop-time experience of mobility and the anti-aging effects of what are often called "vanishing creams." Los Angeles, a city famous for its cult of youth, is the site of this dual transformation in Schevill's tongue-in-cheek lyric. It is speed that vanishes the speaker's "sagging lines of 40" at the same time his "wrinkle-free girl" benefits from Aeterna 27. The freeway thus becomes an unlikely allusion to the ageless realm of Shangri-La. Yet the two will never meet, if his identification of himself with the Flying Dutchman is an accurate rendition of his dream life. That figure, we recall from Wagner's opera, is a sea captain whose punishment for a crime is to sail a ghost ship eternally without ever coming to port. Possibly Schevill recalled the lines from Thomas McGrath's *Letter to an Imaginary Friend*: "Now / In far Los Angeles I hear / The Flying Dutchman in the dry river / Mourning. Mourning."[14]

The poem, in fact, is constructed in the postmodernist manner, sampling and patching bits and pieces of American poetry. The presence of the word "Song" in the title links it to Whitman's "Song of the Open Road" and other "Song" titles in his oeuvre. The reference to "poured, white liberty" for the concrete surface appears to be an adaptation of the "Proem" of Hart Crane's hymn to the Brooklyn Bridge, with its evocation of "*white rings of tumult, building high / Over the chained bay waters Liberty*." And the "golden letters" on the billboard surely are meant to recall William Carlos Williams's experience as a pedestrian: "I saw the figure 5 / in gold / on a red / firetruck." Schevill provides an *hommage* and send-up of these ecstatic neo-romantic moments in canonical American verse about urban experience. The twice-mentioned smog, after all, is in large part the waste product of all that energy being burned by the glory of motion, and unlike wrinkles it cannot be scrubbed away or covered by a magical emollient. It is the incurable disfigurement made from the exhaust of millions of cars. The Flying Dutchman as serial polluter! The pastiche-poem is a wry critique of the modernist worship of machine technology.

"Stick your patent name on a signboard," Hart Crane wrote in *The Bridge*, as mock advice for opportunists on the move on the rivers and railways of America. The advertising sign central to Schevill's poem, like the "Allbran / Billboard" in Randall Jarrell's *The Lost World* already discussed and the "billboard sex" noticed in Carol Muske-Dukes's poem coming up shortly, represents a complex reality for poets of the urban space. As Marjorie Perloff points out in her essay "Signs Are Taken for Wonders: The Billboard Field as Poetic Space," the concision and irresistible impact of written text set against a consumer product or heavenly space inevitably provides competition as well as inspiration for poets who share the wit and rhetoric of persuasion with these messages. Especially in a cultural landscape in which visual images have become the lingua franca of millions of consumers—and nowhere more so than in Southern California—the semiotics of advertisement, no less than their formal design, gives readers pause in their movement over highways place to place. Advertisements tend to encourage the appetitive life: eat our cereal, use our vanishing cream, see our sexy movie. Billboards become, in the poetry of Los Angeles, signs of the presence of Vanity Fair, always propagandizing for some version of the billboard noticed in Azusa next to the Foothill Freeway in Tony Barnstone's poem "The Sermon on Los Angeles": *Life is Harsh. Your Tequila Shouldn't Be.*[15]

Poems like Schevill's and Carol Muske-Dukes's apply the brakes to runaway efforts to identify Los Angeles as a site of the triumph of popular culture, signified by all-too-memorable slogans on vast canvases. The kind of consumerist ideology that infused the Southland following World War II took up where the old boosterism based on fruits and sunshine, oil wells and real estate, began at the turn of the century. Some poets followed the lead of Karl Shapiro in his volume *The Bourgeois Poet* (1964) by embracing the naked poetry he had once disdained. He presented a model of how to romance person, place, and thing in the turbocharged form of prose poems liberated from his once-favored constraints of repetitive cadences and the tyranny of the line. Ron Koertge in "The Pasadena Freeway" lets complex sentences breeze along in a non-linear way:

> Every evening we lift our eyes and know that we are almost home when we cross the dry arroyo that was your maiden name [Arroyo Seco] until—like any luminary—you changed it, honoring the city you wear on your long and lovely self like a sprawling trinket. O, Pasadena Freeway, we have loved you from the beginning, all of us who can hardly wait to hold the sacred wheel and even in our dreams negotiate your movie star curves all night long.[16]

Other poets resisted what they dismissed as camp indulgence in the only way they could, by choosing traditional verse forms and genres that stood fast as an alternative discourse against ever looser and more prose-like measures in praise of the city. They sought alternatives to the pop aesthetics promoted in mass media that increasingly dominated the landscape of Los Angeles. The hot rod and hamburgers and the glamorous curves of the Arroyo Seco could never be preeminent figures in their tropology.

Carol Muske-Dukes

LITTLE L. A. VILLANELLE

I drove home that night in the rain.
The gutterless streets filled and overflowed.
After months of drought, the old refrain:

A cheap love song on the radio, off-key pain.
Through the maddening, humble gesture of the wipers,
I drove home that night in the rain.

Hollywood sign, billboard sex: a red stain
spreading over a woman's face, caught mid-scream.
After months of drought, the old refrain.

Marquees on Vine, lit up, name after name,
starring in what eager losses: he dreamed
I drove home that night in the rain.

Smoldering brush, high in the hills. Some inane
preliminary spark: then tiers of falling reflected light.
After months of drought, the old refrain.

I wanted another life, now it drives beside me
on the slick freeway, now it waves, faster, faster—
I drove home that night in the rain.
After months of drought, the old refrain.[17]

—•—

Carol Muske-Dukes's "Little L. A. Villanelle" seems at first glance the antithesis of a freeway poem. Surely, we think, if you want a sense of velocity, of sweeping forward movement across vast stretches of perceptual territory, you want a free-associating poem of long lines melting at their extreme into prose form as supple as Koertge's specimen above. Muske-Dukes's poem consciously withdraws from the temptation to represent freeway motion by a De Quincey-like syntax of baroque complexity. As Schevill resorts to haiku- or tanka-like stanzas, so Muske-Dukes chooses one of the most traditional fixed forms of the Old World civilization put most at risk by the acceleration of machine technology. A villanelle is closed, not open, in formal structure; it tends to favor repetition as a stylistic and thematic trope. Obsession lies at the heart of its return, tercet by tercet, to a set of phrases and rhymes, as in a minuet of few but varied moves. The villanelle form enacts the sense of cyclical movement belonging to tradition rather than the high-octane, spatially diffuse onward movement of projective verse associated with the urban freeway.

There are several famous villanelles in English, and all are about loss: Dylan Thomas's "Do Not Go Gentle into That Good Night," addressed to his dying father; Elizabeth Bishop's "One Art," about the loss of a partner's love; Ernest Dowson's "Villanelle of the Poet's Road," full of *carpe diem* sentiment about the passing of youth. Muske-Dukes's poem contains a buried, or strangled, narrative of lost love, beginning suggestively by reference to "that night" and more overtly, lines like "he dreamed / I drove home that night in the rain" and "I wanted another life, now it drives beside me / on the slick freeway." It sounds like a breakup poem, a nocturne about *aftermath*, the most familiar temporal key in contemporary romantic poems. The challenge of the lyric is fitting the milieu to the emotion. What does a speaker in this distressed psychological condition notice? That is the question that unlocks the logic of the obsessive repetitions.

"Rain," surprisingly, is the primary and controlling image. Rain is famously rare in Los Angeles except during the period of December to March, and when it comes it surprises the city—"It never rains in Southern California" as the Mamas and Papas sang in an oft-covered ballad. But here the streets are overflowing; the drought is over, but unlike in *The Waste Land* and other poems freighted with archetypal imagery, the rain signifies melancholy, a drought of the spirit. "Rain," "pain," "stain," and "inane" constitute the cheerless "refrain" that holds or constrains the feeling, otherwise likely to be messy, nothing more than the "cheap love song" the speaker hears on the radio. It's a clear segue of poetic logic from cheap love to images of Hollywood. First the Hollywood sign, rarest of images in poetry about the city. The iconic outsize concrete letters on Mount Lee, visible from the Hollywood Freeway, is an object "almost entirely abstract, at once the quintessence and the mockery of the science of signs," according to Leo Braudy's book-length history of this storied structure.[18] The precarious architecture and uncertain meaning of the sign make it precisely the object that would attract the speaker's attention as she speeds toward an uncertain destination. Then another dopey sign advertising "billboard sex," this one with a bloodstained woman's face. Then movie theaters on Vine Street. Finally, the scene shifts to "Smoldering brush, high in the hills." Drought not rain is foregrounded, and the sparks that might ignite a fire. Even in a poem set in the rain, this apocalyptic threat looms in the hills above Hollywood, ready to sweep down and extinguish the life of the city. Possibly this is what is meant by "another life" riding beside the speaker on the "slick freeway," that metaphorical fire commensurate with her anger, grief, and thwarted desire.

The congress of cars on the city's speedways can suggest the anonymity and anomie of separate lives in a hookup culture as well as the jouissance, the extreme and orgasmic pleasure, when all signals are turned to GO. Likewise, the freeway system can serve as a metaphor of the circulatory system of the human body and the arterial movement of both nutrition and disease through the blood. Miroslav Holub, an immunologist, begins his poem "Hemophilia" by conceptualizing the raging movement of infection through the organs:

And so it circulates
from the San Bernardino Freeway
to the Santa Monica Freeway and
down to the San Diego Freeway and
up to the Golden State Freeway . . .[19]

As he points out, the "emergency phone calls" employed to seek help for the disease likewise make use of intersecting lines comparable to the speed and complex interweaving of freeways. And of course the ultimate analogy is poetry itself, arranging lines of language into elaborate patterns designed for the welfare of the consumer.

III

"Poetry is a form of melancholia," Wallace Stevens remarks.[20] "Free" verse came into being along with inventions capable of amazing acceleration, with the promise of an unlocking of the doors of perception and access to cadences of emotion unconstrained by the metronomic measures of meter and the patterned chiming of rhyme. Yet we find that when, for example, Allen Ginsberg motors into Hollywood in *The Fall of America* he is seized by a ghostly apparition of the past, a phantasmagoria of memory that darkens his spirit. He resorts to the *ubi sunt* ("where are?") formula to acknowledge, in hopes of banishing, the deceased figures who are the spirits of place:

Where's Stravinsky? Theda Bara? Chaplin? Harpo Marx?
        Where's Laurel and his Hardy?
                        Laughing phantoms
                            going to the grave . . .

—•—

Grauman's Chinese Theatre's drab sidewalk front's
        concrete footprints, stood there
                stupid, anal, exciting
                    upside down, Crosseyed moviestar'd
        I craned my neck at Myrna Loy & Shirley Temple shoe-marks[21]

Ginsberg's merry ride on the freeway has brought him to this mausoleum of the city where names of the departed swirl through his memory, and even when he sees the prints of living stars he does so cross eyed and upside down, as if a new way of seeing will serve as a lucky charm against his collision with deceased movie icons. He's at the end of the open road, the last frontier, where Hollywood offers to replay his life as a moviegoer just as it offers all of America a retrospective of its powerful dream of success. The next poem in Ginsberg's sequence is "A Methedrine Vision in Hollywood," in which he continues to experience "feedback thru blue void / echoing the Real of Endless Film."

But the following poem, "Hiway Poesy: L.A.—Albuquerque—Texas—Wichita" puts him back on the road again: "up up and away! / we're off, Thru America— // Heading East to San Berdoo / as West did, Nathanael." Like Frank Bidart and Mark Jarman fleeing the exotic spell of the city, Ginsberg speeds south and east as a respite from the ravages of Hollywood. (His reference to Nathanael West doing the same is a bit puzzling, unless he is thinking of West's last car trip, to Mexico on a hunting excursion, before his untimely death in a car crash as he rushed back to Hollywood for the funeral of F. Scott Fitzgerald.) The radio resumes its monitory power, including Nelson Eddy's rendition of "Oh what a beautiful morning." The ghosts of Hollywood flee and the pleasures of moment-by-moment perceptions on the San Bernardino Freeway vivify his spirits. Like Maria Wyeth in Didion's novel, who begins driving on the freeway and sometimes just keeps going until Las Vegas, Ginsberg savors his manic escape from the Medusa-like apparitions of lost time.

Finally, for Ginsberg, the experience of velocity and the certainty of escape are bound up with the paradise of orality and by "the language of movement" enacted by his poem.[22] The book of poems becomes a diary of impressions, part of the genre of travel literature he refreshes in the spirit of Whitman and his friend Jack Kerouac, and of book-length poems like Muriel Rukeyser's *U.S. 1* (1938), J. D. Reed's *Expressways* (1969), and Rosmarie Waldrop's *The Road is Everywhere or Stop This Body* (1978). As long as he keeps driving—or being driven, since he is situated throughout *The Fall of America* in a seat in the VW Bus other than the driver's—he can orate his freewheeling infinite stream of language into his tape recorder and let the flowing sounds of his voice swell the poem into its fluent shape.

Mary Armstrong

FREEWAY SHOOTING

When he felt the punch of the bullet,
he pulled to the left on the wheel,
skid across lanes, hit the concrete
divider and rode it for a hundred yards.
His Candy Apple Red car scraped the wall,
left a line of paint behind him
like an arrow for Exit. Now, blood
pumps from a hole below his left ear;
splatters the window, colors his diamond
stud earring ruby. It is Monday, 5:00 A.M.

Fifteen minutes away, a woman
makes a bed, smooths blankets
in the same hurried way she smooths
her hair. She has learned to be fast,
to keep up with the street.
On the wall by her head, amusement
park banners and sprays of dried flowers
circle a picture of the Holy Virgin.
Its frame is as round as the O sound
the woman will make when she learns
that the dying was quick.

Reporters want statements: something short
from the family. Her voice cracks over
stern English words. "Hard working,"
she says. "Conscientious." His brothers sit
next to her on the bed and nod. "Oh, yes,"
they say, "he was one hell of a driver."

Later, she will cry. She will ask
his brothers how this could happen.
Their faces will tighten

on her question. "Hey," they will say.
"This is the way it is. If you don't want
to be shot, stay the fuck off the freeway,
the streets, the alleys, the driveways.
Stay in your room under the picture
of the Holy Virgin; lock the doors
and the windows. Wait until the blood
is powder in your veins and prayers click
on your tongue like misfires. And then,
when you come out, hold your arms up
over your head and walk backward, away
from this place, as if you were dancing:
as if that is all you intended to do."[23]

—•—

In Mary Armstrong's poem, there is a moment of interruption analogous to Ginsberg's mordant stall in Hollywood, though more macabre. "Freeway Shooting" belongs in the category of poems to be filed under the rubric "Vision of Sudden Death," the second of Thomas De Quincey's chapters in *The English Mail Coach*. In his teased-out narrative the speed and power of the mail coach endangers "the little carriage"; we understand the encounter to be a not infrequent occurrence, a necessary by-product of the Manchester and Glasgow's vertiginous (thirteen miles an hour!) course along the open road after dark. Both parties do what they can to avoid collision, and succeed by diverging at the last second. Fatality has stalked the near-victims, and drives De Quincey's mesmerizing prose, surging forward to bring them all into jeopardy, then backing away intermittently for a sinuously unwinding anecdote or piece of history that holds the tale in suspension. "Freeway Shooting," too, secures our attention by eschewing the devices of linear narrative. We learn almost nothing about the characters in this murder mystery. Who is the victim? Who is the killer? Was there a motive, or just the random violence that pushes up from the momentum of cruising, the Satanic agency of the streets, the city? This is not a police shooting of a fugitive fleeing from justice, as in familiar TV dramas. It is an occasion of original sin, of the depravity of human nature. The freeway is, by urban legend and actual statistics, the perfect landscape for a sniper's motiveless malignity.

The poem artfully begins with the impact of the bullet, a narrative hook that keeps the reader moving through the stanzas to acquire more information. Readers love to play detective, and many canonical poems cannily flatter the sleuthing curiosity brought to the text. The imagery is cinematic: the skid across lanes, the ride up the divider, and then the close-up of the bloody ear. It is every driver's nightmare, the source of *Schadenfreude* when the people of Los Angeles consult the daily news and read or hear of this kind of incident. In the opening strophe we have a clue: the diamond stud earring turned ruby red from the blood pumping out of the hole below the corpse's ear.

It sounds like he belongs to a gang, a gang of drug dealers perhaps, and the killing is a revenge hit. The second stanza cuts to a woman, presumably the victim's mother. The Holy Virgin looks down on her, and when her voice "cracks over / stern English words" we assume that she is Latina. Her other sons don't seem surprised at what's happened. "He was one hell of a driver," they say, as if in one voice. That is part one of his elegy, which continues in the next stanza: "Hey . . . This is the way it is," a credible response, and one the poet amplifies via indirect discourse: "If you don't want / to be shot, stay the fuck off the freeway, / the streets, the alleys, the driveways." The story line effectively ends there, but the poem continues to underscore the abject helplessness of potential victims; it advises readers to be wary, anxious, on and off the freeway. The sense of liberation from spatial constraints endowed by the freeway at 5 a.m. is precisely the psychological trigger for the moral holiday of unsolvable homicide.

Carjackings, drive-by shootings, car-to-car shootings, ritual assassinations, road rage, outbursts of near-riot, or real riot—these are allegorical narratives in the *noir* anthropology of the city. The speech belonging to the actors in this daily tragedy is defiant, profane, resigned; even when the poet lends them an unlikely eloquence at the closure, the speech is the kind of cautionary warning one might hear in the barrio, the ghetto, and also in middle-class precincts where fear of sudden violent death by hostile strangers has always been a fact of life. The fraught situation of freeway peril, and of driving in Los Angeles in general, is sometimes analogized to Tombstone and the O.K. Corral. "[H]ere in Los Angeles / on the freeways / it's like the Wild West / again," Charles Bukowski laments. "[M]any of the drivers carry guns / and if you cut them off / or irritate them in any manner / with your driving, / they simply pull up, point their / guns and begin / firing."[24] The nearest analogy to "Freeway Shooting" is war poetry, especially the poetry of Vietnam, Iraq, and Afghanistan, where daily guerilla combat hardens the hearts of all the participants and results in existential dread.

In a novel or film we would hear a lot more about what it means to be "conscientious" and "hard working" as the mother claims for her son. But he has no profile, no long history like Evelyn Mulwray's in *Chinatown*, shot dead in her speeding car by an officer of the law. The boy has no backstory; he is only a shadow, pocked with red, with a diamond earring.

The fact is, poets seldom write in praise of the wild adrenaline rush of the freeway in the cool manner of Joan Didion's prose. Most poems on the subject conceive of the interchanges as figurative cloverleafs, sending the driver around and around in a cycle of meaningless movement from neighborhood to neighborhood. Unlike the Whitmanian ideal of either being a *flâneur* enjoying the random sensations of a vibrant city, or of hiking the open road like a pioneer or pilgrim, the freeway poem tends to focus on whatever stops or stalls the driver, as trivial and tedious as finding a parking spot or horrific as a car crash or shooting. And the same is true when reckless drivers turn the surface streets into freeways. Popular songs of the 1950s and 1960s sported a narrative like Jan and Dean's "Dead Man's Curve," where a drag race across one of the east-west boulevards puts the singer into the hospital.[25] The sense of liberation that once belonged by poetic association to the freeway is more often displaced to the escape from the city via the freeways onto the Interstate. In such verse scenarios, the popular image of Los Angeles as Autopia receives a corrective rebuke, a repainting of a half-century's visual images designed to boost the seductive allure of the rapture of uninhibited speed.

James Harms

GRIDLOCK

Even in Los Angeles the traffic eases up at noon, particu-
larly heading north toward Palmdale on a Wednesday,
since no one goes where there's nothing to do when
there's a chicken-salad sandwich nearby, the midweek
special at Barney's, coke and french fries included.

But something's wrong. The usual river-hum of cars on
the Hollywood Freeway has been hushed to a horn blast

now and then, the stream of traffic slowed to a standstill, a twelve-mile-long parking lot. Someone rolls away his window and leans out to see what's going on. Drivers exchange looks, the *What's up* of raised eyebrows, shrugs instead of smiles, though a few just shake their heads as they inch their cars politely to the right, to the open shoulder, the offramp just ahead: freedom. But there's always one, in this case a battered Honda Civic, that moves in fits and jerks, the driver beshaded and oblivious, cutting off the more cautious, his insurance long lapsed. He's given the room he needs, the indignity of a cracked windshield his red bandanna, a symbol of the city's largest gang—not Bloods or Crips but the resigned and dispirited, those who've given up and just drive.

The freeway has been closed at Melrose so the men from Brinks can do their job. Red-faced and stoic, forced to wear orange vests, they kneel and rise on the freeway's sticky tarmac picking up over and over what seems to be light, flecks of sun shining on the asphalt. Around them it's just road and blue sky, the oleander and eucalyptus audible in the new silence, California's ubiquitous wind break whispering in a breeze, nearly laughing, though really it's the motorists snaking up the ramp, pointing and snickering, witness at the end of hours and miles of traffic to this latest urban inanity: three men—the driver and two guards—on their knees on the 101 northbound.

And of course the road north leads to promise say the angels fleeing home: the fertile valleys near Modesto, the emerald forests of Marin. The road north is paved with hope for those tired of breathing ozone, of waking with trembles in a doorway, beneath a desk. The road north is littered with coins, dimes and quarters to be exact, for at last a truck has spilled money instead of oil, a bank's worth of loose change just beyond the temporary sign—FREEWAY CLOSED. Someone once said (perhaps it was Tom Hayden) that to solve all its problems L.A. should get its citizenry headed in one direction.

> But someone else (perhaps Tom Wolfe) answered with the literal and obvious: that if all of Los Angeles hit the roads at once there'd be a used car lot the size of Austria, a good idea he said, since then it would be easy enough to pave over the cars, the people, the whole damn city. But if all of Los Angeles heard there was money on the Hollywood Freeway they'd laugh it off as another empty promise—a call back for a sit com, an agent who loves the screenplay—though they might drive by for a look.[26]

—•—

James Harms's "Gridlock," from his volume *Quarters* (2001), collects the thematic points clustered around the general topic of unromantic driving. Lest the poem fall into a grouchy painting-by-numbers indictment of the stereotypical traffic jam, Harms adds one original comic touch. The congestion is caused by a spill of coins from a Brinks truck on the Hollywood Freeway, so the poem becomes a commentary on the California dream of easy money as well as (horse)power. Prose has been the customary vehicle for writing about money in our literature, and the poem unsurprisingly takes the rhythmic and discursive form of a prose poem.[27] In poems like this we are treated to the spectacle of stasis at the symbolic site of mobility. The existential oxymoron of the unmoving movers locked into the bad dream they all dread every time they enter an on-ramp keeps being amplified as more details are added. First, the suspense. How did this grand highway, this figure of "freedom," turn into "a twelve-mile-long parking lot"?

And then, what can be done about it? Nothing but waiting. And while waiting, dreaming about "the fertile valleys near Modesto, the emerald / forests of Marin." The loose change on the freeway points north to the organic, pastoral world. Because of all its natural charms—"the oleander and eucalyptus audible in the new silence, California's ubiquitous wind break whispering in a breeze"– both Northern and Southern California had lured millions of people to the West Coast. But the euphoria over in-migration devolved into bitter resentment by the end of the century, making Harms's poem a revisionist document of cultural change.

Three million people migrated to the Los Angeles area between 1945 and 1965. In the process these new settlers, including ambitious writers, damaged the Horatio Alger dream of fulfillment and good fortune signified in this narrative by the petit bourgeois occupation of authorship. The new class of citizens in L.A. yearn for success defined as "a call back for / a sit com, an agent who loves the screenplay." Writers, including scholars and poets, had settled in L.A. because it offered opportunities for enrichment and status. During the Depression Upton Sinclair wrote a novella, *The Golden Scenario*, unpublished till 1994, in which he put the matter with his characteristic bluntness: "You know, of course, that among the dreams which haunt the souls of film fans—next to the one of going to Hollywood and earning five times as much as the President of the United States—is the dream of writing a scenario and having it accepted and produced."[28] For the screenwriter, as for the poet, *publication*, in the sense of making some internal dreamwork available to the largest likely audience, represents the joyful realization of union and communion, the fluent transmission of words and meaning to a receptive audience. When thwarted, by writer's block, by standards of taste too high or too low, the aggrieved author undergoes the sense of stasis, even of trauma, emblematized by gridlock. Precisely because they were complicit as wordsmiths with the visual media and as drivers on the overloaded freeways, poets seek escape from their sense of feeling stalled on a career track; they dream about a free way with fewer obstacles to forward movement toward Edenic realms.

Harms takes advantage of the open prosaic form, almost journalistic in tone, to drop some names that anchor the poem in Los Angeles and amplify both social and personal themes. The red bandanna of a frustrated driver does "not" mean that he is a member of the "Bloods or Crips"—the negative assumes that the reader leaps to that connection—but signifies his aspiration to make a fashion statement consonant with the presumed glamour of those South Central gangs. Competing sociological viewpoints by Tom Hayden and Tom Wolfe remind us that the abstract principles of a former SDS leader, co-author of the Port Huron Statement and equally famous for political activism in Los Angeles (not to mention his marriage to local celebrity Jane Fonda), are effortlessly subverted by a New Journalist who launched his reputation writing a supercharged essay for *Esquire* about customized cars in Burbank.[29] (Even "Barney's" will resonate on the national level, thanks to the apotheosis of Barney's Beanery by the sculptor Edward Kienholz, who enshrined the restaurant as an installation in 1965.) The two Toms display a professional mobility of special interest to the poet, who finally abandoned his home turf to take a job directing the MFA program in Creative Writing at West Virginia University.

Harms quotes Tom Wolfe as saying about the fantasy prospect of absolute gridlock, every person in Los Angeles taking their car onto the freeway at the same time, that it might be "a good idea . . . since then it would be easy enough to pave over the . . . cars, the people, the whole damn city." A sentiment so vindictive, if also comical, engages the reader as much more than a passive consumer of the text. The rage against the city can be interpreted as remorse for the loss of mobility and the end of the utopian promise of Los Angeles as a privileged space in the history of America. This remorse contributes to a fierce nostalgia for the freewheeling mobility of yesteryear. The poetics of a fluent, fast-moving format in verse and cinema alike, and now in social media of all kinds, remains the most popular contemporary option for writers and readers.

III

A freeway shatters our usual modes of perception by causing us to hurtle past objects and persons with blinding speed. That fact accounts for the enduring viability of poems that use the mimetic form of rapid-fire litanies of imagery lacking coherent connection beyond the contiguity of one perceived figure after another. Thanks in large part to the increasing use of technology that performs the same acceleration in our everyday lives, this brand of writing, what Tony Hoagland calls "the poetics of vertigo," has become a popular verse-form for the generation born into the computer age.[30] Indeed the poetics of high-octane acceleration may be said to mandate the thematics of poems relying on discontinuous form to lend a dystopian aura to poems in this fashionable style. Dana Goodyear's poem "Freeway" is a prime example.

Dana Goodyear

FREEWAY

Alongside this, a river: somewhere head-
waters, somewhere a mouth.
It begins with thought and ends with speech,

while the road just drains and drains, gray
nervous miles. I drive all day under a strike surface
scratched by skywriters' mistakes, through the city

bleeding silver like a video game,
past Nadaland, past Mojave, toward the bodies
decomposing in the quiet valleys

killers used to ranch. Behind me,
in my mind, the lurid birds of paradise
bend their orange faces toward the pool

to drink, but the pool is full
of flames, and the trees are ash shadows,
and the sky's so dark night-blooming whites

release themselves to moths
too singed to reach them. The yellow vine
presses its wax ear against the warping glass,

and the deck chairs, pale and worked
as skeletons, somehow hold their ground.[31]

—•—

As one of the most recent poems on this subject, "Freeway" can be read as a representative text that absorbs the conventions of the genre outlined above and points forward to future poems treating the freeway in both literal and metaphorical modes. Goodyear proposes no argument, no thesis, no story line. The genderless speaker drives all day, "cruising the bleak arterials of dismal L.A. backwaters," in the words of Thomas Pynchon.[32] This motoring intelligence becomes the receptor and chronicler of disturbing sensations. Unlike the deliberate coordination of syntactical unit with the line in poems of freeway speeding by Eloise Klein Healy and Wanda Coleman already quoted, the congeries of dissociated images is full of cinematic jump cuts, breaking the syntax of the phrase and sentence into multiple lines and across stanzas, halting for a line or two over utterly strange images like "the lurid birds of paradise" that "bend their orange faces toward the pool // to drink, but the pool / is full of flames." Vivid images of this kind punctuate the poem, but they don't slow it down. The dizzying, random movement of the wandering eye is brought into conjunction with the "strike surface / scratched by skywriters' mistakes," an inspired mirroring of the aerial and terrestrial condition of literal and literary waywardness. The poem offers a compendium of correspondences or objective correlatives; it is a work of sophisticated literary construction steeped in postmodern practice and theory. At the same time it answers a simple question: "What does this rural area beyond the civic center actually look like?"

Goodyear has written the author that "'Freeway' began with some lines I wrote a number of years ago, driving back to L.A. from near Death Valley, where I had been doing some reporting. Later I read about the possible exhumations at the Barker Ranch (where the Manson Family went after their murder spree)."[33] That the desolation of landscape has some historical roots in the moral desolation symbolized by the Manson murders follows from poems like those of David Wojahn and Frederick Seidel discussed in the earlier chapter "Hollywood, 'Here' and Everywhere." The "bodies / decomposing" in this Gothic hideaway point forward to the poem's closure where the deck chairs are imagined as "skeletons" in the macabre scenario of the speaker's fevered imagination.

In its original publication in Issue 2, 2011, of *Slake*, a Los Angeles literary journal, "Freeway" featured a Part 1, later excised, as long as the present version. The poem as we now have it constituted Part 2 in *Slake*. In both parts the freeway serves as a connective figure for the totality of regional topography in Los Angeles, not just the basin but the suburbs, desert, and farmland. Syncretic in structure, this landscape poem presents in streamlined form the motifs and themes of a metropolis that began by advertising its citrus orchards and its golden coastline but now surrenders to the entropy of aging and irresistible return to the primeval ooze, "the world's agglutinative // slough, its shuck and mud and food, / effluvia and fuel," as the *Slake* version puts it. A young city is revealed in flashes of lyric shards as decadent, all-too-vulnerable to the destiny enforced by geological and historical circumstances. It's understandable that escape from this morass by means of the freeway has become an essential convention of freeway literature. What was once the major attraction of the growing metropolis, "Autopia," has now become the agency of release from its "hedonic damages"—a new idiom for loss of value and affect—in the new century.

In a new historical era when social media, especially, have raised anxieties about changes in discourse, in the shared fragmented language of an entire literate generation, it is worth dwelling on the notion that a condensed form of articulation may be putting increased pressure on poets to dissolve the customary transitions of lyric poetry. Tony Hoagland comments, "Judging from current magazines and books, vertigo ('a sensation of whirling and loss of balance . . .') is the preeminent topic of contemporary poetry. It may be the dominant stylistic inclination as well. In the context of our time and place, this artistic focus—of speed and rapid (or no) transition—makes perfect sense."[34] Though he does not mention it in his essay, Hoagland's source text is Charles Olson's classic manifesto "Projective Verse," with its all-caps exhortation, "ONE PERCEPTION MUST IMMEDIATELY AND DIRECTLY LEAD TO A FURTHER PERCEPTION . . . keep it moving as fast as you can, citizen. And if you also set up as a poet, USE USE USE the process at all points, in any given poem always, always one perception must must must MOVE, INSTANTER, ON ANOTHER!"[35] This mode of hyperkinetic assemblage was formerly deemed "cinematic" in tribute to the montage structure of film, though many of its earliest advocates and artists, such as Griffith and Eisenstein, called attention to film's sources in poetry itself. By indirection, in other words, modern poetry had become "Los Angelized" by its association with the film industry commonly signified as "Hollywood." In poems like Goodyear's the city's freeways are credited with a similar power to enforce sensations of vertigo for writer and reader as a new normal, a dynamic state of consciousness increasingly shared by the community of readers/spectators/drivers.

One senses a new mythology in the making. Not surprisingly, the chief manifestos for that new manner of worship and faith, whether written as piety or satire, are more likely to be inscribed in the orderly form of a tract or gospel.

Dana Gioia

THE FREEWAYS CONSIDERED AS EARTH GODS

These are the gods who rule the golden land.
Their massive bodies stretch across the countryside,
Filling the valleys, climbing the hills, curving along the coast,
Crushing the earth from which they draw their sustenance
Of tar and concrete, asphalt, sand, and steel.

They are not new, these most ancient of divinities.
Our clamor woke them from the subdivided soil.
They rise to rule us, neither cruel nor kind,
But indifferent to our ephemeral humanity.
Their motives are unknowable and profound.

The gods do not condescend to our frailty.
They cleave our cities, push aside our homes,
Provide no place to walk or rest or gather.
The pathways of the gods are empty, flat, and hard.
They draw us to them, filling us with longing.

We do not fail to worship them. Each morning
Millions creep in slow procession on our pilgrimages.
We crave the dangerous power of their presence.
And they demand blood sacrifice, so we mount
Our daily holocaust on the blackened ground.

The gods command the hilltops and the valleys.
They rule the deserts and the howling wilderness.
They drink the rivers and clear the mountains in their way.
They consume the earth and the increase of the field.
They burn the air with their rage.

We are small. We are weak. We are mortal.
Ten thousand of us could not move one titan's arm.
We need their strength and speed.
We bend to their justice and authority.
These are the gods of California. Worship them.[36]

—•—

The worship of speed manifested by new technology has a long ancestry, as indicated earlier. Whitman all but imagined God as the engineer of his "type of the modern" in the poem "To a Locomotive in Winter," and in 1929 Sinclair Lewis featured, with transparent irony, the automobile manufacturer Sam Dodsworth as a high priest of the new religion. Gazing around Grand Central Station, he imagines it as a new cathedral:

> He fancied that this was veritably the temple of a new divinity, the God of Speed.
>
> Of its adherents it demanded as much superstitious credulity as any of the outworn deities—demanded a belief that Going Somewhere, Going Quickly, Going Often, were in themselves holy and greatly to be striven for. A demanding God, this Speed, less good-natured than the elder Gods with their faults, their amours, their vanity, so easily pleased by garlands and flattery; an abstract, faultless, and insatiable God, who once he had been offered a hundred miles an hour, straightaway demanded a hundred and fifty.
>
> And with his motor cars Sam had contributed to the birth of this new religion . . .[37]

Reyner Banham had also contributed to the new mythology in his Platonic model of Autopia in 1971. The philosopher kings of his Republic were the architects who had endowed Los Angeles with a freeway system that constituted a radical new infrastructure in the city, changing the life of its inhabitants ever afterward. As we have seen, this new fact on the ground inspired both positive and negative responses from poets. Dana Gioia's "The Freeways Considered as Earth Gods" from his volume of 2012, *Pity the Beautiful,* addresses its contemporary significance. Gioia constructs a myth to revise, and undermine, the primal scripture. Composed in the form of a devotional appreciation of the freeway system, it pretends to annunciate the gospel of speed and mobility according to Banham as if written by the master himself. It attempts the difficult task of describing as a matter of faith, or dogma, the claims of the new technology upon the populace it serves. Those who have studied the history of "The Industrial Muse," as it was once called, know that every world-changing invention of the post-Renaissance era has been divinized by (some) enthusiastic poets in tones both rhapsodic and didactic. Hart Crane's oracular claims for the Brooklyn Bridge rank as exhibit A, but lyrics about the airplane, the automobile, dams, and even nuclear technology, fill the anthologies of poems about science and machinery with rapturous homages, not without qualms, for new monuments of social engineering. There is a sense in which Gioia's poem can be read straight as advocacy for the glory of motion, the *magna vivimus* celebrated by De Quincey at the inception of the industrial era of Western civilization. In the declarative sentences arising from the chorus of true believers we hear the chant of the faithful who submit happily to the new gods who are ever-present in their daily experience.

Freeways are not agencies of human will, according to the poem, so much as they are evolutionary forms that manifest to city dwellers the potential for an enhanced kind of power. Like the computer and the entire cyberworld of robotics and artificial intelligence, the freeways now dominate the social systems from which they originated. How could this usurpation be otherwise than natural in the scheme of things?

> We are small. We are weak. We are mortal.
> Ten thousand of us could not move one titan's arm.
> We need their strength and speed.
> We bend to their justice and authority.
> These are the gods of California. Worship them.

The last two words in the poem's final line mimic the closure of Gerard Manley Hopkins's sonnet "Pied Beauty" which considers the awesome power of God to impose marks of differentiation upon objects in nature including human beings. "Praise him." the poet and Jesuit priest commands. Gioia, also a Catholic, dramatizes throughout the poem the self-abasement of humanity as it divinizes its own Creation as "the pathways of the gods."[38] To worship the freeways is to flatter themselves even as they attribute to their invention the sublime powers formerly assumed by a transcendent God or gods. The poem seeks to mortify human pride by allowing the speakers to deify themselves as god-makers even as they surrender their former privileged status in the Great Chain of Being.

Gioia's poem is an artful exercise in rhetoric. It consecrates the freeways toward the effect of critiquing them. It reminds each reader why it is they respond so ecstatically to the opportunities for speed, when they do, and why they rage against the instruments of gridlock and "blood sacrifice" they have welcomed into their everyday lives under the illusion that freeways are sacred signs of a perfect world. Sometimes the poet's mask slips and he reveals his scorn for the Banham gospel, as in the use of the word "holocaust" and the protest in stanza five against the ruin of California's gardens in the making of sustainable roadways on the order of the 405 and the 110. But the poem leaves a memorable impression, as poems in this oracular voice often do. At once the ultimate in whoring after strange gods *and* in expressing justifiable piety for a Creation that affects the thoughts and actions of the citywide congregation, "The Freeways Considered as Earth Gods" elevates the debate over traffic to a new level.

The poem reminds us how scarce religious poetry is in the literature of Los Angeles. Joel Kotkin, in his brief history *The City*, claims that one of the three sustaining characteristics of great cities throughout history has been the binding power of the sacred, manifested in the dominance of churches, synagogues, and mosques, among other religious institutions, in the streets and civic centers. But when poets writing about Los Angeles summon religion, and faith itself, we are more often treated with images that expose the deformation of the spirit rather than its pious exercise. In what is arguably the most searching examination of the religious condition of Los Angeles, Dorothy Barresi's volume of 2010, *American Fanatics*, the poet begins a kind of pilgrimage through the city that begins at the site of Aimee Semple McPherson's Foursquare Church in Echo Park and ends at an unlikely shrine, the Motion Picture and Television Home for the Aging in Woodland Hills. As in Gioia's poem, machine technology satisfies the craving for spiritual sustenance:

> who among us has not eaten or drunk of
>
> glamour's damnation
> watching the old
> black and white movie stations
>
> flicker to our sleeplessness?
> If we knew that we kept them alive
> just by watching
>
> would we look away?[39]

The answer to that question is No; the pathology of modernity is such that we submit gladly to the new gods who take control of our consciousness. In such ways, the freeways, like the movies and television, emerge triumphantly in the mythology of Los Angeles as redemptive figures deserving of praise.

IV

Diane Wakoski

THE ORANGE

Driving through the desert at night in summer
can be
like peeling an orange,
the windows rolled down, the prickly scent
of mesquite and sage
blowing through the car, the
perfume
of the twilight shadowed earth lingering;
the acrid spray of the peel,
with its meaty white pillow
nestles into your fingers.

You are driving from Los Angeles to Las Vegas,
running from your loneliness, an empty house,
an ocean which brings neither father nor lover.

For one hour, the wind streams through
your car, a
three-year-old Pontiac you have named Green Greed;
for one hour, the scent of all the desert
plants makes you feel
loved, makes you
forget you have no one
to talk to. You do not care about the
myth of the West, about
the City of Angels and its beaches.

You are not yet even slightly
interested in
gambling.

You are 32 and feel you have a destiny. Somehow
in that car,
on that night, alone on the wind-cooled highway between California
and Nevada, for one hour,
the fragrance of sage, especially,
made you complete,
moving swiftly over your face, through
nostrils, the car, you warm,
from desert day fire.

You were not even looking
yet, for Beethoven in Las Vegas,
Snake Mother in the desert.
Your life was over, or
had not yet begun. Did you see
a map of Michigan filling your hand
as you peeled the big navel orange,
the one which glowed like fireflies
that wink
in Michigan summer nights?
The white membrane, the orange raindrop
textured meat of the fruit
saturating your hands with sugar
as you drive, as you drove,
as you remembered one
beginning?[40]

—•—

Escape from L.A. is a dystopian film of 1996 that imagines the city reinvented as an island prison from which the entire population of convicts yearns to be liberated. John Carpenter's script is not a model of clarity but it does communicate the agony of those who feel trapped by technological and political forces and who conspire in 2013 to break free from a demonic setting and go somewhere else, anywhere but L.A. As we have seen, some poets share that nervous aversion to the local deities who "rule the golden land," in Gioia's phrase. Diane Wakoski, born in Whittier in 1937, has written nostalgically about Southern California, but paradoxically some of her most intensely felt meditations on Los Angeles have come in her poems about leaving the city, both for short-term residencies and teaching positions in New York, Virginia, and elsewhere before her permanent residency at Michigan State University. In "The Orange," she clings to a talismanic piece of fruit as she leaves L.A. and hurtles eastward toward her professional destiny in Michigan. Some freeway has taken her beyond the city limits, and now the faster Mojave Freeway opens her senses to the desert scents of mesquite and sage. Driving serves as a means of encapsulating the poet in a bubble, a metallic carapace, that both extends and relieves the negative personal and cultural associations clinging to the identity of Los Angeles. That identity, according to cultural critic David Rieff, depends on "decontextualization," the sense of being immune from past and future, independent of community, of relationship, even of place:

> There has never been anything like this in the history of the world: every man and woman an Icarus. But the sun has not melted their wings yet, even though, as one wag put it, in Los Angeles "ecology is constantly struggling to keep up with mythology." Call it consciousness or false consciousness, mindlessness or bliss, nobody could have imagined that it would be possible to so completely decontextualize people, or that the internal combustion engine would make this atomization seem like a gift.[41]

The space within the automobile is like a womb, a delivery system into the new beginning of life, a transition space preceding growth and development outside the aura of the megalopolis. "You do not care about the / myth of the West, about / the City of Angels and its beaches," Wakoski writes, addressing herself as an Other, a second person, migrating toward Las Vegas and then East Lansing, to be redeemed and reborn.

Velocity is central to the poem; the desert fragrance is described as "moving swiftly over your face," a sign of felt urgency and the expectation of reward. Here again the topography of Southern California nourishes the psychological change Wakoski celebrates as she sheds her Californianess. It is conventional in narrative that the protagonist, the "hero with a thousand faces" in Joseph Campbell's formulation, crosses some desert region marking the desperation of his or her fugitive flight from the Great Wrong Place toward a nourishing landscape of pleasure or spiritual restoration. The desert can be a terminus, an ambiguous destination in itself, as in the lives of some biblical prophets and saints. But more often it is the wasteland in which desire is mortified and bad behavior sanctioned or shrived in advance of reaching the "Boon of Understanding," as Campbell calls it. For Wakoski's purposes, the ambiguous symbol of the desert is Las Vegas, just across the border from California. Las Vegas serves as Vanity Fair in most depictions of the region, most famously in Didion's novel *Play It As It Lays*. "You are not yet even slightly / interested in / gambling," Wakoski reminds her alter ego. "Lost Wages," as it was called in my boyhood, became the preeminent symbol of ruined fortunes and ruined lives, before the Nevada city morphed into the family-friendly entertainment capital it is today. Like Tijuana or Palm Springs, Las Vegas is a sibling city to Los Angeles, a reflector of its values, an index of its excesses. Wakoski has written often, especially in her volume of 1995, *The Emerald City of Las Vegas*, about the gambling capital's seductive lure, from which almost no American is immune.

But the semi-magical orange keeps her from stalling in the desert way-station. It perfumes the car with its scent and saturates her hands with sugar and the stuff of Vitamin C. It sponsors in her consciousness a sensitivity to colors and textures. Like some western American version of the golden bough, it carries her into a realm of consciousness where she can see "a map of Michigan filling your hand / as you peeled the big navel orange." It is a Michigan habit to identify places in the state by holding up one's right hand, which does indeed have the shape of the state, and pointing to the appropriate spot. ("Port Huron is here, in the thumb.") Michigan is a state famous for its apples and cherries; oranges are a foreign product. On one level the orange represents the memory, the persistent being, of Los Angeles County when it was more agricultural. A poem by Edward W. Barnard published in 1895, "A Ballade of California," celebrated the orange as "the golden fruit of the Hesperides" and enthused over "groves of gold bound in a zone / Of bloom as honey-sweet as Hybla's own."[42] But here too the ecology has failed to keep up with the mythology. The orange, along with the vanishing orange groves in Southern California, is a sign of exile, of the afterglow of the light on the beaches and farms Wakoski has abandoned for the opportunity to work productively in the Great Lakes state, the Eastern time zone.

In a poem full of symbols, the orange is worth dwelling upon for a moment. It is sometimes called the salvation of the Southern California area, for it drew millions of people, over a century, to grow and pick and distribute the uniquely tasty navel oranges so perfectly adaptable to the climate and soil of the southland. Before aerospace factories, real estate developments, and oil wells replaced most of the orchards, especially during World War II when workers streamed into the area to staff the war materiel factories, orange groves reigned as the preeminent symbol of the fertility and sensual pleasures of the region. Orange County persuasively claimed the title of The Big Orange before it migrated in the 1970s to Los Angeles as a counter-idiom to The Big Apple touted by New York. Now the old Sunkist boxes with their bright pictures of lemony light and green fields are nostalgia items for sale at antique boutiques. But the oranges persist in the imaginations of those like Wakoski who grew up in Orange County near the fields (see her volume of 1972, *Smudging*) and uses them as geospatial figures for her origins. In her book *Medea the Sorceress* (1991) "The Orange" is accompanied by a hand-drawn map showing the trajectory of travel originating in the aptly named Point Dume on the northern tip of the cusp of Santa Monica Bay and proceeding through Las Vegas to East Lansing, and all the way across the Atlantic to Vienna, the Old World capital of high culture.

As in all Wakoski's poems, the lineation is erratic and sometimes defiantly so. It follows the presumably improvisatory compositional strategy associated with William Carlos Williams and Charles Olson, and with the San Francisco Renaissance. In making a line like "your car, a" or "interested in" she ostentatiously violates the customary practice of traditional poetry, including free verse, to make the contents of the line echo some older prosody, not to mention prescriptions like Shelley's to "load every rift with ore" when measuring out significant content line by line. Her mentor is almost certainly Charles Bukowski, not a member of the Beat Generation, who is most identified with the poetics of Los Angeles. Many imitators in the city have reproduced this free verse form of what detractors call "chopped prose," and hailed it as a means of mimicking the offhand lifestyle of Establishment-hating poets in a city eager to espouse a local verse style to match.

It's rare in modern literature to find Los Angeles glimpsed in a rearview mirror. The whole point of freeways was to deliver people to various parts of the city in a cycle of the voyage out and the bliss of return. Poets have registered their discomfort with the city by seizing upon this chief icon, what Reyner Banham called "the tutelary deity of the City of Angels," as a mode of ecstasy as well as a mode of convenient mobility to a desired local destination. Not all poets wish to record their experience of being in transit, of course. But how well the freeway suits the restless imagination of authors in perpetual search of new places on the map and new thresholds of visceral pleasure. And how cautionary are some of their depictions of these often-clogged arteries that sometimes lead to fatal terminuses.

FIVE

South Central: The Lofty Towers and the Plains of Id

> These central flatlands are where the crudest urban lusts and most fundamental aspirations are created, manipulated, and, with luck, satisfied.
>
> —REYNER BANHAM[1]

> *for you, los angeles—you at my jugular*
>
> —WANDA COLEMAN[2]

The term "South Central Los Angeles" referred to communities south of downtown in the long arc of flat urban space east of La Brea Avenue between the Santa Monica Freeway to the north and the Century Freeway to the south. Central Avenue bisects this space, and gave its name to the former designation of the area. The City of Los Angeles changed the official name to South Los Angeles in 2003 in order to purge the negative associations with the inner-city riot in Watts in 1965 and the widespread violence in 1992 following the trial and acquittal of policemen who beat up Rodney King. "South Los Angeles" supposedly directs more attention to upscale communities like Baldwin Hills, West Adams, and the University of Southern California. The civil disturbances and gang warfare at and after the historical juncture of 11–15 August 1965, and their dominance of the nation's headlines, constitute the chief reason this area and its literature came into global prominence.

A multitude of books and essays have pondered why and how Watts and Compton, the template communities for civil rebellion (or "insurrection" or "uprising" or "civil unrest" or "riot"—take your pick) in urban sites throughout the country, turned into a "ghetto" and thence to a center for African

American resistance to the city's Establishment. The rise and worldwide celebrity of gangsta rap emanating from the streets of South Central, and the prominence of some muckraking movies, especially *Menace II Society*, *Colors*, and *Boyz N the Hood*, contributed to a notoriety that continues to define the entire region, now mainly Latino and home to a variety of racial and ethnic groups. This complex cultural history deserves the full attention of every reader.

I

Elizabeth Alexander

STRAVINSKY IN L.A.

In white pleated trousers, peering through green
sunshades, looking for the way the sun is red
noise, how locusts hiss to replicate the sun.
What is the visual equivalent
of syncopation? Rows of seared palms wrinkle
in the heat waves through green glass. Sprinklers
tick, tick, tick. The Watts Towers aim to split
the sky into chroma, spires tiled with rubble
nothing less than aspiration. I've left
minarets for sun and syncopation,
sixty-seven shades of green which I have
counted, beginning: palm leaves, front and back,
luncheon pickle, bottle glass, etcetera.
One day I will comprehend the different
grades of red. On that day I will comprehend
these people, rhythms, jazz, Simon Rodia,
Watts, Los Angeles, aspiration.[3]

—•—

I want to begin my discussion of poetry about South Central, however, with the unlikely figure of Igor Stravinsky (1882–1971). My license to do so is "Stravinsky in L.A.," the opening poem in Elizabeth Alexander's book *Body of Life* (1997). The poem is designedly off the subject of civil disorders and racial conflict, a counter-statement to the despairing spirit of place constructed by writers we shall soon sample. Its focus on a redemptive site in the city intends to compel readers to re-imagine a district that suffers from stereotypes as deeply engraved as those of Venice Beach and Hollywood Boulevard.

No significant poem about this area of Los Angeles can be written in ignorance of the riots and their socioeconomic causes. This hard fact of literary composition does not disable a poet, however; on the contrary, it compels originality in subject matter, point of view, and rhetorical structure. It invites the poet to do what she does best: to surprise the reader with a linguistic tapestry that presents an entirely fresh conception of local materials customarily drawn from news stories, textbooks, and the prevailing clichés of rap and hip-hop. Whatever else it does, "Stravinsky in L.A." assists readers in adjusting their psychogeography as a means of cultural healing.

"Stravinsky in L.A." brings into conjunction the great modernist composer during his period of residence in Los Angeles, more precisely West Hollywood, and the idiosyncratic towers built by another immigrant, Sebastiano [Simon] Rodia (1879–1965), in Watts, between 1921 and 1948.[4] The poem does not claim that Stravinsky could see the towers from his hilltop house at 1260 North Wetherly Drive, but their presence in the same metropolitan conurbation is part of his consciousness as he undergoes an unsettling experience of color and sound that leads him to an aesthetic and moral resolution embracing not only Rodia but the community of color and the whole of Los Angeles. Both artists have created experimental structures of massive weight and repute; both have fulfilled their "aspiration" to construct what Reyner Banham, writing about the towers, describes as a "dream monument."[5] Separated by many miles into communities that define the extremes of social class, they reach an accommodation, a bonding, in Stravinsky's reverie. It is significant that Alexander, an African American poet who has written extensively about black experience in America, does not assign a speaking or thinking role to Rodia; he is mute, and virtually invisible.[6] Rodia was an Italian immigrant, not a Negro, but his residence in Watts serves Alexander's purpose in connecting the two idiosyncratic artists; Rodia's speculative distance from West Hollywood becomes an object of Stravinsky's reverie as he considers the "chroma," the hues and saturation, of his own domestic situation and his art.

Stravinsky was one of the most Old World of European artists who settled in Los Angeles. A native of Russia and a longtime resident of Paris, where he composed his most innovative masterpieces, he became a key figure in the history of the twentieth-century avant-garde, not only for the music itself, but for the music's association with poetry. T. S. Eliot wrote admiringly of the collage structure of *The Rite of Spring* in a review for *The Dial* of a performance in 1921, and then went on to revise *The Waste Land* under its influence.[7] Stravinsky cultivated poets and occasionally collaborated on projects with them, as with W. H. Auden for the opera *The Rake's Progress* and Dylan Thomas for a setting of "Do Not Go Gentle" in what came to be a posthumous tribute, *In Memoriam Dylan Thomas* (1954); he also composed *Three Songs from William Shakespeare* (1953) in the same period. Early on, Stravinsky incorporated Negro folk music and jazz rhythms into his work; in 1946 he composed *Ebony Concerto* for clarinet and ensemble for Woody Herman's swing band. Arriving in Los Angeles in May 1940 he would certainly have kept his eyes open for phenomena like the Watts Towers and appreciate how they made a difference in aesthetics, how his own medium of sound would and should reverberate in tune to the existence of Rodia's paradigm-shattering towers of steel rods and reinforced concrete, all of its surfaces tiled with collages of broken glass, pottery, seashells, and building materials. At least, this is the premise of Alexander's poem.

Stravinsky is that familiar figure in the literature of Los Angeles, the genius who migrates from the East and absorbs the atmosphere of his adopted home at the same time that he changes the cultural dynamics there by the power of his creative intelligence. Stravinsky came west because of Hollywood and suffered the same difficulties as most European artists who immigrated before and after him. His protracted argument with Walt Disney over the use of *The Rite of Spring* in the film *Fantasia* has become the stuff of legend. He withdrew from the movies to compose his work in a colony full of transplanted European authors, conductors, and composers—Sergei Rachmaninoff (very briefly), Arnold Schoenberg, Ernst Toch, Erich Wolfgang Korngold, Erich Zeisl, Hanns Eisler, Darius Milhaud—and performance venues for sophisticated audiences (the Hollywood Bowl, the Greek Theatre, UCLA). He embodied the exile's temperament and some of the dandyist habits of the nineteenth-century artist—hence the "white pleated trousers" and "green sunshades" in Alexander's poem. Robert Craft remarked in a memoir that Stravinsky became Los Angelized as he settled into the city: "The composer's aloofness had given way to an informality in his relations with people, as well as in his habits of daily life, style of dress, and entertaining. . . . Now he wore denim trousers, ate hot dogs in diners, and hobnobbed with Hollywood's rank-and-file orchestra players."[8] The poem begins by sketching a few details expressive of his sensibility, and then moving into his mind to speak in his first-person voice. He tells us directly that he has left behind the minarets of Russia for a different species of tower, one that he has not yet "comprehended"—a word that appears twice in two lines—but that he *will* comprehend once he is able to translate the colors emanating from the towers, indeed from Rodia's whole surrounding environment, into audible, then musical form. That is his "aspiration," the breath of his creative ambition.

In the poem Stravinsky is estranged from Watts; he has a distant conceptual prospect of it, but the geographical situation makes it remote, if tantalizing. He cannot report from the ground; he can only deliberate on the aesthetic lessons of the landmark monument built by an itinerant construction worker with no academic training in architecture. Alexander has emphasized that the poem honors Rodia as someone who constructed his artwork from local materials as a tribute to the community that adopted him.[9] "Stravinsky in L.A." is one limited perspective on an area that by 1996 had received abundant onsite bulletins. We have to understand the poem, in large part, as an attempt to withdraw from the massive attention to the riots and the way the morbid fascination of a large public with the violence of 1965 and 1992 had obscured all that the Watts Towers symbolized for Watts and the rest of Los Angeles alike. The 104-foot-high towers, too, "aim to split / the sky" but not materially, not violently; they represent the art-spirit of a community divested of its glamour by historical events but committed to creative alternatives to conflict. Possibly, Alexander is thinking of the way "syncopation" coming from Watts in her own time in the form of hip-hop presented "the different / grades of red" Stravinsky would have recognized from his early years in Russia, when the streets ran red with Bolshevik banners and the blood of revolutionary activists and victims of pogroms.

Alexander begins an early lyric about Miami, "I could go to any city / and write a poem."[10] The trick is to contrive a coherent point of view on significant objects in the landscape. (See "Robeson at Rutgers" and "Monet at Giverny" in the same volume.) "Stravinsky in L.A." presents an exile's perspective. The uprooted composer, acknowledging Russia only fitfully in his increasingly abstract compositions, reports on the way his sensorium is bombarded with visual and aural sensations, such as the "palms" and "sprinklers" that exemplify the popular imagery of his adopted city. Hollywood is nothing but bits and pieces of color, red and green "noise" vibrating in the heat. That the only "noise" specified in the poem is the "tick tick tick" of lawn sprinklers suggests how alienated Stravinsky is from the usual urban uproar of factories, cars, outdoor media, the chatter of crowds. In her "Poem for Barack Obama's Presidential Inauguration" Alexander begins by remarking, "All about us is noise. All about us is / noise and bramble, thorn and din, / each one of our ancestors on our tongues." But the composer does not live in such a loud urban milieu, nor in such a deep cultural heritage. If Los Angeles is going to become an adopted homeland for this cosmopolitan artist, Stravinsky must locate some architectural substitute for the domes and minarets of Moscow and Saint Petersburg, some looming monument commensurate with the imago of his youth that nourished his own aspiration to erect a dream masterwork composed of sound that will make real and permanent what he has lost and abandoned.

"Look for color everywhere," Alexander urges at the end of her poem "Today's News" in *The Venus Hottentot* (1990). The Watts Towers are remarkable for their bold colors, tiled together from broken store-bought commodities like blue Milk of Magnesia bottles, green 7 Up and Canada Dry bottles, and fragments from the nearby California Clay Products Company. Colors are like musical notes in this poem, but in keeping with its eminent subject, sound remains at the forefront of the composer's consciousness. The hiss of the locusts conjures in his sonic imagination the sun's "red / noise." Stravinsky's new home was part of the desert bioregion, and every day provided a time-frame for locusts. Now there is abundant water, but the "tick, tick, tick" of the sprinklers presents a counter-rhythm to the soft shades of green generated by the culture of irrigation that distinguishes the Hollywood hills from the small dry lawns of Watts. The poem gains from being spoken aloud so that, for example, the sharp enjambments and percussive plosives hammer at the ear. Alexander captures the tension of oppressive heat and liberating water in the only pronounced couplet rhyme in the poem, when the "seared palms **wrinkle** / in the heat waves" but "**Sprinklers**" mock the desert climate with their refreshing mechanical sound.

International and interartistic in his sympathies, innovative in his compositions, Stravinsky paradoxically became one of the émigré artists most associated with Los Angeles. Allen Ginsberg, entering West L.A. after a cross-country car trip, utters first the question, "Where's Stravinsky?" [see page 138] The answer is, Stravinsky is part of the myth-history of high culture assimilation that defines the elite section of the city. For a black poet like Alexander to enter his consciousness and share his artistic aspiration in a praise song in modernist form is to declare independence from the essentialist version of Blackness in the protest literature of the Black Arts movement of the 1960s and afterward. Themes of immigration, exile, and assimilation underlie the crosstown vista in this condensed lyric, which ends in the line "Watts, Los Angeles, aspiration" like three emphatic musical beats. The poem teaches us, with its complicated syntax and mixture of artistic references, how to re-vision a contested terrain as rigidly stereotyped as any in the public imagination.

But what about the *actual* Watts? Was there any Stravinsky who emigrated to South Central in the first half of the twentieth century? Or any homegrown genius who created surreal mosaics from street language comparable to what Rodia shaped in steel rods and pipes, wire mesh, porcelain, and fragments of Batchelder and Malibu tiles? Not until 1965 was there a stirring of creative fervor among local poets, and as they looked back to an earlier period before the riots, they wondered what kind of world had disappeared in the flames. (Fortunately, the Towers were saved, as they had been saved from the wrecker's ball in 1959 after a civic agency recommended they be torn down.) Was it a genteel Eden of one- and two-story houses and neat lawns and gardens of sunflowers and nearby playgrounds, settled by citizens of European descent and populated after World War II by contented African American blue-collar workers and their families, as both whites and blacks had reason to assert?[11] Michèlle T. Clinton sounded a disenchanted note in her first book of poems, *High Blood / Pressure* (1986):

> it don't seem like it ever was
> a functioning community,
> don't seem like it coulda been more than a myth,
> a wish, a desperate hallucination,
> that black people could love each other
> in the cool & dark of Watts America
> 1966.[12]

The black population that labored in the nearby shipbuilding factories, at Bethlehem Steel, Goodyear, Firestone, North American, Pacific Electric, and General Motors, in meatpacking plants and makeshift farms, have little or no prelapsarian state of being. Poets like Clinton present Watts as always already historical and oppressed, and their rage against whites and each other is an indelible presence in the literature of the post-1965 period, such as we have it. But the myth cannot be simply waved away as a "desperate hallucination." If South Central is ever to be *re*habilitated, if it is ever to *re*cover and be *re*deemed from the fires of insurrection, it will need some primal story of prosperity to secure the scar of representation, to stanch the blood flow and dampen the fires originating in 1965.

Those in quest of an upbeat backstory can find one in RJ Smith's account of what was then called Bronzeville in *The Great Black Way: L.A. in the 1940s and the Lost African-American Renaissance*. Smith sketches a world comparable in its identity to Harlem in New York, Paradise Valley in Detroit, and Chicago's own Bronzeville. Jobs were plentiful and poets took notice of the good times, as in a poem by John Kinloch: "Life is. / A job. / At North American. / It is. The banging / And busting. / Of big machines."[13] Though some talented youth who grew up in Watts, such as Arna Bontemps, had fled to the superior culture of Harlem, and though there were dissenters aplenty before and after the city was annexed by Los Angeles in 1926, there was also a sentiment of contentment during the post-Depression era. There were youth gangs, to be sure, but these were gangs of white men full of class and race resentment. The Spook Hunters, especially, show up occasionally in the literature and police records of the period.

Walter Mosley sets his novel of 1992, *White Butterfly*, in 1956, and, historian that he is, reminds the reader of what has been forgotten:

> We drove quite a ways down Central Avenue. That was before the general decline of the neighborhood. The streets were clean and the drunks were few. I counted fifteen churches between 110th Street and Florence Boulevard. At that corner was the Goodyear Rubber Plant. It was a vast field with two giant buildings far off to the northern end. There was also the hangar for the Goodyear Blimp there. Across the street sat a World gas station. World was a favorite hangout for Mexican hot-rodders and motorcycle enthusiasts who decorated their German machines with up to three hundred pounds of chrome piping and doodads.
>
> Naylor drove to the gate of the Goodyear plant and flashed his badge at the guard. We drove to a large asphalt parking lot where hundreds of

cars were parked neatly in rows like they were on sale. There were always cars parked there, because the Goodyear plant worked twenty-four hours a day, seven days a week.[14]

Like his evocation of the "jazz heyday" in Watts and the exuberant presence of "showy residents" linking Hollywood with South Central, Mosley's passage intends to lay down a floor on which later authors can undertake a reclamation project.

Of course Mosley is not disclaiming the negative forces of racism and class exploitation; on the contrary his novel seethes with revelations of white bigotry and injustice. Mosley sends his detective Easy Rawlins from site to site in South Central and portrays the residents unsentimentally. The prostitutes, the thugs, the riffraff of the bars—these types come in all shades from Nordic white (like the title character, a UCLA undergraduate who lives part-time in the black underworld as a stripper) to deepest black. Chromatic and violent, this world is the shadow of the doomed prosperity evoked in the passage.

In *High Blood Pressure* Clinton dismisses the nostalgia that lights up retrospective vistas like Mosley's, which come with the occasional brushstroke of boosterism: for example, "that golden sort of sunny day that they only get in southern California" (Mosley, 37). Her lyrics have some warm glimpses of childhood in the ghetto but when Clinton gets a job in a more prosperous section of Los Angeles she reverts to a gloomier tone of voice.

So when I do the weekend chill out
with white middle management,
if I say I'm from Watts
even the men get quiet,
'cause they know what I am then,
refuge[e] nigger, possibly brutalized,
now quieted & relieved for the view their company affords.[15]

In both passages Clinton attempts a distancing maneuver in the manner of Alexander, but she is pulled back by self-knowledge to the mean streets, with their tidal claim on her affections and their threatening memories of bad behavior chiefly by males who lord it over everyone: white thugs with a badge, black thugs with irresistible muscle, whites and blacks in the Mayor's office with no clue how to meet the needs of their constituents.

II

The poets who came to prominence in the wake of the 1965 riots, as witnesses to and commentators about Watts, were all African American. We have no significant poetry about the black community written by non-blacks, at least until the rise of Latino and Asian American authors in the same area. White poets with a strong political consciousness turned to the Vietnam War for subject matter, and there was certainly plenty of material in those killing fields to sustain their anger at authority and fill their poems. After 1965 the search began for a native informant who could describe and interpret not just South Central Los Angeles but all the ghettos from coast to coast. Was there a figure like Langston Hughes walking through Harlem taking notes about the dreams deferred? Or Bob Kaufman, writing his Beat and offbeat poems in the late 1950s and early 1960s up north in Bayview, the black district of San Francisco? Or Gwendolyn Brooks, who had articulated the complex community life of South Side Chicago beginning with *A Street in Bronzeville* (1945)? Or Robert Hayden, who preserved in his lyrics and narratives indelible images of Black Bottom in Detroit during the first six decades of the twentieth century? At least one poet emerged from the fires of Watts prepared to answer those crucial questions: What is Watts actually like? What fuels the rage that causes districts like Watts to explode? What language is available to a poet who undertakes this mission?

The bard of South Central, the most trustworthy and eloquent guide to the region, is Wanda Coleman (1946–2013), who began writing, she tells us in an introduction to *Greatest Hits 1966–2003*, during "my coming-of-age in the Los Angeles of the 1960s, considering the impact of those fires that burned during the Watts Riots (August 1965). Because of those fires, I shifted my creative pursuit from singing to writing, hoping I had something original to offer."[16] Coleman attended Budd Schulberg's Watts Writers Workshop, and then published seventeen books and several chapbooks, garnering significant notice including fellowships from the Guggenheim Foundation and the National Endowment for the Arts, an Emmy in Daytime Drama writing, and the 1999 Lenore Marshall Poetry Prize awarded by the Academy of American Poets. She was nominated for the 2001 National Book Award for her volume *Mercurochrome*. As with any poet who has composed more than a thousand poems, her work is uneven; some of it has that willed, repetitive flavor that stains the reputation of most prolific poets, including two other L.A.-based authors in the stable of Black Sparrow Press, Charles

Bukowski and Diane Wakoski. But Coleman has a stylistic range beyond theirs and a capacious sense of form that gives her glimpses of life in South Central an originality and scope worthy of more critical examination and more respect. I have written elsewhere about Coleman's contribution to the genre of Hollywood Poetry and her sense of Los Angeles overall.[17] Here I'll turn my attention to her evocation of Watts, an area of only two and a half square miles but one of the most pungent reputations in America.

Wanda Coleman

WHERE I LIVE

at the lip of a big black vagina
birthing nappy-headed pickaninnies every hour on the hour
and soul radio blasting into mindwindow
bullets and blood
see that helicopter up there? like
god's eye looking down on his children
barsandbarsandbarsandbarsandbars
where i live
is the gap filled mouth of polly, the old black woman
up the street whose daughter's from new orleans and who
abandons her every holiday leaving her to wander
up and down the avenue and not even a holiday meal. she
collects the neighborhood trash and begs kindness in
doorways/always in the same browns, purples
and blues of her loneliness—a dress
that never fades or wears thin
where i live
is the juke on the corner—hamburgerfishchilli smells
drawing hungry niggahs off the street and pimpmobiles
cluttering the asphalt parking lot. pool tables in the
back where much gambling and shit take place and
many niggahs fall to the knife of the violent surgeon.
one night me and cowboy were almost killed by a stray
bullet from some renegade low riders and me and
kathy used to go down and drop quarters

and listen to al green, and the dudes would hate
my 'sditty ways and call me a dyke
'cause i wouldn't sell pussy
where i live
is the night club working one to six in the morning.
cigarette burn holes in my stockings and wig full of
cigarette smoke. flesh bruised from niggahs pinching my
meat and feeling my thighs, ears full of spit
from whispers and obscene suggestions and mind full of
sleep's spiders building a hazy nest—eyes full of
rainbows looking forward to the day i leave this hell
where i live
avoiding the landlord on the first and fifteenth when he
comes around to collect the rent. i'm four months behind
and wish i had a niggah to take care of me for a change
instead of taking me through changes. this building which
keeps chewing hunks out of the sides of people's cars and
the insane old bitch next door beating on the wall, scaring
the kids and telling me to shut up. every other day she calls
the cops out here and i hope they don't run a make on me
and find all them warrants
where i live
the little gangsters diddy-bop through and pick up
young bitches and flirt with old ones, looking to
snatch somebody's purse or find their way into somebody's
snatch 'cause mama don't want them at home and papa
is a figment and them farms them farms them farms
they call schools. and mudflapped bushy-headed entities
swoop the avenues seeking death
it's the only thrill left
where i live
at the lip of a big black vagina
birthing happy-headed pickaninnies every hour on the hour
the county is her pimp and she can turn a trick
swifter than any bitch ever graced this earth
she's the baddest piece of ass on the west coast
named black los angeles[18]

—•—

"Where I Live," from *African Sleeping Sickness* (1990), will serve as one guide to the neighborhood and an index of Coleman's art. It's a poem that will not be to everyone's taste; it is naked poetry to an extreme degree. The poem opens, and closes, with a bravura metaphor intended to shock the casual reader of loco-descriptive poetry: Watts, or "black Los Angeles," is imagined as "a big black vagina." On one level, the metaphor intends a sociological point, that the district teems with babies, with "nappy-headed pickaninnies" generated by a prolific sexuality ("she can turn a trick / swifter than any bitch ever graced this earth") and a permissive social welfare system ("the county is her pimp"). This figure of speech is Coleman's version of the standard characterization of the multitudinous city in poetry—Paris as the "fourmillante cité" in Baudelaire or Wordsworth's comparison of London to an anthill in *The Prelude*. Her concluding lines evoke the spirit of "The Big Easy," the cognomen of New Orleans, and stray perilously close to an association with the popular phrase "black hole," the astronomical realm of some infinitely dense mass of dark matter. In tone and content the trope is reminiscent of Audre Lorde's lines:

> I was born in the gut of Blackness
> from between my mother's particular thighs
> her waters broke upon blue-flowered linoleum
> and turned to slush in the Harlem cold[19]

"Every hour on the hour," Coleman writes, more "pickaninnies" come into an already densely populated cityscape defined by violence reported on soul radio and symbolized by the police helicopters patrolling the post-riot territory.

Coleman's packed lines always offer plenty of ambiguity to unpack. One asks, Does the word *pickaninnies* have invisible ironic quotation marks around it? Are we to read it as we do "bushy-headed entities" later in the poem, who "swoop the avenues seeking death"? Are these the terms used casually in Watts, are they imported from the white world to reflect the disdain for burgeoning and brutal life in black neighborhoods? And how deliberately are "soul radio" and helicopters and "pimpmobiles" meant to represent the colonizing machine technology in a district like Watts, answering back to the more positive images of urban technology in (white) modernist poetry: the firetruck and the Bridge, the swoop of the Buick, the skyscrapers of New York and Chicago, the "Railroads and Freight Handler to the

Nation"? The helicopter, especially, resonates for an American audience that has drawn into their nervous system the sound and sight of invasive copters in films like *Apocalypse Now* about Vietnam and *Boyz N the Hood* about South Central. That those machines can be termed "god's eye," a superhuman surveillance operation, links the agency of control back to the Puritan panopticon, the spirit of one nation spied upon by an angry God. The Watts Towers, a more forgiving figure in the cityscape, are not visible to helicopters, nor in Coleman's visual survey of the flat and dry field on which the district has been erected.

Coleman is not interested in machinery; she focuses her poem on sexuality, on appetite. The diction is reductive and demeaning in line with the opening metaphor. Coleman studs her poems with scatological language that draws a boundary line, like the restrictive covenant that fenced off white areas of the larger city, around the repeated motif, "where i live": niggahs, shit, dyke, pussy, spit, bitch, snatch, pimp, piece of ass. Rap music has established this formerly unspeakable kind of language as the dialect of the tribe expressive of the down-and-dirty lifestyle of a captive territory filled with privation and rage. This is not the language we hear in poems and songs about West L.A. and the beach, though Coleman has made it clear that the private patois and behavior of Hollywood mirrors that of Watts to a considerable degree. But who has the moral right to hold these idioms at arm's length? Eric Partridge reminded us back in 1948, in *Shakespeare's Bawdy*, of the astonishing number of tropes referring to body parts and sexual acts in the oeuvre of the greatest Anglophone author of all time. Shakespeare, he claims, is a "dirty-minded" poet, though of course nobody, including Partridge, would be satisfied with that term to describe the totality of his work.[20] Some poets have a Shakespearean or Swiftian sensitivity to the body's anatomy, appetites, and wastes, and a willingness to deploy them; Coleman is one of them. She would subscribe to a remark by the narrator of Saul Bellow's novella, "Him with His Foot in His Mouth": "Real candor means excremental and genital literalness."[21] It is not her scatological language per se that should disturb us, then, if it does, but the corrosive view of social life implied by her relish in using so many profane terms and figures of speech.

Black writers, from the century's beginning, had been implored by many in the community not to run down the race but to uplift it. Not to take notice of the negative sites of the Negro milieu, not to stress the obscene and anti-social in local customs and speech, but to isolate for inspection the praiseworthy, the dignified, and the virtuous. Coleman's practice is to present a speaker who protests the debauchery that offends her moral imagination. She makes use of the high tradition to underscore her disgust, as when she offers this iambic pentameter line to characterize the experience of landscape while driving through Watts:

> barsandbarsandbarsandbarsandbars

Bars have usurped the presence of churches in black neighborhoods, if we can trust Walter Mosley's description above. In this wasteland of sin and crime, where the "night club" and gambling dens attract "little gangsters" who pick up "young bitches" for their pleasure, the presence of "god's eye" in the form of police helicopters sounds like a saving grace. While rap artists constantly rage against the cops on the beat, Coleman constructs "Where I Live" to fill out the scene in a reportorial way, flashing her poetic license, faithful to the actual sensibility of the district's victims.

Coleman offers herself, as speaker, as the chief victim, whose "meat" keeps being pinched and whose landlord hounds her for the overdue rent. She too has a shady past if those "warrants" are what we think they are. And as in many of her poems, Coleman puts a spotlight on old women who cannot cope with the city's brutality (again like Baudelaire). First there is Polly, the "old black woman" who wanders the streets "and begs kindness" from the less deprived. The figure returns in a more demonic form as the "insane old bitch next door beating on the wall." She too is a figure for Watts, driven to distraction and madness by the random and ruthless psychic wounds inflicted by "this hell / where i live." Person by person, site by site, Coleman "blackens" the nostalgic image of pre-riot Watts just as Alexander revises Coleman by relocating value in the aspirations of residents, using the Watts Towers as an inspiring symbol of reconstruction.

No poem in this mode will ever make it into the *Norton Anthology of Contemporary Poetry* or *The Vintage Book of Contemporary American Poetry* or the (Oxford) *Anthology of Modern American Poetry*. Coleman can and does write sculpted poems of well-ordered lineation and disciplined tone that please the eye and ear trained by the canonical tradition of poetry in English. (I do not mean just orderly quatrains and metered verse, as my references to modernist practice make clear.) "Where I Live" is disorderly, messy, carnivalesque. It shows its impatience with its subject matter; it expresses "attitude" with deliberate defiance of all the norms of taste. Its sentences sprawl across the lines rather than fitting themselves into some kind of artful—that is, deliberate and cadenced—design. In the most obvious way the poem mimics its subject matter by making itself ugly, malproportioned, promiscuous in its catalogue of images and in its rush of statement. It eschews standard English punctuation. It is a jeremiad and claims truth as its purpose, not the so-called decorum of art.

A useful contrast is Claude McKay's Shakespearean sonnet "The Harlem Dancer" (1922), which pleases the reader by its subtle articulation of a refined sensibility, stanza by stanza, and its sophisticated presentation of the dancer as a symbol of Harlem itself, exploited and brutalized by "the wine-flushed, bold-eyed boys" who gaze lustfully at her and throw coins on the stage to humiliate her. Coleman tends not to hold the focus on a single figure and document a speaker's changing perspective toward it; she hurries forward, presenting an overwhelming quantity of data, in order to depict a thrill-seeking locality marked by prolific variety and inevitable transgressions. She is Watts's raucous answer to the more genteel and ingratiating Harlem poets: McKay, Countee Cullen, and Langston Hughes.

"Where I Live" focuses on a particular neighborhood in Los Angeles, but like so many other poems by Coleman it implies an identification between Watts and the larger metropolis. "Los Angeles has replaced New York, in the public mind, as the nation's most criminal and ungovernable metropolis," David Wyatt asserts.[22] If that is so, then Watts, and all of South Central, can be said to have become "Los Angelized" in the sense defined by Thomas McGrath in *Letter to an Imaginary Friend* (see Introduction). And the prosody of poems like this one has also become Los Angelized, deromanticized in the service of truths that put off the cosmetics of euphemism and orderly form. She might say, with the rapper DJ Quik in "Born and Raised in Compton": "But I ain't doin' nothin' but claimin' my city . . . Yes, I'm definitely freestylin', all the while still profilin'." By holding the mirror of poetry up to the Caliban-face of Greater Los Angeles, Coleman renders a public service anchored in the history of protest literature.

"[Y]es, it's insanity / writing poetry in Los Angeles," Coleman sighs in another, later poem.[23] She writes constantly on this theme, that the obsession with composing poems, which in some privileged places remains a source of pure joy and professional advancement, drives black poets to unremitting anger as they torment themselves repeatedly in the feedback system of contemporary American publishing. That poets are marginalized by society in all cases, and minority poets are doubly penalized in places like South Central, is the burden of her extraordinary poem "Clocking Dollars" (too long to reprint), which presents a full-scale self-portrait of a *poétesse maudite* undergoing steady humiliations in the modern city.[24] Innovative in form and modernist to a fault in its social critique, it expresses more comprehensively than any poem of its kind the situation of the distressed poet in the era of late capitalism.

A prose poem, the appropriate medium for a tirade of this kind, "Clocking Dollars" mixes together bits of verse, song, anecdote, parody of bureaucratic language, and a stream of inspired punning. It is the verbal equivalent of the Watts Towers in its mosaic form. Coleman makes a comedy of language, for example in finding a plethora of synonyms for "money," from the title through "smackers," "moolah," "Vitamin M," "filthy lucre," "solid green," "new cabbage," "simoleons," "clams," "double sawbuck," "new notes," "ducats," "dinero," and many more down to the "greenbacks" in the last line. Money flows freely to some black makers of lyrics, she wryly observes, if they have "Bleached skin, a nose job and 'natural rhythm.'" Michael Jackson and rap artists seem to prove that equal opportunity exists for ghetto dwellers, but she claims to speak for almost all of her fellow citizens of Watts when she testifies to the opposite case. "Open my pages and read my bleed," she demands. Specifically, she itemizes how she is disadvantaged by five conditions: race, class, sex, the distraction for readers and scholars of dead rivals, and finally, "regionality." Most readers simply don't want to read about South Central, though they may enjoy hearing songs about it. But "regionality" refers to Los Angeles in general, so often discounted in the mainstream institutions of poetry. Yes, there are benefits that come with what Coleman calls the "Niggah-of-the-Minute syndrome," and a small window of attention during Black History month (February), but Coleman is front and center in testifying that the attention is fleeting and illusory. She has personal experience to counter the pieties of political correctness, so often advanced by the academy and public relations offices in the poetry establishment.

Coleman makes her case partly by stories, the appropriate content for a prose poem. She tells us about her angry dispute with "some Koreans who'd purchased a popular ghetto burger stop." She speaks with an "old Yid" over lunch at the Hollywood Boulevard eatery, Musso & Frank's. And she narrates a dream in which she finds a "Ulysses S. Grant" (a fifty-dollar bill) in a desk and internalizes the accusation of theft from a white male. Coleman has written abundant poems in which she presents herself as under suspicion, by other minorities as well as her own people, simply for existing in a black skin. Money is usually the means of rising above such indignities but her line of work is a barrier to upward mobility. We can read the mangled verse quotations in "Clocking Dollars" as further speculation on whether this barrier can be overcome. She travesties a song The Beatles and The Rolling Stones made famous, "Money (That's What I Want)":

money don't get everythang—it's true
what it don't get I can't use

Her version is "*money iszant everything but / it's way out ahead of whatev-ah's in second place.*" The Beatles rose from a poor neighborhood in a port city into worldwide celebrity and almost unimaginable wealth. They are legitimate role models for the aspiring poet. The original song was composed by Barrett Strong, a black musician from Mississippi, and recorded by Tamla (later Motown) in 1960. Strong's earning potential was enhanced when he wrote other songs for Motown including "I Heard It Through the Grapevine" and "Papa Was a Rollin' Stone." And the final quotation in the poem's closure has a recognizable literary antecedent:

the want that thru the greenbacks drives the power
drives my rage

Dylan Thomas was probably not thinking of money when he composed "The force that through the green fuse drives the flower / drives my green age" but he certainly felt the "want" of money in his Welsh town and had to hustle all his life to turn his poetry into gold. In such quotations Coleman stakes out her claim that art and cash are indivisibly connected, especially in regions of deprivation. She simultaneously deconstructs the pieties of the poetic tradition and calls attention to the primal need for money underlying poetic testaments of the recent past.

Also of note is another quotation, isolated as a stanza and italicized:

live rich, love easy, die asleep in bed with a smiling corpse

The famous original line is "Live fast, die young, and leave a good-looking corpse," spoken by the young thug Nick ("Pretty Boy") Romano in Willard Motley's novel of 1947, *Knock on Any Door,* and recirculated in the 1949 film with John Derek as Romano. Motley was a light-skinned Negro who passed as white and who wrote in this novel about Italian-Americans in Chicago growing up in a slum and turning to crime. The best gloss for Coleman's revision of the line is her earlier passage, remarkable for the internal rhyming and the other sound effects she employs to give it a hip-hop beat:

> Chump change: for the ghetto parasite there's hope in dope—luxury cars, Cuban cigars, rubbing noses with movie stars, high-priced likker no need to dicker when the Feds come around to jump your ticker. It's a shame, a disgrace, but they'll tell you to your face: the top's reserved for the White Queen's race.

This kind of jazzing or speeded-up syncopation, as well as the burlesque of mainstream literature, is the ghetto's answer to mainstream linguistic structures. It is an experimental abstraction of the prevailing tradition, in the manner of Stravinsky working over the nineteenth-century masters. By toning up the rhythms and diction to a comic level, the poem disarms critics on all sides, black and white, middle class and underclass. Seeming to protest the privileges belonging to "the White Queen's race"—and what an ambiguous figure *that* is!—the passage throws most of its punches at the upwardly mobile "ghetto parasite" who cashes in as if he or she hustled the system in wonderlands like Las Vegas and Tijuana. Like those outliers of Los Angeles, Watts offers "hope in dope," the specter of heroin, crack, PCP, and other street drugs peddled for high profits.

"Clocking Dollars," then, is an entertainment that critiques poets' conventional and often tiresome obsession with their craft and reputation. But it is also a genuine complaint for all its goofy wordplay. The poem keeps its eyes on the prize, which is not equality and justice per se but the tangible reward system for the minority poet who learns the rules of "cant, jargon, and slang" favored by the grant-giving literary establishment. Like Martin Amis's novel *Money*, mainly set in Los Angeles, "Clocking Dollars" sends up the indelicate subject of so much American prose going back to *Poor Richard's Almanack* by Benjamin Franklin. Making the sentences snappy while fitting the advice to the location (as in Philadelphia, so in South Central), the poem performs the resistance of a resilient colony to its imperial master.

III

The Watts riot of 1965 in fact extended well beyond Watts, as did the iteration of its insurrectionary text in the 1992 Rodney King riots. This landmark event can be described in many ways but for our purposes here I want to characterize it—and I am hardly the first to do so—as a realization of the visionary painting "The Burning of Los Angeles" that plays a central role in the image structure of Nathanael West's novel of 1939, *The Day of the Locust*. In that novel Tod Hackett, a set and costume designer for a Hollywood studio, works intermittently on a large canvas that the narrator tells us established his reputation in later years. The painting depicts the massive upsurge of ordinary citizens in a rage-filled frenzy of destruction. These are the city's id, the personification of barbarism unleashed by the humiliations and oppressions they have had to bear. At the end of the novel these same types of humanity appear at a film premiere on Hollywood Boulevard and trample everything that resists their desperate efforts to achieve recognition and ecstasy. They embody purely and simply the aggressive power of the liberated multitude.

In the final paragraphs of the novel, as he descends into a fugue state of delirium in the midst of the mob, Tod is "able to think clearly about his picture, 'The Burning of Los Angeles' . . . Across the top, parallel with the frame, he had drawn the burning city, a great bonfire of architectural styles. . . . Through the center . . . came the mob carrying baseball bats and torches." Bored to the point of extremity by their life in Los Angeles, these maddened creatures are "No longer bored, they sang and danced joyously in the red light of the flames." These masses are not the labor protestors of John Steinbeck's *In Dubious Battle* or the lynch mob of William Faulkner's *Light in August*, or the outraged rioters in Ralph Ellison's *Invisible Man* (a scene based on the Harlem Riots of 1943), to cite examples in which the righting of perceived wrongs in savage justice underlies the clamor. There can be no remediation for West's angry misfits. There is no definable enemy, only the neurotic dreams and libidinous desires that have driven most of the crowd across the country to the so-called paradise of Los Angeles, and humiliated them upon their arrival.

"The city burning is Los Angeles's deepest image of itself," Joan Didion remarks in a "Notebook" published in *Slouching Towards Bethlehem*. She makes the connection of West's novel and the 1965 riot, noting, "For days one could drive the Harbor Freeway and see the city on fire, just as we had always known it would be in the end."[25] Poets adopted the resonant phrase as a subject heading for their depictions of a scorched and wasted city, in its material and psychological aspects. One thinks of contrary labels like "The

Windy City" or "The City of Brotherly Love" coined in homage to other American places; but "The Burning City" hardly seems appropriate for a seacoast metropolis favored rather than disfavored in local propaganda for its temperate weather, natural bounty, and utopian dreams—its light not its heat. But Jack Hirschman in his poem "The Burning of Los Angeles," written in 1962 before the riot but after devastating fires in Griffith Park and the Hollywood Hills (May 1961) and in the Santa Monica Mountains and Bel Air (November 1961), claims that West rightly prophesied an apocalyptic fate for the city. Daringly, Hirschman characterizes the wildfire as a giant female figure spreading her witch-like powers of destruction across the mountains and lowlands:

> Supple up there licking the tops of the trees
> chewing the hair offa them
>   A deer came down a canyon with
>   a piece of her and done
>   A palomino came down his mane was her and he died
> at the edge of the gutter
>   with jacarandas died with cries
> of muskrats leaping from trees
> thumps of rabbits on stone
>   Screeches and whine of
> sirens of engines ambulance spotlight
> out of the awe of my eye[26]

Giving the fire a human form anchors the figure in a literary tradition that recalls most explicitly a favorite literary character in the 1960s, Orc, a mythic spirit entirely made of fire which stands as the symbol of revolution and flaming youth in William Blake's narrative poem *America*. Orc *is* America, burning up all the rotted laws and restrictive moral codes of its parent and imperial power Albion. Hirschman's poem, full of surreal riffs, treats the firebrand as an erotic superwoman who lays waste both the wilderness and the city for unspoken reasons; but the speaker's fascination with her powers, his seeming desire to be consumed by her, is in keeping with Tod's complicity with the violent and untamable forces that drive him to madness by the end of West's novel.

That authors have recourse to the language of eroticism for their descriptions of all-consuming conflagrations reverses the conventional troping of sexual passion as a fire in the blood. Hirschman presents his incendiary female figure as the transformed image of nature itself, of the Motherland, customarily allegorized as female. Likewise, T. C. Boyle, in his novel centered on Mexican immigration, *The Tortilla Curtain*, represents an uprush of fire in the high canyons above Los Angeles as "roiling in bright orange beauty, mesmerizing, seductive, the smoke unraveling round the edges as if whole empires were aflame. . . . It leapt to the trees like the coming of the Apocalypse."[27]

Samuel Maio's volume *The Burning of Los Angeles* (1997) contains an epigraph from West's novel and a poem with that title, but the poems seek to establish a pre-apocalyptic landscape, a site primed for lordly wrath but not yet ablaze. The virtue of his method is to highlight scene by scene the actual geography and cultural features of the different neighborhoods. Disneyland, the middle-class suburbs, the Hollywood of Whiskey a Go Go, and other sites, including the interiors of houses steeped in domestic violence, provide evidence of alienation and despair. The locations as a whole constitute Cities of the Plain, as with Sodom and Gomorrah, that deserve divine punishment. Coming upon a poem titled "South Central L.A." one expects to read a representation of the riots, but Maio, speaking in the first person, recounts instead a general apprehension of peril in the inner city as he guides our attention from University Park, home of the University of Southern California, toward the more dangerous locations east and south of the wealthy college and its rich fraternities:

> My neighbors get richer by the day.
> And during the vast, sordid night
> The circling police helicopters
> Obscure the gunshots and screams.
> The gang rapists and car thieves
> Outrun them and sleep disquietly
> As any of us behind barred windows
> And steel doors hoping we're safe.[28]

Maio cedes the subject matter of riot to black poets, despite the opportunistic title he gives his volume. And in doing so he follows the lead of most white commentators on events in the Los Angeles ghettos during and after the 1960s. White poets were wary of speaking for the victims, who so often in their rhetoric identified whites, even white authors, as antagonists.

Oddly enough, the same is largely true of black poets, who shied away from the specific events belonging to the two riots in South Central. Information about the motives, actions and reactions, and aftereffects of the 1992 riots can be found in Anna Deavere Smith's one-woman play *Twilight: Los Angeles*, based on interviews. For novelistic treatment of the same materials Walter Mosley's *Little Scarlet* (2004) and Joseph Wambaugh's *The New Centurions* (1971) provide a police-eye view of the 1965 riot. There is an empty space, a haunting absence in literary history, which the epic story of South Central in the latter half of the twentieth century ought to occupy. There is no major work equivalent even to Gwendolyn Brooks's brief sequence "Riot" or Maya Angelou's generic poem "Riot: 60's" about uprisings in other cities. *Black Fire: An Anthology of Afro-American Writing*, edited by LeRoi Jones and Larry Neal in 1968, scarcely notices Watts in the course of its massive attention to violent resistance in Harlem and Newark. The "burning" of actual buildings in South Central, the killing of 34 people and the arrest of 3,952, was an epoch-making historical occurrence; the fire in the mind, the fierce antinomian spirit bred by the riots, did linger and swell to enormous psychic weight in verse about South Central after 1965. But little trace of such verse can be located in printed books.

No grand theories are necessary to account for this virtual absence. Put simply, those artists who felt motivated to chronicle and document the war of African Americans, and other minorities, against the white power structure, and other minorities, set their lyrics in rhymed four-beat lines and sang their outrage rather than speaking it. Rap fascinated listeners of all colors because of its intricate and forceful language, as opposed to the equally declamatory genres of heavy metal and punk, in which the clear articulation of complex diction was the last thing on the minds of singers and audiences. In a social context of the return of the repressed, the minority art of poetry, facing the hardest times in centuries at the cash register, roared back into public view and seized the center of the cultural scene. Albums from rap artists sold tens of millions of copies—Tupac Shakur's albums have sold some 75 million units as of 2010—while page poets like Wanda Coleman, as she testified in "Clocking Dollars," could do no better than publish in fugitive literary journals that only paid her two copies of the issue in which her poems appeared.

An extended discussion of gangsta rap in this chapter would put too much bias on a small albeit world-famous group of lyricists. Bias in the sense of a built structure that leans further in one direction than is desirable. The "architecture" of South Central itself has always been a matter of debate. To all appearances pre-1965 Watts and Compton, and indeed all the black areas south of the city, had the look of somewhat more prosperous suburbs like Lawndale and Lakewood. "Despite the restrictive covenants that so limited black mobility in the years after World War II," David Wyatt writes, "the Urban League had even rated Los Angeles first out of sixty-eight cities in terms of the ten basic aspects of Negro life."[29] Change came very quickly, however. Thomas Pynchon characterized Watts in 1966 as "a pocket of bitter reality" and analogized "the miles of heavy industry that sprawl along Alameda Street" as a "gray and murderous arterial which lies at the eastern boundary of Watts looking like the edge of the world."[30] The public image of the entire area was transformed further by the police repression that followed upon the explosion of crack use and sale throughout the southland. The language of rap and the corrosive visuals in music videos, video reportage, and film narrative heightened the sense of a fortress community under siege. Robin D. G. Kelley describes the ghetto in the 1980s as

> an overcrowded world of deteriorating tenement apartments or tiny cement-block, prisonlike projects, streets filthy from the lack of city services, liquor stores and billboards selling malt liquor and cigarettes. The construction of the ghetto as a living nightmare and gangstas as products of that nightmare has given rise to what I call a new "ghettocentric" identity in which the specific class, race, and gendered experience in late-capitalist urban centers coalesce to create a new identity—"Nigga"[31]

The "Nigga" is the first-person narrator of almost all gangsta rap songs about "Black Los Angeles." He (rarely she) presents himself as a racialized subject with a vengeance.

Rap songs tend to the bitter, and occasionally the murderous. Singers take on rap aliases, personae who perform the identity of outlaws, gangsters, pimps, thugs, revolutionaries, lording it over innocent gawkers who accidentally cross their path. The poets light the fire of antisocial rhetoric and their listeners (and now readers) are warned to stay clear. Here are passages of a seminal text in the genre, "How to Survive in South Central," as sung by Ice Cube on the soundtrack of the film *Boyz N the Hood*:

> Just to be safe don't wear no blue or red
> cause most niggaz get got

in either L.A., Compton or Watts
Pissed-off black human beings
So I think you better skip the sight-seeing
And if you're nuttin but a mark
make sure that you're in before dark
But if you need some affection mate
Make sure the bitch ain't a section eight
cause if so that's a monkey-wrench ho
and you won't survive in South Central

Now you realize it's not all that it's cracked up to be.
You realize that it's fucked up!
It ain't nothing like the shit you saw on TV.
Palm trees and blonde bitches?
I'd advise you to pack your shit and get the fuck on;
punk motherfucker!

—•—

Rule number three: don't get caught up
Cause niggaz are doing anything that's thought up
And they got a vice
on everything from dope to stolen merchandise
We discern
cause South Central L.A. is one big yearn[32]

In these last lines the strain of finding a rhyme produces a telling phrase: South Central is "one big yearn"—but so is all of Los Angeles, and everywhere else in the world as well. As with Wanda Coleman's poem "Where I Live," the needs of human nature are simplified by an angry speaker down to their most appetitive level. Power. Sex. Notoriety (a debased version of Fame), Money, Thrills. These troubadours swagger and vaunt their profanity-filled message that life is a jungle, always addressing their audiences, winking at the audacity of it all, with maximum braggadocio. The white rapper Eminem delivers the same message from the depressed areas of Detroit—and all over the world posses and bands form in hopes of repeating the formulas and the trajectories of success hammered out by N.W.A. and its offshoots "straight outta Compton."

South Central, in this telling, is a remote kingdom of infinite danger and thus of mystery and elemental passions. Its bards invent transgressive masks to cast themselves as subhuman, inhuman: "I am a nightmare walkin, psychopath talkin / King of my jungle, just a gangster stalkin," declares Ice-T in "Colors."[33] Tupac Shakur, who was killed by enemies unknown at the age of twenty-five, has been called "the standard-bearer of the West Coast rap scene" because of his prolific and poetic dreamscapes of South Central. His apologia for his poetics has an altruistic sound to it: "I'm not saying I want to rule the world, but I know that if I keep talking about how dirty it is out here, somebody's going to clean it up."[34] Yet he self-mockingly acknowledged the cynical nature of his art; writing under the alias Makaveli, he spoke in "To Live & Die in L.A." of his songs as "Makin' money off of cuss words, writin' again / Learn how to think ahead, so I fight with my pen." The world of predation and sadism summoned in gangsta rap, and the corresponding use of offensive speech to manifest the imagination of personal and social degradation, has paradoxically elevated singers like Tupac to a cultural status well above the listeners and now readers of their resistance poems.

It is not what you see on TV sitcoms, dramas, and reality shows, not the world of Malibu and Beverly Hills and all the other Hills. The sexual exploitation in rap does not match the world of genteel pornography studios in San Fernando Valley, as in the film *Boogie Nights* or Carolyn See's nonfiction study *Blue Money*. It is the Hobbesian realm of dreadful combat and unending jeopardy. Some of it genuinely warns the listener away from the 'hood, some of it openly postures and mau-maus the middle-class white teens who not so secretly admire the warrior pose of the members of N.W.A. and their latter-day posses. The preferred scenery for these narratives is not the interiors of South Central but the streets where most of the actions take place. From their original format of mock battles between singers for boasting rights, the MCs (masters of ceremonies) took their invective to the police and to women, using the crass misogyny of thwarted adolescence to signify anger against the world. Rap songs document how communities of blacks, victimized by unemployment, police brutality, deterioration of civic services, crack peddlers, and the seeming inevitability of long prison sentences, fight back. Half of Dr. Dre's song "The Day the Niggaz Took Over" is given to sound clips from news coverage of the fifty-six baton blows to the body of Rodney King and the ensuing riots.[35]

So far the ghettos see limited economic benefit from having this unruly identity foisted on them. But poetry itself has benefited from the infusion of so much vehement and inventive language, according to rap's advocates. "In the past thirty years rap has led a renaissance of the word, bringing a return to poetry in public life," claim Adam Bradley and Andrew Dubois.[36] Certainly, rap burned down the house as surely as the real fire of riot. And like Orc, Blake's figure of both creative and destructive energy, the rap poets have arguably helped to turn the Plains of Id (as Reyner Banham calls South Central) into some reformed Ego, or Superego. In any case, the 'hood has changed significantly like so many other residential areas in Greater Los Angeles. An influx of immigrants has eased tensions overall as a new ethnic mix, replicated in more and more neighborhoods, has contributed to a new mentality to tone down the Manichean version in gangsta rap. (More enlightened police commissioners and cops on the beat have also done some good.) How much of the twenty-first-century poetry of South Central will be retrospective, returning to the scenes of the conflicts to reexamine the causes and consequences of all that Black Fire, and how much will be multicultural to reflect the new demographics, remains to be seen. In the post-apocalyptic era of this contested region, street poetry, the timely manifestation of African oral tradition, is likely to take some surprising turns as the sites of conflict are re-visioned.

IV

Those mutations are likely to follow a trajectory that we examined in the case of Hollywood, and will see repeated in the following chapter on Latino poetry, in which a particular district becomes transformed into a general concept, a manner of behavior, a diasporic condition, as Hollywood Boulevard assumed the abstract form of The Movies in the course of time. Black poets who have withdrawn from the radical politics represented by gangsta rap fostered in Watts and Compton have nevertheless carried forward the imperative of the Black Arts aesthetic to tell the story of race in America with or without recourse to a rhetoric of acrimonious complaint and protest. As always, the practitioners of this twenty-first century poetics cannot be herded into narrow categories. Some of them—and Wanda Coleman is one of their models—return in poems of translucent clarity to stories of roots, of ancestors, of community solidarity. Others build upon the achievement of mentors like Robert Hayden, Gwendolyn Brooks, Sterling Brown, and even Countee Cullen in order to construct a tradition as energetic as the Black Arts Movement of the 1960s but insistent on finding alternatives to the Movement's aggressive rhetoric. Some poets have made use of the avant-garde poetics of the 1990s and thereafter to regain the spirit of play that informs hip-hop but became formulaic and doctrinaire in the styles and structures of that popular medium.

Place and location serve this new poetry, in all of its diversity. One gets a sense of the range in *Rainbow Darkness: An Anthology of African American Poetry* (2003), edited by Keith Tuma. The essays and poems in this collection appreciate the topography of many American regions, and not just those visited in recent decades by violent protests. As with the cinema of the 1980s onward, one sees a reaction against the glamorization of the outlaw figure rising in Orc-like triumph from the ghetto. Los Angeles had long suffered from the feedback system in which popular novels about Western outlaws and urban gangsters were adapted to films of the *Jesse James* and *Public Enemy* genres, only to engender in the 1960s not only actual rebels but the threatening lyrics that fed off the fantasies and energies of media conflict against established order.[37]

I must confine my comments here to one representative poem from *Rainbow Darkness* about Los Angeles that moves the center of gravity for African Americans in the city somewhat to the north and west, reconstituting the terms of the cityscape poem in innovative ways. Here is the full poem:

Harryette Mullen

#6 SEPULVEDA

Arrival at terminal laxative. In and out with fries. Fox mauls hill.
A colored crowd. Sad cactus left over from family nursery's going
out of business sale. The drive-in movie was a used car lot, then a
flea market, now it's condos. *Botanica* across from coffee shop near
Cuban restaurant where workers gather for lunch. A few blocks
down, you can get five different *mole salsas* and wire dollars to
Oaxaca. At pancake palace I hop on the bus across from all night
news guy. Today's special veggie burger at Hot Diggity, home of the
Y2K dog. Turn right past blank soldier and bland sailor. A white
cross for each life lost. Pencils, toothpicks, chopsticks. Trees in
this wood, all cut down to size. Pay a large sum for a large bag of

popcorn. End of the line, everyone out. Grab a *Daily Bruin* and run.
It's okay, the crazy people on the bus aren't talking to themselves.
They're speaking on their cell phones.[38]

—•—

Since the publication in 2009 of *American Hybrid: A Norton Anthology of New Poetry*, edited by Cole Swenson and David St. John, much conversation among poets and critics has ensued about the viability of a third way in the history of modern American poetry. The anthology features poems that keep their distance from the most extreme experiments associated with Language Poetry and other theory-based poetics, while still adhering to the fundamental imperative of all such movements to Make It New, to freshen the readers' perceptions and consciousness by manipulating language in an intellectual and innovative manner. The anthology seeks to defamiliarize not only language itself but its contents—for example, the experience of urban places.

Harryette Mullen's poem is a textbook case of such a confluence and mixture of earlier styles. (She appears in *American Hybrid*, but not with this poem.) Most obviously, the fourteen-line poem calls attention to both the conventionality and the resourcefulness of the traditional sonnet form, with its play of grammatical and syntactical shifts and permutations. One might say that Mullen has crossed the sprung rhythm sonnet form of Gerard Manley Hopkins with the discontinuous, unrhymed free verse form of some walker in the city like Frank O'Hara or Langston Hughes. The poem is essentially a chronicle of someone on the move down a major thoroughfare, calling attention to the sights without editorializing about their status as metaphorical signs of ethnic changes in the West Side.

As always in good sonnets, pleasure-inducing wordplay abounds. Filling the poem with incomplete sentences and fractured enjambments communicates the hurried, moment-by-moment sensations of a mental note taker on the move. "The notes for the poem are the only poem," Adrienne Rich wrote at a point in her career when she was speeding up her lyrics and narratives in the manner of cinema.[39] The first line puts the reader on notice that puzzle solving will be an important constituent of the pleasure derived from tracking this antic picaresque of a poem. The speaker has arrived at LAX, airport code for Los Angeles International Airport. The code word has long been treated as a joke about the laidback character of the city—its lax rules for conduct in places that afford leisurely interludes of long duration. Mullen extends the code word to "laxative" to emphasize the purgative qualities of such casual lifestyles, and more fundamentally the recourse to the restroom at the terminal building after a flight punctuated by frequent hot and cold drinks. "In and out with fries" records one cycle of consumption and purgation, playing off the ubiquitous In-N-Out Burger fast food restaurants headquartered in Irvine and located throughout the southwestern United States. "Fox mauls hill" is a play on the Fox Hills Mall near the terminal, a center for upscale consumption. The building of the mall involved the destruction of a neighborhood and natural space, following a historical pattern of urban development in the city, as we have seen. It's the way of the world, how lovely old trees are winnowed down to toothpicks and chopsticks. The poet notices such signs of transformation—the disappearance of the Studio Drive In Theater is another example—but she does not lament the inevitable; her poetic form messages us that she takes pleasure in the variety of new businesses and new products she notices as she maneuvers her way by means of the Culver City Bus Line #6 green bus north on Sepulveda Boulevard from the airport to her place of employment, the UCLA campus where she picks up a copy of the undergraduate newspaper. One almost expects some line like "with her face on it" as an homage to the clearest model for this kind of peripatetic topographical poem, Frank O'Hara's tribute to Billie Holiday, "The Day Lady Died."

In the pages of *Rainbow Darkness* this seemingly blithe poem serves a polemical purpose by subverting the kind of anguished lyric typified by Wanda Coleman's "Where I Live" and "Clocking Dollars," not to mention the rage of N.W.A. and Ice Cube. Mullen changes the subject in both meanings of that word. She speaks as a professor of literature at one of the city's elite educational institutions, and she praises the plenitude of the contents of the enriched environment that she enumerates with obvious approval: *Botanica*; the Cuban restaurant; the cantina where you can get "five different *mole salsas*" and make contact with Oaxaca; the "pancake palace" that is probably Dinah's Family Restaurant, a mainstay on Sepulveda Boulevard for generations; but for other tastes there's the "veggie burger at Hot Diggity" and a large bag of popcorn as well. Food serves as a sign of what is left out in older poems from South Central, where bars stand in for restaurants. The thematic tilt in the poem toward Latino references reflects the profound demographic changes that have brought Harryette Mullen to Los Angeles from Alabama and Texas, part of the diaspora out of Africa by way of the

South into a multicultural or "rainbow" world that welcomes constant revisitation in poems. If we know the history of the Sepulveda family's hostility to the native peoples in the nineteenth century, a story of the Californios ranchers versus the original Native American tribes on the land, the name of the major thoroughfare takes on a coloring of dramatic irony.

Finally, one feels an enhanced sense of uplift in the poem's closing couplet, a bow toward Shakespearean sonnet structure: "The crazy people on the bus aren't talking to themselves. / They're speaking on their cell phones." When Robert Frost published "The Telephone" in 1916 making use of the new invention as a metaphor for communication with God (he speaks into a flower head), he was registering the need of poets to keep current with technology in order to create new ways of speaking very old sentiments about God, nature, and humanity. A century later the cell phone has become ubiquitous in poems as in real life, and most often with the same intentions as when Frost, Thomas Hardy, T. S. Eliot, William Carlos Williams, Langston Hughes, and other poets imported topical materials into their dramatic lyrics: to highlight the new channels of communication being formed by social media. Mullen's poem seeks to persuade us that we do well to pivot our attention away from what Mike Davis calls the "carceral" or "fortress" sites of warring communities in L.A. to the more joyful nodes of connection and consumption: airports, restaurants, buses, universities, malls, even cell phones. "It's okay," she reassures us. One doesn't want to put too much of a smiley face on this or any of Mullen's poems, but as a bellwether of twenty-first-century hybridity, "#6 Sepulveda," like "Stravinsky in L.A.," seems to mark a turn in the ethnopoetics of Los Angeles.

SIX

Californios, and the Fertile Blood of Poetry

> Yo recuerdo los antepasados muertos.
> Los recuerdos en la sangre,
> la sangre fértil.
>
> —LORNA DEE CERVANTES[1]

I

A logical strategy for this chapter on the ways poets have imagined the Latino presence in Southern California would be to use the foregoing chapter as a template. For ghetto read barrio; for protests against racist victimization against one minority, substitute another minority, brown for black. Lay over Ice Cube's anthem "How to Survive in South Central" with the equally cautionary classic by Cheech and Chong, "Born in East L.A."

> I don't belong here in downtown T.J.
> Cause I was born in East L.A., olé
>
> I crawled under barbed wire, swam across a stream
> Rode in six different trucks packed like a sardine
> Walked all day in the burning sun
> Now I know what it's like to be born to run

There is plenty of truth in such a one-to-one rhetorical structure, as Latino, mainly Mexican-American, authors attest. Important prose texts such as Oscar Zeta Acosta's *The Revolt of the Cockroach People*, Gloria E. Anzaldúa's *Borderlands / La Frontera: The New* Mestiza, Luis J. Rodriguez's *Always Running: La Vida Loca: Gang Days in L.A.*, and Luis Valdez's *Zoot*

Suit, all of them widely studied in schools across the nation, formulate Chicano identity in terms of oppression by a dominant white society. Beginning in the mid-nineteenth century this elite class of white latecomers to the Golden State solidified its power over a subordinate ethnic group and herded it into overcrowded districts, limiting its opportunities not only in real estate but in the councils of civic decision-making as well as entertainment and media venues. George J. Sanchez has told this story to good effect in *Becoming Mexican American: Ethnicity, Culture, and Identity in Chicano Los Angeles 1900–1945*. Another scholarly work focused on literary history is Rafael Perez-Torres's *Movements in Chicano Poetry*. That Latino poetry did and does document the same dynamics as African American poetry, often asserting solidarity with kindred minorities in the ongoing struggle, makes for a neat congruence in extending the formulas and conventions from the previous chapter to this one.

And yet to do so would be to sideline and diminish differences between the two groups that deserve to be highlighted and analyzed. The chief historical difference, of course, is that Southern California once belonged to the territory that the Viceroyalty of New Spain, centered in Mexico City, colonized and developed. These colonizers, who subdued a Native American population and imposed a Spanish Catholic culture on the land, have been known as "Californios" since the 1920s. As the very name El Pueblo de la Reina de Los Angeles suggests—not to mention Santa Monica, San Diego, San Francisco, Santa Barbara, and other sites along El Camino Royal—the mission structure of Hispanic hegemony populated most of California with an identity and language distinct from the ethnic white forces that usurped the land in turn and eventually brought it under the control of the United States government. The canonical poem on the subject is Lorna Dee Cervantes's widely anthologized elegy "Poema para los Californios Muertos" (Poem for Dead Californios). In this melancholy lyric, the poet visits the ruin of a refuge for Mexican citizens and laments, partly in Spanish and partly in English, the dispossession marked by a memorial plaque and by the absence of what had once sustained cultural identity for "ancient Californios." The sentiment is faithful to the spirit of the state's (unofficial) founding text, the novel *Ramona*, by Helen Hunt Jackson, in 1884, which dramatizes the displacement of both Native American and Hispanic American figures (in the form of two lovers) by an irresistible white occupation supported by military force.

Let me further illustrate this historical situation by personal reference. I grew up in Culver City, an enclave of Los Angeles south and west of downtown and east of Venice and Santa Monica. Culver City is most famous as the home of Metro-Goldwyn-Mayer (later, Sony) studios and of the nearby Selznick (later, Desilu) studios—and, further down Washington Boulevard, the Hal Roach studios, now a site for light industrial buildings, including studios providing content for YouTube. The region had formerly been part of the sprawling 14,000-acre domain called Rancho La Ballona claimed by Agustin Machado in the nineteenth century. In the early twentieth century Harry Culver, a real estate developer, engineered a sale of one portion of the Rancho to himself. The new owner changed its identity to a white community with restrictive practices that kept out blacks, browns, and other minorities. My parents had lived in the West Adams district in the mid and late 1940s, and then moved across the redline of La Cienega Boulevard into Culver City. Neither in my elementary school, nor in the city's only junior high school nor in the city's only high school, was there a single black student, and there were very few Latinos. One of the latter was the scion of the Machado family, whose presence at Culver City High School was an eerie reminder of a not so distant past. Had the scenario of local history played out differently, he would have been the Prince of the City.

Mexico was the ghost at the banquet in those years of postwar prosperity. In elementary school we studied its history, especially its missionary activities up and down the coast. We sampled its language and food, performed its dances, fashioned its costumes, and got a glimpse of its art and architecture on field trips to the county museum and other institutions. But after the sixth grade, this attention to the Hispanic past gave way to a nearly exclusive focus on British and American history and civilization. We read *Julius Caesar, Silas Marner,* and *David Copperfield* in our high school literature classes, and spent time with poems like *Elegy in a Country Churchyard* and *The Eve of St. Agnes*. I don't recall reading a single assigned text about Latin America. Mexico ceased to exist in our worldview despite its proximity and the largely invisible population of Chicanos concentrated in eastern parts of Los Angeles we never visited.

With one exception. Tijuana, or T.J., loomed large in the fantasy life of almost every adolescent male and no doubt in the female imagination as well. A few hours drive to the south, Tijuana was a borderland that lured young and old because of its reputation as a city of sin and vice, especially of sexual license. As Las Vegas catered to grown-ups, above all for its gambling, so Tijuana became legendary among teenagers for its whorehouses (one never heard any other term; "brothel" was a word I learned at college), its cantinas with their lewd acts of striptease, its abortion clinics, its easy access to alcohol and drugs including pharmaceuticals illegal in the States, its tuck and roll car upholstery services, and its pornographic comic books and playing cards passed hand to hand in secondary schools by males in that generation. Garrett Hongo recalls in his Los Angeles poem "96 Tears" such a moment: "the time [his friend] Higashi brought in the deck / of Tijuana playing cards to sophomore gym." An excellent portrait of a Los Angeles teen's rite of passage in Tijuana during the 1950s is Leslie Epstein's essay in *The Movie that Changed My Life*. In his case, the movie is a porn flick at a Tijuana whorehouse intended to encourage visitors to sample the merchandise. In addition, Tijuana offered horse races, prize fights, bullfights, cockfights, dogfights. The cockfight scene in Nathanael West's *The Day of the Locust*, organized by Miguel, the charismatic Chicano—he is the one character who successfully seduces the otherwise standoffish Faye Greener—can be read as an introjection of Tijuana into the life and consciousness of the Ivy League–educated protagonist Tod Hackett, who indulges in rape fantasies involving Faye throughout the novel.

Curtis Zahn

TIJUANA

In all that thin, squalid, exploited valley
There exists no security, only the stoic
Freedom of the economically damned, and
Everywhere hangs listlessly the olive-eyed
Color of greasewood smoke. Here, crab-grass
Rebounds under the lifted hooves of melancholy
Cattle, but it's crew-cut, it's sparse, dry
And creamed with dust. And manzanita thinks
Adolescent thoughts about willow, knowing too
The peculiarized smell of corrugated tin
Roofs that defend from rare rain, the radios
Which talk all day long of things
Nobody will be able to buy.
Here they grow soft, small men with musical hearts

And wives gone fat with poverty's diet, and absurd
Dogs that caricature a civilization
Ground thin between two restless nations, and
Slowly pulverized by shock of opposed ideologies.

A wire fence makes it Mexico, but God
Has never been asked. And the vegetation
Does not change its citizenship overnight, nor do
The animals, and even the river
In its winter plumage, traffics casually
Across the International Line, bringing home
The raw sewage deposited there when
Good Neighbors built the fence
And created an incident, and
Caused a city, a roadside beggar whose hat had
Better stay away from his head.
But no, the birds need no passports
And coyotes can cross and re-cross; the
Tourists too. Only the residents are immobilized;
Frozen to the north by
The sprawling verbiage of passport wordage
And turned back south and east by centuries
Of sterile desert, and held to the western
Beaches by the Pacific's restless combers.
Tijuana? One can get into but not out of it
And into it from the whole world
Have come seekers, drifters, escapees;
Wanted men and unwanted women come here
For the final stalemate. Their shoes—
Their city shoes frozen by dust, and
Stomachs bleached by begged tacos shot with horsemeat—
Here to dry up while drinking and stealing
And waiting. Converting their German, French,
English, Chinese into the oiled, grey
Pidgin Spanish of bordertown; to wait
Beside the flagrant streets for new faces
Come to be horrified by sin, and to
Grovel in the spectacle

Of abortion and absorption. And to hear
Lame, warped, U.S. made guitars, chord-wrecked
By Indians too poor to fatten
Their dogs for the eating.[2]

—•—

Curtis Zahn's poem "Tijuana," then, belongs securely within the working mythology and behavioral patterns of the city of Los Angeles. Published in the Autumn 1951 issue of *The California Quarterly*, it was reprinted in *Poets of the Non-Existent City: Los Angeles in the McCarthy Era*, edited by Estelle Gershgoren Novak, an anthology of authors who vied unsuccessfully with East Coast postwar poets to achieve some place in the sun of public attention. As noted in my Introduction, very few of the poems in the anthology are set in Southern California. In retrospect it is arguable that the poets' avoidance of place and local history limited the range of their vision and language. But "Tijuana" is an exception. Essayistic and full of compelling detail, it is arguably the most artful poem in the anthology. Curtis Zahn (1912–90) attended the University of California, Berkeley, and San Francisco State College before World War II; he became a conscientious objector during the war and served a year in a federal penitentiary. He worked for the *San Diego Tribune* for a while, giving him regular access to Tijuana. Later in life he settled in Los Angeles and worked intermittently on the preparation of a collected volume of his poems, which never appeared.[3]

"Tijuana" draws from a long line of Anglophone literary and cinematic treatments of Mexico, almost all of them negative. These texts set in opposition white and Mexican characters and explore how the cross-border contact breeds resentment and brutal violence. They establish the context informing Zahn's reportorial account of a place that deeply unsettled him. D. H. Lawrence's novel *The Plumed Serpent* (1926) and his long story "The Woman Who Rode Away" (1928), for example, examined the primitivism that white women throughout Lawrence's work find appealing, and in the latter case, fatal. In Lawrence's view, and those of his peers, cruelty arising from the poverty of the natives, and from a culturally indulged will to power, made the tribal Mexicans rapacious, predatory, dictatorial in their regional and sexual politics.

These themes appear in another early novel about Mexico, B. Traven's *The Treasure of the Sierra Madre* (1927), faithfully transferred to the screen in 1948. Graham Greene's travel book *The Lawless Roads* (1939), renamed *Another Mexico* in its American edition, along with his novel *The Power and the Glory* (1940), likewise critiqued the banditry and anarchic social dynamics of the country, especially the rural world of villages and small towns. Another classic narrative set in Mexico, and this time in a border town like Tijuana, is Orson Welles's film *Touch of Evil*, though, as Joseph McBride points out, Welles "shot the film in the hellish city of Venice, California." Since the 1950s the most powerful American novels about Mexico are those of Cormac McCarthy, who lived for many years in the border city of El Paso and has demonized Mexico as a world of drug gangs, freelance outlaws, overwhelming violence, and corruption. I need hardly add that in all the works mentioned above, the iniquity of the white characters is the dominant theme in the narrative. Tilted one way or another, the burden of evil actions draws the characters on either side of the border into a shared sinfulness and moral squalor. The prominence of drug running, gang warfare, and undocumented immigration in recent years has guaranteed that films like *Traffic* and *No Country for Old Men*, as well as fiction like T. C. Boyle's *The Tortilla Curtain*, will continue to shape the public imagination for some time to come.

Of American poems about Mexico by canonical white American authors, two are worthy of special note. Archibald MacLeish's book-length narrative *Conquistador* (1932) retells the story of the conquest of the Aztec civilization by Hernán Cortés in the sixteenth century. A Pulitzer Prize–winning volume, though neglected in recent decades, MacLeish's poem drew heavily from the classic account of the conquest by Bernal Díaz del Castillo, a soldier in Cortés's army. A Hollywood film of 1947, *Captain from Castile*, endorses the military venture of Cortés, as portrayed in swaggering manner by Cesar Romero and his second-in-command Tyrone Power. William Carlos Williams had retold the same brutal story in one chapter of *In the American Grain* (1925) titled "The Destruction of Tenochtitlan." Williams's late long poem "The Desert Music" (1954) tells of a visit across the border from El Paso to Ciudad Juárez. Williams focuses intensely and repetitively on an image that has come to be regarded as the dominant icon of the entire poem. Traveling across the bridge into Mexico, he spots "a form . . . / torpid against / the flange of the supporting girder." He sees the same human form, perhaps dead, while returning to El Paso: "an inhuman shapelessness, / knees hugged tight up in the belly // Egg-shaped! // What a place to sleep! / on the International Boundary. Where else / interjurisdictional, not to be disturbed?"

"Tijuana" is the product of firsthand observation but it is also overdetermined by texts like those listed above. Interestingly, though, its one deliberate intertextual reference is to Robert Frost's "Mending Wall"; I refer to the line "Good Neighbors built the fence," which echoes the final line of Frost's narrative of two rural neighbors north of Boston meeting to replace stones and boulders fallen from the wall between them: "Good fences make good neighbors." Frost's line is ironic but that did not stop the U.S. government from borrowing it as a title for its Good Neighbor policy in the 1930s. Zahn no doubt has in mind also the description of the speaker of that line as a "stone savage armed," a moment of demonization that calls our attention to the speaker himself, who clearly is projecting his own hostility upon the laborer on the far side of the wall. Zahn's poem openly includes desperate tourists and asylum seekers from various countries and cultures—"German, French, / English, Chinese"—as complicit with and constitutive of the ambiguous moral practices of the borderland. Tijuana is a hybrid of ethical states of being, a way station for men and women eager to change their status by entering the United States, legally if possible. Tijuana's identity has much to do with its being not-the-U.S., though from the perspective of Los Angeles it is importantly not-Mexico either. It is a liminal public space, "unique in time / Like Athens or Baghdad," as Karl Shapiro writes of Hollywood. In crucial ways, 1950s Tijuana was like Hollywood, a fantasyland where the performance of often taboo spectacles were made available to visitors of all ages.

One hears Shapiro's voice in the opening of Zahn's poem, especially in the formulation, "Here, crab-grass / Rebounds under the lifted hooves of melancholy / Cattle. . . ." and "Here they grow soft, small men with musical hearts." The echo in this reportorial verbal formula, by no means unique to Shapiro, is of lines from "Hollywood": "Here may the tourist . . . Rest from his dream of travels" and "Here all superlatives come true." In both poems hyperbole is the rhetorical trope of choice. In "Tijuana" the sense of deprivation is absolute: "There exists no security," "the residents are immobilized," the desert is "sterile," the waves are "restless," the streets are "flagrant." All the "new faces / Come to be horrified by sin, and to / Grovel in the spectacle / Of abortion and absorption." The ending combines deprivation and depravity: "Indians [are] too poor to fatten / Their dogs for the eating." As a poem of place, "Tijuana" achieves its effects by its tone of disgust, its choice of unsavory details and downward comparisons. Tijuana emerges as the bad suburb, cursed by God and man ("economically damned") in its history, geography, and social structure. This is not the land of opportunity, but of *frustrated* opportunity, of oppressive greasewood odors like the stench of Hell, of a river carrying nothing but the "raw sewage" of humanity, and of men and dogs "that caricature a civilization."

(One might expect a period after "civilization" at the end of the first strophe. But Zahn continually writes beyond the ending, intensifying the critique of this forlorn place. A clause of ambiguous reference follows the word "civilization":

> Ground thin between two restless nations, and
> Slowly pulverized by shock of opposed ideologies.

Clearly "civilization" is the subject of that clause, yet the "soft, small men," "Wives gone fat with poverty's diet," and even the "absurd / Dogs" also are being "ground thin" syntactically by the two nations, and "pulverized" like so much processed meat. Those dogs return in the poem's last line as figures of all victims, as denatured as the "Pidgin Spanish" exchanged in the marketplace.)

As we have seen, writers about Los Angeles divest the city in many ways of its pretensions to civilization. The greasepaint glamour of Hollywood, the borrowed pomp of Venice, the naive triumphalism announced by the construction of Autopia, the enforcement of illegitimate white power against South Central, these are obvious and easy targets for the moral indignation of poets and fiction writers alike. "Tijuana" is something different. It denounces the world on the other side of the wire fence, a world all too vulnerable to the wit and outraged tone that makes the poem so vivid and memorable. Every one of the abundant adjectives intensifies the degradation of this grotesque landscape. "Tijuana" exploits the "exploited" without registering a consciousness of piling it on. It's a poem that could not be written as it now exists if it sought publication today. Yet it would be a mistake to exercise political correctness in our judgment, especially if we recognize "Tijuana" as an expression of moral anguish in the Baudelaire and Eliot tradition. How can such a "bordertown" be allowed to exist? is the cry from this poet, who walked those streets and reported in newspapers about social evils that needed correction. And people who remember Tijuana from the 1950s, when this poem was written, might claim that it does not do justice to the negative aspects of that locale. It does not speak directly of prostitution, for example. To the extent that the poem demonizes the gateway from Mexico into the U.S., and by extension the Latinos (and not just Latinos) who pass through it into El Norte, it contributes to the painfully vexed assessment of the Latino presence in Southern California. The poem is an ugly gauntlet thrown down before citizens of the U.S. and Mexico alike, challenging readers to make reforms and to reconceive the cities and civilization generated from this alpha site and "final stalemate" that Los Angeles cannot disown.

Yet recent scholarship about Tijuana has emphasized not the contrast of Tijuana and Los Angeles but their sibling identity. Especially as immigration has altered the demographics of polynuclear Southern California in general, Los Angeles itself is more and more described as precisely the kind of fraught crossroads for a multinational and polyglot population inscribed in Zahn's troubled poem. "Los Angeles has been a border city since its founding," Greg Hise asserts. "It has been and remains a site where people, artifacts, and ideas from around the globe converge, a place where residents and newcomers, Californios and Yankees, Chinese and Molokans, African Americans and Filipinos created a hybrid or metis culture and city."[4] Tijuana may be conceived as a shadow self of Los Angeles, an alterity that directs attention to the speaker's implied critique of his own privileged prospect as a tourist crossing the line to the forlorn city beyond the border. Those border crossings are now described by scholars not as Jekyll and Hyde transgressions into the dark side, but reciprocal exchanges of cultural influences that sponsored some of the dominant cultural texts of the twentieth century and beyond. Tijuana had become after World War I a center for Los Angeles's black music culture. "If LA was the black music Mecca of the West, then Tijuana was its southern Medina," Josh Kun declares.[5] Tijuana, according to recent studies summarized by Kun, had become so hospitable to aggrieved artists from South Central that Los Angeles took on the character of a suburb and mirror image of Tijuana. Tijuana was a place of "progressive racial beliefs" not just a refuge for drinkers during Prohibition and a resort city for boxing and horse-racing enthusiasts. The poetry of that association of oppressed minorities exists in the song lyrics carried between the two regions by performers like Jelly Roll Morton, who composed popular tunes at his post in Tijuana's popular Kansas City Bar.

From the Mexican perspective on nineteenth- and twentieth-century history, the crossing of the borderland is a modern version of the movement in some ancient texts toward the Promised Land, a journey perfectly consonant with white America's most cherished myth of nationhood. The literature of this crossing to El Norte is, or could be, comparable to the stirring narratives of the Middle Passage and the Great Migration in the African American canon. David Rieff estimates it "as close to epics as the modern world has seen, the stuff of legend and myth."[6] But white authors of Zahn's generation do not and cannot see it that way, sympathetic as they usually are to the anguish of immigrants. Zahn's resistance to the transgression—in the neutral sense of the word—across an international boundary takes the form of a diction steeped in the sordid history of Mexico-U.S. relations, and to the necessarily degraded faces and destinies of newcomers in the land. (As John Steinbeck had depicted in *The Grapes of Wrath* the revulsion extends to white migrants from the American heartland.) By stigmatizing a distressed place and imagining it as a tainted inferno of a fallen world, Zahn cannot help but throw suspicion onto ethnic peoples eager to transfer nationalities for the sake of a better future. His poem challenges revisionist narratives of Mexican-American relations and, more to our purposes, sets difficult terms for poems coming in its wake.

II

The borderland is a place, a location, and it is also a state of consciousness, a condition of "life on the hyphen" in the phrase popularized by Gustavo Pérez Firmat.[7] Mexican-American, Cuban-American, Hispanic-American, these are the bifurcations that define and confuse identities within the Spanish-language community as well as between language groups. *De dónde eres*—"Where you from?" —is the common salutation when Latinos encounter each other. It is also the title of Gina Valdés's poem that enacts the divided self of an enforced bilingualism.

Gina Valdes

WHERE YOU FROM?

Soy de aquí
y soy de allá
from here
and from there

born in L.A.
del otro lado
y de éste
crecí en L.A.
y en Ensenada
my mouth
still tastes
of naranjas
con chile
soy del sur
y del norte
crecí zurda
y norteada
cruzando fron
teras crossing
San Andreas
tartamuda
y mareada
where you from?
soy de aquí
y soy de allá
I didn't build
this border
that halts me
the word fron
tera splits
on my tongue[8]

—•—

As with Lorna Dee Cervantes's poem quoted at the head of this chapter, this one deliberately provokes English-only readers, who may be tempted to turn the page wherever it appears in order to escape the implied critique of their linguistic limitations. The effect is similar to encountering words and phrases in a variety of languages in the modernist poetry of Pound, Eliot, and William Carlos Williams. If the reader complains, "it's not fair to publish a poem using language I can't understand," the poet's riposte is likely to be, "if you're not educated enough to read poetry as cosmopolitan as mine, go elsewhere." As poetry, like all communication, becomes increasingly globalist, increasingly multicultural and multilingual, poems like this one will certainly become more standard, more widely read and understood, more often sites of debate over the poetics of the twenty-first century.

The very short lines of Valdés's poem call attention to themselves as marks or signs of opposition in the ethnography of the poet's homeland(s). She answers the question, "Where you from" by splitting her answer into a balance of contraries, "Soy de aquí / y soy de allá." The speaker grew up (crecí) both in Los Angeles and in Ensenada, a few miles south of Tijuana in a Mexican state tellingly named Baja California. Her identity breaks across the border ("frontera") between the two countries with their different majority languages. On two occasions the word "frontera" is broken across two lines to enact her divided consciousness. Commentary about the poem necessarily falters in treating the matter of *voice*. Voice derives from the confident assumption of identity, all the more so when the identity is a masked one. Once the continuity of linguistic tradition is broken into languages set in uncertain relation, the reader feels the dissonance of the poet's internal disturbance. Likewise, we infer, the personality of the city, of Los Angeles specifically, must be oppositional, conflictual, lacking the customary confidence of designated spokespersons who are agents of continuity within the urban milieu.

The internalized border is both like and unlike the situation faced by a bicultural and bilingual person from any country in the world. As with the split between Yiddish and English in my own family background—the grandparents speaking mainly Yiddish and a little English, and the grandchildren speaking English and a little Yiddish—two kinds of experience are undergone, or in Valdés's term *tasted,* in the everyday movement between language groups. Such versatility is a reason for satisfaction and an origin of creative thinking. But Yiddish is not a nationality; at most it's a neighborhood in numerous foreign lands remote from the U.S. Mexico is nearby, a stone's throw from San Diego and El Paso. Language can be a barrier, a force of contention, a carrier of prejudice. An English-only reader occupies the sense of split identity of the Chicana author during the time he or she reads this poem. For the duration of traversing its linguistic fissures, one feels as if walking on the fault summoned by the poem's reference to San Andreas, watching two bordering but distinguishable worlds trembling at the verge of irreconcilable division.

Gary Soto

GOOD BUY IN BEVERLY HILLS

My realtor friend says, The house is haunted.
The owner died in a hot tub, his wife in a lounge chair.
The middle child collapsed with his head in the stove.
And the dog, a bothersome yakker poisoned one night,
Is buried in the yard. The yard is overgrown with weeds
And berry bushes. Crickets and mosquitoes thrive,
And turd-colored toads multiply daily by fours and fives.
I flick on the light switch in the den
And the darkness lays crumbled like a body on the floor.
The room is airless. Dust doesn't climb more than an inch before it
falls.
What's that? I ask of the bolts on the wall. My realtor friend smirks.
For your pleasure, he says, and flicks an invisible whip. I picture
A portly man in a leather thong, flinching before the whacking begins,
His mouth terrorized with three shades of lipstick.
His cock is holstered in a leather pouch.
Jesus, I say, and I ask, So this is Beverly Hills?
My friend smiles and shows me the master bedroom,
Where, he says, the dead circulate and knock in the walls.
I picture the dead with their dead pooch. They ask repeatedly,
Who did this to us, Fluffy? They're sitting on the bed's edge,
The husband and wife, the son with his lungs basted with gas.
The dead go away, come back, go away with nothing to report.
How much for this place? I ask my realtor friend,
Who licks a thumb and flips through his clipboard.
With so many dead, with these spirits weeping at night,
A pretty penny. A high for the producer, the director,
A high for the once-pretty faces with everything,
The car, the ski rack on the car, three homes in two countries,
Everything except talent and a place inside them for a soul.[9]

—•—

Turnabout is fair play. If Tijuana is the Medusa head that Latino poets have turned away from in their assimilation to the barrios and non-barrio spaces of Southern California, so are those spaces, many of them elite and prosperous, fair game for scrutiny and satire by the Californios who recognize decadence when they see it. Los Angeles invites the debridement of moral correction, as we have seen. More often than not it depends upon its immigrants and visitors to lay bare its corruptions by the power of suasive rhetoric. I choose to read Gary Soto's poem "Good Buy in Beverly Hills," from *One Kind of Faith* (2003), as one such attempt at cultural critique. Soto is arguably the best-known Chicano poet in California. His debut volume, *The Elements of San Joaquin* (1977), explored in a straightforward lyric voice the territory of the Great Central Valley. His was and is a communitarian poetry, with sensitive portraits of ordinary people living in mainly agricultural locations and engaging in everyday activities raised to importance by Soto's sympathetic gaze. He has achieved his reputation not by formal innovations but by the sharpness of detail and no-word-wasted economy of his dramatic lyrics. Manual labor is a central concern in his poems, as it is not in so much of contemporary poetry. His faithfulness to milieu, and to the mainly congenial spirits in the neighborhoods of his farming community, has made him a moral center in California (and national) poetry, a person with believable judgments and a code that is undismayed by bad behavior that he records faithfully and sometimes doggedly but most often with good humor. "Soto writes with a pure sweetness free of sentimentality that is almost extraordinary in modern American poetry," remarks Andrew Hudgins on the back cover of Soto's *New and Selected Poems* (1995).

"Good Buy in Beverly Hills" is one of Soto's best poems set outside the boundaries of his northern California homeland. Because the first-person narrator is a character in the poem, it is necessary to refer to "the speaker" rather than name the author in discussing the poem. Otherwise we might get distracted by wondering why Gary Soto is looking to buy a house in one of the wealthiest sections of Los Angeles, a white enclave populated by professionals who would consort ill with the Soto we know from his straight-talking working-class poems of the previous thirty years. The persona who speaks the poem has undertaken a by-now-familiar journey from some distant place and—to the extent that he trails associations with the pastoral world of the Central Valley—from some earlier and simpler time in the American past. Soto does not paint the speaker as a mysterious stranger, however; it is the former inhabitants of the house he inspects who are revealed as strange, and strange in a way that belongs to the fallen fortunes of an elite community. A poet like Luis J. Rodríguez could not write a satire like this—he could not even feign a tone of voice in which to utter "So this is Beverly Hills." (The tone is that of "I'm shocked, *shocked*. . ." but Rodríguez is unshockable.) The bard of Fresno and points north, however, can negotiate this comic scene with pitch-perfect aplomb.

The scene is one of what Emily Dickinson called "sumptuous destitution." The house is fancy and very expensive even with its sordid reputation and reputed ghosts. By the end of the poem we understand how soulless and perverted its former occupants had been. "Perverted" is the precise word, for the speaker shows his dismay at the realtor's revelation of how the "master" of the house, in his airless den, turned away from nature as it is customarily understood in order to revel in sadomasochistic rites involving leather whips and a "leather thong." The natural world around this man seems to have been contaminated by his spirit, as in a tale by Nathaniel Hawthorne. Weeds, mosquitoes, "turd-colored toads" surround the house; one supposes that the "berry bushes" produce inedible and semi-poisonous berries. The property is a haunted waste land, where the domestic supports of life—hot tub, lounge chair, stove—are the agencies for death of a kind that makes the reader suspicious. Was there criminal intervention here, as with the poisoned dog? Had this family made itself "bothersome" to the wrong people? We know only that these dead cannot lie still; perhaps they have crimes to expiate beyond the master's taste for corporal punishment. How can the earth receive a man whose mouth has been "terrorized" with "three shades of lipstick" and his cock "holstered in a leather pouch"? (These two lines are placed at the exact center of the poem.) And who would wish to cross the sill of a house with such memories?

Soto is having fun with the sounds as well as the images. "Pooch" chimes with "pouch"; the "flick" of the whip touches the "flinching" man in the next line, and the "flip" of the realtor's "clipboard" resolves the worth of the property; "basted with gas" and "pretty penny" join other instances of soundplay to give the poem an antic as well as a sardonic character. But there is nothing genial about the final lines, which are corrosive and moralistic, bringing the poem into a sibling relation with Curtis Zahn's climactic take on Tijuana. The speaker is informed that though he might expect the price to be low because all three of the residents died on the property, and because "these spirits" weep at night according to our expectations for unhappy ghosts, the house is expensive because previous occupants have included a producer, a director, and "once-pretty faces"—presumably actresses. The price is high because the dead predecessors had the signature fixtures of an enviable American life: "The car, the ski rack on the car, three homes in two countries, / Everything except talent and a place inside them for a soul." Location, location, location. Beverly Hills is the most prestigious address in Los Angeles. It has instant recognition value among filmgoers across the country (*Beverly Hillbillies, Beverly Hills Cop, Down and Out in Beverly Hills*), as well as fans of the popular TV series *Beverly Hills 90210*. What would any follower of the American Dream pay for such an enviable celebrity address? And what does that say about their values?

The title puns on the terms "good buy" and "goodbye" to underline the dark humor of real estate transfers: one family's goodbye is another's good buy. The potential buyer has no trouble imagining the depraved scenes of the past. "I picture" them, he says twice, and perhaps he overstates them because he too has a lurid imagination, giving the dead producer "three shades of lipstick" to enhance the color scheme of the whole composition. And for more effect he imagines the people turning to the dog for answers to their agonized relation to their bodies. Beyond the essentially comic scene we might hear echoes of other titles with the resonant word "goodbye": *Goodbye to All That* (Robert Graves), *Goodbye to Berlin* (Christopher Isherwood), *Goodbye, Columbus* (Philip Roth), *The Long Goodbye* (Raymond Chandler, and also *Farewell My Lovely*). What is left behind, or "kissed off" in the fine idiom, is an entire way of life, often appalling, sometimes pathetic, but always emotionally troubling, returning with the libidinal energy of the repressed as ghostlike presences. At the furthest edges of meaning, this haunted house contains the tormented and secretive libertinism of decadent Los Angeles. It is a narrative illustrating how pleasure, death, and money form their various combinations in a privileged part of the world. The poem inverts the critique of Mexico in the work of writers like D. H. Lawrence, Graham Greene, B. Traven, and Cormac McCarthy.

The dark underside of life in this famed Los Angeles community is irremediably vile, perhaps made more vile by the perpetrators' wealth. We sense an overwhelming ennui at the center of this life, something alien not just to San Joaquin Valley but to our sense of the good life in the good place, the utopia formed according to our desire for virtue, moderation, simplicity, and a dependable happiness. That violated "hope of heaven"—to cite the title of John O'Hara's 1938 novel about Los Angeles—permeates many exposés of the city, as we have seen. The situation described by Soto is reminiscent of a scene in Joan Didion's novel *Play It As It Lays,* in which Maria Wyeth, a small-town girl (not even a town but a single street), has come to Los Angeles and fallen into a degenerate lifestyle with her director husband and his tormented friends, the homosexual producer BZ and his wife Helene:

> "I can't take this, Helene." BZ was wearing tinted glasses and for the first time Maria noticed a sag beneath his eyes. "If you can't deal with the morning, get out of the game. You've been around a long time, you know what it is, it's play-or-pay."
>
> "Why don't you go tell that to Carlotta [BZ's wealthy mother]," Helene whispered.
>
> Maria closed her eyes at the instant BZ's hand hit Helene's face. "Stop it," she screamed.
>
> BZ looked at Maria and laughed. "You weren't talking that way last night," he said. (164)

Last night's orgy, fueled undoubtedly by the cocaine all the characters partake of constantly, is emblematic of white mischief far from the barrio. Latinos don't exist in Didion's rarefied world; their resentment has no voice or presence. And of course there is no suggestion that the first-person speaker in Soto's poem is Latino. The poem has been scrubbed clean of ethnic markings. If there were such markings we would be tempted to read the poem as an allegory of reterritorialization, of Reconquista, the taking back of real estate misused by unworthy Yankees and its return to the former owners, the Californios.

III

Latino poetry is filled—how could it not be?—with *ressentiment,* a term popular in political theory that means, or includes, "an oppressive awareness of the futility of trying to improve one's status in life or in society." It is a fancy term for "class resentment," for the sense of being exploited by those who have usurped one's heritage as a human being and profited unjustly by one's labor. *Ressentiment* divides the world into geographical locales, especially in urban poetry. The upper-class estate Soto presents in "Good Buy in Beverly Hills," with its dungeon of secret vices and its presumed emptiness much of the year, being one of "three homes in two countries," is emblematic of genteel corruption among the wealthy. An obvious geographical contrast would be the fields and farms of San Joaquin, or the cannery rows and kindred work spaces of northern California. A more generalized space would be the factories in which Latinos, often lacking papers to prove they are in the country legally, work for sub-minimum wages. Soto's comic poem "Mexicans Begin Jogging" plays out a scene of such a factory being raided by La Migra, the Border Patrol, and the boss waving at him to run:

> "Over the fence, Soto," he shouted,
> And I shouted that I was American.
> "No time for lies," he said . . .

It's significant that Soto uses his own name in this anxiety dream of a poem. It is a confession of his secret shame and sense of transgression in simply being different. He knows that California has a history of Relocation Centers and bigotry toward the "wetbacks" and racially suspect. He begins running, or "jogging," that is, pretending to be joining his superiors in recreation rather than fleeing the prison or exile that awaits those who fail to dissemble successfully.

> What could I do but yell *vivas*
> To baseball, milkshakes, and those sociologists
> Who would clock me
> As I jog into the next century
> On the power of a great, silly grin?

According to the poem, identity politics mandates that no Latino genuinely feels "American"; they live forever with the dread of having their ethnic and national origins revealed and punished. "Soto" carries a psychic message into our century, to alert all citizens of the divide between not just haves and have-nots—for a significant percentage of Latinos are prosperous—but between those who wear the mantle of authenticity and those who fear in the depth of their souls that they are and will always be strangers, their presence contingent on the permission of their elite co-occupiers of the land to maintain lawful residence. An ingratiating grin is the politic alternative to a raised fist.

Jimmy Santiago Baca

THESE HANDS

These hands that now sign
through cell bars
to my lover below on the street,
        built your city—
        they shovel sand in wheelbarrows,
        mix the mortar, set the bricks,
        cook your food, pick the vegetables,
        hoe the rows,
        serve the food, iron your clothes,
        carry your infants,
        tutor your teenagers,
and then we are told to leave, get out of sight,
we don't want to see you.
        Until, there is more work to do—
        and these hands,
        still flashing signs through the cell bars
        polish your luxury cars,
        weed your gardens,
        till your soil,
        construct your buildings,
        your offices, wash the windows,
        vacuum, make your furniture,
        wash and dry your clothes,
        spoon feed your ailing parents,
        shop for groceries for you,
and then you tell us we don't belong,
we are the reason for your faltering bank accounts,
we are taking your jobs away.
And then at dawn,
as our hands sign our dreams of a better life
through cell bars to our wives and children on the street,
the sun rises over the smoggy ruins of L.A.
        the glittering sodom-stroking city,

and these hands hose down your sidewalks we laid,
empty the trash you made,
clean up your mess after cocktail parties,
cater to your lavish lifestyle,
dye your graying hair,
trim your cracked cuticles,
make you look younger,
give you the easy life, we do your work,
take your sins,
heft your wrongs on us,
pray for you,
worry about you,
and then we're told to get out, don't be seen,
and cops prowl the streets with clubs and guns
raking us in to jails
because we're told we are to blame for all your problems.
Beware of your hypocrisy,
these hands will turn on you.[10]

—•—

Prison is the ultimate locale of captivity in the poetry of *ressentiment*. In Latino narratives jail time is like the visit to the underworld in the classical epic. These contemporary versions of Hades are moments of death-in-life, of protracted isolation and growing bitterness. Jimmy Santiago Baca (born 1952) spent five years in prison for drug possession, and wrote his first poems during that experience. Not all of his poems about incarceration are spoken in his own voice, and "These Hands" may be said to be written in the collective voice of "The Latino" in the manner of Langston Hughes's "The Negro Speaks of Rivers." Like the article "the," which implies a universal experience of the race, "These" hands record the protest of an entire ethnicity. As with so many poems written in Los Angeles "These Hands" has an absolute clarity, in its syntax and diction, and in its thematic statement. Commentary hardly seems necessary, but precisely because it expresses so vividly and persuasively a vision of exploitation central to Latino life in the barrio and mixed neighborhoods, it deserves extended notice as well as praise for its overall structure and grace notes.

"These hands" (later "our hands") serve as title and first words of the poem, before the indented section supplies the predicate and fulfilling information extending the emblematic value of the hands. The hands "sign" as a mute person would depend on sign language or as a chimpanzee would communicate with its trainer. The image is a resonant one in literature and narrative generally: the "lover" on the street gazes upward for a glimpse of some beloved figure in a poignant vignette of emotional and physical estrangement. But "these hands" have more than this visual function; they make a political point when they are joined grammatically to a line like "built your city" and the building is further amplified in the lines that follow, all using the indented left margin. Many poets let their lines move around on the field of the page for particular effects, or no effect but the novelty of breaking the tyranny of the left margin. In Baca's poem the indented material, which keeps to the new margin, is a catalogue of the fundamental experience of Latino laborers who sustain the civilized dynamics of a city that neglects or disdains the benefits of working-class toil. The synecdoche of hands recalls the *bracero* or "strong-arm" program begun during World War II, when the U.S. and Mexican governments contracted to import workers from south of the border to aid in manufacturing and, especially, agricultural labor. When the poem returns to the far left margin, the "you" figures, who seem to be directly addressed by the poet, have their say, in indirect discourse, and it's consistently an ungrateful and narrow-minded sentiment of resentment for the presence of a sub-class that should be appreciated, if there were perfect or even reasonable justice in the world.

In Curtis Zahn's poem visitors to Tijuana are "horrified by sin," and yet they enjoy the benefits of being serviced by the hungry population of desperately poor Mexicans. Likewise, the middle and upper classes of Los Angles depend upon the services rendered by Latinos who are both an essential and reviled part of the urban mix. Immigrants are told "you don't belong," and even while they carry out all the tasks of everyday life, even "spoon feed your ailing parents," the paymasters are busy figuring out how to deport them back to their Spanish-speaking homelands. Indeed, the *quantity* of jobs undertaken by these hands is evidence of the irrefutability of the basic argument. The poem is a timely intervention, to use the common idiom for political verse, in a national debate raging throughout the country. Most readers who disagree with the moralistic tone of the poem will not consider theirs a "lavish lifestyle" or an "easy life," but the weight of all those enumerated jobs redefines what work is, whether it is weeding the garden or praying for employers who fall ill.

We "heft your wrongs on us," the speaker declares. An ugly saying about Tijuana in my youth was that "the Mexicans suck the money from us, and we suck the self-respect from them." By adopting the Christian perspective of listing how Latinos take the society's sins upon themselves, Baca is trying to reveal to the unwitting how from a point of view both humane and spiritual—indeed, divine—the money earned in lowly service is redemptive for the elite of whatever ethnic identity. Latinos "clean up your mess" and not just after cocktail parties. Rightly seen, the humble work performed by the labor pool is a counterpoint to the wasteful play of those who have made of their rich neighborhoods a version of Tijuana, a site of fallen nature. "The smoggy ruins of L.A.," too, is a God-forsaken "glittering sodom-stroking city."

If so, then the prophetic tone of voice, muted somewhat in the body of the poem, emerges logically in the final couplet:

> Beware of your hypocrisy,
> these hands will turn on you.

Language here fails the poet. The poem does not need to wag a finger in the reader's face, having demonstrated the structure of hypocrisy plain as plain can be. The shock word "Beware," especially, has a genealogy perilous for the contemporary poet. Coleridge could get away with a legitimate prophetic tone in "Kubla Khan" when he foresees a readership susceptible to the divinely inspired poet's enchantment: "And all should cry, Beware! Beware! / His flashing eyes, his floating hair!" Lewis Carroll would parody these Romantic adjurations in "Jabberwocky": "Beware the Jabberwock, my son! . . . Beware the Jubjub bird . . ." And Sylvia Plath, likewise, has her tongue firmly in cheek when she intones at the conclusion of "Lady Lazarus" the mock-incantation

> Herr God, Herr Lucifer,
> Beware
> Beware.
>
> Out of the ash
> I rise with my red hair
> And I eat men like air.

In a poem of such patient detail, Baca's threat that hands "will turn on you" is vague to the point of being evasive. Is it actual violence in the form of riots he has in mind? Does he intend to breathe spirit into a workers' revolt that would reconquer the land formerly settled by Californios and "eat men like air"? Is he speaking as a prophet of Aztlan, the dreamed-of kingdom of Latino dominance in Southwest U.S.? If he is to utter the loaded word "Beware" he is obligated to envision the future with more specificity, or the command rings hollow.

IV

Richard Garcia

VERNON

Vernon of brick smokestacks, of circuitous
slaughter houses, of meat packing, of heavy
and light industry, of wrong exit.
Vernon, where I found myself not
on the way to the airport.
Vernon, where the ribbon of concrete
that resembled the freeway entrance
was just the skeleton of a Roman aqueduct.
Vernon, where I slammed on my brakes,
effectively trapping the only pedestrian
in Vernon against a bridge railing.
"Do you know the way to the airport?" I said.
"Do you know the way to the airport?" he said,
apparently frightened into echolalia.
"No, but I do know the acrid smell of fear,"
I replied, as I sped off while watching him
mouth my words in the rearview mirror.
I thought of the murdered convict stuffed
into a fifty-gallon drum and shipped via UPS
to an animal rendering plant in Vernon.

VERNON, I cried out as I sped between warehouses
and self-storage facilities, as my wife's plane
flashed Fasten Seat Belts and flight attendants
were making sure all seats were in an upright position,
trays latched back, GOD HELP ME, I'M IN VERNON.
Vernon, a painting by de Chirico: a solitary tower,
an archway, shadows leaning against pylons,
a plaster face reflecting sunlight from the bottom
of a well representing an abyss of despair.
Vernon, where I prayed my wife's plane would be late,
that she would step carefully from the hatch
through the rubbery mouth of a landing dock,
prepared to apologize for my long wait
and never know that I too had come vast distances
and emerged through a tunnel, had been face to face
with Vernon, my own private Vernon,
Vernon of no entrance, no exit, closed ramp,
under construction, detour, go back, severe tire damage.[11]

—•—

As downtown Los Angeles increasingly morphed into a Latino city, its white citizens abandoning districts like Boyle Heights and gravitating to suburban or "edge" communities at some distance from the Civic Center and East L.A., poets of Latino, mainly Mexican, descent could be expected to speak with more confidence not as subordinate figures in the cityscape but as the heirs to an established metropolitan culture, including its wary or disdainful attitudes toward antisocial transgressors in their midst. The perspective of many Latino poets on the twenty-first-century city is justifiably proprietary, more like Gary Soto's than Jimmy Santiago Baca's. The privileges of a newly assumed status, as authors and citizens, are varied, but humor is certainly a part of many poets' strategy. Richard Garcia's "Vernon" has become a regional favorite, precisely because its antic contents make it perfect for oral performance and classroom study, guaranteed to appeal to high school and college students wary of page poetry. Its versification offers no superficial difficulties and its thematic texture does not intimidate readers who appreciate its attitude even if they don't catch the kind of intertextual references

I will be noting as I read through what is surely the only poem in existence about this locality off the beaten track of daily life for almost all Angelenos. As with Gary Soto's poem on Beverly Hills, this one sits uneasily in an essay about mainly Chicano verse. I will argue, however, that it is a quintessential document of the new Latino poetics.

Until a full-scale political scandal involving Vernon and its neighbor city Bell erupted into view throughout the country in 2011, Garcia's comic tale of some hapless speaker finding himself lost in Vernon depended for its success on nobody knowing much, or anything, about a place so vehemently derided. The poem was an inside joke directed mainly at residents of East L.A., as well as motorists from around the county who had been warned away from Vernon for years. Probably British readers felt the same sense of *Schadenfreude* reading John Betjeman's tirade against the factory town of Slough in 1937, which begins, "Come, friendly bombs, and fall on Slough! / It isn't fit for humans now." (Betjeman and his heirs apologized for the poem in later years when faced with an outraged population of real citizens.) Betjeman became infatuated with the notion of Slough as a symbolic place, a site of evil tendencies in Britain's modern culture. He was no doubt thinking of William Blake's crusade against the "dark Satanic mills" erected throughout England during the Industrial Revolution. Blake's animus shows up in at least one masterpiece of American poetry, Allen Ginsberg's "Howl," in the obsessively repeated word "Moloch" that flavors the second part of the poem:

> Moloch whose mind is pure machinery! Moloch whose blood is running money! Moloch whose fingers are ten armies! Moloch whose breast is a cannibal dynamo!

The repetition of "Vernon" as a leitmotif in Garcia's poem, both in lower and upper case, hammers into the reader's consciousness that the capitalist nightmare of the twenty-first century, the heart of darkness in Greater Los Angeles, can be imagined as this factory city five miles south of downtown but strictly nowhere in the everyday public lexicon.

When Vernon became a touchstone for political corruption in 2011 the civic furor drew attention to the fact that the "scandal-tainted city," as it came to be called, contained almost exclusively a vast number of meatpacking plants, warehouses, slaughterhouses, seafood-processing facilities, and metalworking businesses. Its residential population was minuscule, boasting only about 100 residents sprinkled among 1,800 businesses. Los Angeles County Supervisor for the First Ward, Gloria Molina, said of Vernon, "It is a company town masquerading as a city."[12] Vernon is part of the industrial capital of Southern California, which includes Watts, Compton, Carson, Lynwood, South Gate, City of Industry, and Huntington Park. The scale of corruption revealed in the investigation staggered even the most jaded crime reporters and forever fixed the identity of Vernon as an exploitative and venal place on the map, a rendering plant more than a community of souls, a "cannibal dynamo" in Ginsberg's phrase.

When the speaker of Garcia's poem finds himself taking the "wrong exit" from the freeway he realizes with horror that he has blundered into the Great Wrong Place in Southern California. The situation recalls the opening chapters of Tom Wolfe's novel *The Bonfire of the Vanities*, when the protagonist takes a wrong turn in the Bronx and drives into a mess of racial and legal trouble. Garcia, in what sounds like an autobiographical narrative, pointedly does not enter into a Third World barrio or ghetto. He encounters a built environment of "brick smokestacks" and roads like "the skeleton of a Roman aqueduct." The affect of this territory reminds him of "a painting by de Chirico." With his mind's eye fixed on the freeway and the airliner bringing his wife safely home, he has unwittingly crashed across the temporal border into a cityscape of dreamlike premodern structures and early modernist re-creations of ghost cities abandoned by their former workers, "a solitary tower, / an archway, shadows leaning against pylons." (The tower and shadows suggest Giorgio de Chirico's most famous work, *Nostalgia of the Infinite*, circa 1912.) He has broken through to the obverse image of Los Angeles as Shangri-La, the mortmain of a desolate cultural past occupied by timeworn architectural forms, bereft of human life. When he meets "the only pedestrian / in Vernon" he gets no directions but only the apprehension of fear still discernible as he drives away and watches the receding figure in his rearview mirror. The pedestrian is what the speaker would have become if he lived in Vernon, an alien victim of "my own private Vernon," from which there is "no exit," no easy passage into localities still possessed by the upwardly mobile version of the American Dream.

Is there a poet who has not written a poem something like this one, in which he or she crosses a boundary line into a demonized suburb of civilized life and feels in their throat a scream akin to that of Edvard Munch's iconic figure lost in the "abyss of despair"? For Curtis Zahn this moment came in Tijuana. Gary Soto's persona encountered the ghosts of former oppressors in the aristocratic demesne of Beverly Hills. Jimmy Santiago Baca reported on the injustices of modern Los Angeles from the vantage of a jail cell. Like Soto and Baca, Garcia turns the tables on Zahn, finding in the dark world of white-owned and white-operated Vernon an extremity matching that of Tijuana. (The demographics of Vernon show that residents identified themselves in 2011 as 98 percent white and 43 percent Latino.) Vernon becomes the caricature image of the Latino poet's fear; it is the antiworld of the sterile past navigated by his ethnic clan, ever present as a trap to reclaim and imprison him in an ultra-proletarian existence. "Vernon" presides in the imagination of the multiethnic community of poets and readers in Los Angeles because it testifies to their anxieties about immigration, assimilation, and degradation, in their separate selves, in their city, and in their nation.

"Vernon" belongs to a genre that might be called the "lost in America poem," by no means limited to authors of hyphenated or bifurcated identity. The speaker finds himself or herself in a "labyrinth" or "maze," almost always urban and dominated by fences and massive constructed forms prompting anxiety, fear, and outrage. Gina Valdés traces the malaise back to the first fraught entrance into the U.S.: "The Border / a wall of barbed lies, / a chain of sighs, a heart / pounding, an old wound."[13] Subways sponsor such emotions, as do massive office buildings, factories, prisons and other carceral institutions. In "Heart of Hunger," Martín Espada tracks a Latino's frightened progress from the borderland through a bus station, gas station toilets, into "the towering white clouds of cities": assembly lines, sweatshops, steel mills, and finally "city jails."[14] "Under L.A. International Airport," by Simon J. Ortiz is another such poem. The Native American speaker finds himself staggering from tunnel to tunnel, confused by the oppressive presences of "jet drones, bland faces, TV consoles" and much more, until he doubts his identity as an American and even as a human being.[15] Likewise Luis J. Rodríguez describes the clamor of work in a Los Angeles foundry: "The blast furnace bellows out a merciless melody / as molten metal runs down your back / as assembly lines continue rumbling / into your brain, into forever, / while rolls of pipes crash onto brick floors."[16] Judy Lucero, who signed her poems with her prison identification number rather than her name, wrote wrenchingly of captivity in a mental facility. An in-depth reading of Latino literature reveals compelling affinities with seminal texts by Franz Kafka, Louis-Ferdinand Céline, Jean Genet, and the field of science and fantasy fiction stretching from Thomas Pynchon's *The Crying of Lot 49* and *Gravity's Rainbow* to the alarmist texts of Cyberpunk.

V

"Vernon" does not trouble the reader. Garcia does not wield the stiletto heel of a woman's shoe at his admirers, like his mother in the poem "El Zapato," who introduced him at an early age to the violence of domestic life. His poems are entirely assimilated, with an ethnic edge that more often, as in "Vernon," disguises a prophetic howl against the Moloch of the modern world with an ingratiating grin. Lyrics of resentment from minority communities, including the Jewish community, will continue to indict the majority culture forever, but poems like Soto's and Garcia's, especially, demonstrate a confident sense of settling into the so-called border areas in which their authors were once stigmatized as interlopers and aliens. From the border city of Tijuana up to the northernmost region of Alta California, the changing poetics of Latino authors have brought them closer to the mainstream of public poetry, comfortable enough on native grounds to construct a dystopian version of the city and civilization they identify as home.

Most Latino poets, however, are not publishing defiant poems characterizing the urban environment as a dystopian or infernal site, even in fun. They are focusing their attention on matters more domestic, more home- and family-oriented. They are defining their lives and their art by the quality of attention they command for their immediate surroundings. Partly as a bridge to the next chapter of this book, on the subject of interior spaces in the landscape of Los Angeles, I want to discuss a poem with subject matter so venerable, so long-standing in the tradition of mainstream poetry, that readers may miss the "alternative" aspects of its testimony about living in the city.

Aleida Rodriguez

MY MOTHER'S ART

In my dream, my mother sat on the floor,
painting several small pictures of Los Angeles.
I recognized City Hall, poking up like a giant Rapidograph pen
behind some low yellow buildings
on which the sun burned fiercely.
And the Ambassador Hotel,

its long awnings and withered glamour,
a bluish evening seeping up its faded façade.
The paintings lay around her on the floor
and she was clearly enjoying herself.
I admired them with surprise
for I had never known my mother could paint
at all, never mind so well.
How had I never known this?
That my mother was a great artist?
And that she did it so naturally,
so casually, just sitting there on the floor,
her work, the obvious product of her delight,
all around her?[17]

—•—

In the nineteenth century a daughter's poem in praise of her mother might summon for regard generic images of the mother at her spinning wheel, or baking bread at the stove, or teaching her children some skill like reading or drawing. In the twentieth century mothers are more often depicted as professional women, active in offices, factories, showrooms, "manning" the counters or executive suites of shops and businesses. Rodríguez's poem, published in her prize-winning inaugural volume *Garden of Exile* during the last year of the twentieth century, looks both backward and forward. Or rather it dreams backward to construct an identity for the speaker's progenitor, who was *not* a painter but who becomes one in the wish-fulfillment fantasy of the poet who is obviously seeking an identity for herself. Mother and daughter are bonded in this dream as sister artists, siblings devoted to representation and pious regard for places of historical significance. The poem provides them with a "floor," a word that ends three different lines in this brief poem, after a personal history of migration.

As is so often the case with poems about Los Angeles, the domestic interior receives scant notice. The dreamer's eye does not rest on furnishings, on appliances, on the layout and coloration of rooms. Her eye, like the painter's, is focused on the exterior landmarks of Los Angeles treated in the "small pictures" (akin to short poems) scattered on the floor. The most striking image appears in the third line: "I recognized City Hall, poking up like a giant Rapidograph pen." The longest line by far in the poem, the strange simile ostentatiously calls attention to itself. (In poetry workshops students are told to turn their manuscript on its side and chop off the tops of "skyscrapers" that rise too high above the surrounding, three-, four-, and five-beat lines.) The Rapidograph pen is a trademarked name for an instrument used by architects to design buildings like City Hall. The simile is an accurate one for Los Angeles City Hall's tapered elongation from base to apex. And a fine metaphor as well. City Hall writes the laws and codes that literally construct the municipal reality affecting every citizen. The image of the pen binds together the mother's and daughter's art with the Promethean power of the city's monumental edifice. Time past and time future coalesce in this suggestive image.

City Hall does not, however, dominate the landscape, either in reality or in this representation of it "poking" its head above "low buildings." This is not a skyscraper poem of the kind we identify either with Carl Sandburg's "Skyscraper" or with New York poems, beginning with Sara Teasdale's lyric of 1915, "From the Woolworth Tower." The Woolworth Building was the tallest structure in the world in 1915 and worthy of the Romantic claims made for it by poets searching for an image of modernity and cultural power. Teasdale exults in "the millions of humanity beneath us" as she and her partner look out over the city at night. But Rodríguez disdains that kind of post-Nietzschean rapture; she juxtaposes the traditionally female space of the domestic room to the erection nearby, and then turns to a more modest structure of vastly different social valence.

The Ambassador Hotel, a mid-Wilshire gem, belongs only to time past, for it was demolished in 2005, a few years after the poem's publication. The lumpy words "Rapidograph pen" give way to soft liquids and fricatives: "low yellow," "long awnings," "evening seeping up its faded façade." More than most poems, this one improves by being spoken aloud so that the *feel* of the past as it absorbs the older parent becomes manifest. Described as "withered" and "fading," the glamorous hotel, site of many Academy Awards presentations and of the assassination of Robert F. Kennedy, represents the bygone or lost world of twentieth-century Los Angeles. These two locations introduce but they do not "frame" the poem, which turns back to focus for the remainder of the lyric on the speaker's admiration for the imaginary work by her predecessor creator.

Does it matter that the poem was written by a Latina? And not a "Californio" nor a "Chicana," not born in California or Mexico, but in Cuba. Are there ethnic markings in the poem that connect it to an explicit prose poem about origins elsewhere in the volume, "My Mother in Two Photographs among Other Things," in which the poet gazes at a "newspaper photo above the caption 'Family of Cuban Expatriates Reunited Here'" and notes that "I am the only one gazing at the camera, my face twisted into a complex curiosity"? She does not foreswear "emblems of the exile," but she seems to herself to be already fascinated by the future prosperity promised her by assimilation into the United States. She will write herself into the identity of her adopted land, a city not upon a hill but in a basin. Nature will provide the continuity she requires for artistic expression:

> Earth's language is a continuous current,
> translating the voices of my early trees along the ground.
> I can't afford not to listen.
> They find me islanded in Los Angeles,
> surrounded by a moat filled with glare,
> and deliver a lost dictionary of delight. (9)

In this first book, Rodríguez depends on visuals for her best effects. "Why I Would Rather Be a Painter" is the title of the section in which "My Mother's Art" appears, along with many still lifes and self-portraits. Exile provides the speaker with the opportunity to create a new self in keeping with new "scenery," for example, the "live oak, mock orange, pine, and eucalyptus" that replace her daily fare as a child of "*ciruelas, naranjas agrias*" and "*mamoncillos*" that endowed her with a lexicon she will not leave behind. She paints herself as a figure of good fortune, root and branch a hybrid of binational identity. *Garden of Exile* is one text in the epic story of Latino migration to El Norte, attentive to local places and monuments, part of the heritage handed down from mother to daughter across the boundary break of the twenty-first century.

SEVEN

Interiors: Kinds of Sanctuary

> The space we love is unwilling to remain permanently enclosed. It deploys and appears to move elsewhere without difficulty; into other times, and on different planes of dream and memory.
>
> —GASTON BACHELARD[1]

I

Thanks to the largely benevolent climate and a century of boosterism celebrating the outdoor attractions and spectacles of Southern California—the beaches, deserts, and mountains, the freeways and open-air stadiums, Disneyland and Universal Studios theme parks, Griffith Park and the Santa Monica Third Street promenade—the exteriors of Los Angeles and environs have become fixed in the public imagination as the essential sites of the region. Even the fiction writers have focused on outdoor surfaces, recreational sites, and vistas rather than off-street life. *The Day of the Locust* gives us detailed descriptions of interiors, but who remembers them? It is the mob riot on Hollywood Boulevard, the movement of nineteenth-century infantry through the studio lot, and the facades of homes disguised as "Mexican ranch houses, Samoan huts, Mediterranean villas, Egyptian and Japanese temples, Swiss chalets, Tudor cottages" up and down the slopes of the canyons that remain memorable to the reader. When we pass through the doors of dwellings in this novel, the insides reveal themselves as drab and poorly furnished just like the bleak inner lives of the characters.

Poets have shied away from evoking the splendor and misery of inner architecture and intimate relations of public and private spaces, as the poems I have analyzed to this point suggest. Yet there is a way of arguing that the scene of rumination in Robert Hass's "Old Movie with the Sound

Turned Off" is a paradigm for the imaginative possibilities of confining the subject-speaker behind protective borders. (A classic model would be Samuel Taylor Coleridge's "This Lime-Tree Bower My Prison.") The writing desk, the figure of the beloved at *her* writing desk, and most of all the televised movie drawing the mind's eye back into history—these images and situations point to the rhetorical strategies and advantages of the domestic mode. As in fiction where the furnishings and décor provide significant clues to the psychology of the characters, so in poetry the living room, the media room, the children's room, the bedroom, even the patio, have the power to evoke the mysteries, the enchantment, of the country or city. I intend in this chapter to move from outside to inside and observe what is hidden, what is discovered, what is valued in the various domains presented as simulacra of either the home or self-chosen enclosed spaces in the Los Angeles community.

Gaston Bachelard's landmark study of the phenomenology of claustral structures beloved of poets, *The Poetics of Space* (1958), provides some useful clues as to why interiors are so often cherished in poetry. "The first, the oneirically definitive house, must retain its shadows," Bachelard remarks.[2] For his psychoanalytical purposes, this alpha dwelling is the child's vividly remembered chamber of joys and afflictions, the shadows of which linger in the psyche from the inception of consciousness till death. Sites of comfort, safety, and love consort in our memories with the jealousies and anxieties that merge, to use Bachelard's terms, "felicitous space" with "hostile space" to create a psychic arena charged with contrarieties. Refuges and shelters can and do become threatening spaces in the course of reverie. Even the objects arranged neatly, or not, in drawers and closets may return in memory as disturbing images called forth by troubles in mid- or later life. Yet all these potent emblems play less of a role in poems about Los Angeles than one might expect, perhaps because relatively few of the city's inhabitants spent their first years in the city, and/or because of the impoverished nature of the first house. The aura and amplitude of the indoor spaces in, say, the novels of Tolstoy, Wharton, Proust, Nabokov, Woolf, and Salinger bear no resemblance to the standardized urban and suburban houses built on a grid and offering few amenities. I grew up in one of these minimal houses, and so did D. J. Waldie, who comments in his history of Lakewood, *Holy Land*:

> The critics of suburbs say that you and I live narrow lives.
>
> I agree. My life is narrow.

From one perspective or another, all our lives are narrow. Only when lives are placed side by side do they seem larger.[3]

Not enough poems exist about the first functional house to compose an ample tradition or school of magical remembrance. So many dwellings, even those summoned in dream like Aleida Rodríguez's in the previous chapter, resemble the bare stages in Samuel Beckett's plays. The constant reader's eye is turned outward in poem after poem toward Los Angeles's remarkable buildings and surroundings. Poems about Los Angeles tend to appreciate the home away from home, in actuality or in imaginative texts, rather than the ancestral domicile. We must look to those estranging retreats, mainly public venues, to construct a useful psychogeography on this essential subject.

Victoria Chang

GAMBLE HOUSE

We toured your rooms of ton
and beam, of ram, of mortise-
and-tenon, of ten thousand.

Your pegs swollen from holding
wood, the opal of your lights
like minced stars, your panels

in the great room pronounced
their thunder each night while
the Gambles read by light or

watched your fires retire.
Some mornings the oven
smoked with the eddy of breads,

braiding up the stairs, wafting
under Persian rugs. But what
business did we have here—

of gambled to greatness, of black
to blaze, of scrap to starling?
What business did we have

preserving this maze of chambers
into a landmark, while bombing
another into a footprint?[4]

—•—

Victoria Chang's restive lyric on Gamble House, in Pasadena, from her debut volume *Circle* (2005), is a recent entry in what must be one of the least popular genres in Anglophone poetry: the formal or informal tour of a famous house. Ben Jonson's "To Penshurst" and Andrew Marvell's "Upon Appleton House" grace the list of seventeenth-century examples, but very few distinguished titles come to mind as we proceed down the eighteenth and nineteenth centuries and into the twentieth, when W. B. Yeats's meditations on the estates of Coole Park reintroduced the reading public to a rhetorical mode derived from neoclassical models. What makes modern poets uneasy about the genre is probably the reader's unhappy familiarity with the competing discourse of tour guides, in printed, bodily, or mechanical form, which dispense a mass of data beyond one's ability to keep it in mind. No poet wants to imitate the prefabricated narrative of a tour; a lyric of resistance may seem the only plausible response. Contemporary poets tend to form their stanzas at cross-purposes with the orderly mentor who marches visitors through rooms speaking of family history and histories of furniture.

Gamble House is one of the most popular sites of its kind for visitors to the Los Angeles area—it requires only a short drive up the freeway to Pasadena—and most longtime residents have paid it a call. Built in 1908 as the winter home of David Gamble, of the Procter & Gamble Company of Cincinnati, it mixed the Arts and Crafts tradition with a diversity of European and Asian styles. The architects Charles Sumner Greene and Henry Mather Greene clearly intended the house to be put on display like the grand mansions in Manhattan, New York, and Newport, Rhode Island. Possibly they imagined that it would be written about admiringly by some Henry James of the late twentieth century. Robert Gamble became a member of the Anglo-Saxon oligarchy that ruled Los Angeles in the first decades of the twentieth century. He too, like Mulholland, Doheny, Otis, and Griffiths, wanted to be immortalized by a handsome memorial. Poets can be forgiven for refusing to be conscripted for this task, except in an act of subversion.

Chang announces her resistance in the first disorderly stanza. She addresses her remarks to the house as to a powerful antagonist. Impatience with facts, with words, roughs up the first ten lines, rendered as bits and pieces of language wholly insufficient to describe the house's charm for an audience of readers. Rhyme is internal and erratic. Words like "ton" and "ram" seem randomly and nonsensically dropped into the stanzas. The poem settles down in the sentence beginning "Some mornings," but the fierce interjection, not once but twice, of the question roiling in the speaker's mind—"what / business did we have here [?]"—jerks the reader back into a skein of incoherencies: "of gambled to greatness, of black / to blaze, of scrap to starling." The poet defaces the mild pleasures itemized before her outburst, like Picasso impulsively painting African masks over the pretty faces of the demoiselles of Avignon, or Emil Nolde fashioning sketches full of tonal instability with just a few brushstrokes. Chang means to challenge Gamble House, to protest it, to resist the rhetoric that belongs to the Craftsman tradition and the prestige of the patrons who anchored their name and reputation in this building. Gamble House becomes the occasion for a counter-statement, a refusal to honor the settlers' self-admiring and self-defining proprietary culture. In a few discontinuous gestures, Chang has reimagined Gamble House as a latter day version of Timon's Villa, which Alexander Pope excoriated for its ostentation in the turbulent couplets of "Epistle to Burlington."

The poem's closure puts the matter baldly:

> What business did we have
>
> preserving this maze of chambers
> into a landmark, while bombing
> another into a footprint?

The meaning of this passage is somewhat opaque. "Maze" certainly registers the confusion and disorientation registered by the speaker in her incoherent litany of nouns. She has made the poem into a maze with the intention of devaluing Gamble House as a meaningful "landmark." *Webster's Dictionary* defines "landmark" as "a structure of unusual historical and usually aesthetic interest, especially one that is officially designated and set aside for preservation." The city of Pasadena has indeed designated Gamble

House as a primal site of its own historical identity, and of California's. The University of Southern California administers its daily operations. The house is a metonym, a part that aids us in comprehending the whole. Chang suggests that to the extent we move inside the house, the maze, and defer to its status as a sign of the power structure that built and sustains house and city, we submit to its power as spectacle. The agitation of the poem embodies a rebellious rejection of an imposed set of values and standards of taste.

And what's wrong with the culture that built Gamble House? It is here that Victoria Chang, who has shown herself in other writings very conscious of the bifurcation of identity signified by her name, presumes to speak for those who have been victimized by the symbolic House full of comforts and civilization but also lordly and imperial in its political hegemony. The words "bombing / another" carry too much of a burden of reference to make a clear connection to historical examples. Some war has been going on ever since Gamble House was constructed, it is always ongoing. "We" of the U.S. continue to disfigure foreign enemies on their own grounds; we place our "footprint" on the soil, and bodies, of other people, in the current understanding of the idiom. Readers are compelled to supply examples from their historical memory. The bombings of Hiroshima and Nagasaki, which reduced human bodies to shadowy prints on the sidewalk, as well as Operation Rolling Thunder in Vietnam, and the Shock and Awe campaign of "rapid dominance" directed at Iraq in 2003, are likely to stir in readers' memories while reading these resentful lines. Is this an oblique reference to Friday's footprint in *Robinson Crusoe*, a foundation narrative of colonialism? Chang's minimalist stanza suggests but does not explain why a Chinese American writer would feel compelled to dismiss the charms of Gamble House as a deception, a disguise, a power move as suggestive as King Minos of Crete's construction of the labyrinth.

However one interprets the poem, it raises questions about the way interior spaces can stir powerful feelings reaching into the political unconscious. One does not have to read very far into the history of the Chinese immigrants in California to understand the vehemence in the closure of this poem. The exploitation of Chinese coolies by railway companies and farm owners, the stigmatization of Chinatowns as centers of depravity and criminal activity, the prejudice codified in the state of California's anti-miscegenation laws barring marriage between whites and Asians, repealed only in 1948—these and other historical forces underlie the lack of respect for Gamble House manifested in the formal structure of the poem. The ambivalent poems on

Mao Zedong and the Chinese Revolution in Chang's second volume, *Salvinia Molesta* (2008), amplify our understanding of the speaker's strangled rhetoric in this anti-lyric. Yes, the poem is over-condensed, the ending too emphatic. The speaker does not do full justice to the genuine claims upon her attention proffered by Gamble House, a valuable museum of lost time. But the poetics of space exist in order to give expression to surprising connections between the individual and the locality, between past and present. In its halting and fragmented syntax and imagery, "Gamble House" troubles the reader's conditioned respect for a city proud of its orderly landmarks and eager to display them to strangers.

One of Chang's most successful poems in *Circle* is "Lisa Fremont," in which she identifies with the heroine of one of the most claustral of all motion pictures, Alfred Hitchcock's *Rear Window*. A fashion model with a crush on a dashing photographer confined to his room in an apartment complex because of a leg injury, Lisa Fremont experiences a gradual amplification of her understanding of the world by means of her growing intimacy with her disabled boyfriend and her gradual cooperation in his quest to bring to justice a murderer whose guilty actions the photographer has witnessed during his voyeuristic spying on neighbors across the court. "How strangely her many selves paradox one another," Chang remarks. In other poems Chang scrutinizes the solitary figures in Edward Hopper paintings of a hotel room, an office at night, a room in New York. And in a section titled "Limits" she ponders the fate of Lady Jane Grey in the Tower of London, the most troubling figure of solitude in an enclosed space. But Lisa Fremont remains her chief object of study: "I love how nothing in her minds her state, / how she lets others, much later, mind for her." Chang's attitude toward this complex young woman, and her admirer, is a prime example of the poetics of interior space.

Garrett Hongo

THE UNDERWORLD

Under the cone of flurried light
blued with cigarette smoke,
we sat in the false, morphined shade
of L.A.'s old Orpheum,

a once lavish Fox now gone to skinflicks,
horror fests and community matinees,
laughing at the silliness on-screen—
two comics, a black and a Jew,
both Afroed and dressed in chicken outfits,
trying to rob a suburban bank.
The black housewives around us
laughed too, nursing and cooing
at their infants who bawled
during the lulls and gunfight scenes,
shushing their older ones
who jounced in their seats, miming
the robot-dance or tossing popcorn, bored.
A few rows up from us was a stagpile
of the unemployed, bachelors in their twenties,
middle-aged fathers graying in cigar smoke,
all of them dressed in satins and polyesters
softly gleaming in the spill-light from the screen.
There was one in particular—a ghetto blade
in green velours—he wore a purple hat too,
and its feather, a peacock's unblinking eye,
bounced and darted, faintly luminous in the dark.
He cackled through the escape and arrest scenes,
calling out to his partners
phrases I couldn't quite make out,
then laughing and muttering deep *Yeahs*
in the rhythm of the talking around him.
I suppose they shared a thrill of recognition,
that old slap five and *I heard that*
from the street-corner session,
but something passed among them,
a common pain or delight in, just once,
another's humiliation. It was Monday
or Thursday, and though no rain
was coming down in the streets
outside that I could see,
everybody seemed nonetheless well.
My friend talked about the opulence around us—

coal-black interior walls frescoed
with a chain of demons intertwined,
the stalled parade of aisle and exit lamps
(red grottoes, archipelagoes of colored light)
and plush chairs with their flower-carved fabric
and scalloped backs, the gabled balcony overhead—
everything so ornate and particularized,
designed on a theme of descent
into an irretrievable world—
summer afternoons of phosphates and cowboy serials,
or love made more than potential,
corporeal on-screen, a starlet's hair
undone and almost in your lap, *so real*
that the soul stirred in the body
like a river of cold light sliding
through a forest petrified in winter.

When we left, shuffling out behind
the small crowd lighting up their Kools,
almost embarrassed to be seen
in the harsh house lights, everyone went quiet
from the dissonance of our being there.

We stepped outside to the chill blast
of the low desert turning to fall,
city buses hissing and squeaking by,
slurs of Spanish and disco and rap,
a cop's traffic whistle, a street vendor's call,
the day's last, feeble light
streaked in the eyes, fuzzy Giotto halos
like the stiff, polyester hats
on the shimmering, mingled throngs of the poor.[5]

—•—

"The Underworld" by Garrett Hongo, from his first volume *The River of Heaven* (1988), is a frequently anthologized lyric set in the Orpheum Theatre in Los Angeles. The derivation of the theater's name from Orpheus, the classical Greek god of poetry, is serendipitous for Hongo's purposes. This downtown movie palace, recently restored to its original splendor, opened in 1926 and served as a venue for live performances as well as cinema offerings of high and low quality. Its gilded décor, plush seats, expensive carpets, and large glittering chandeliers gave it a tone of luxury unrivaled even on Hollywood Boulevard. Mimicking the theater's embellishments in its style, the poem features sinuous sentences, full of high diction, winding through mainly four-beat lines in long stichic passages. The poem aims to lull the reader into a trance of pure escapism, lifted in spirit by the pleasing melodies, just as the theater itself acted as a museum of sumptuous artifacts working upon the imagination of the spectators. At first glance, the poem is neo-romantic, beginning with the steadily expanding prepositional phrase outward—"Under the cone of flurried light . . ." The uncommon adjectives and equable voice promise to restore to the common reader the pleasures of poetry-as-music violated by the coarse howls and hysterics of so much anguished postwar verse.

But Hongo is not writing a symphonic poem, nor a sublime one. He immediately complicates his description of the theater in the second line, "blued with cigarette smoke," not blued with the blue flowers of Romantic verse, mirroring the cloudless sky. And then the main clause:

> we sat in the false, morphined shade
> of L.A.'s old Orpheum,
> a once lavish Fox now gone to skinflicks,
> horror fests and community matinees,
> laughing at the silliness on-screen—
> two comics, a black and a Jew,
> both Afroed and dressed in chicken outfits,
> trying to rob a suburban bank.

"False, morphined shade" is itself an elegant formulation, especially the word "morphined" which contains echoes of Keats's description of his semiconscious condition in "Ode to a Nightingale," absent-minded "as though of hemlock I had drunk, / Or emptied some dull opiate to the drains / One minute past." The furnishings of the Orpheum intend to erase the ugliness of reality but working against the narcotic effects is the fact that the theater has degenerated into a showcase for lowbrow shadows, like the fallen images in Plato's cave, and, further, that the pictures dancing on the screen are deliberately ridiculous, a travesty of the classical "underworld" motif pictured on the interior walls of the theater and praised in a later passage of the poem.

If the poem's speaker simply lamented the hijinks of Richard Pryor and Gene Wilder (the film is *Stir Crazy*), the poem would be more conventional and less interesting. But he and his companion are laughing at the ethnic farce of it all—he a Japanese American watching a black and a Jew in an unlikely multiethnic camaraderie. The participial phrases keep extending the sentence so that all aspects of the scene, highest to lowest, get jumbled together as a complex affect. From the beginning, we are alerted to the resistance Hongo is mounting toward the conventional poem about movies and moviegoing. The second sentence amplifies the psychological situation, as the speaker takes stock of the audience with a clinical gaze. The satire is mild and pictorial, as it notices the "stagpile" of unemployed men "graying in cigar smoke, / all of them dressed in satins and polyesters." The fabrics call attention to a certain unnaturalness (i.e., not cotton or wool), a lapse of good taste, that is elaborated in the character of "one in particular" singled out for his denatured dress code:

> a ghetto blade
> in green velours—he wore a purple hat too,
> and its feather, a peacock's unblinking eye,
> bounced and darted, faintly luminous in the dark.

The customary idiom is "gay blade" but Hongo need not and does not choose a sexual orientation for the flamboyant figure he isolates and sketches for the reader's amusement. The word "ghetto" injects into the poem a gritty fragment of Los Angeles from which one might wish to escape into the glamour of the Orpheum, especially if one were dressed in colors and combinations likely to offend the citizens of a place like Watts or Compton. Hongo would have chosen the word "barrio" or some other verbal clue rather than "ghetto" if he wanted to indicate a different racial identity. Inside the theater this sport becomes part of the "silliness" as well as the free and easy racial integration on screen. The "blade" exhibits his power to attract attention as if he were as outrageous and comical as Pryor and Wilder. And if he enjoys making a spectacle of himself, who can blame him? Not the speaker of this poem.

This figure appears in the scene as more than local color or period realism. He is a symbol for what is permitted in the protected interior space, as opposed to the public agora, of a city wrestling with racial tensions and ambiguities. Transfer him to the public space of a Harlem street, and the comic situation assumes a stronger polemical edge than in "The Underworld." Here is Helene Johnson, a poet of the Harlem Renaissance, in "Bottled":

And yesterday on Seventh Avenue
I saw a darky dressed fit to kill
In yellow gloves and swallow-tail coat
And swirling a cane.

When this "darky" begins a slow dance on the street, the speaker is embarrassed at the public and racial humiliation of it all, and she responds wishfully by mentally transporting him back to Africa:

And somehow, I could see him dancin' in a jungle,
A real honest-to-cripe jungle, and he wouldn't have on them
Trick clothes—those yaller shoes and yaller gloves
And swallow-tail coat. He wouldn't have on nothing.

—•—

And he'd have rings in his ears and on his nose
And bracelets and necklaces of elephants' teeth.
Gee, I bet he'd be beautiful then all right.[6]

No transformation of this kind occurs in "The Underworld," unless one counts the metamorphosis of Pryor and Wilder into chickens with Afro hairstyles. The era of zoot suits is over, the era of hip-hop array has not yet begun. So the "ghetto blade" remains a figure of strange and ornamental artifice like the theater he frequents and the poem he inspires.

The passage beginning "My friend talked about the opulence around us" broadens the field of vision and enlarges the theater to symbolic status. For a moment the trope of Los Angeles as a place of tinsel and kitsch recedes in favor of a genuine homage to the fantasy of achieved and "*corporeal*" (note the italics) pleasure, "*so real*" (more italics) that a moment of ecstasy shudders in the poem. The lurid downtown theater in the film *Mulholland Drive* comes to mind.[7] How long can a contemporary poet sustain such a spiritual epiphany by means of diction elevated to Renaissance or Romantic pitch:

"*so real* / that the soul stirred in the body / like a river of cold light sliding / through a forest petrified in winter"? Hongo makes it last for another strophe, all the way to the end of the poem where the sounds and sights of the downtown street carry another charge of supernal beauty:

> slurs of Spanish and disco and rap,
> a cop's traffic whistle, a street vendor's call,
> the day's last, feeble light
> streaked in the eyes, fuzzy Giotto halos
> like the stiff, polyester hats
> on the shimmering, mingled throngs of the poor.

How rare this transfiguration of the everyday is in the poetry of Los Angeles! After the satirical notice of the "ghetto blade" and the audience of unemployed, one expects the ironies and condescension to intensify; but the return of the "hats" motif in a finer tone, as halos on the heads of the poor, sanctified by the respectful allusion to Giotto, provides a satisfying and upbeat closure to a poem that traverses a range of moods and attitudes. The interior world has succeeded in its task of giving the poet fresh eyes to see the beauty he must have overlooked while focused on the "silliness" onscreen, though even that convivial farce must have contributed to the vision of a better world—a vision travestied in Helene Johnson's poem about the "poor shine" dancing in the streets of Harlem.

There are many intriguing poems set in movie theaters; Philip French and Ken Wlaschin devote 76 pages to them in *The Faber Book of Movie Verse*. In that anthology, however, there are only two poems about a theater in Los Angeles, one by myself about Grauman's Chinese Theatre and featuring a review of *Superman*, and Charles [Harper] Webb's "Further Decline of Western Civilization," set in the "Odium in Hollywood," a purely imaginary venue for two lousy films that are the focus of the entire poem.[8] The Chinese, which declined in glamour and aura when the Mann syndicate bought and renamed it, appears in poem XLV of David St. John's novella in verse, *The Face* (2004), as a setting for the speaker's nausea when confronted with a memory film of his own troubled relation to a romantic past. Likewise, Hongo seizes upon the metaphorical possibilities of the world-within-world of the Orpheum Theater frescoes that ostentatiously display the "theme of descent / into an irretrievable world," not the Golden Age of myth but the remembered ecstasy of romantic passion evoked in our memories of adolescent moviegoing by the "starlet's hair / undone and almost in your lap." The painterly descriptions of the classical world, with their sexual motifs in the foreground, achieve a second life in this Los Angeles landmark theater. In the entire panorama of the poetics of space, this soul-stirring location shines in the projected pleasures of that "river of cold light" available to the entire community, whether as a mockery of their desire or a fulfillment of it.

The conventional decompression and melancholy upon leaving a movie theater is familiar to all readers. A character in John Fowles's short story "The Woman in the Reeds" says to his companion, "You know what it's like sometimes when you come out at the end of a film? You feel we're all nobodies; just a lot of nobodies they can do what they like in front of. We can never be like they are."[9] Hongo's poem advises that moviegoers shift their gaze and their aspirations from the silly presences on the screen to the irradiated dreamers in the audience and carry that heightened sensibility into the streets where a kind of electrical charge of spiritual light moves among the passersby. This is a generous and persuasive rendering of the dynamics between interior and exterior realms of being. And if we take the Orpheum as a type of all theaters, in the nation and around the globe, then Hollywood's claims for a civilizing mission sound less risible, less self-deceiving.

Hongo's poem is a strategic advance beyond the standard-issue movie theater poem typified by John Hollander's "Movie-Going" and Frank O'Hara's "To the Film Industry in Crisis," as well as Edward Field's nostalgic evocations in the book *Variety Photoplays* and John Allman's in *Loew's Triboro* (2004), two books with the names of New York movie theaters as titles. In those poems there is a tone of adoration approaching camp, as the classic genres and stars of the 1930s and 1940s pass before our eyes. The Los Angeles poem both imitates and subverts the tonality of such nostalgic East Coast poems, challenging the reader to rethink the relation of the film image and the spectatorial consciousness.

II

A similar rhetoric of subversion can be found in Denis Johnson's poem "The Supermarkets of Los Angeles," which has in its crosshairs one of the most famous poems set in the Golden State: Allen Ginsberg's "A Supermarket in California." Ginsberg sets his poem in an unnamed location that we know to be the Bay Area. "Shopping for images," he steps into a market and notes the peaches, avocados, tomatoes, and artichokes, and also the ghosts of Manhattan's homosexual pantheon, García Lorca and Walt Whitman. The poem becomes increasingly somber as the lonely poet leaves the fruits of the earth behind and strolls with the shade of Whitman outside the market, both of them "dreaming of the lost America of love," the emotional abundance equivalent to the fruits and vegetables of the lighted interior world of the market.

That is one take on California, the tangible cornucopia. In Denis Johnson's poem no food item is mentioned; instead a two-way television above the aisles reflects back the watchers' gaze while behind it some ghostly agent monitors the scene for shoplifters. These faces, "so tiny // in the relaxed fist of / Los Angeles . . ." usurp the attention and fill the last half of the poem. Johnson alters Ginsberg's romantic scenario by making the love scene narcissistic, as befits the self-admiring city of Los Angeles. The phrase that follows the one quoted above is "hearing / Los Angeles singing // to the murdered." It was Whitman who proclaimed "I Hear America Singing," but in L.A., in 1976, all of the elements of urban life have been reshuffled by the ubiquitous presence of television, of visual media in general. The media panopticon following upon the 1950s and 1960s operates to track down crime, in settings like markets where all the shoppers are potentially guilty. Johnson has turned the Whitman-Ginsberg tradition inside out, revealing interiors as empty of any object except one's own hungry countenance captured in the gaze of the ceiling eye.[10]

What is true of the magic lantern world of cinema is no less applicable to the world of sports. One of the finest evocations of the ecstatic pleasures of indoor spectatorship is Quincey Troupe's homage to Earvin "Magic" Johnson of the Los Angeles Lakers in "A Poem for 'Magic.'" Rhapsodic in tone, this fan's letter addressed to his idol documents an evening at The Forum when Johnson's amazing ball-handling thrilled the speaker and a huge crowd. The poem is descriptive and evocative, lacking the thematic depth of Hongo's poem, but conveying in a rich vernacular the opportunities for crowd splendor:

> you cartwheel the crowd towards frenzy
> wearing now your electric smile, neon as your name

—•—

& so we cheer, rejoicing with you for this quicksilver, quicksilver, quick-
silver
moment of fame, so put the ball on the floor again, "magic"
juke & dazzle, shaking and baking down the lane
take the sucker to the hoop, "magic" Johnson
recreate reverse hoodoo gems off the spin
deal alley-oop-dunk-a-thon-magician passes, now
double-pump, scissor, vamp through space, hang in place
& put it all in the sucker's face . . .[11]

Most sites in Los Angeles, as we have seen, offer few opportunities for full-throated celebration, but The Forum and now The Staples Center are venues that can galvanize a mass audience seeking refuge from the home TV screens that fall short of prompting spectators to stand up and cheer. The poet's task is to manifest the *vox populi* by channeling the slang of the neighborhood basketball courts into the sprung rhythm of these volatile lines and to let their cumulative effect simulate the "frenzy" of watching a perfect athletic performance. Reading the poem, we feel like we can hear the rafters ring.

David Wyatt remarks on "the peculiarly overdeveloped ability of Californians to frame experience as a spectacle."[12] In Southern California the culture industries, including what we now more commonly refer to as the "media industries," stage these spectacles with manic intensity, as if the population must be distracted or diverted constantly in order to fight off the boredom of urban and modernized life. The Orpheum and The Forum, Disneyland, the Hollywood Bowl, the Rose Bowl, The Greek Theatre, the Ramona pageant, Knott's Berry Farm, Hollywood theme parks, the art exhibits during Laguna Beach's Sawdust Art Festival, the Music Center and the Walt Disney Concert Hall, surfing competitions, and parades on and around Olvera Street—all of these and many more exert their seductive spell on millions of visitors annually. Even the downtown train station is a tourist destination. Poets visit these public attractions and register their responses. Indeed, one of the chief values of poetry as a medium is that it brings the solitary creative temperament into immediate contact with the crowd-pleasing recreational venues. "Literature is in part the business of finding new angles at which to enter reality," Salman Rushdie has written.[13] The poem, on the page or on the portable monitor, proceeds from the interior space of the psyche and stands apart from actual locations even if it pretends to re-present them accurately. Except at a poetry reading, almost always an interior occasion, the poem shares its privacy with only one person. That is both its limitation and its invulnerable advantage in the rivalry with entertainment vehicles and venues.

Poems that focus on the indoor, the modestly enclosed, the domestic and erotic, assert their descriptive language against the immense and crowded forces of urban dynamism. Such poems fall back upon scenery with few characters and activities of perennial, universal modality. Bachelard has written eloquently about the poet's recourse to nature for images and symbols of the solitary or self-contained—the nests, burrows, glades, and gardens secreted from the much-traveled roads of mass attention. In the city, natural places are transfigured into asylums with rural associations designed for patrons of a quieter caste and temperament. In the poetry of Charles Gullans the companionable sites of refuge are familiar and convivial, with none of the manic energies of the Orpheum and Forum. He confines his poetics to the classroom, the restaurant, the bar, the small party in a living room, and the bedroom where "Eros the Terrible" removes the inhibitions of polite intercourse. There is no city in the world where these modest and often moralistic poems could not be set. The culture of fantasy, the thrill of mobility, the neo-romantic opportunities supposedly so prominent in the literature and life of Los Angeles, recede in his work into the reportorial diction and Horatian tone of an acute observer. Robert von Hallberg, in *American Poetry and Culture 1945–1980*, remarks, "Along with Edgar Bowers and Turner Cassity, Gullans helped [the] traveler's theme, the degradation of eros, to evolve into a sub-genre, the barroom poem of jaundiced courting."[14] True, but this is an incomplete account of Gullans's range. Especially as he aged, this mild-mannered UCLA professor moderated his physical hungers in order to share with a small readership his observations on the life that begins at twilight.

Charles Gullans

ANOTHER LOCAL (THE CHARTHOUSE)

Westwood, or Coronado, Malibu,
It scarcely matters. They are all the same,

The same appeal to casual luxury,
The same polite and handsome, youthful crew,
Spectacular in their vitality,
Around the margins of whose consciousness
One finds a place to be. They live their lives;
And you have yours, thornier, older, gnarled,
As theirs will someday be. Meanwhile they work,
And you are part of it: they wait on you.
They chat and argue, sometimes they discuss
The bar and business, sports, the books they read,
Life at the beach, their friends, their larger aims.
Acute and commonsensical, they know
More of the world than I did at their age.
They are engaging and respectful. My grey hairs
And my bald head are not ridiculous,
Even to me, in such an atmosphere,
At once intelligent and tolerant.
And one expands a little from the chill
Of more abrasive climates. I relax.
They are so very much themselves that I
Almost become myself, almost let go.
There is a model here. After a time,
We do not change. We learn to bear ourselves,
And bear the burden of our friends, and they,
They bear us, too, with equal fortitude.
Our problems are not solved. They are survived
With grace and caution, day by careful day.[15]

—•—

"Another Local (The Charthouse)" is part of a sequence of four poems, "Down at the Local," published with another sequence, "Los Angeles Place Names," in *The Bright Universe and Other Poems* (1983). The Chart House, which officially separates the proper noun into two words, is a franchise fish house and bar found in choice locations in the Southland. "They are all the same" makes note of its ubiquitous presence, not just as a company brand but as a kind of "local," as Gullans always calls the bars he frequents. The word is British slang for a pub. Hollywood offered some notable and unique restaurants in its heyday, some extinct (Ciro's, The Brown Derby, the Coconut Grove), some still in business at this writing (Musso & Frank's). A "local" is a neighborhood venue with middle-class clientele. Gullans notes the "casual luxury" of the décor without itemizing or describing it. His gaze fixes immediately and for the length of the poem on the servers, to whom he surprisingly attaches the epithet "Spectacular in their vitality." (But "polite"; this is not a Bukowski-style hangout.) The poet situates himself at the margins of their consciousness, an outsider and observer taking mental notes. Employees, or "crew," they act in the poem with the free and easy manners of customers. Of course they are "respectful" to the poet who breathes a sigh of relief: "My grey hairs / And my bald head are not ridiculous . . ." He has found his comfort zone, his refuge from a youth-oriented society bearing down on him harder on the streets of Los Angeles than it would elsewhere.

"They are so very much themselves that I / Almost become myself, almost let go. / There is a model here." The repetition of "almost" measures the distance of age between himself and the crew, but also between what he can acknowledge to himself and what he can act upon as a "self" whose libido we know from other poems is identical to those in the room with more outward vitality. Waitstaff are one thing, friends another. The poem closes on a cautionary and stoical note as he reminds himself that though "After a time, / We do not change," our unchanged and unchangeable desires can become a burden to our friends, as their trailing needs are a burden to ourselves. "Careful" is the keyword in the closure: don't follow the spirit of place and indulge in pleasures off-limits to people of your age and profession. That is a home truth, a "local" truth, appropriate to the restaurant he has chosen in a city obsessed with looking and acting young. In other poems, the poet comes home from such an outing with a male partner and the space of the bedroom becomes a site for abandonment of prudence and caution, a yielding to Dionysus rather than Apollo. But in some he shrugs off advances and returns home alone, secure against the temptations of the appetitive city.[16]

What counts in this poem is the sense of intimacy and moderate satisfaction appropriate to a favorite restaurant. The poem on fine dining has a long history beginning with Horace's praise of the unique comforts of the table, especially if prepared by a friend who has invited the poet to supper. Situating the dining room in a restaurant, in an urban space, permits the poet to become more private, more anonymous; he can enjoy the spectacle of the quick-darting waiters and persuasively meditate on the lessons his contemplation of their beauty brings home to him. Like an airport or market, the restaurant brings constant change of view without unsettling the visitor. The full sentence "I relax" reflects the trusting nature of the place better than any long passage. We are a long way here from the "Burning of Los Angeles" that dominates the imagination of so many authors who fix the image of the city in its most apocalyptic guise.

Also noteworthy for our purposes is Paul Monette, a gay poet of greater range than Gullans, and by the time of his death from AIDS in 1995 a spokesman about the disease. Known to a national audience, more for his prose than his poetry, he compiled an oeuvre of verse among the most distinguished by Los Angeles writers. In his sequence *Love Alone: Eighteen Elegies for Rog* (1988) Monette composed a tribute to his deceased partner Roger Horowitz, with one eye on the classical tradition of the elegy, adapting and transforming its customarily male lament for a fellow male (a shepherd, a college friend, a fellow poet) in order to make the ceremonies of domestic life in Los Angeles serve as the contemporary equivalent of the conventional pastoral romance.

The key poem in the volume is "The House on Kings Road," too long to present here in full and too complex to analyze passage by passage. Kings Road takes its grandiose name from El Camino Real, the grand highway of the Hispanic missionaries running up the coast of California. Monette is referring, however, to the long street winding through West Hollywood and extending above Sunset Boulevard, a favorite site for large estates going back to the era of silent film. Monette positions his own home well down the economic strata from the manse of "Bacall and Bogie in living noir / champagning away from the forties at 1600 / *Here's looking at you kid*" and mentions Chevy Chase and Steve Martin as upstart homeowners on the block in place of Hollywood royalty. Names of famous people roll through the stream-of-consciousness poem that jams sentence fragments together in syntactical rupture without punctuation in the manner of James Merrill in *Scripts for the Pageant* (1980) and James Joyce in the Molly Bloom soliloquy that closes *Ulysses*. Joyce and Merrill are unmentioned, but allusions to Cavafy, Sophocles, Dickens, Shakespeare's Juliet and Lear, Plato, Jean Follain, and Thoreau maintain the high cultural status of the elegy. The house, too, is endowed with metaphysical and even mystical power; it is "safe harbor / for the heart" and a reward to the deserving for all of life's effort:

the dream house

is worth it it got you somewhere die in
its shady yard bougainvillea rippling
like a coral reef gold on the west windows

It was a love nest, a sanctuary for a community of two. The outside world of "bachelor flats" is depicted as an alien and deprived space, "noplace air-shaft rooms stacked with *Playbills*." Gay life in the Hollywood Hills might be brash and seductive, but it fails to satisfy in several ways. The purpose of the poem is to assert and define the superior qualities of the house on Kings Road, even if the contract lists the occupants as "single man" and "single man" rather than the married couple Monette insists he and Rog manifestly were and, after Rog's death, remain.

This cherishing of the house on Kings Road is a point worth underlining. Like the ocean and freeway, the orange groves and the La Brea Tar Pits (not really tar but asphalt), the freestanding house has an elite place in the iconography of literary Los Angeles. In *Borrowed Time: An AIDS Memoir*, Monette, a classicist, provides a close-up of this *locus amoenus:*

> A stucco thirties cottage high in a box canyon above the Sunset Strip. There's a view of the city lights through the coral tree out front and between the olive and the eucalyptus across the way. In square footage it's about the size of a two-bedroom on Seventy-ninth and West End [New York City], the sort people kill for. Out back is a garden court shaded by Chinese elms and a blue-bottom pool that catches the sun from eleven to three.[17]

Modest, seemingly rural in its pastoral amenities, the house is imagined as a magic castle; it provides a perfect "anchorage" against the roiling, hurried, and distracting world of Los Angeles. In retrospect, after Rog's death, Monette remembers his constant daily prayer, "Thank you for this . . . thanking the darkness for the time we'd had—the ten years, the house, the dog, the work" (48–49).

Monette, in other words, rejects the culture of cruising the gay bars and hustling prospects. He is not on the streets searching out rough trade or persuadable runaways from the Midwest. A countercultural figure among gay authors, he identifies with Dickens as a recorder of the psychogeography of his time. "[T]he quill on Dickens's desk is exactly where / he laid it," he remarks. And that is so because Dickens immortalized himself and his city, and thereby caused his possessions and his house to be preserved. Monette aspires to the same condition: "let the brief museum / of Kings Road be all mine." Will his domain ever be shown to tourists as "Monette's House" as the dwelling up the road is forever Bacall and Bogie's House? Elegies are all about making judgments and making promises. At the end of the poem Monette turns toward the past, that paradise of love, and summons scenes of himself and Rog at their everyday activities, including time in the bedroom, "taking a nap curled like spoons on / a rainy Sunday terror and evil banished / like the snakes in Ireland." The final dithyramb must be quoted at length. Here the non-coincidence of line and sentence is extreme, a reflection of disorderly grief raised to a wild pitch. The rapid rhythm of emotional phrases roughs up the tradition of the elegy no less than Victoria Chang distorts the conventional poem of praise directed at a distinguished estate:

> you cried *What happened to our happy life*
> staring blind out over the garden Rog
> it's here it's here I know because I am
> the ghost who haunts us I am the last window
> sir tread lightly who bargains for this house
> you are sporting with kings on a high road
> despite the sifted gray of time where things
> are atomized the white chairs under the elm
> the wall of books laid brick by brick the lamp
> pooling on the blue-bound Plato as we held
> our ground through August let the material go
> what you cannot buy or have in your name
> is the ghost of a touch the glancing stroke
> as a man passes through a room where his love
> sits reading later much later the nodding head
> of the one on the other's shoulder no title
> usurps that place this is its home forever[18]

So much can be unpacked from this defiant yet pathetic passage of mourning! On one level it might be said to take real estate as its subject matter. Rog is dead, and Monette foresees his own death from AIDS closing in on him (he died seven years after this poem was published). The house and garden must be transferred to other occupants. Monette does not imagine himself in the future as a ghost; he *is* a ghost already and the proof is the urgent, denatured poem he deeds to his readers in which his voice speaks *d'outre tombe*. Rog has gone the way of other ghosts from Kings Road, and however much he returns by means of reincarnation as a procession of words on the page, or in the moments his name is uttered as part of some spot of time in a poem such as this, he is no less spirit-like than the author who declares that he is stopping time and insisting that the new homeowners have no abiding claim on his property, real or imaginative: "no title / usurps that place this is its home forever."

Grief is a rare subject for poets, or authors generally, in Los Angeles. Their gaze is more often on entertainments and spectacles than the ruins of time, as we have seen. Evelyn Waugh's novel *The Loved One* is a burlesque of grief in Southern California because Waugh considered the iconic cemetery of Forest Lawn and its ideology a blasphemous travesty of actual disconsolation. Only *A Single Man*, by Waugh's fellow Briton Christopher Isherwood, honors the rites of mourning with the solemnity we associate with the literary tradition beginning in Ancient Greece and Ancient Israel. Monette and Isherwood provide alternatives to the stereotype of the gay hustler as we find him in John Rechy's popular and purple novels. But then, Rechy does not live in West Los Angeles as Isherwood and Monette did. His haunt was Hollywood, the terrain Wanda Coleman called "celluloid fairyland" in her sequence "Art in the Court of the Blue Fag."

Stanley Plumly has argued that

> The dominant feeling, the resonant tone in American poetry, right from the start, has been . . . elegiac, melancholic, meditative, aggressively expressive, and romantic, which is why truly early modernists like William Wordsworth and John Keats have become iconographic influences within our American canon.[19]

In his cadences of nostalgia and grief, the almost sobbing tone of his run-on lines, Monette situates his Los Angeles dwelling in the main line of poetic achievement in American poetry. More than his simple cottage and arboreal yard, the Kings Road domicile, with its Mediterranean and English antecedents, rises to a cosmopolitan significance, just as his poem and memoir call attention to autumnal shadows in the landscape of the national canon.

III

Carol Muske-Dukes

THE IMAGE

I turn on the television and he is
there, on-screen, in profile—
turning to stare full-faced at me.

A scripted wind lifts his hair,
he gazes outward and through me.
It seems he is a traveler, bored,

at a cocktail party on a terrace high
above a strange city. A beautiful
woman enters the frame, smiling,

throws her arms around him from
behind. It's clear now that he is
playing a happy husband or a lover.

He laughs again, gently extricates
himself from her embrace. That
woman holding him holds his life

in her hands, but his life is nothing
more than what he chooses to give her.
An exit line thrown over his shoulder.

A practiced emphatic smile. What he
chooses has in turn been chosen for him.
So later in the script, after they argue

in bed, she stares at the stripes of morning
light falling through the blinds across
his back and knows that he is only there

conditionally—and that the conditions are
not hers. It has been written long ago that he
longs to leave. Still, anyone with eyes could argue

the opposite. He longs to stay. Look at the
unspoken desire—the bands of light tightening
across the body even in its attitude of flight. The

tousled dark hair, the curve of the back, the
powerful muscles unresisting finally, the body
begging to be detained. Even though he sleeps

turned to the wall, she can imagine his
expression: the eyes wide open, perhaps
lit with expectation in that face he shows no one—

hidden from the lens, yet still an object of regard.[20]

—•—

For reasons of continuity I will close this chapter by turning to a poem by Carol Muske-Dukes, from her volume *Sparrow* (2003). Because of superficial resemblances to Robert Hass's "Old Movie with the Sound Turned Off," and because like Monette's it is situated in an upscale neighborhood, it frames my discussion of the mystification present in interior spaces in Los Angeles. "The Image" requires us to know that Carol Muske married the stage and screen actor David Dukes (not to be confused with the white-supremacist David Duke) and wrote about him memorably before his early death, as in the poem "Last Take" in which she visits him on a movie set and, with a chilling *sang-froid,* watches him get killed by a professional assassin in retake after retake. So when "The Image" opens "I turn on the television and he is / there" we know immediately who "he" is. Not knowing about David Dukes would make this into a different kind of poem.

What makes the poem original is that the reader is not directed to a location away from the speaker's house, as the narrative of the TV movie unfolds, but deeper into the intimate rooms of the speaker's own life history with the actor on the screen. The movie is all too recognizable to her as an image of her happy life with the protagonist, just as the actress in the movie inevitably becomes a stand-in for the poet herself. She wills the screen to become a mirror so that she can relive, not without pain, the romantic scenes of what sounds like a soap-opera-style film. This direct connection would not be feasible in a theater—certainly not one as opulent as the Orpheum. However, the privacy of the house, of the room into which his voice has called her, guarantees an undistracted psychic connection of considerable power. Tercet by tercet readers are drawn into the dynamics of this act of recovery, in which the ghost who dwells in the house as a survivor makes fleeting contact with the ghost who rises as if by magic from the grave, and troubles both his screen lover and her romantic double, his grieving widow.

Something profound about how the designs of time and fate take harrowing turns in a media culture is being represented in "The Image." And some reverse form of the Orpheus-Eurydice legend is being adapted for twentieth-century consumption. The poem invites the reader to journey to the "underworld," as in Garrett Hongo's poem where the artwork on the walls reminds the audience that they have chosen the steep descent down from the surfaces of everyday life. The poem is about interiors and subterranean spaces—of the home where the heart is and the unconscious where the departed lie in wait before they reappear in their former habitation. "The Image" is a spot of time that could have been set almost anywhere, but it is entirely appropriate that we feel assured that it is set in the fountainhead of media culture, the city where a working actor for films and television would naturally find his home. This too is an "L.A. Story" of death and resurrection by the power of art, first by the resources of screens and then by the inscription of elegy.

The poem is titled "The Image" for complex reasons. The beauty and enduring psychic presence of the husband mandates an afterlife for the speaker of never-ending remembrance. The deceased appears in his permanent bodily image in the poem's poignant conclusion:

Look at the

Unspoken desire—the bands of light tightening
Across the body even in its attitude of flight. The

> Tousled dark hair, the curve of the back, the
> Powerful muscles unresisting finally, the body
> Begging to be detained.

As in Robert Hass's poem this one turns off the sound to enhance the visual corporeality and intensity of the phantom apparition. Commanded to "Look," the speaker and reader bond together as spectators of the image even as the verse exhibits a design featuring enhanced sound devices: the rhyme of "light," "tightening," and "flight," with their alliterative repeated plosive "t" effects down to the important word "attitude" and minor words like "at" and "its." And then the sentence fragment that holds the male figure in an intransitive stillness even as the content makes clear that he cannot resist the movement of the film toward conclusion. Important trochaic words like "Tousled," "Powerful," and "Begging" are front loaded at the beginning of lines, where capitalization lends them even more prominence. Plosive "b" words—"back," "body," and "Begging"—are resonant hooks for our attention and the speaker's accumulating remorse. The speaker stops time to create a picture, as if it were hanging on the wall rather than moving on the screen. Television—the culture's infinite repository of images—usurps the traditional place and function of portraits in the interior space of the living room. Static family pictures do not arrest the poet, if indeed they exist on the shelves or hang on the walls. In this sense too the television is a consciousness and a time machine, the daimon of all interior spaces (including the unavoidable replays on Jumbotron screens in sport and concert venues).

Muske-Dukes's poems often interrogate matters of class and privilege, and arguably "The Image" does so by means of the movie, set "at a cocktail party on a terrace high / above a strange city." The unrhymed tercets carry a hint of Dante's inferno, the region of ghosts, not least because the poem situates the deceased in a world where he is "still an object of regard," not just of the grieving spectator-speaker but of the woman in the film who is scripted to watch him as he exits first the party and then the bedroom and eventually her life altogether. The poem is about a woman (the speaker) turning into an image as well by means of her art. She too is a filmmaker, a creator and processor of figures and scenes, animating the dead who have left behind the luxury that characterizes not only social class in Los Angeles but the earthbound habits of bodily pleasure and artistic production.

It must be emphasized that the poem is fundamentally a meditation on the boundary of art and life, and the same is true for the entire volume, *Sparrow,* which marks moments when David Dukes as actor steps out of the poet's circle of life and begins an impersonation that makes him figuratively deceased to her in his new incarnation:

> When you crossed under
> The arc of the proscenium, you were already dead
>
> to me, yet more alive than ever. (8)

Roles are eternal; they exist in a Platonic realm awaiting new bodies to perpetuate them. The so-called little death of sexual consummation is superseded in poems like "Actor," "The Illusion," "Ovation," and "The Empty Chair" by the repetitive surrender of the partner to a celebrity that inspires cheers from the audience and bows from the beloved, but also premonitions of that day when he dies into the image of his art-form, a state of being that no longer has a location in Los Angeles, except when mediated as a form of self-knowledge, as in this haunting poem.

Topographical poems like the Virgilian georgic, according to John H. Johnston, specialize in representing "terrain, soil, weather, seasons, plant and animal life."[21] The "city poem," by contrast, most often follows the speaker from street to street as he or she catalogues the distractions of passing vehicles, pedestrians, fronts of houses, factories, and commercial buildings open for business. Only when the poet steps behind closed doors is the verse likely to take on the enhanced subjectivity and moral assessment that comes from the solitary, sustained gaze at people and objects isolated from the turbulent bombardment of momentary phenomena street after street. Not every "interior" poem will fulfill the pastoral character and slow-time elaboration of lyrics sampled in this essay. But this too is Los Angeles, well off the busy streets of unfamiliar neighborhoods.

Futurists writing about Los Angeles call attention to the inevitability of a newly shared consciousness of interior spaces, as population density encourages more people to spend more time indoors, away from the ever-burgeoning traffic, in residential patterns of development tending to the vertical. Congestion on the freeways and main arteries will increasingly determine the distances people are willing to travel, not to mention the rising costs of visiting entertainment venues. Perhaps the glamour of high-rises like the Westin Bonaventure Hotel and Frank Gehry's Walt Disney Concert Hall, postmodernist icons rivaling the freeways that sweep around them, will achieve an ascendancy in the public image of Los Angeles. Suburban and rural alternatives will continue to beckon those who seek a collective space with front and back yards, whether on a horizontal grid or freestanding in natural surroundings. And, because of technological changes, especially the ubiquity of social media, as well as social patterns of cocooning and withdrawal from the openness of the urban commons, the poet's dwelling, and therefore the poet's creative imagination, is the territory where more and more poems about the city are likely to be set in the future.

EIGHT

Exteriors: Signs of the Endtime

> Only a catastrophe gets our attention. We want them, we need them, we depend on them. As long as they happen somewhere else. This is where California comes in. Mud slides, brush fires, coastal erosion, earthquakes, mass killings, et cetera. We can relax and enjoy these disasters because in our hearts we feel that California deserves whatever it gets. Californians invented the concept of life-style. This alone warrants their doom.
>
> —DON DELILLO, *WHITE NOISE*[1]

I

All lives take place in a constant exchange of interior and exterior situations. It's not simply a matter of moving between the domestic realm and the out-of-doors. The garden, so beloved of poets, is often a space fenced in and adjoining the domicile so that no useful distinction, topographically, can be drawn between the flower or vegetable beds and the garage, back porch, patio, or lanai supplementary to the main housing unit. Without thinking much about it we all pass constantly across the liminal space from inside to outside, and then advance further outside. The subject of David Hockney's famous painting *Beverly Hills Housewife* (1966) stands at the house's border, outside of the living room demarcated by a sliding glass door, but inside the patio space between house and pool—an in-between space with its own decorative features, such as a Courvoisier chair and a modernist sculpture. If our eyes go right to the woman caught within these zones with no clear definition, we can understand how the poet Dick Barnes finds it necessary to sympathize with this emblematic figure seemingly lost in a wilderness of mirrors: "In case you thought it was so easy being / a Beverly Hills housewife."[2]

The swimming pool became an icon of Southern California before it spread across the country as a middle-class amenity. Not just a functional place for family recreation, it swiftly achieved symbolic status as a mark of social class aspirations. Those like myself who came of age in 1950s Los Angeles will remember the first swimming pool in our middle-class neighborhood, following upon the first television on the block, and how the newly popular owners became the envy of the less fortunate. A fixture in advertisements, movies, and paintings of the period, the pool did not lend itself to poetry; it lacked resonance and gravitas, especially compared to the sublime surf within easy reach. But the backyard pool, it now seems obvious, holds a unique place in the public imagination precisely because it is an exterior phenomenon lodged within the penumbra of the overarching house, literally walled off from the neighbors' children who may be tempted to play near its concrete borders or plunge into its apparently safe but actually perilous depths. The swimming pool became an agora for friends and family members—a selective, intentional community set off from the anonymity and randomness enforced by the zoning patterns of Los Angeles real estate. The pool certainly appealed to David Hockney, who put it on the cognitive map of art connoisseurs with his near-obsessive attention, in photographs, drawings, and paintings, to the lines and angles of poolside architecture, the central figure of the blue pool itself, and the frequent presence of naked young men in postures of enjoyment.

David Trinidad

HOCKNEY: BLUE POOL

Los Angeles,
California:
a summer afternoon.
One boy sunbathes
on a yellow towel
beside the pool;
another stands
at the end of
the diving board,
gazing downward.
Palm trees sway
in the blue water.
Overhead, a few

clouds float by.
To the right,
sprinklers lightly
spray the green
lawn. The sunbather
slips off his red
and white striped
swimsuit and rolls
over; the other
boy dives into the
pool. The artist
snaps a photograph
of the splash.[3]

—•—

This is a poem to which we might give the same title as Carol Muske-Dukes's lyric in the previous chapter: "The Image." In fact, the poem partakes of the poetics of the Deep Image movement of the 1960s and thereafter, in which the poet attempts to conjure a mystical sensation by focusing on some natural object or objects. Readers familiar with James Wright's canonical poem "Lying in a Hammock at William Duffy's Farm in Pine Island, Minnesota" will notice some similarities with that litany of images, as well as the poem's ambition to picture the condition of happiness in a specific location. Also, the skinny lineation and radical enjambments of Trinidad's poem will recall Charles Bukowski's poem analyzed earlier, and some of my reservations about his methods apply here as well.

This report filed as "Los Angeles, / California" complicates the conventional depiction of a natural scene in interesting ways. Most important, it re-creates in the ekphrastic mode not a scene the poet has witnessed but a scene from a photograph remade into a painting. In fact, the poem aspires to the condition of painting, with its palette of colors and its stationing of objects and people. It recalls some of Wallace Stevens's metapoetical poems, such as "A Study of Two Pears," in which the reader may be unsure whether it is the actual pears being described or an artist's "study" of them on canvas: art and life achieve a union of ontological effect. The poem's author, in any case, retracts himself in favor of the imagery assembled by Hockney. The poem is a species of photograph: objective, mimetic, minutely detailed. It is a poem about its own making in the form of another work on paper: the photograph that snaps shut the poem itself.

The poem, like the painting, is a celebration of the leisure community of gay youth in the act of hedonistic play. Hockney is preserving an image of the happy homosexual lifestyle he celebrates in his writings (especially his memoir of 1976, *My Early Years*) as well as his graphic productions. Hockney's depictions of this milieu made a splash, so to speak, in the dictionary sense of "a striking show or an ostentatious display." The double entendre embedded in the poem's last word, as in the frequent figuration of the splash in Hockney's artwork, lends significance to the casual displays of flesh in the poolside scene. The poem does not include a didactic comment on its images (as James Wright closes his poem by remarking "I have wasted my life") and the short lines militate against any kind of sustained discursive commentary. The cool surface—and the poem is all surface—helps to validate Hockney's daring assertion of the privileges enjoyed by himself, in his Hollywood Hills home, and his companions and patrons as nouveau riche entrepreneurs, the stars of their very own pictures. And part of their exterior world of palms and sunshine and bodies of water is the pleasure of exhibiting themselves as nudes in their restricted neighborhoods.

Timothy Steele

DAYBREAK, BENEDICT CANYON

Thick fog has filled the canyon overnight
And turned it to a sea of milky gray:
The steep-sloped chaparral and streets below
Are drowned from view; hilltops across the way
Form a low-lying archipelago
Upon the fog's smothering gulfs and shoals.
The scene, in the uncertain predawn light,
Recalls those Chinese landscapes on silk scrolls

In which mists haunt ravines and clouds surround
Remote peaks fading to remoter skies.
The scene suggests, too, the apocalypse
The earth may suffer if sea levels rise.

This very deck could be a ghostly ship's
And I a lone survivor, cast by fate
Out on a flood as lifeless and profound
As the one Noah had to navigate.

Yet soon this world's specifics will revive
And banish fanciful analogies.
Some mourning doves, on airily whistling wings,
Will light in canyon-overhanging trees;
Damp breeze will test the tensile strength of strings,
Jeweled and soaking, that a spider's spun;
Cars snaking up along Mulholland Drive
Will flash their windshields at the rising sun.

The fog will drain; the canyon will evince
Toyon, buckthorn, and yucca, and restore
The ceanothus thickets that hide deer;
Houses will surface on the canyon floor.
The only ocean will be south of here
And glimpsed through a green hollow in a ridge,
Pacific in its sunny sparks and glints
Beyond San Pedro's Vincent Thomas Bridge.[4]

—•—

To live in the hills, with a deck or a pool or patio as a bridge to the outer world, is to keep a perilous balance, as in Timothy Steele's "Daybreak, Benedict Canyon" from *Toward the Winter Solstice* (2006). Before we appraise the content of this meticulously designed lyric, we should pause to admire its formal intricacy. The rhymed eight-line stanzas recall the sculpted perfection of, for example, Yeats's poems in ottava rima, "Sailing to Byzantium" and "Among School Children." In this case the poem presents a variation on ottava rima, in its rhyme scheme and especially in its eschewal of a final couplet for each stanza, which in Yeats's work creates the effect of a resounding closure, like the lid snapping on a box, in his famous analogy. Still, the rhymed stanzas preserve the gravity and stately pace of the lyric as it proceeds stage by orderly stage to its meditative finale. Of special note in the rhyme scheme is the chime of line one with line seven in each stanza. To withhold the rhyme for so long is to credit the reader with patience and an attention span capacious enough to discern and *feel* the unusual pattern as a tonal variation from the norm. The pleasures derived from the melodic pentameter rhythm are varied by the frequent substitution of two-stress or spondaic feet: "Thick fog," "steep-sloped," "low-lying." There is an abundance, perhaps an overabundance, of liquids and nasals to manifest the lovely scene being described, but the surprising eruption of plosives at key moments, such as the "p's" in "apocalypse," the key word in the poem, prick our attention and recall us from a trance of pleasurable reading. At all times we feel the commanding intelligence of a deliberate technician, working against the free verse practice of most Los Angeles poets.

"Daybreak, Benedict Canyon" is a dawn song, but rather than begin by praising the freshness of immediate sensations upon waking, the joyful escape from the fog of dreams and the fog of unconsciousness, this poem records the obscurity of vision awaiting the poet upon leaving the house—and gazing into the exterior world from his deck. Benedict Canyon is a large ravine in the Santa Monica Mountains, descending into Beverly Hills, heavily forested, and populated mainly by white professionals who have benefited from higher education. It is a place of privilege to which most young Angelenos aspire. But it is also vulnerable to fire and its inhabitants live in constant anxiety during the summer and fall seasons, especially in times of drought. During these times it's likely that the first thing every occupant does upon awaking is stroll outside to take a look at the sky and sniff the air. Breezes from the nearby Pacific Ocean carry a mixed charge; they are welcome relief from hot weather and for bringing scents of the natural world, but they have the potential to whip the smallest fire into a devastating conflagration. And homeowners have to contend with other images of peril: earthquakes, mudslides caused by heavy rains. Geologists foresee tsunamis rushing in upon the whole coastal region in an irresistible flood.

So the "thick fog" that opens the poem does not have the same thematic value as, say, the yellow fog that J. Alfred Prufrock notes as he wanders the streets of some archetypal American city in T. S. Eliot's poem, or the fog that enters on "little cat feet" in Carl Sandburg's imagist poem. Nor is it the picturesque "fog drift" that Robinson Jeffers watches from his house in Carmel in the poem "Boats in a Fog," all but concealing the shadowy fishing boats making their way under the cliffs. The ocean fog (not smog) in Steele's poem is symbolic from its first appearance, a figure of artifice reminiscent of "Chinese landscapes on silk scrolls." This analogy not only announces the poet's credentials as a connoisseur but establishes the habit of mind that discovers tropes in all phenomena. The speaker of Steele's poem begins to detach the image of fog from its natural, climatic sources and ponder the suggestibility of the image for a fantasy of apocalypse. What if the sea of fog were the actual ocean overwhelming himself and his city? The poet imagines himself as a "lone survivor" in the midst of universal catastrophe. Again, this reverie is culturally specific; the poet is "cast by fate" in both major meanings of the word "cast." He is potentially a castaway in a drowning world, but he is also cast by fate, a Noah-to-be, in a scriptural drama of biblical proportions. For a moment, he feels himself a prophet in the doomed history of Los Angeles, an agent in one of the many scenarios of absolute catastrophe generated by pulp novelists, tract writers, and filmmakers about the city.

To say as much is to indicate how Steele's ability to conceptualize Los Angeles grew in sophistication from the modest pictorialism of poems like "Near Olympic" and "At Will Rogers Beach" in his volume of 1986, *Sapphics Against Anger*. The first two octaves of "Daybreak, Benedict Canyon" resemble the detailed sketching of these early poems: fanciful, whimsical, painterly. But halfway through the poem, a major thematic and dramatic turn occurs, signaled by the important conjunction "Yet." This rhetorical structure recalls the design of Thomas Hardy's great poem of 1899, "The Darkling Thrush," also in eight-line stanzas, which shifts halfway through from melancholy brooding upon the corpse of the nineteenth century figuratively spread out before him, to at least a tiny intimation of "illimitable joy" for the future. (The twentieth century did not, alas, live up to the thrush's presumed annunciation.) The rising sun of "Daybreak, Benedict Canyon" dispels the fog and the gloomy thoughts it sponsored and restores to the poet the familiar images of his environment: mourning doves, spider webs, and the human presence represented by cars moving along nearby Mulholland Drive cresting the mountain canyons. In the final stanza the register of actual objects becomes a catalogue of vegetation, a prelude to the houses that "surface" from the dwindling fog in a daily miracle of resurrection. The poem ends resonantly with the prospect extending toward the vanishing point of a distant landmark, the Vincent Thomas Bridge spanning Los Angeles Harbor between San Pedro and Terminal Island. Bridges are one means by which humanity defeats the ubiquity of the watery world. As in Hart Crane's poem about the Brooklyn Bridge, they connect community with community, earth and sky, mortality and divinity. Steele makes no such claims in his poem but he relies on the reader's memory of poems like Crane's to lift the spirit out of its fears of the future, fears of some tidal wave that might transform Los Angeles into an inland lake.[5]

In the two poems discussed above, then, Trinidad and Steele undertake themes of controlled and uncontrolled water, the swimming pool and the deluge, that this book's first essay, "The Pacific Ocean of the Poets," surveyed to some degree. In his study *Water and Art*, David Clarke has hypothesized that "water, as a substance which is itself without fixed form, may have found a particular relevance for our era of fluidity and dissolution."[6] David Hockney became the public face of Los Angeles art in large part because he features water in its most domestic and orderly form, as a site for hedonic pleasure comparable to the beach but more exclusive and with no sand or tar. Hockney has made the body of water and the human body into a utopian fit, a merging of culture and nature that fulfilled the British immigrant's expectations of the American Dream. Trinidad's modest poem pays tribute to this successful master-stroke.

Steele's poem is more ambitious, more visionary. It is not a poem of eighteenth- and nineteenth-century intentions, of the kind explored by W. H. Auden in his monograph *The Enchafèd Flood*. Nor does it offer iconography like John Everett Millais's depiction of Ophelia drowning, Jules Verne's heroes diving twenty thousand leagues under the sea, or J. M. W. Turner's wild seascapes in a war of elements. Nor is it an essentially comic poem of the desert and the sea like the sequence in Mary Kinzie's *California Sorrow* (2007), in which T. S. Eliot's meditations on water are burlesqued in an account of his visit to the original "In and Out burger place" in Corona Del Mar along with many of the artists in the modernist pantheon. Steele's intimations of being overwhelmed, of suddenly being underwater, does recall the threatening deluge portrayed by Wordsworth in his dream of the gathering flood and the Arab Rider in Book 5 of *The Prelude*. Steele's elegant lyric is a realm of order, a fortress of language, a measured sigh of relief for being saved one more dawn from the tsunami likely to be unleashed by The Big One.

II

The Big One. Only those who grow up in California and/or live there for long periods know how ubiquitous the chatter is, daily and persistently, about the prospect of a devastating earthquake. It is part of the social imaginary, the complex of aspirations and anxieties that shape a city's sensibilities and account for much of its self-definition, ideology, and daily behavior. The fact that the city was built, and continues to be developed, in defiance of the predicted catastrophe along the San Andreas and/or other fault zones that silently govern the future existence of Los Angeles, speaks to an *amor fati* among its residents. The compensating obsession with calamity informs much of the popular culture by which the city is defined. Films like *The War of the Worlds* (1953), which depicts in one scene the destruction of Los Angeles City Hall, and *Kiss Me Deadly* (1955), which concludes with a nuclear device going off in a Malibu beach house, were followed by an abundance of apocalyptic movies directed at a mass audience entertained by images of devastation in the city. And not just Los Angeles: a so-called megaquake would take down many coastal areas south and north of the city. In a memoir the poet John Haines recalled an earthquake that hit Long Beach on 10 March 1933, killing 120 people:

> I had just finished eating my supper when my bed began moving violently across the room. I heard a terrible grinding and shaking, the sound of things spilling and breaking, cries from elsewhere in the house. I remember screaming for someone to save me, the world was ending. . . .
>
> The next morning, the car packed full, we left Long Beach. Our house had become unsafe, and we had to move. We drove slowly through the damaged city, past the heaped rubble of old buildings, past barbed-wire barricades set up by the National Guard, sentries and deserted streets. I saw my school, St. Matthews, a brown stucco pile that had collapsed the night before.[7]

Like the same earthquake described by John Fante in his novel *Ask the Dust* (1939), this one undermined the sense of living in a protected social community; it inspired a morbidity of imagination brought on by a momentary loss of faith in the future ("the world was ending") with repercussions for the child's/adult's inner map and inner calendar. For the public at large, the traumatic memory of fatal temblors like the one in Long Beach and an earlier quake that destroyed the commercial area of Santa Barbara in 1925 sustains the imagination of disaster forever.

The San Francisco earthquake of 1906 remains the primal shock that informs commentary on The Big One in the discourse of Southern California. David L. Ulin assesses the impact of that event:

> The San Francisco earthquake is a watershed in California history, an essential turning point in the narrative of the state. It represents, in many ways, the genesis of contemporary California, the origin of our identification of the place as earthquake country. As a fractured landscape of devastating possibility, where hope and terror may abruptly coincide.[8]

Ulin focuses his book, *The Myth of Solid Ground* (2004), on the many individuals and institutions currently invested in predicting a repeat of the 1906 devastation, especially in vulnerable Southern California, where an abundance of geological faults and constantly occurring tremors—thousands during the last few years—create a psychic landscape of oncoming doom.

A memorial volume issued immediately after the San Francisco quake by The Bible House in Chicago, begins its first chapter, after a portfolio of photographs, by quoting from 1 Kings 19:

> And he said go forth and stand upon the mount before the Lord. And behold, the Lord passed by, and a great and strong wind rent the mountains, and brake in pieces the rocks before the Lord, but the Lord was not in the wind; and after the wind an earthquake; but the Lord was not in the earthquake.
>
> And after the earthquake a fire; but the Lord was not in the fire; and after the fire a still small voice.

In this passage the Lord has manifested His sublime power to His fearful prophet Elijah, but not with a menacing purpose; rather, He speaks quietly and encourages His servant to help repair the damage to the kingdom of Israel resulting from its lapsed belief. Likewise, the earthquake of 1906 is described, in this book and others of an evangelical cast, as a catastrophe of huge dimensions, but also a "scene . . . of unspeakable grandeur."[9] A history of Vesuvius and Pompeii is appended to the volume to secure the parallel between the work of the "fire fiend" of classical and modern periods. Romanticism fed upon the last days of Pompeii as a foretype of modern Europe's dissolution in the aftermath of the French Revolution, though no experience of the ancient world matched the Lisbon earthquake of 1755, which was interpreted variously as God's punishment and a wholly natural phenomenon free from divine intervention. Californians inherited preconceptions and interpretations dating back thousands of years, renewed periodically; San Francisco in 1906 took form as the sign and template of worse to come. Residents became accustomed to living on the edge, obsessed with the drawbacks of exceptionalism and the harrowing continual expectation of catastrophe.

Burton Pike notes, "The fascination people have always felt at the destruction of a city may be partly an expression of satisfaction at the destruction of an emblem of irresolvable conflict."[10] Even before the attack on the World Trade Center in 2001, the skyscrapers of New York City had become such an emblem or symbol, and their destruction a terrifying omen inspiring reactions by authors and the general public that wavered between vindictive rage, despair, and a strange exultation. One feels that throb of ambivalence in the fictive scenario of two aerial assaults upon New York City, H. G. Wells's account in his novel *The War in the Air* (1908) and Alexander P. de Seversky's in his non-fiction polemic *Victory Through Air Power* (1942).[11] The literature of Los Angeles, as we have seen, has been nourished by intertextual connections to the earliest prophetic and apocalyptic imaginings of catastrophic endings to some utopian vision too good to last. The American city, in its history and in its self-descriptions, has been a place of sometimes hardly endurable conflict. Scorn, even hatred for the city marks the poetry arising from each settlement, if only as a resistance to the partisan celebration of this privileged spot on the globe. Nature has always manifested its power both as a garden of delights and as a nemesis for those who enjoy, and degrade, its bounty. Writers often contemplate a swift resolution to the city's agonies, its failure to live up to its earliest promises of joy, its fall into crime, corruption, and degeneracy. The San Andreas Fault, which stretches for 700 miles from the Mendocino coast north of San Francisco to the Mexican border, has become the city's ambiguous emblem of final affliction, a byword of future fatality.

Quakes are not so common in California, despite their reputation, that poets have felt obligated to respond to them. San Francisco itself has seen no major quake since 1906; those of 1989 and 2010 are customarily described as "mild" and "moderate." But poets have registered the anxiety caused by even small temblors, in their metaphors and in their direct lyric engagements with the subject. A representative example is "Quake" by Henri Coulette, printed here in full:

Henri Coulette

QUAKE

Jack Donne and Raymond Chandler, like shattered pigeons, fall,
All thud and blunder, quintessential California.

A name like Richter gives a signature to fear,
And palm tree rats now hearken to the lisp of God.

The swimming pools of Eden suddenly are empty.
Bertolt Brecht's spectacles lie splintered on the floor,

For all the world is made of glass and makes to break,
And shines like stars without a heaven, and makes to cut.

Alas, O children of paradise, it comes to this:
This bed thy centre was, that is a midnight mouth.[12]

—•—

The style of this condensed and allusive lyric could not be less "Californian," as we now define that category. It conforms to the tradition loosely associated with T. S. Eliot, Allen Tate, and Ezra Pound, and with the practice of The New Criticism, which favored an allusive lyric style fenced off from the free-verse "barbaric yawp" of Whitman and the more naked poetry of Whitman's successors and imitators. Coulette was one of many poets in Southern California who espoused the poetics of the eastern establishment as a bulwark against what they considered an overly relaxed vernacular poetics based on the rhythms and prosodic structures of prose. Such poets sought an educated audience, not a mass audience, comfortable with wide-ranging references and sometimes hermetic utterances full of suggestion but not always entirely legible. Such verse is commonly called "conservative" or "reactionary" but these political labels serve little purpose in literary history.

John Donne (1572–1631) was the beau ideal of The New Criticism, having been extravagantly praised by T. S. Eliot for his exceptional versatility as a craftsman and his deep understanding of human nature. Donne's sensibility seemed especially apt for a post–Great War generation that appreciated the Renaissance poet's sensitivity to profound and unsettling changes in his historical period. Donne's response in "An Anatomy of the World" to the new science represented by Galileo and Copernicus—"all coherence gone"—became a catchphrase for the new century shaken to its core by Darwin, Marx, Freud, and Einstein, and by radical changes in machine technology and social organization. And so, his name came easily to Coulette as he sought a figure for the collapse of faith in the stability of self and society following upon the predicted earthquake. Likewise, the last line of the poem echoes the final line of Donne's signature love lyric "The Sun Rising": "This bed thy centre is, these walls thy sphere." Donne's confident assertion that, though all else may prove unstable, subject to the whims of "kings and desperate men" as well as accidents of nature, the romantic couple will survive as the axis upon which the world turns, seems as suspect to the demoralized speaker of Coulette's poem as Raymond Chandler's depictions of the triumph of good over evil in his detective novels. Collapse is the inescapable condition of "quintessential California." After the quake, as after the fall, "the swimming pools of Eden" live under the sign of inevitable destruction.

It is Charles F. Richter rather than Copernicus whose science now dominates the cosmopolitan metropoles. (The Richter scale measures the intensity of earthquakes.) And Bertolt Brecht, who lived in exile in Los Angeles for many years and wrote many wry lyrics about Hollywood in particular, is offered as a modern equivalent of Donne. Brecht depicted the disorder of society, certainly, but with the inner faith that a solution was possible: Communism, or Marxism more generally. The earthquake is a social and economic fact as well as an accident of nature; it is the genuine game-changer in human affairs and makes a mockery of progressive and utopian schemes of all kinds. The wisest of our time are revealed as tree rats when an emergency strikes, "For all the world is made of glass and makes to break." The odd locution "makes to break" and "makes to cut" is readable as a testimony of pessimism, a confession that humans are alone in the world, without the benefit of that "still, small voice" of God promising some happier scenario for the future. The poem withdraws from the "children of paradise" any possibility of local pride based on the milieu of palm trees and swimming pools—

the good life touted in so much promotional literature. What is genuinely exceptional about Los Angeles is its apocalyptic fate, the "midnight mouth" that *will* swallow the city.

Coulette's poem is a radical experiment in the Eliotic method of mixing statement and allusion to present both an emotion and a vision. Intended as a rebuke to readers who prefer, indeed insist upon, the blandishments of mass culture, "Quake" comes close to parodying the "mosaic style," as this verbal shorthand was sometimes called. Couplet laid upon couplet, this immensely concentrated composition presents a daunting surface to the reading public. All poems about earthquakes challenge literary structures, agitating readers who are troubled by the effort of moving from a comfort zone into a rhetorical world less legible, more metapoetic. Coulette's poem is not without a shading of humor, a taunting challenge to the reader's complacent status as a consumer of the long centuries of useless literary culture.

The presence of wit and humor in conjunction with earthquake is most famously displayed in *Candide,* Voltaire's satire on Enlightenment optimism after the Lisbon earthquake of 1755. Dr. Pangloss justifies the earthquake to Candide who lies helpless under the rubble. Voltaire's earlier work "Poème sur le désastre de Lisbonne" had some wit but no humor. Modern authors almost by definition seek a tone for their poems more ironic and more sardonic than their predecessors, as if softening up readers for the disabling punch. Debora Greger, in "Piranesi in L.A.," offers one reason to join Dr. Pangloss in looking on the lighter side:

> optimistic as this city where what's built wrong
>
> goes down to earthquake, mudslide, wrecking ball
> before age has its chance.[13]

The jerry-built will not outlast the geological shock, and the well-built will follow soon after. Like the buckling freeway in the poem by Charles Harper Webb that follows, "what's built wrong" seems to belong to the Los Angelized landscape that offered some levity amidst narratives of mayhem ever since Nathanael West heaped scorn on houses made of plaster and paper rather than brick and hardwood.

III

Charles Harper Webb

YOU MISSED THE EARTHQUAKE, BILL

One instant I was asleep in bed; the next,
I was bucking and bouncing like a tuna
on the floor. Power-transformers flashed
like bombs; then black poured in. "Oh shit, oh shit,"
I prayed until the jolting stopped. Alive,

my house standing—as far as I could tell—
I groped for clothes, and stumbled into them
outside, where car-alarms whooped
and caterwauled in pre-dawn chill. The yellow
feelers of flashlights twitched up and down

the black trees, black sidewalk, black street.
Art Campo's radio reported freeways buckled,
buildings down, exploded gas lines,
spewing water mains. We tried to think
we were lucky as aftershocks rolled in

like bowling balls. When I think of you, Bill,
I usually think of some good things you're missing:
redheads, pow-wows, barbecues, thunderstorms,
the Hubble telescope tuning in a cosmos clear
enough to see the souls in heaven. (I didn't

see you.) But the dead miss bad things too—
getting fired from a good job, which I just was,
or dumped by a woman you love,
which I was too, or trapped in your apartment's
rubble or your mini-van, screaming

as chunks of overpass crush it, then you.
I thought I heard your kids crying three blocks
away as darkness grabbed our homes and shook,
your wife—still hating you for Jane in Idaho—
screaming "Goddamn it, Bill, why aren't you here?!"

A cop was motorcycling through silvery fog
when a freeway bridge dropped out
from under him. Dying, he missed a week
of sixteen-hour shifts, rescues, crushed bodies,
looters, gapers, gorgers on misfortune.

He might've liked those things, who knows?
We never know what we've enjoyed till we look back.
He was too startled, probably, to enjoy
his arcing flight, then too afraid. But what
a ride he must have had, Bill, what a ride.[14]

—•—

The title of Charles Harper Webb's poem "You Missed the Earthquake, Bill" registers a seismic tonal shift from the poetics of Coulette. This poem is "Southern Californian," as one might expect from a poet identified as a tutelary spirit of place ever since he coedited with Suzanne Lummis an anthology, *Stand Up Poetry: The Poetry of Los Angeles and Beyond,* in 1990.[15] The anthology presented its Southland poets as a school-with-a-style; the title owed something to New York poet Edward Field's first book of poems *Stand Up, Friend, With Me,* a Lamont Award–winning volume from 1963, as well as to the idiom "stand-up comedy," carrying associations with Lenny Bruce, Mort Sahl, Richard Pryor, George Carlin, Joan Rivers, and other irreverent monologists. In an introduction Webb cited humor as the heart and soul of this new school, again using Field as a role model. (The title of Field's book is addressed to his penis.) The Los Angeles School, in other words, presented itself as an offshoot of the New York School: it too goes on its nerve, to cite Frank O'Hara's description of his poetics, and delights in performance style and structure. It is a school attuned to the "bop prosody" of the Beat poets, and one can hear in many poems of this and other anthologies of Los Angeles verse the echoes of (northern) California poet Lawrence Ferlinghetti and frequent visitor to Los Angeles Allen Ginsberg. In the same volume from which "You Missed the Earthquake, Bill" is drawn, *Reading the Water* (1997), Webb addressed an adulatory poem to Ginsberg, "Invocation to Allen as the Muse Euterpe." He begs a favor from this bohemian muse:

> . . . Help me quit griping and celebrate L.A.: its corpse-blue sky,
> its Bel air and Beverly hills, its gurus and gangbangers, beaches and
>   waves into which, diving, you taste seven million bowels.
>
> —•—
>
> Help me to sing of Hollywood pushers and peep shows and aging stars
>   ground underfoot, of Angelyne, "famous for nothing," who looks
>   down like God on rush hour with her abuse-me eyes above her
>   continental chest's wide divide.[16]

The carnivalesque content of Ginsberg's poems is an inspiration for Webb, and for his contemporaries who since the mid-1970s have published numerous volumes with the same robust comedy if not the same graceful form.

The premise of Webb's poem is that earthquakes are something to laugh about as well as shudder at. This temblor was not The Big One, the dreaded 8.-plus catastrophe, but a substantial one, the Northridge quake of January 1994, which registered 6.7 on the Richter scale, caused 72 deaths and 9,000 injuries, and cost 20 billion dollars. More than any quake in recent decades it raised anxieties about the future, causing an uprush of punditry and graveyard humor, and a discernible narrative thread of proximate jeopardy in many Hollywood movies and TV dramas of the '90s and '00s. Webb's use of the earthquake is characteristically complex. The jocular title gives way to some farcical language in the opening stanzas: the speaker is "bucking and bouncing like a tuna." "Oh shit, oh shit,' / I prayed" and then car alarms "whooped / and caterwauled in pre-dawn chill." The aftershocks roll in "like bowling balls." Webb seeks to effect a subversion of discursive style and good taste by means of extravagant rhetoric suited to the occasion. After all, big earthquakes burst the bounds of everyday geological behavior; if you want to mimic their disruptive effects, for journalistic as well as comic purposes, you go for the excessive simile, the impolite profanity, the exclamatory adjective. These are a survivor's idioms, designed to lure the reader into the poem and its extraordinary dramatic occasion.

The poem deepens in the fourth stanza. From a personal report, it turns to elegy, as it draws into its circumference of concern the deceased figure of Bill, who has escaped the terror but also the vivifying excitement of the quake. Webb is performing a difficult rhetorical exercise here, preparing the reader for what will be an upbeat attitude about a policeman who fell to his death when a freeway he was riding buckled. In the historical record this man's name, Clarence Wayne Dean, has been eternized at the site of the accident: this stretch of the Antelope Valley Freeway is now known as The Clarence Wayne Dean Memorial Interchange. "The dead miss bad things too," the poet temporizes, which is cold comfort to the cop's survivors, and there is no attempt in the poem to gloss over or sentimentalize the pain of Dean's leaving a life sketched in glowing colors in the fifth stanza.

The poem is heading in a direction that is putatively consolatory; it will make claims beginning in the penultimate stanza about the mordant satisfactions of premature decease. The poem first offers some slight recompense for the cop who will miss the ordeal of cleaning up after the catastrophe; but the real leap comes when the poem considers the image of the cop hurtling through the air after the freeway collapsed under him. "But what / a ride he must have had, Bill, what a ride." For a moment all the thrill of riding the freeways, examined in an earlier chapter, is condensed into this single dramatic line and a half, reminiscent of James Dickey's contrarian strategy in his long poem "Falling," in which the moments a stewardess falls to her death after being sucked through a door of the airplane are dilated to vast dimensions, ending with a transcendental moment of ecstasy as she hits the Midwestern fields of grain.

But there is an analogy closer to the locale and relevant to the focus of this book. In her novel *Golden Days*, Carolyn See imagines a nuclear attack on Los Angeles that turns most of the city into a "charnel house," leaving a small band of survivors, including the narrator of the novel. Destruction on this scale is the worst fate anyone could imagine for L.A. or any city. And yet the narrator, Edith, asserts in despite of reason that this misfortune is a *felix culpa*, a fortunate fall:

> I stood up and put out my arm to quiet her. "*No!*" I said. "Some people say these are the bad times, but *I* say they are *good* times. We have brav-

ery! We have love! We have the future. We have the Beginning! We have the present! Listen to *that* word, the Present."[17]

If such a claim, seemingly mad, can be made about a nuclear strike, then arguably it can be made about the death of any individual (Bill, or the cop) or any collateral victims. The dead will not be offended, and though the loving survivors can never be consoled, the mass of readers, the citizenry at large who are the self-selected readers of the poem, must be offered a conceptual refiguring of the significance of such a death. The poem looks to a future nourished by the blood of those who died unwillingly, as all people die under such circumstances. As with A. E. Housman's popular lyric "To an Athlete Dying Young," the sentiment is outrageous, unacceptable, yet somewhere in the unconscious it carries a parcel of tragic joy, stoical and ecstatic at the same time. Contra-historical and contra-traditional in its defiance of the customary pieties, it has the insouciant tone and content of stand-up comedy routines, for which nothing is sacred.

Dorothy Barresi

SOME QUESTIONS WE MIGHT ASK

I

This morning after the earthquake
I lay in bed listening.
First light, and the studs in the walls
and the crossbeams settled down again,
the water pipes and heating ducts,
carpet nails, each
low thing groaning.
                    Cubes began dropping
one by one from the automatic
ice cube maker down the hall.
The electricity in my alarm clock hiccupped off, then on.

2
At what age are we no longer considered
too young to die?
I thought about my sister Ellen.
At thirteen and twelve and fifteen,
she beat me with a fuzzy bedroom slipper,
her eyes gone to bored, peevish discs.
I can't always call it abuse. The lack of love

she had for me had reasons, and those,
reasons of their own.
Still, in low moments, cast down,
I can hate myself without trying, and my decent,
mute, and muddled parents
for the failures she found in me.

But it wasn't a clear case of anything.
Not like the story of my friend's youngest sister, who,
without language or recourse,
amidst bears and wicker and ruffles, curled
into a brine shrimp—tiny
pink nothing—
each time her father slipped soundlessly from her room.
Years like that.
Then, when words came, years more,
and not one change
or day in the crazy world to tell.

3
Listen. Here is a fact about personal safety
I like to keep in mind.
If a leash or silk tether tied us,
like a sine wave snapped
back from the invisible future,
to everyone who held
our safety in hand: every teacher and lawyer, parent,
crossing guard and fast
food cook, every pharmacist, spot welder, pilot and so on,

we couldn't walk down the street without tripping
and falling on our faces.
After the earthquake this morning
the glass in the windows flexed
subtly, intermittently—
a faint murmur of steel in the day
urging us onward,
and our reluctances,
which is said to be one of the seven
easiest words in the English language to say: *murmur*.

4
I took a drink of water.
Later, doing dishes left from the night before,
I imagined the suds pearlescent
DNA molecules
mounting each other for the steady air.
It occurred to me then: idiot!
I should have crawled under something heavy, my writing desk,
or braced myself upstairs
in the upstanding, rectilinear
safety of a doorway.

5
I'd been surviving by accident all day.
Like this one last theory
buzzing my brain,
that cats and dogs leave home for the scrub

and creosote hills above Sunland and Thousand Oaks
a few days before a temblor hits.
Later, picked up
in record numbers by the county, they're counted,
and after a decent interval,
claimed or gassed;
                    and the coyotes, too, have their feast.
To know something's coming, anything, sub rosa
in the meat and tender

architecture of our paws!
Of course we have no such wild sense,
but what if we did?
Leave or howl, diminish—on all fours at the concrete river—
where would we go next?
How far away from home is safe?
Face on the river,
who will tell us to stop when we finally arrive?[18]

—•—

Perhaps the premier poem about earthquakes in Los Angeles is Dorothy Barresi's "Some Questions We Might Ask," from her volume of 1996, *The Post-Rapture Diner*. Barresi teaches at California State University, Northridge, and so she was perfectly positioned to document the Northridge earthquake of 1994. Her response has the stoical urbanity of so much Los Angeles poetry. In fact, the prosaic, de-dramatized style, full of somber tonalities, might be claimed as a period style in American poetry of the *fin de siècle*. It fits well the attitude assumed by an artist who does not put on the bardic posture of Romantic and Modernist poets but descends in tone to the commonsensical, companionable manner of dignified conversation. As with Webb's poem, the opening of "Some Questions We Might Ask" is cool and offhand, as if it were the blasé chitchat of a wit innocent of even the idea of trauma. The central event is introduced in a prepositional phrase, "after the earthquake," reporting in a seemingly uninflected voice, on the verge of bravado, the aftermath of what she must have feared was The Big One. The wry tone of "The electricity in my alarm clock hiccupped off, then on" suggests that the shaking was no big deal, but the meditation that follows registers the rising anxiety stirred in her by the warning sign of larger destruction to come.

Unlike the crossbeams, she cannot settle down. She considers the injustice of life, to which the violence of earthquake contributes. The first question she asks is "At what age are we no longer considered / too young to die?" After the aftershocks fade, she tries to displace the quake by the force of memory, summoning adolescent terrors to screen the injuries she and her city have suffered in the night hours. For "lack of love" and even "abuse" she can at least blame herself. And she's luckier than her friend's youngest sister who had suffered molestation from her father in the night. Part 2 of the poem succeeds in lightening the personal implications of the disaster; the speaker lay safely in bed whereas her friend's unfortunate sister had no such comfort. Such rationalization is a normal coping mechanism akin to Webb's celebration of the cop's wild ride; but in Part 3 the earthquake snaps back into prominence as a threat to "personal safety." The drama of the poem resides in the obsessive presence in her memory of this potentially mortal threat to her and her family, and how her strategies to *not* think about it take on evasive dimensions, as when she considers how the word "murmur" is one of the easiest words in the English language to say. Distracting thoughts crowd her brain at the beginning of Part 4, but the inescapable danger comes roaring back into her consciousness:

> It occurred to me then: idiot!
> I should have crawled under something heavy, my writing desk,
> or braced myself upstairs
> in the upstanding, rectilinear
> safety of a doorway.[19]

So far the poem is entirely interior: she remains inside a house and her subject matter proceeds as reverie inside her brain. Glimpses of the exterior world, where the earthquake's effects lurk, are mainly diversionary, ways of not thinking about what is most proximate to her secluded state and most awful to contemplate.

But the final strophe, Part 5, succumbs to the irrepressible vector of her obsession that points outward. Cats and dogs, she remembers, as "theory" not fact, are sensitive to foreshocks and leave home for "the creosote hills above Sunland and Thousand Oaks / a few days before a temblor hits." But there is no safety in such flight, she reminds herself as part of the self-reproach initiated by the earthquake. Coyotes terminate the lives of these pets more surely than would the shaking of the earth. And what if they escape the predators? They're rounded up and either "claimed or gassed." Now the misgivings, the anguish of helplessness, gathers speed and mass till the final line. What if we had the prescient instincts of cats and dogs, where would we escape to? In the final passage of despair, humans are imagined as crawling on all fours like animals and making their way to the "concrete river"—the Los Angeles River paved after a disastrous flood in 1938 to prevent future flooding. Would that be far enough away from Northridge to escape the quake? "How far away from home is safe?" And who would tell the now four-footed figures face down at the river's edge that they have reached safety? A poem that began in the cool tone of assurance ends in abasement and terror, full of questions about the contingency of our pathetic condition living atop an increasingly worrisome pattern of faults. (The Northridge fault was previously unknown.)

It is noteworthy that the poem locates violations of safety not in the streets of the city where afflictions from crime, traffic accidents, and fire overtake the innocent, but in the interiors of the putatively safest place in the world, the home. Yet this cold comfort stalks the speaker as she directs our attention beyond the hearth out to the woods, the concrete river, the inhospitable outdoors where the coyotes signify a predatory nature painful to consider. For readers *anywhere* in the country, or the world, these lessons enacted in Los Angeles bear upon everyday life, all the more so because they are spoken in a supple lineation with plentiful asides and nuances. The urbane poem invites us into the private life of the speaker, who has been shocked into an understanding that the earthquake exposes non-geological fault lines underlying confidence and consciousness alike.

Would it stretch the boundaries of interpretation to identify the traumatized speaker of Barresi's poem as a figure for the entire population of Los Angeles? To speak with victims of an earthquake like the Northridge strike (my mother was one, shocked awake by the collapse of the chimney and front part of her house) is to hear the pattern of auto-critique outlined above. To think on this topic is to be full of sorrow, to adapt Keats's line from "Ode to a Nightingale." Efforts at consolation by locating reasons for relief give way to a catalogue of counterexamples, fearful conjectures, alarmed prophecies. The rhetoric of self-persuasion collapses into its rebuking opposite, just as Keats's speaker in the ode descends from an ecstatic vision of the "Queen Moon" and "starry Fays" into a recognition that he has been desperately *not* talking about a forlorn condition of mortality and that all his eloquence cannot forestall the fact of death that has been his barely repressed subject all along. Such is the testimony of those who begin their discourse in denial, but bravely break through or give way to a recognition of what is waiting in their future. That The Big One *will* come is the specter that every sustained commentary devolves to in the conversations I have experienced with Angelenos. This is the communal voice that David L. Ulin identifies as the fundamental identity-forming narrative behind every Los Angeles life.

For those who live in Los Angeles, in proximity to large geological faults, Barresi's poem, like Charles Harper Webb's, performs the public service of one of Mithridates' daily drops of poison, strengthening his digestive and circulatory system against a larger dose served up by the inevitable assassin. "Some Questions We Might Ask" asks the pertinent questions ("How far away from home is safe?") but also, and with more resignation than Webb's poem, carries the antidote of reassurance. "First light" does finally break after the night terrors, though daytime brings more terrors to mind. The poem troubles the reader, yet the existence of the poem is proof that one remains, for the time being, in whatever humiliating posture, a survivor.

The poems of Coulette, Webb, and Barresi address the inevitability of The Big One that haunts the imagination of the citizens of Los Angeles. Is it the end of the world, as the child John Haines cried out fearfully, or is it a dreaded event that will mark the beginning, for good and ill, of a new phase in the history of Los Angeles, as it did for San Francisco in 1906? However much we resist or reject the sense of jeopardy and/or the *amor fati* expressed in such poems, we now have them in our psychic armamentarium, fortifying us for any of several catastrophes that can and will occur in the twenty-first century. Mike Davis has provided a squirm-inducing catalogue of such potential horrors in *Ecology of Fear*. Global warming and other climatic changes threaten to raise the Pacific Ocean six to nine feet, inundating the coastal areas periodically. And the various tsunamis and earthquakes in Asia have provided vivid images of wholesale destruction during the last several decades.[20] The U.S. Geological Survey in 2011 issued warnings about "a superstorm" during the coming years that would cause $300 billion in damage and wipe out one-quarter of the homes in the state of California. The normally consoling genre of the "nature poem" is shadowed in Los Angeles by the prophecies of erasure contained in such publications.

IV

To conclude a book-length study of Los Angeles poetry, and an essay on the psycho-geography of its exterior, with the rubble and mayhem of earthquake and flood, would follow the lead of key texts on the city, which arrange their sequence of scenes and commentary to flow toward a morbid and melancholy closure. Not all poets have fallen in line behind this structural and ideological formula, however. What if, they ask, Los Angeles is not sufficiently summarized as a Babylon or "Chinatown" infused with crime and corruption from top to bottom, and facing a future of being overwhelmed by fire, flood, earthquake, or worse? The genuine pleasure of living in the city, as evidenced by its increasing population and the genial tone of much popular culture about the neighborhoods and lifestyles of its citizenry, is one of the streaming motifs of its verse. I will focus on a poem by Joy Harjo that presents an apocalyptic format of an entirely different kind, one that owes much to the early boosterism and celebratory character of some lyrics but with a spiritual thrust missing from almost all poems about the city. That "The Path to the Milky Way Leads through Los Angeles" is one of only two poems about Los Angeles in the 1,210 pages of *The Norton Anthology of Contemporary Poetry* suggests that this lyric may have already achieved canonical status, and may serve as both a beacon and target for future poets formulating their responses to a city more and more difficult to represent persuasively.[21]

Joy Harjo

THE PATH TO THE MILKY WAY LEADS THROUGH LOS ANGELES

There are strangers above me, below me and all around me and
we are all strange in this place of recent invention.

This city named for angels appears naked and stripped of anything
resembling the shaking of turtle shells, the songs of human voices
on a summer night outside Okmulgee.

Yet, it's perpetually summer here, and beautiful. The shimmer of gods
is easier to perceive at sunrise or dusk,

when those who remember us here in the illusion of the marketplace
turn toward the changing of the sun and say our names.

We matter to somebody,
We must matter to the strange god who imagines us as we revolve
together in the dark sky on the path to the Milky Way.

We can't easily see that starry road from the perspective of the crossing

of boulevards, can't hear it in the whine of civilization or taste the
minerals of planets in hamburgers.

But we can buy a map here of the stars' homes, dial a tone for
dangerous love, choose from several brands of water or a hiss of oxygen
for gentle rejuvenation.

Everyone knows you can't buy love but you can still sell your soul for
less than a song to a stranger who will sell it to someone else for a profit
until you're owned by a company of strangers
in the city of the strange and getting stranger.

I'd rather understand how to sing from a crow
who was never good at singing or much of anything
but finding gold in the trash of humans.

So what are we doing here I ask the crow parading on the ledge of
falling that hangs over this precarious city?

Crow just laughs and says *wait, wait and see* and I am waiting
and not seeing anything, not just yet.

But like crow I collect the shine of anything beautiful I can find.[22]

—•—

Harjo is a Native American poet, and in interviews she has described her angle of regard on all subjects as grounded in her ethnic background. Of special note are comments in an interview that express her fidelity to a countercultural sense of place. Laura Coltelli is the interviewer.

LC: Since language has an importance of its own in Indian culture, what's the contribution or influence, just in terms of language, to mainstream American literature?

HARJO: What I think of immediately is the denial, the incredible denial of anything other than that based on the European soul in American literature. Anything else is seen as "foreign" or not consciously integrated into what is called American literature. It could be ethnocentrism backed by a terrible guilt about what happened in this country.

LC: So what's the contribution, just in terms of language, to mainstream American literature?

HARJO: That's a difficult question, one that will take me many months to consider because I'm always thinking about what I can add to the language, as someone of this background—dreams, and so on. I consider first a certain lyricism, a land-based language.

LC: The spirit of place?

HARJO: Yes, the spirit of place recognized, fed, not even paved over, forgotten. Sometimes I feel like specters of forgotten ones roam the literature of some of these American writers who don't understand where they come from, who they are, where they are going. The strongest writers have always been the ones with a well-defined sense of place—I don't mean you have to be a nature writer—I'm thinking of "nonethnic" people, like Flannery O'Connor.

LC: What about imagery?

HARJO: Oh sure, imagery. That's definitely part of it.

LC: A new feeling of landscape, perhaps?

HARJO: Or a knowing of the landscape, as something alive with personality, breathing. Alive with names, alive with events, nonlinear. It's not static and that's a very important point. The Western viewpoint has always been one of the land as wilderness, something to be afraid of, and conquered because of the fear.

LC: The so-called wilderness.

HARJO: Yes, it depends on your viewpoint what wilderness is. For some the city is a wilderness of concrete and steel, made within a labyrinth of mind.[23]

These remarks are a shrewd commentary on assumptions about American culture that have dominated so much poetry, beginning with Whitman's endorsements of Manifest Destiny in poems such as "Song of the Pioneers" and "Song of the Broad-Axe." In this view, the terrain beyond the borders of white civilization is signified as "wilderness" and all the natives therein are alien figures deserving of conquest and domination, for their own good. Native Americans are stigmatized as antagonistic to the march of progress from Eastern cities to the Western frontier. Urbanization therefore results in the ghettoizing of aliens and the creation of an oppressed and depressed population of victims. The Los Angeles sections of N. Scott Momaday's novel *House Made of Dawn* (1968) present depictions of a disconsolate band of Native American drifters in the city, as does the documentary film *The Exiles* (1961). For Native Americans the city is in fact the moral wilderness warned against in their primal texts. For them to assimilate into the often perverse culture of the city is to deform their identity, personal and ethnic, and render themselves to the world as caricatures, as depicted in Nathanael West's grotesque portrait in *The Day of the Locust* of "Chief Kiss-My-Towkus," who has left the reservation and joined the group of deracinated drifters who hustle merchandise and exchange wisecracks on Hollywood Boulevard. Such people have constructed a "labyinth of mind" out of their conflicted understanding of their roles in the city. For such people, for all readers, poets can offer some guidance out of the labyrinth. Harjo casts herself, in the interview and the poem, as an Ariadne with an intuitive sense of the nonlinear exit from the jungle of cities. Her totemic ball of thread is lyrical language, winged words.

The format of the poem substitutes strophes of prose utterances for the strict lineation of traditional verse. Sentences run on like biblical verses, and only occasionally is there a line that insists on its integrity as a complete unit, as with "We matter to somebody." Here Harjo follows the contemporary practice of relaxing cadences and syntax to achieve something of a chanted, dithyrambic effect. The poem creates distance from the formal conventions of the Anglo-American tradition. Yet the poem does not give up on recognizable lineation, line breaks most of all, but strives for a balance of old and new, English and American, in the commonly understood latter-day traditions of modern speech.

The poem is directed most of all to a reader who feels lost, estranged, a victim of the metropolitan wilderness rather than one of its authentic citizens. It begins by consoling such readers that "we are all strangers in this place of recent invention." These readers are immediately narrowed in the second strophe to Native Americans, who feel like they have lost their spiritual and emotional contact with their community, living and dead. The fortuitous circumstance that the city is named for angels directs the poet's strategy of summoning, in rituals of remembrance, the old gods in the shadows of dawn and dusk. "We matter to somebody" is the emphatic message derived from the poet's apprehension of presences in the markets and streets of this recently established city. One hears an echo of Elizabeth Bishop's line "Somebody loves us all" from her poem "Filling Station," in which the speaker interprets the presence of a big begonia, an embroidered doily, and the rude arrangement of oil cans to spell out ESSO-SO-SO-SO as evidence of aesthetic labor for the benefit of passersby, an act of altruistic communitarianism akin to poets' steady work of composition. But Harjo's claim is grander. "We must matter to the strange god who imagines us as we revolve / together in the dark sky on the path to the Milky Way." Here the galaxy, of which our solar system is a part though we may not feel a sense of solidarity with it, becomes a type of heaven-haven, a destination for the pilgrim soul whose progress has been halted in the city that bears the name of angels.

Having laid down a fairly conventional scheme of redemption, Harjo further defines her specific vision of the contact between the terrestrial and celestial. Everything around us participates in the higher level of being, she claims, and she enforces her point with some humor. When we contemplate "the crossing of boulevards" the last thing evident to our senses is the order of the cosmos, amid the honking of horns and the noise of construction. The inescapable chatter of the media new and old, "the whine of civilization," drowns out our apprehension of the music of the spheres. Who thinks of the cosmic origin of matter when biting into a hamburger? "But" she argues—and the poem now turns into an overt act of suasion, a moral directive—"we can buy a map here of the stars' homes . . ." The hoary pun of movie stars and heavenly bodies still contains a primitive identification that remains revelatory after all the generations of celebrity worship. And if we want love, we can get a fragment of it from dialing a service that provides oral gratification of our desire for contact, and more than that if one is willing to pay for it. Money is a medium for "rejuvenation," the poem claims, tongue in cheek. We can buy what we need, including poems that affirm our access, one way or another, to the true goal of all our striving. And Los Angeles deserves credit for that much assistance, no matter how mercenary its materialist motives day to day.

And then the final turn in the poem occurs. Crow is a tutelary deity in some Native American legends, and though it is not exactly an "angel" it performs services to humanity. Harjo's crow is not to be confused with Ted Hughes's "Crow" in his book- length narrative of that title, published in 1970. His "Crow" is often malevolent, a figure of the demonic and of post-nuclear apocalypse. Harjo's "crow" is closer to the real thing, naturalistic rather than archetypal. Harjo playfully compares her song to the crow's cawing, and watches him strut around "on the ledge of / falling that hangs over this precarious city." If this were the "Crow" of Ted Hughes's poems "Crow Tyrannosaurus," "Crow Blacker than Ever," and "King of Carrion," the ground would quake under the feet of the congenial speaker; but this black bird has more in common with Thomas Hardy's thrush or Wallace Stevens's thirteen manifestations of birds of dark color. "Crow just laughs and says, *wait, wait and see*." It's easy advice to take and the poem closes with the speaker agreeably stating that she is waiting as instructed, not yet undergoing a revelation, not yet moving toward the stars, "But like crow I collect the shine of anything beautiful I can find."

That emphatic last line has the sound of a manifesto, and one directed, intentionally or not, at readers who have retreated from the obligations and pleasures of poems about people, places, and things. One function of poetry is to restore to our thinking selves a vivid sense of the circumambient world. Los Angeles, Harjo writes in the opening line of the poem, is a place of strangers, of migrants, of orphans in the universe alienated by being uprooted from familiar locations. Poetry seeks, on one level, to estrange us from the everyday, to defamiliarize the world so as to lend us new eyes and ears. But in the great tradition of landscape poetry coming down from the classical era, such revelations are most often formulated as a result of patient observation and precise description. Poets cultivate a presentness to the world and proceed with their inventions on the basis of empirical evidence. The achieved poem represents a balance of actuality and an active intelligence. The "shine" she discerns in "anything beautiful" derives from a union of diverse sources of light.

Starlight belongs to the stars, Harjo seems to say, but in sunny Los Angeles where it is "perpetually summer" she can be grateful for the daily benison of nurturing light; just looking at its reflections in the things of this world, regarding it with undistracted attention, she finds a firmer place in the firmament. The *fear* of living in "the city of the strange and getting stranger" is like the fear of earthquakes, the fear of car crashes, the fear of assault by strangers, the fear of wipeout in the surf, the fear of whatever is threatening in everyday life. Harjo uses her tutelary gods to overcome her anxiety of being an outcast. One can imagine Eve making the same kind of affirmation not only from the garden but from the first city she locates or helps to construct. Los Angeles is a transit point, provisional as our lives, but offering no less access to the eternity we seek than any other sacred site. On the freeways, at the beach, in Hollywood or South Central, we wait and hope for transfiguration, as our sages and guardian angels have instructed us.

NINE

Conclusion

This book has argued that despite the lingering charge that Los Angeles has been insufficiently brought into focus by its poets, there persists among them an invigorating desire to examine closely the sites, persons, and presumed identity of the city, if only to compensate for the long absence of high quality loco-descriptive poetry about the region. In conversations and correspondence with poets who have written about L.A., whether they live there or not, I've heard constantly the sentiment that the city is extraordinarily attractive to the eye and mind and challenging to the poetic imagination. It offers provocative surfaces to match its historical depths. It compels attention and like all inspirational subjects it encourages linguistic enterprise. Whether in or out of fashion, poems that model for readers fresh views of remarkable locations maintain a lasting value. Probably it is this infatuation with place that lends such poems a retro glamour pleasing to readers who grew up with the modernist tradition. I refer to the poetics evoked, for example, by William Carlos Williams's "Preface" to *Paterson*: "To make a start / out of particulars / and make them general. . . . Sniffing the trees, / just another dog / among a lot of dogs," and by the manifesto declared by Virginia Woolf's character Lily Briscoe, a painter, in *To the Lighthouse*: "to be on a level with ordinary experience, to feel simply that's a chair, that's a table, and yet at the same time, It's a miracle, it's an ecstasy."[1]

My contention in this book has been that, beginning with objects as familiar as trees, a chair or a table, a freeway or a beachfront, poets engaging Los Angeles interiors and exteriors have constructed a canon of texts evoking the past, present, and future of this city. If the reader is a resident, or anticipates a visit, then his or her recognition of the location being described in such poems amplifies their satisfaction with living in *that* place or *any* place capable of being so legitimated as a vital source of authenticity, of revelation, even of ecstasy. A useful commentary on this psychological process appears in Walker Percy's novel *The Moviegoer*, when Binx Bolling, the narrator, takes his cousin to see the film *Panic in the Streets*, set in the city where they live, New Orleans. He remarks on her curiosity about his joyful responses in the movie theater:

> She refers to a phenomenon of moviegoing which I have called certification. Nowadays when a person lives somewhere, in a neighborhood, the place is not certified for him. More than likely he will live there sadly and the emptiness which is inside him will expand until it evacuates the entire neighborhood. But if he sees a movie which shows his very neighborhood, it becomes possible for him to live, for a time at least, as a person who is Somewhere and not Anywhere.[2]

Just as Binx claims that the streets and docks of New Orleans are more real if you are a resident and see them depicted in a film, so Los Angeles becomes more fascinating, more present to the imagination, thanks to the poems written to inscribe its locations deeply into personal and collective memory. As in Binx's case, the individual undergoing this ceremony of identification and legitimization feels less lonely in the universe, companioned now with more of the eidetic imagery of a tangible reality. Other cities' readers of poems about Los Angeles will be happy in knowing that everyday reality can sponsor profound engagements of subject and object in satisfying works of art. If, as scholars often argue, the modern lyric poem commonly represents a standoff between the poet's sense of solitude and the overwhelming crowdedness and accelerating flux of the modern and postmodern world, this stabilizing process of certification, a testimony to our ability to imagine Anywhere as Somewhere (and vice versa), restores a vital sense of pleasure in living.

I have written this book as if it were a Los Angeles novel and the poems are characters who interact in very human ways to their co-presence between covers or on a screen. Los Angeles should be more firmly anchored, more interesting, more satisfying to intellectual curiosity, for those who have considered carefully the poems in this and kindred books. To the extent that the poems contain history—of the city, of the nation, of the whole of human time—they amplify the knowledge of persons, places, and things brought into vivid existence by the poet's sensibility and craft. Just as Robert Lowell, when he gazes on the Boston Common in "For the Union Dead," includes in his sustained description the Civil War and the prehistoric "dark downward and vegetating kingdom / of the fish and reptile," so poets in Los Angeles, for all their predilections for the distractions of a media-haunted environment, demand of their readers a capacious space- and time-consciousness essential for an active appreciation of everyday existence. Poets model for us in their stylistic choices as well as their imaginative reach how to visualize and meditate on the varieties of human experience. Even the poems that profess alienation tend to militate against it in their meticulous observations and linguistic flair.

Standing on the borderline between past and future, at the juncture of the Lost World and the New World, poets who have taken up temporary or extended, perhaps lifelong, residence in some neighborhood of Los Angeles have jousted with received ideas about the city, especially its ideologies of boosterism and *noir* identity. Both ideologies derive from the myth of the California Dream, which now extends across the multicultural body of the city's various communities. Poems that record in poetic form the texture of experience anywhere in the city preserve for present and future readers an endangered heritage, aesthetic and civic. An oft-quoted statement by Walter Benjamin is irresistible in this context:

> The past can be seized only as an image which flashes up at the instant when it can be recognized and is never seen again [. . .] every image of the past that is not recognized by the present as one of its own concerns threatens to disappear irretrievably.[3]

In Los Angeles, a city stigmatized as having insufficient memory of its locations, poems act as a family album, one to a household, as each reader assembles over time the images that preserve a way of life—theirs and others'—from oblivion. For all their anxieties about the apocalypse, Angelenos have at their instant recall the means of salvation from the fate they most fear.

This book has asked the vital question, What particular value do readers extract from poems about Los Angeles? To the extent that we search for a single style or voice in such poems, as we tend to do when we identify something called the New York or Boston school, we diminish the vitality of a city's poetry by insisting on a small center and a vast periphery as the literary criterion of value. Poets can be cunning self-promoters when they claim in manifestos or in the way they review each other's work in influential journals and websites that some handful of poets represents the spirit of place, and that poets of equal talent or genius belong at the distant margins of critical consideration.

Anthologies, wittingly or unwittingly, often purvey such judgments in their commentaries and their selections for inclusion and exclusion. True, the sum total of such effects does construct a literary theater of ultimate merit. The galaxy of critical discourse depends upon such compact discriminations in order to compose a coherent history, in the certain knowledge that the pantheon created by canon-makers *will* become subject to debate, and warring camps *will* attract publicity and respect for their champions. It would probably help the poets who find Los Angeles amenable as subject matter if clear battle lines and dogmatic claims had received more attention during the last sixty years.

But something more subtle and complex has occurred, and a category like "the poetry of place" enables us to see by glancing sidelight as well as direct gaze how a city mandates certain styles and topics. Bill Mohr, for example, in the introduction to his anthology *"Poetry Loves Poetry"* (1985), emphasizes the *light* in Los Angeles as a vital constituent of the city's visionary poetics. In part, this claim is a tribute to the temperate climate that has helped to define the city's *look*, its contrast to the look of other American cities. It was the remedial quality of the sunshine and favorable climate in L.A. that helped to empower the film industry, another constituent element of the city's fundamental sense of itself.[4] Mohr argues that Los Angeles poetry can be best defined as "existential," though the term remains too vague in application to be of precise value. I am more attracted to claims that Los Angeles authors are so sensitive to the nuances of cultural imperatives inherent in places like the Pacific Ocean, the freeway, Hollywood, South Central, etc., that the places rendered are as resonant, as symbolic, as those in the great poetries we study and cherish. Poets of the region learned their craft in large part by studying the craft of their predecessors, as all poets do, but with a difference arising from the unique geographical setting. They discerned sermons in the stones of the built environment, and in the natural world so prominently displayed to them in the activity of the four elements of nature: earth, air, fire, and water. Like Poe's domain of Arnheim, and Stephen Yenser's evocation of "Shangri-L.A.," as we glimpse those realms of wonder in the brief excerpts I use as epigraphs to this book, this city of angels has always been most effectively measured by its *strangeness*, its beauty and its terror.

I am loath to suggest that it is not so much the light as the darkness that now defines Los Angeles poetry. I did not begin this project with that assumption—quite the opposite. I had hoped to construct a sequence of cityscapes in the manner of Walker Percy's genial narrator in *The Moviegoer*, though always aware that Binx Bolling constantly acknowledges a darker vision of New Orleans when the "malaise"—his term—overtakes him. But as I've asserted intermittently, the artists of Los Angeles—the painters, filmmakers, fiction writers, and song writers—have constructed a history and prophecy that have tended to push elegiac, conflictual, and disconsolate poems to the foreground of attention. Whether or not poetry is a form of melancholy, as Wallace Stevens claimed, melancholy has arguably become the dominant tone of contemporary poetry about the city.

In *Made in California: Art, Image, and Identity, 1900–2000*, the catalogue for a millennial exhibition at the Los Angeles County Museum of Art, Howard N. Fox articulates the prospect for the twenty-first century, emphasizing that the downbeat view of L.A. in the fine arts speaks to the dour state of California and the nation. His concluding paragraph is worth quoting in full as a touchstone of much recent commentary on the subject:

> California remains one of the most imagined places in the American psyche. Although situated on the western edge of the national map, California is central to the mythology of America. Its history over the past century, embodied in the legacy of its arts, narrates a psychodrama of national dreams and nightmares. The Golden State is no longer the epitome of the regional and parochial fantasy that it once seemed. Earlier envisioned as a Garden of Eden, California has been portrayed more recently in both popular and critical forums as a Tower of Babel. As life in California—increasingly presumed to mirror the nation's character and to presage the world's destiny—continues to evolve in its fitful and unfathomable manner, its extraordinary accommodation of all that is new and beyond traditional cultures may prove to be its greatest strength. And the arts will doubtless continue to offer keen insights into the significance of "real" and imagined California.[5]

Some alarmist texts, including several by Mike Davis, as well as David Rieff's *Los Angeles: Capital of the Third World* (1991) and Peter Schrag's *Paradise Lost: California's Experience, America's Future* (1999), elaborate on the underlying causes of Fox's pessimism. Even Kevin Starr, the equable historian of the state of California, acknowledges "the ominousness of the real" as he surveys the geological, social, and cultural forces militating against the California Dream in the twenty-first century.[6] As readers and citizens we should take such pessimism seriously, while always embracing the caveat in Fox's last sentence: that the arts will offer us both the most complex reasons for a gloomy prospectus on the present and future *and* the creative means to resist the temptation of succumbing unduly to visions of the city and state in such negative terms.

Those who urge the consolatory power of art, and its social function, often have recourse to Thomas Hardy's line from "In Tenebris—II": ". . . if way to the Better there be, it exacts a full look at the Worst." Poets have not been shy about presenting the worst, as we have seen, and of doing so to enact that species of tragic knowledge that underlies all the arts, including the arts devoted to place and location. Unlike the large spectacles in theaters and concert halls, poems work upon us in confidence, in solitude, as we gaze at page and screen. Poems possess charges of insight that alter our mood, and serious readers have reasons to seek from even the most somber of them both solace and an empowering energy. Hardy's own peculiar and moving poems have taught us how to look at everyday scenes as complicated by a first-rate sensibility.

The city's physical presence, as well as its day-to-day life and its historicity, continue to be periodically available in verse, as in fiction, painting, and film. It's not easy locating these poems, however. They rarely appear in the most visible literary journals, where Eastern and Midwestern poetry continue to carry more cultural cachet. Online websites provide plentiful outlets for poems about every American locality, but as with so much content in digital form, the needle in the haystack rarely presses for special attention. It might be useful to select for illustration one recent poem from a Los Angeles literary magazine and one from a book published by a university press—increasingly an indispensable venue for distinguished verse. The first strives for a *timely* and the second for a *timeless* perspective. The Fall 2011 issue of *The Los Angeles Review*, with a stunning color photo on the cover of fire sweeping across the mountains above the San Fernando Valley, contains at least one exemplary text for our purposes, Nik De Dominic's 9/11 poem, "September, Los Angeles."

Nik De Dominic

SEPTEMBER, LOS ANGELES

—for Erik Wennermark

The traffic is light today, unusually.
Usually it cries through the windows by morning,

slouching along Sunset toward Beverly Hills.
My roommate is hung over: usual. Okay,

we're both hung over: too much Jack Daniel's
and the bottle of Tylenol PM we split

to kill the hang over from the too much Jack Daniel's—
usual. And it didn't work. It never does.

My roommate's girl calls, a fat chick
from the valley, with Betty Page bangs

and thick black glasses, a prepackaged walking cliché
who tells us to turn on the TV.

We are in baggy shorts and stained t-shirts,
the collars stretched out, loose nooses.

We haven't done laundry in a while
and we've run out of toilet paper—

three weeks now.
And we smell vaguely of shit

though we used to shower after every time.
It's Orson Welles on the TV,

so we both call Kinko's to see
if we have to go into work

and we do because we're in California
and the traffic is clear

and we don't know anyone else
anywhere else because we are from California

and it's a big state. But we decide, collectively,
not to go in today. We go to the Pic N' Save instead

and smoke cigarettes in the bed of his truck.
At the edge of the lot, we put together paper gliders

I bought on my credit card because
we'd already blown through our checks that month.

We talk about how he should leave his fat girlfriend,
and I should leave mine. I fit panel A into slot B,

working the thick pieces into each other. We speak
in the language of pornography: cum-shots and Nikes.

We never mention the dead. We drive back to our apartment complex,
The Hollywood Arms—two tall buildings that share a courtyard—

and smoke Camels in the cul-de-sac, and float our paper gliders up
toward the roof of the buildings and watch as the plates turn

on themselves, and finally we decide to light them up
and then there's nothing left but soft ash

falling from the pink sky. We brush ourselves off and walk
down the street. Night has already loosed the day,

and people are sitting on their stoops. Drowsing,
I know it was a sunny day, and I imagine

a sky full of glass, glinting.
I imagine I know beauty.[7]

—•—

Suzanne Lummis, the author of "Shangri-La" (see Introduction), told me that she regularly read her poem aloud before audiences, but after the events of 9/11 she could no longer do so because of the lines taunting New York for its unhappy experience of dismal weather. New York became a virtually untouchable subject in the poetry of Los Angeles during the first decade of this century, all the resentment and jocular rivalry suspended in the shadow of the World Trade Center's ruins. De Dominic's poem tries to break the spell, at the same time that it presents a vision of L.A. in keeping with the characterization of the city active in popular culture on both coasts. Unlike most of the significant poems about 9/11 written in the emotional period directly following the catastrophe, this one takes advantage of the decade's passage to lower the temperature of the rhetoric, to move from earlier prophetic and political content to a more relaxed narrative structure and slacker tone for its effects. No contemporary reader will fail to notice that the poem enacts the style and psychological turns of what has become the dominant literary form of recent decades, the confessional memoir.

De Dominic has acknowledged in a letter to the author that the poem is autobiographical to some extent. He was a high school dropout who gravitated to Los Angeles with the ambition of becoming an actor. Reading the work of Charles Bukowski and Bret Easton Ellis, he sought to "echo those voices as much as possible." In 2001 he was twenty years old, feckless, cynical, more or less like the speaker of the poem. Years later, when he undertook the task of recalling his responses to 9/11 he saw a way to characterize his generation and his chosen location. Is the poem, then, a genuine record of his experience? We have sampled in this book a range of lyric speakers from the determinedly personal to the pointedly impersonal. A century of literary theory has established the perils of identifying the actual poet with the artifice of the constructed voice in a lyric poem. Yet how irresistible it is to designate the speaker of Mark Jarman's poem "The Supremes" as Jarman himself or of Wanda Coleman's poems as Coleman herself. (Not to mention the obsessively autobiographical Paul Monette and Charles Bukowski.) But we have also noticed how poets like Lummis and Gary Soto and Joy Harjo, as well as the performers of gangsta rap, veer toward voices and agency at some distance from the artifice of a candid, self-referential script. The omnipresence of film, fiction, and song in the city's constructed sense of itself has encouraged poets to stage fantasy versions of encounters with authentic places and perplexing issues. Sophisticated illusions of that kind can meet with a cool reception from readers who want a real person to speak in sincere language about real events—no bending or ironizing the tone to disguise the recognizable dynamics of city life. But the viability and aesthetic value of poetry depend on the reader's granting to poets like De Dominic the option of self-disguise.

I used the adjective "slacker" above for the tone of "September, Los Angeles," but in fact the whole poem is an expression of attitudes and behavior belonging to a (noun) slacker. The speaker and his roommate are the kind of lowlife featured in a popular genre of Los Angeles literature: hard-drinking, pill-popping, cigarette-smoking, unsanitary, sexist, running up debt for their few amenities. Nathanael West would recognize these alienated types, now proliferating on reality TV and YouTube video. The speaker of this poem is savvy enough to write an exposé of his life for the benefit of upscale readers. He does not pretend to understand the deeper meaning of what has happened on that September day; he can't talk about it but he mimics what he has seen on TV by making and then burning paper gliders and watching the ash falling from the sky. He makes no mention of watching the events on television; clearly they are beyond his comprehension. Only in the final lines does he assert, or pretend, that he undergoes one of those compensatory moments common in the poetry of 9/11: suddenly "I imagine I know beauty" at the fleeting thought of fiery catastrophe he cannot summon words to describe or contemplate directly ("We never mention the dead."). The exculpatory last line works the same way as the allusion to Orson Welles, as if to say that he has, or aspires to, a sensibility superior to the desperate one he presents in detail, but he cannot *feel* the pain of others, nor can he persuasively articulate it. Or perhaps he revels in his anomie, like Dostoevsky's Underground Man, who exclaims: "'Sluggard'—why it is a calling and vocation, it is a career."[8] Being from Los Angeles, he implies, he has not been intellectually nourished sufficiently to comprehend the complex meaning of an event like 9/11. He chooses to evade the subject altogether because he and his roommate "have to go into work."

This speaker is ill-prepared for the twenty-first century. He is no empire builder or dreamer; he professes no ambition, nor does he claim any marketable skill. On one level he and his friend are the pathetic victims of trash culture proliferating outward from Southern California, dumbed down by the irresistible addictions of smoking, drinking, drugs, pornography, and the daily grind of mere subsistence as the bums or bottom dogs of their milieu. "Betty [*sic*] Page" is the most accessible reference point for him, along with Jack Daniel's. His is no stalwart Emersonian self-reliance. Like the traffic he personifies as the dominant presence of his environment, he slouches along on the road of life, working at Kinko's, himself a replica version of the authentic human creation he half-yearns for, half-rejects. "He is representative of some L.A. figure . . . who traffics in signs not always understanding what makes them signs," De Dominic has written.[9] The fact that I can get exasperated with this speaker as I write about him is one measure of how successful the poem is in evoking him as a paradigm of the new class trucking along in the underbelly of the city. The jerry-built structure of unrhymed couplets, its phrases cobbled together with monotonously repeated copulatives like "and" or "so" remind us of the debased speech, shaky architecture, and infirm social codes that Los Angeles has always been accused of manufacturing. This is pure existential composition, the one-damn-thing-after-another vision that replicates lifestyles and consciousness stigmatized in intellectual media as fundamental to the identity of the city.

Has De Dominic captured the *Zeitgeist*, the spirit of the age? Has he updated and amplified the metaphor of Los Angeles as dystopia so often summoned by the poems reprinted in this book? What he has depicted is one of those bleak landscapes so familiar to readers of Los Angeles literature. A place, as David L. Ulin writes, "where people live in disconnection, as unrooted as dust upon the surface of the world."[10] The events of 9/11 were genuinely apocalyptic, and seen universally as prophetic of atrocities to come. For a moment, pundits declared hopefully that the frivolity, shallowness, and cheap irony of American popular culture had been violently terminated, and that once again life would be earnest and real. How well this hope has been realized, I leave to the reader to judge.

A poem like "September, Los Angeles," is heuristic; it serves to promote discussion about the serious matters it raises, even in so oblique a fashion. It does not so much beg the question as proffer it provocatively: What kind of diction, what idioms, what linguistic organization has the best chance to break through the daze of media bombardment and represent the splendors and miseries of the places we live in? What kind of poem will sharpen our sensitivity to the changes that leap into existence at a quickening pace? I have argued in this book that poetry observant of the tradition, innovative in its language, self-conscious in its interpretive takes on everyday incitements, stands the best chance of arousing and permanently sustaining our interest in the complex dynamism of a heteropolis like Los Angeles. And so it is with this strange, disjointed poem that disdains the status of elegy but draws us into meditation on the Babel of Los Angeles.

Poems about cities usually turn out to be more dour than one expects, even when the original intention seems to have been celebratory, as with Hart Crane's *The Bridge* and William Carlos Williams's *Paterson*. In the Introduction to this book I argued that to be "Los Angelized," in the sense asserted by Thomas McGrath in his book-length poem *Letter to an Imaginary Friend*, was to be caught up in "the entropy of the failing system," driven pell-mell into the condition of a contemptible extra in "the movie at the end of the world." The fiction of Los Angeles displays the heritage of a *noir* tradition with a vast and ever-growing audience. Poets have derived considerable visionary energy from that tradition, and some of them have written with immense force and emotional precision about states of mind and states of urban sites using a poetics in which style and voice seem to be driving the inner narrative to a state of extremity. But this is not the whole story. Resistance to the very scenario I have just outlined characterizes the city's verse as well. I'd like to close this book with a poem emblematic of a counter-force in the city's process of self-definition.

Patty Seyburn

SURF

The ocean inhales hot air from the desert
after the sun goes down. Early morning, hot and cool air collide
to fog. Intimate. Indifferent.

Before the marine layer lifts, surfers paddle out
to await the arrival of their language,
sets and crests, faces and breaks, swells, blue arcs to tame

though each lull says, *this is just a reprieve,*

no room for perfidy.
And the lithe boys are powerless among these words
that would drag them into a curl with no remorse—we'd feel better

if nature would feel at all.
A tintinnabulation of pebbles
assumes the agnostic's position: *courageous, reckless, whether or not*
you're here does not affect us

and still, the boys return in quiet camaraderie,
hoping for a glimpse of speech by low-tide,
when again they're stripped of senses, oblivious to the ocean's argot

—labial, dentate, glottal—

shapes to fill as salt water assaults lip and limb.
And when the sea bores of proselytes, it leaves
memory of tone and rhythm, the only way we know

when to end one word, begin another.[11]

—•—

If Nik De Dominic's poem "September, Los Angeles" is constructed around the concept that falling towers in a great city constitute *history*, and that the street vernacular summoned by the common man to cope with catastrophe will inevitably fall short of meaningfulness, Patty Seyburn's poem "surf" offers another way of thinking about language and locality. "surf" returns us in a long feedback loop to some of the poems featured in the chapter of this book about the Pacific Ocean as a primal source of inspiration for writers about this or any body of water. Seyburn's book of 2002, *mechanical cluster* (making all letters of a book title and poem title lowercase has become a fashion in this generation) records the poet's experiences growing up in Detroit as well as her residency in Southern California as a professor of English at California State University, Long Beach. The dialectical journeys of her imagination back and forth between Michigan and California recall

Diane Wakoski's repeated movements between these two states, as well as the transcontinental contents of work by New York poets who have found congenial ground on either coast. As we have seen, Los Angeles has been constantly redefined by émigré authors in all genres who have settled for a long or short stay in L.A.

Seyburn does not specify the precise location of her poem. This is the generic surf, the ocean stretching up and down the California coast, the "Western sea" that Whitman hymned without laying eyes upon it or hearing its mystical speech—"the ocean's argot" in Seyburn's phrase. Surfers paddle out into the waves "to await the arrival of their language." What they hear cannot be translated; it possesses "tone and rhythm" but not meaning. It can only be experienced as a strangeness of utterance compelling a response of unique and pleasurable diction: "A tintinnabulation of pebbles," for example. (These "lithe boys" will later find that strange word in Poe's sound-poem "The Bells.") The surf's sounds are beyond articulation and beyond definition. When the boys return for more surfing they enjoy a recurrence of that mystical sense of experience bereft of man-made language. We have seen the same claims made in Mark Jarman's poem "The Supremes." The fricative word "surf" has no identifiable origin, and is probably derived from the sound of the swell of water, an example of language absorbed directly from natural sources. Eventually, the surfers abandon that watery fountainhead of unique sensory fulfillment; and when they do so they retain only a "memory of tone and rhythm" available for the making of songs and poems. They make civilization, they construct cities as well as verses, they educate others in all the disciplines including the one that cannot be taught.

"surf" is shaped as a coherent narrative of the essential story of the human race: our linguistic engagement with the ineffable, the superhuman. If the essential poetry of California as a state of being can be said to begin with Robinson Jeffers's volume *Flagons and Apples* (1912), with its attention to the Southern California beaches, and his subsequent chronicles of living on the sea-edge, then the century that follows his efforts has extended his missionary zeal to connect Land and Water by means of a neoromantic rhetoric, an elevation of diction and an extension of poetic attention so that justice is done to the city in every literary manner. In this way the consciousness of poets and readers has been "Los Angelized" in a way very different than the political activist Thomas McGrath anticipated.

"surf" is written in the middle register favored by most of the poets I have treated in this study. It is not the plain style of Bukowski, always "easy to understand" (see page 109), nor the patrician, ornate style of a Derek Walcott when he writes about sites other than L.A. Nor does "surf" declare like Walcott that "the sea is history"; this stretch of the Pacific is pre-historical as it is pre-conscious, pre-linguistic. The poem does not attempt to mimic the pre-linguistic by means of pseudo-diction, a futile enterprise. It reconstructs in analytical terms the conditions of the interchange between mind and water, as Wallace Stevens does in his positivist meditation on how "the meaningless plungings of water and the wind" contribute to verbal form in the song of the woman in "The Idea of Order at Key West." It numbers among its readers not only the "proselytes" who withdraw from the ocean carrying surfboards but readers who enjoy a rhetorical performance that demonstrates what can and cannot be communicated about the experience of wordless rapture. If the Pacific Ocean is the defining entity of all coastal locations in California, shaping the public imagination by its visceral effect on those who indulge in its pleasures, then it can rightly claim to be the alpha and omega site of the poetic quest. For these reasons "surf" takes its place as a counter-example to Nik De Dominic's "September, Los Angeles," no less a document of twenty-first-century Los Angeles.

In his essay on *fin de siècle* art in Los Angeles quoted above, Howard N. Fox recurs to the early twentieth-century notion of L.A. as a "Garden of Eden." Poetry about the city since the 1920s has been disdainful of that boosterish claim; certainly "surf" does not fall under that rubric. And yet, readers cannot be blamed for yearning backward, as well as forward, for some archetype of the city other than the *Blade Runner* or *Turner Diaries* scenarios of a dystopian future. Is a vision of the Golden Age inaccessible to contemporary poets? What happened to that Ur-world before gridlock, ethnic hostility, police brutality, civic corruption, drugs, despair about global warming, earthquakes, fire and flood, anxiety about immigrants, about the so-called "neo-feudalism" overtaking an unbalanced economy? Before the "media manipulation" of our brains that Tony Hoagland decries and relates to the poetics of vertigo? Perhaps that intelligible world never existed except as a promotional come-on. And yet, even the casual visitor to Los Angeles, certified with all the defenses against this supposed dystopia, *will* yield to its astonishing and inexhaustible beauty and dynamism. Can we say that there is a deficit of lyrics about its worldly satisfactions? As our envoi, our last glance backward to the once and forever landscape of Eden, the dream of innocence and joy, I quote the opening stanzas of Dana Gioia's poem "Los Angeles After the Rain":

Back home again on one of those bright mornings
when the city wakes to find itself reborn.
The smog gone, the thundering storm
blown out to sea, birds
frantic in their joyous cacophony, and the mountains,
so long invisible in haze,
newly risen with the sun.

It is a morning snatched from Paradise,
a vision of the desert brought to flower—
of Eve standing in her nakedness,
immortal Adam drunk with all
the gaudy colors of the world,
and each taste and touch, each
astounding pleasure still waiting to be named.[12]

Adam was the first poet; he gave names to everything surrounding him in that idyllic bower he inhabited for so little time. The language certified his existence in a place made more orderly and hopeful for his presence. What would he (and more so, she, Eve) have said about Los Angeles, so often advertised as the reincarnation of their original, lost paradise? In every precinct of the city, and elsewhere in the world, fallen poets continue to generate the many voices that will make Los Angeles more meaningful, and more satisfying, to our imagination.

TEN

Twenty More Poems About Los Angeles

Buckley, Christopher. "Lost Angel." *Fall from Grace*. Kansas City, MO: BkMk Press, 1998. 29–32.

Clary, Killarney. "Clouds of birds." *Who Whispered Near Me*. New York: Farrar, Straus & Giroux, 1989. 9.

Coke, Allison Adelle Hedge. "#4 Southwest Chief/L.A. Central." *Off-Season City Pipe*. St. Paul, MN: Coffee House Press, 2005. 38–39.

Dickey, James. "Exchanges . . . being in the form of a dead-living dialogue with Joseph Trumbull Stickney (1874–1904)." *The Strength of Fields*. Garden City, NY: Doubleday, 1979. 48–56.

Digges, Deborah. "Media Years." *Late in the Millennium*. New York: Alfred A. Knopf, 1989. 36–38.

Eshleman, Clayton. "Gorgeous George Comes Pounding Down the Beach." *Under World Arrest*. Santa Rosa: Black Sparrow Press, 1994. 155–57.

Halliday, Mark. "Yvette Vickers." *Thresherphobe*. Chicago: University of Chicago Press, 2013. 23.

Hofmann, Michael. "Venice Beach." *Poetry* CCI, no. 6 (March 2013): 505–7.

Levis, Larry. "The Oldest Living Thing in L.A." *The Selected Levis*. Rev. ed. Ed. David St. John. Pittsburgh: University of Pittsburgh Press, 1997. 182.

Locklin, Gerald. "Low Tide Floodtime: Winter 1969." *"Poetry Loves Poetry": An Anthology of Los Angeles Poets*. Ed. Bill Mohr. Santa Monica: Momentum Press, 1985. #37 (unpaginated).

Mazur, Gail. "Fracture Santa Monica." *Zeppo's First Wife: New and Selected Poems*. Chicago: University of Chicago Press, 2005. 169–70.

McGrath, Campbell. "California Love Song." *In the Kingdom of the Sea Monkeys*. New York: Ecco / HarperCollins, 2012. 24.

Mohr, Bill. "The Murals." *Hidden Proofs*. Los Angeles: Bombshelter Press, 1982. 32–33.

Pillin, William. "The Bulldozer Promenade." *To the End of Time: Poems New and Selected (1939–1979)*. Los Angeles: Papa Bach Edition, 1980. 167.

Prado, Holly. "Monkey Journal 2004—2005." *Monkey Journal*. Huntington Beach, CA: Tebot Bach, 2008. 3—48.

Rhoads, Brady. "Los Angeles." *Bear Flag Republic: Prose Poems and Poetics from California*, ed. Christopher Buckley and Gary Young. Santa Cruz, CA: Greenfield Review Press/Alcatraz Editions, 2008. 321–22.

Schjedahl, Peter. "To Pico." *"Poetry Loves Poetry": An Anthology of Los Angeles Poets*. Ed. Bill Mohr. Santa Monica: Momentum Press, 1985. #1 (unpaginated).

Simon, Maurya. "The Sea Sprite." *The Geography of Home: California Poetry of Place*. Ed. Christopher Buckley and Gary Young. Berkeley, CA: Heyday Books, 1999. 340–41.

St. John, David. "Hollywood Salvation." *The Auroras*. New York: HarperCollins, 2012. 10–11.

Uyematsu, Amy. "1110 on My Transistor Dial." *Stone Bow Prayer*. Port Townsend, WA: Copper Canyon Press, 2005. 54–56.

Notes

Preface

1. James D. Houston, *Californians: Searching for the Golden State* (New York: Alfred A. Knopf, 1982), 222.

2. Fredric Jameson, "Reading Without Interpretation: Postmodernism and the Video-Text," *The Linguistics of Writing: Arguments Between Language and Literature*, ed. Derek Attridge, Alan Durant, Nigel Fabb, and Colin McCabe (Manchester: Manchester University Press, 1987), 222. Jameson extended his critique of the "new kind of flatness or depthlessness" he perceived in all postmodern artistic forms, including poetry, in his classic text, *Postmodernism, or The Cultural Logic of Late Capitalism (Post-Contemporary Interventions)* (Durham, NC: Duke University Press, 1991), 9. Marjorie Perloff has synthesized this line of thinking into its most comprehensive form in *Unoriginal Genius: Poetry by Other Means in the New Century* (Chicago: University of Chicago Press, 2010).

3. Ron Silliman, "The Chinese Notebook," *Anthology of Modern American Poetry*, ed. Cary Nelson (New York: Oxford University Press, 2000), 1112 [Entry # 117]. Though Silliman scorns the realistic tradition in poetry, he demonstrates in his prose memoir *Under Albany* (Cambridge, UK: Salt Publishing, 2004) an enthusiasm for vivid autobiographical detail in his depiction of his early life in the Bay Area. Likewise, Lyn Hejinian, another Language poet, produced a classic of regional literature in her memoir of growing up in northern California, *My Life* (Los Angeles: Sun & Moon Press, 1987).

4. Jed Rasula, *This Compost: Ecological Imperatives in American Poetry* (Athens: University of Georgia Press, 2002). "I do think of poems as ecosystems," he remarks, and later, "The work of poetry is less to entertain images than to pass human order through the mulching of language" (7, 90).

5. Bill Mohr, *Hold-Outs: The Los Angeles Poetry Renaissance 1948–1992* (Iowa City: University of Iowa Press, 2011), 3, 123. Even Mohr, an enthusiastic advocate of the city's poetry, raises the question about labeling poets after their often temporary residence:

"[I]s 'Los Angeles' a code word for marginality, an ironic inflection of [the poets'] relationship to the culture at large as well as to the layers of poets and artists elsewhere, both experimental and traditional? Above all, what advantage do we gain by categorizing them as Los Angeles poets?" (42).

6. Guy Debord defines the term as "the study of the precise laws and specific effects of the geographical environment . . . on the emotions and behavior of individuals" in his essay "Introduction to a Critique of Urban Geography" (1955). The essay can be found, along with an illuminating history, in the Wikipedia entry for "psychogeography." Guy Davenport's phrase provides the title to *The Geography of the Imagination: Forty Essays* (Boston: David R. Godine, 1997).

7. Leonard S. Bernstein, "Los Angeles," *The Black Snowman* (London: Abelard-Schuman, 1971), 24.

Introduction

1. Thomas McGrath, *Letter to an Imaginary Friend, Parts I & II* (Chicago: Swallow Press, 1962 & 1970), 124. All citations in the text are to this edition.

Amy Wilentz provides a recent gloss on McGrath's statement: "Although I came from Perth Amboy, New Jersey, I really grew up in California, like all Americans." *I Feel Earthquakes More Often Than They Happen: Coming to California in the Age of Schwarzenegger* (New York: Simon & Schuster, 2006), 148.

2. Randall Jarrell, Letter of August 1954 to Philip Vaudrin and Harry Ford, *Randall Jarrell's Letters*, ed. Mary Jarrell (Boston: Houghton Mifflin, 1985), 401. By contrast, James M. Cain had noted in an essay of March 1933 that the citizens of Los Angeles spoke excellent English, and "These people read, they know what is going on in the world." See *Writing Los Angeles: A Literary Anthology*, ed. David L. Ulin (New York: Library of America, 2002), 113.

Robert Peters offered a much-discussed rebuke to Jarrell's kind of snobbery by imagining a seemingly dopey married couple, Dick and Jane, sitting on their beach patio and trying to grapple with John Ashbery's long difficult poem, "Litany." Dick, a plumber, and Jane, who recalls how in college she much preferred playing tennis to any "tennis oath" (an allusion to an inscrutable poem by Ashbery), do in fact come to appreciate the poem. Their sprightly dialogue became a paradigm of support for poetry in Los Angeles. See Robert Peters, "Dick and Jane at Home in Southern California," *The Great American Poetry Bake-Off*, 2nd series (Metuchen, NJ: Scarecrow Press, 1982), 2–15.

3. Estelle Gershgoren Novak, *Poets of the Non-Existent City: Los Angeles in the McCarthy Era* (Albuquerque: University of New Mexico Press, 2002), 5.

4. Ibid., xvii.

5. Alfred Kazin, *A Writer's America: Landscape in Literature* (New York: Alfred A. Knopf, 1988), 8.

6. The most recent at this writing is *London: A History in Verse*, ed. Mark Ford

(Cambridge: Harvard University Press, 2012). See also *All That Mighty Heart: London Poems*, ed. Lisa Russ Spaar (Charlottesville: University of Virginia Press, 2008), and *The Norton Book of London*, ed. A. N. Wilson (New York: W. W. Norton, 1993).

7. Kevin Starr, in his history of Los Angeles in the 1920s, *Material Dreams* (New York: Oxford University Press, 1990), has singled out Jacob Zeitlin's career as the paradigm of a talented young poet, Russian-Jewish, emigrating from Texas to the West Coast, who failed to find a voice other than that of a second-rate Carl Sandburg. Lacking an original perspective on the cityscape and a modernist style, Zeitlin gave up poetry and settled for a distinguished role as editor, bookseller, and intellectual leader in the cosmopolitan milieu of a city still in the first generation of its cultural emergence. Starr calls attention as well to Hildegarde Flanner (1899–1987), who unlike Zeitlin advanced from a jejeune first volume in 1920 to an increasingly sophisticated poetics fully at home in the dynamic society of Los Angeles, especially marked by her pleasure in writing about the automobile. See *Poems: Collected and Selected* (Santa Barbara: John Daniel, 1988).

8. James M. Cain, "Paradise," first published in the March 1933 issue of *The American Mercury*. A convenient reprint is *Writing Los Angeles: A Literary Anthology*, ed. David L. Ulin (New York: Library of America, 2002), 130. The future tense is crucial. At present, Cain remarks, "life takes on a dreadful vacuity here" (117), but he sees reasons to believe that the epic story of American movement westward gives Los Angeles the best chance of any American city in the twentieth century to achieve greatness.

9. Carol Muske-Dukes, *Married to the Icepick Killer: A Poet in Hollywood* (New York: Random House, 2002), 6. The narrator of Jack Kerouac's autobiographical novel *The Dharma Bums* (1958) remarks that "a regular hell is L.A. . . . the only thing to do was to get out of L.A." [Chapter 16]. In Kerouac's cosmology northern California and Mexico are paradises with an urban inferno of smog, foul odors, and intense heat sandwiched between them.

10. Edmund Wilson, *The American Earthquake: A Documentary of the Jazz Age, the Great Depression, and the New Deal* [formerly titled *American Jitters*] (Garden City, NY: Doubleday Anchor Books, 1958), 381. As with the spread in *Life* magazine, Wilson showcases the evangelist Aimee Semple McPherson as the spirit of place. The poet Daniel Mark Epstein has provided reasons for this reputation in his biography *Sister Aimee: The Life of Aimee Semple McPherson* (Boston: Mariner Books/Houghton Mifflin Harcourt, 1994).

11. Norman Mailer, "Superman Comes to the Supermarket," *The Presidential Papers* (New York: G. P. Putnam's Sons, 1962), 33.

12. "City of Dreadful Joy" is from Aldous Huxley, *Jesting Pilate: The Diary of a Journey* (London: Chatto & Windus, 1926), 269. "A Gobi of suburbs" is from Mike Davis, *City of Quartz*, New Edition (London: Verso, 2006), 47. Davis is characterizing the view of the anti-fascist exiles in Los Angeles, such as Brecht and Adorno, who "complained bitterly about the absence of a European (or even Manhattan) *civitas* of public places, sophisticated crowds, historical auras and critical intellectuals." A. M. Homes does not intend

her characterization to be negative. She remarks on the preceding page, "it feels like one of the most American cities in America right now." As she well knows, American poets from Poe to Ashbery feel very much at home in the surreal. *Los Angeles* (Washington D.C.: National Geographic, 2002), xvi, xv.

13. Kevin Starr, *Material Dreams: Southern California Through the 1920s*, 69.

14. Linda Gregerson, "Rhetorical Contract in the Erotic Poem," *Radiant Lyre: Essays on Lyric Poetry*, ed. David Baker and Ann Townsend (Saint Paul, MN: Graywolf Press, 2007), 44.

15. Suzanne Lummis, "Shangri-La," *In Danger* (Berkeley: Roundhouse Press, 1999), 22–23.

16. David Fine, *Imagining Los Angeles: A City in Fiction* (Albuquerque: University of New Mexico Press, 2000), 41–42. One hears the chime of names, Lummis and Loomis, in West's character Mrs. Loomis, as described above.

17. The phrase comes from an editorial by Lummis in *Land of Sunshine* 2, no. 2: 34. I am grateful to Marie Jaqueline Pelzer for calling this material to my attention. Suzanne Lummis has pointed out that her grandfather is best understood as a crusader for social justice and compassion for Native American and Hispanic populations, not inherently racist despite some propagandizing for European-born immigration into the Southland. Lummis's book *The Spanish Pioneers* (1893) makes the most extended case for the Hispanic version of Saxon culture favored by the author. Conversation with Suzanne Lummis on 24 February 2012. In *Inventing the Dream: California through the Progressive Era* (New York: Oxford University Press, 1984), Kevin Starr emphasizes that Lummis envisioned a Hispanicized Anglo-Saxon culture for the Southwest and adopted a lifestyle for himself based on the Spanish model.

18. James Hilton, *Lost Horizon* (1933; Pleasantville, NY: Reader's Digest Association, 1990), 62, 79, 116. Though Hilton wrote *Lost Horizon* in Woodford Green, Essex, he spent periods of time in Hollywood working for the studios, and died in Long Beach. L. Frank Baum wrote almost all of the Oz books just off Hollywood Boulevard.

19. Wordsworth's line is in *The Prelude*, Book VII, 621. Baudelaire's expostulation is the opening line in "Les Sept Vieillards" [The Seven Old Men].

20. Many popular songs have etched this image of blond beauties into the national consciousness. Katy Perry's smash hit of 2011, "California Gurls," celebrates the species but without any of Lummis's irony: "Toned, tanned, fit, and ready," the girls of this anthem celebrate their good luck in living in the "Wild, wild west-coast" of "Venice Beach and Palm Springs." The obvious source for this song is the Beach Boys' "California Girls" about "the cutest girls in the world."

21. Linda Gregerson, *Radiant Lyre*, 51.

22. Suzanne Lummis, "Introduction, Los Angeles Poets Mini-Anthology," *Malpaís Review* 1, no. 2 (Autumn 2010): 26.

23. John H. Johnston, *The Poet and the City: A Study in Urban Perspectives* (Athens: University of Georgia Press, 1984), xvii.

24. David Barber, "Funicular," *Wonder Cabinet* (Evanston: Northwestern University Press, 2006), 68–70; Josephine Miles, "Maxim," *Collected Poems 1930–1983* (Urbana: University of Illinois Press, 1998), 137; Tom Disch, "In Defense of Forest Lawn," *Yes, Let's: New and Selected Poems* (Baltimore: Johns Hopkins University Press, 1989), 18–19; Ann Stanford, "Union Station," *Holding Our Own: The Selected Poems of Ann Stanford*, ed. Maxine Scates and David Trinidad (Port Townsend, WA: Copper Canyon Press, 2001), 26; Martha Ronk, "The San Gabriels," "The Sierras," *State of Mind* (Los Angeles: Sun & Moon Press, 1995), 12, 30.

25. James Harms, "The Dodgers, 1958," *Freeways & Aqueducts* (Pittsburgh: Carnegie-Mellon University Press, 2004), 47.

26. See Scott L. Bottles, *Los Angeles and the Automobile: The Making of the Modern City* (Berkeley: University of California Press, 1991). Bottles argues that Angelenos so much preferred driving their own cars to mass transit that support for streetcars dwindled, making their extension throughout downtown and into the suburbs infeasible. The "ghost" of this debate nourishes Harms's poem about the moral dimensions of radical change in the city.

27. Fyodor Dostoevsky, *Notes from Underground*, section II, first paragraph. In the classic Constance Garnett translation the word is "towns" not "cities." But the narrator is speaking of St. Petersburg, so the latter word is the more sensible translation.

28. Michael Connelly, *Echo Park* (New York: Little, Brown, 2006), 60.

29. Ry Cooder, *Chavez Ravine* (Nonesuch, 2005). Cooder sets some of the short stories in his collection *Los Angeles Stories* (San Francisco: City Lights Books, 2005) in Chavez Ravine.

30. W. J. T. Mitchell, "Introduction," *Landscape and Power*, ed. W. J. T. Mitchell (Chicago: University of Chicago Press, 1994), 1, 13. Mitchell's essay in the volume, "Imperial Landscape," explores the relation of landscape and violence in ways pertinent to my project.

1. Pacific Ocean

1. Brenda Hillman, *Cascadia* (Middletown, CT: Wesleyan University Press, 2001), 18.

2. David Fine, *Imagining Los Angeles: A City in Fiction* (Albuquerque: University of New Mexico Press, 2000), 252.

3. David Orr, "Beach Reading," *Poetry* 190 (July/August 2007): 316.

4. Mel Weisburd, "Along the Coast," *A Life of Windows and Mirrors: Selected Poems 1948–2005* (Marina Del Rey, CA: Conflu:X Press, 2005), 76.

5. Gail Wronsky, "Tonight, Walt Whitman, the Pacific," *Dying for Beauty* (Port Townsend, WA: Copper Canyon Press, 2000), 58.

6. *The Collected Poetry of Robinson Jeffers*, Volume Four, ed. Tim Hunt (Stanford: Stanford University Press, 2000), 404. In his early poem "At Playa Hermosa" Jeffers had

emphasized "my quiet by the sea" and remarked that "Strange and ominous peace abides" (31). In later poems about the Pacific, he favored less pacific descriptions in favor of an energized, arousing body of water.

7. The phrase occurs in Part 4 of "Origins." Derek Walcott, *Collected Poems* (New York: Farrar, Straus & Giroux, 1986), 14.

8. *The Collected Poetry of Robinson Jeffers*, Volume Four, 392.

9. Robinson Jeffers, "Birds," *The Collected Poetry of Robinson Jeffers*, ed. Tim Hunt (Stanford: Stanford University Press, 1988), Volume One, 108.

10. Mark Jarman, "The Supremes," *Bone Fires: New and Selected Poems* (Louisville: Sarabande Books, 2011), 88–90.

11. Mark Jarman, *Body and Soul* (Ann Arbor: University of Michigan Press, 2002), 12. Jarman is responding to a quotation from Kenneth Clark: "Facts become art through love, which unifies them and lifts them to a higher plane of reality[.]"

12. Jane Tompkins, *West of Everything: The Inner Life of Westerns* (New York: Oxford University Press, 1992), 14, 4. "In Westerns the obsession with landscape is finally metaphysical," Tompkins remarks (4).

13. Dorothy Barresi, "Surfing as Meditation," *The Post-Rapture Diner* (Pittsburgh: University of Pittsburgh Press, 1996), 65–67. For an East Coast "meditation" on the subject see Barbara Guest, "A Handbook of Surfing," *Selected Poems* (Los Angeles: Sun & Moon Press, 1995), 42–50.

14. William Irwin Thompson, *At the Edge of History* (New York: Harper & Row, 1971), 6. "Rich fantasy life" is on page 4.

15. Derek Walcott, "Summer Elegies II," *The Arkansas Testament* (New York: Farrar, Straus & Giroux, 1987), 95–96.

16. Derek Walcott, "The Sea Is History," *The Star-Apple Kingdom* (New York: Farrar, Straus & Giroux, 1979), 25.

17. Lord Byron, "Childe Harold's Pilgrimage," Canto Three (xxv, 3). Byron's Romantic meditation on Venice exerted a profound influence on urban poetry, not least on Walcott's anti-romantic poems like this one.

18. Cited in Humphrey Carpenter, *A Serious Character: The Life of Ezra Pound* (Boston: Houghton Mifflin, 1988), 326.

19. Bill Mohr, *Hold-Outs: The Los Angeles Poetry Renaissance 1948–1992* (Iowa City: University of Iowa Press, 2011), 62 *passim*.

20. Lawrence Lipton, *Bruno in Venice West & Other Poems* (Van Nuys, CA: Venice West Publishers, 1976), 6. For further information about Lipton and his milieu, see John Arthur Maynard, *Venice West: The Beat Generation in Southern California* (New Brunswick and London: Rutgers University Press, 1991).

21. Umberto Eco, *Travels in Hyperreality*, trans. William Weaver (New York: Harcourt Brace Jovanovich, 1983). The pilgrimage to locate works of imitation and replication in the title essay finds its full requital in Southern California, where the Movieland Wax Museum, Forest Lawn, Knott's Berry Farm, the Getty Villa (in Malibu), Disney-

land, and (further up the coast) the Hearst Castle at San Simeon provide definitive examples of the "absolute fake."

22. Karla Kelsey, review of *The California Poem* in *Double Room* 5 (Winter–Spring 2005), http://webdelsol.com/Double_Room/issue_five/Eleni_Sikelianos.html.

23. Eleni Sikelianos, *The California Poem* (Minneapolis: Coffee House Press, 2004), 140. Page numbers in the text refer to this edition.

24. One could imagine a Southern California poet answering Sikelianos in kind by focusing on malevolent trends shared by northern and southern parts of the state. In *Where I Was From* (New York: Alfred A. Knopf, 2003), Joan Didion surveys the proliferation in the north of prisons, defense industries producing nerve gas and other weapons, and franchise outlets (Wal-Mart, McDonald's, Baskin-Robbins, Holiday Inn, etc.) that have transformed the region into Robinson Jeffers's worst nightmare. See especially pages 170–88.

25. Alice Fulton, "Of Formal, Free, and Fractal Verse: Singing the Body Electric," *Feeling as a Foreign Language* (Saint Paul, MN: Graywolf Press, 1999), 51.

26. Kevin Starr, *Material Dreams: Southern California Through the 1920s* (New York: Oxford University Press, 1990), 20.

27. Lewis MacAdams, *The River: Books One, Two & Three* (Santa Cruz, CA: Blue Press, 2007), I.23. The book is unpaginated, so that numbers in my text refer to section and numbered poem.

MacAdams's crusade has helped to produce one benign effect. In late May of 2013 the Los Angeles River opened a 2.5 mile section for unrestrained public recreation, including kayaking. See www.cnn.com/2013/06/01/travel/los-angeles-river/index.html?hpt=hp_t2.

Another remarkable long poem about the Los Angeles River is Jacqueline De Angelis's thirty-eight-part sequence, "Atwater," in *Another City: Writing from Los Angeles*, ed. David L. Ulin (San Francisco: City Lights, 2001), 135–48. The poem begins by asking, "Where do I enter?" and thereafter ponders both the seductive and mystical appeal of the river, as of the Pacific. "*What if the river is liquid god?*" the speaker asks. She declares that the mouth of the river is Playa del Rey, not in fact correct (not since 1824) but metaphorically suggestive as a more poetic merging of bodies of water. A more dispiriting take on the river, dramatized as a site of drug-taking, an escape from nature, is Luis J. Rodríguez, "The Concrete River," *My Nature is Hunger: New and Selected Poems 1989–2004* (Willimantic, CT: Curbstone Press, 2005), 20–22.

28. Charles Wright, "California Dreaming," *The World of the Ten Thousand Things: Poems 1980–1990* (New York: Farrar, Straus & Giroux, 1990), 116. To be fair, Wright has written some fine imagistic and meditative lyrics about Laguna, such as "Laguna Blues" (23), "California Spring" (30), and "Laguna Dantesca" (31). Brenda Hillman discusses "Laguna Blues" in a special issue devoted to Wright of *Northwest Review* 49, no. 2: 46–49.

29. Susan Suntree, *Sacred Sites: The Secret History of Southern California* (Lincoln: University of Nebraska Press, 2010), 99–100.

30. See the interview with Mike Davis in *Unmasking L.A.: Third Worlds and the City*, ed. Deepak Narang Sawhney (New York: Palgrave, 2002), 29.

2. *Hollywood*

1. Delmore Schwartz, "Metro-Goldwyn-Mayer," *Last & Lost Poems*, ed. Robert Phillips (New York: New Directions, 1989), 22.

2. Michael Tolkin, *The Player* (New York: Vintage, 1988), 13.

3. Karl Shapiro, "Hollywood," *Selected Poems* (New York: Random House, 1968), 44–45.

4. Karl Shapiro, *The Younger Son* (Chapel Hill, NC: Algonquin Books of Chapel Hill, 1988), 69. As in the poem, Shapiro follows the lead of Nathanael West in *The Day of the Locust* in his long catalogue of bizarre structures: "an A & P grocery store was built to look like a gothic cathedral, a shoe store made into a gigantic shoe, gas stations with gardens and fountains, an orange juice stand a two-story orange with a one-story leaf stuck on the top" and so forth. Photographs of many such curiosities can be found in Jim Heimann, *California Crazy & Beyond: Roadside Vernacular Architecture* (San Francisco: Chronicle Books, 2001).

Charles Reznikoff, another Jewish poet, Brooklyn-born, was living in Hollywood during Shapiro's trek down the Boulevard. In his verse sequence "Autobiography: Hollywood," he eschews the cultural touchstones Shapiro favors, and speaks constantly instead of birds, flowering plants and bushes, and of course the lofty palms. He expresses pleasure in the sunshine and disdains movie people. He soon returned to New York where the Yiddishkeit made him feel more at home. See *Poems 1937–1975, Volume II of The Complete Poems of Charles Reznikoff*, ed. Seamus Cooney (Santa Barbara: Black Sparrow Press, 1977), 38–47.

5. A convenient reprint is Bertolt Brecht, *Journals* [excerpt], in *Writing Los Angeles: A Literary Anthology*, ed. David L. Ulin (New York: Library of America, 2002), 290.

Both an American citizen and an émigré from Paris, Henry Miller would present a critique of American mass culture comparable to Nathanael West's and the Frankfurt School's in *The Air-Conditioned Nightmare* (New York: New Directions, 1945). Worth noting, however, is his moment of praise as he descends the Cajon Pass into San Bernadino at the end of his drive across the continent: "Then comes a burst of green, the wildest, greenest green imaginable, as if to prove beyond the shadow of a doubt that California is indeed the Paradise it boasts of being" (245). Shapiro would later identify Miller as "The Greatest Living Author." See *In Defense of Ignorance* (New York: Random House, 1960), 313.

6. *Writing Los Angeles*, 285. In the mid-1920s Moyshe-Leyb Halpern traveled from Silesia to Los Angeles with expectations akin to Brecht's. He, too, suffered disappointment: "I came out to this tropical land, / A sick man in search of a cure / Only to be sliced

into pieces, / Dished out like honey-cake at a Bar Mitzvah." I quote from the poem "Los Angeles," trans. Julian Levinson, *Jewish Currents* 68, no. 1 (Autumn 2013): 57–61.

7. Rita Barnard, *The Great Depression and the Culture of Abundance: Kenneth Fearing, Nathanael West, and Mass Culture in the 1930s* (Cambridge: Cambridge University Press, 1995), 184.

8. Susan Sontag, *Styles of Radical Will* (New York: Farrar, Straus & Giroux, 1969), 9.

9. Randall Jarrell, *The Complete Poems* (New York: Farrar, Straus & Giroux, 1969), 289. If *Poetry Los Angeles* were arranged thematically rather than geographically, one chapter would be devoted to the motif of "the lost world"; plaintive poems about Hollywood places and figures would constitute a significant portion of the essay. I would include as well a section devoted to James McMichael's book-length poem *Four Good Things* (Boston: Houghton Mifflin, 1980), in which the poet retraces his early life in Pasadena. The meticulous specificity of topographical detail re-creates not just the look but the psychic feel and local history of this unique Southern California suburb. McMichael's memory poem can usefully be read alongside John Espey's equally realistic evocation of early Pasadena in his novel *The Anniversaries* (1963), which culminates in chapters about the first Rose Parade.

10. The circumflex appears atop the second "a" in the *Complete Poems* but is customarily placed above the "o."

11. Robert Hass, "Old Movie with the Sound Turned Off," *Time and Materials* (New York: HarperCollins, 2007), 79–80.

12. Robert Duncan, "Ingmar Bergman's SEVENTH SEAL," *The Opening of the Field* (New York: Grove Press, 1960), 93–94; Richard Howard, "George Meredith on *Woman of the Year*," *Talking Cures* (New York: Turtle Point Press, 2002), 55–57.

13. Walter Benjamin, "The Work of Art in the Age of Mechanical Reproduction," trans. Harry Zohn, *Illuminations*, ed. Hannah Arendt (New York: Schocken Books, 1969). Benjamin writes, for example, "Even the most perfect reproduction of a work of art is lacking in one element: its presence in time and space, its unique existence at the place where it happens to be. . . . The presence of the original is the prerequisite to the concept of authenticity" (220).

14. James M. Cain, "The Widow's Mite, or Queen of the Rancho," *Vanity Fair*, August 1933, 22. *Vanity Fair*, a Condé Nast magazine published in New York, focused principally on Broadway as a hub of the universe, but it was uncomfortably aware that Hollywood had usurped the glamour from the Great White Way. How grudgingly they must have published along with Cain's article a lavish two-page artwork of forty-nine famous movie stars sitting on the Malibu beach. The jealousy of *Vanity Fair*'s editors can be seen in the snide contributor's note accompanying a piece by Cain in the April 1933 issue: "He has accepted movie gold and is living in the Land of Sunshine, Fruit, and Flowers." Cain deliberately disowned this cliché characterization of himself and the city in an essay, "Paradise," published in the March 1933 issue of *The American Mercury*: "Wash out,

then 'the land of sunshine, fruit, and flowers.'" A convenient reprint of "Paradise" is in *Writing Los Angeles: A Literary Anthology*, 108–30.

15. Robert Polito, "Barbara Payton: A Memoir," *Hollywood & God* (Chicago: University of Chicago Press, 2009), 5–11; Alexander Theroux, "Thelma Ritter," *Michigan Quarterly Review* 42, no. 1 (Winter 2003): 59–60; Michael C. Ford, "The Disappearance of Deanna Durbin" and "Depression in D-Minor: The Voice of Dorothy Dandridge," *Emergency Exits: The Selected Poems, 1970–1995* (Modesto, CA: Amaranth Editions, 1998), 111, 79.

Polito's placement of his prose memoir in a volume of poetry recalls Robert Lowell's inclusion of a much longer prose memoir, "91 Revere Street," in *Life Studies* (1959). A comparison of the two texts would tell us much about cultural changes in the fifty-year interval, especially the rise of a celebrity subculture culminating in a volume of poems that re-creates the fervor of devotion, always with a hard edge of irony and condescension, for figures like Paris Hilton, Elvis Presley, and unnamed ex-stars and groupies. The tableau of damaged figures in *Hollywood & God* brings to mind *Les Fleurs du Mal* and the Catholic sensibility of their creators.

16. Wanda Coleman, "Los Angeles Nocturne," *Ostinato Vamps* (Pittsburgh: University of Pittsburgh Press, 2003), 24–25.

A novel by Michael Connelly published in the same year as Coleman's poem presents the *noir* landscape of Hollywood with equal vividness: "Hollywood was always best viewed at night. It could only hold its mystique in darkness. In sunlight the curtain comes up and the intrigue is gone, replaced by a sense of hidden danger. It was a place of takers and users, of broken sidewalks and dreams. You build a city in the desert, water it with false hopes and false idols, and eventually this is what happens. The desert reclaims it, turns it arid, leaves it barren. Human tumbleweeds drift across its streets, predators hide in the rocks." *Lost Light* (Boston: Little, Brown, 2003), 153.

17. Rita Dove, "Hattie McDaniel Arrives at the Coconut Grove," *American Smooth* (New York: W. W. Norton, 2004), 92–94.

18. Robert Alter, *Imagined Cities: Urban Experience and the Language of the Novel* (New Haven and London: Yale University Press, 2005), 30. A performance poem that captures this sense of the phantasmagorical in the process of relating a Hollywood success story with extraordinary good humor is Doug Knott, "Sunset Strip Self Improvement Affirmations," *The Outlaw Book of American Poetry*, ed. Alan Kaufman (New York: Thunder's Mouth Press, 1999), 577–80.

19. Raymond Chandler, *The Little Sister* (1949; New York: Vintage Books, 1988), 184.

20. Gary Snyder, "Night Song of the Los Angeles Basin," *Mountains and Rivers Without End* (Washington, DC: Counterpoint, 1996), 62–64.

21. Rock music and Hollywood scandal revived the theme of dying young identified with the Romantic movement of the late eighteenth and early nineteenth century, enshrined most famously in the suicides of Werther in Goethe's novel *The Sorrows of Young Werther* and of Thomas Chatterton in England, and in the early deaths of Byron (1788–

1824), Shelley (1792–1822), and Keats (1795–1821). Jim Morrison's death-haunted poems beginning in his years as an undergraduate at UCLA evolved organically into songs celebrating "The End."

22. David Wojahn, "History Being Made: Melcher Production Studios, Los Angeles, 1968," *Mystery Train* (Pittsburgh: University of Pittsburgh Press, 1990), 40.

See my discussion of Amy Gerstler's prose poem "Slowly I Open My Eyes," from her first volume, *Bitter Angel*, in which the criminal figure imagines himself as a messianic crime boss—"Jerusalem Slim on his final night in the garden. Mr. X, Dr. No, The Invisible Man. All the same guy, different movies. It's a city of delinquents: my disciples." *The Misread City: New Literary Los Angeles*, ed. Scott Timberg and Dana Gioia (Los Angeles: Red Hen Press, 2003), 133–36.

23. Diana Trilling, "The Death of Marilyn Monroe," *Claremont Essays* (London: Secker and Warburg, 1965), 242. The context offers some exoneration. Speaking of writers who blamed Hollywood's "vulgarity and greed" for Monroe's suicide, Trilling writes, "I share their disgust with Hollywood, and I honor their need to isolate Marilyn Monroe from the nastiness that fed on her, but I find it impossible to believe that this girl would have been an iota better off were Hollywood to have been other than what we all know it to be, a madness in our culture."

24. See http://hotelcaliforniameaning.com. Joan Didion reports that Camarillo, the state psychiatric facility in Ventura County, is "sometimes said to have provided inspiration to the Eagles for 'Hotel California.'" See *Blue Nights* (New York: Alfred A. Knopf, 2011), 40.

25. Frederick Seidel, "1968," *Poems 1959–1979* (New York: Alfred A. Knopf, 1989), 41–43.

26. Quoted in Richard Rayner, *A Bright and Guilty Place: Murder, Corruption, and L.A.'s Scandalous Coming of Age* (New York: Anchor Books, 2010), 32.

27. *The Paris Review* 190 (Fall 2009): 149. The interviewer, Jonathan Galassi, refers to Seidel's "willfully disagreeable poems" (139). Michael Hofmann takes note of Seidel's "bold, inflammatory, defamatory gestures" and his "aggressively schizophrenic vocabulary" so often featuring "the headlines and personalities and atrocities" of the contemporary era. "So Goddamn Glorious," *Poetry* 194, no. 5 (September 2009): 452, 453, 454.

28. A convenient reprinting is Frederick Seidel, *Poems 1959–1979* (New York: Alfred A. Knopf, 1989), 91.

29. Pauline Kael, *5001 Nights at the Movies* (New York: Holt, Rinehart and Winston, 1982), 54. David Trinidad has written several interesting poems relating contemporary fascination with the Manson killings to celebrity culture. See especially "Sharon Tate and Friends the Moment Before" and "The Shower Scene in *Psycho*," *Dear Prudence: New and Selected Poems* (New York: Turtle Point Press, 2011), 95 and 268–78 respectively. See also Clayton Eshleman, "Still-Life, with Manson," which relates the Manson gang to Nazi youth as portrayed in Luchino Visconti's film *The Damned*. Clayton Eshleman, *What She Means* (Santa Barbara: Black Sparrow Press, 1978), 61.

30. Cited in E. P. Thompson, "Homage to Thomas McGrath," *TriQuarterly* 70 (Fall 1987), 128–29. Thompson's fifty-one-page essay is part of a special issue, edited by Reginald Gibbons and Terrence Des Pres, entirely devoted to McGrath's life and work.

3. *Bukowski*

1. Letter from Charles Baxter to Laurence Goldstein, 24 April 2011.

2. Archibald MacLeish, "Years of the Dog," *Collected Poems 1917–1982* (Boston: Houghton Mifflin, 1982), 376–77. "And what became of him? Fame became of him."

3. Stephen Holden, "Poet's Grim Prophecies, with Drama and Music," *New York Times*, 29 November 2010, C6.

4. Charles Bukowski, *Bone Palace Ballet: New Poems* (Santa Rosa, CA: Black Sparrow Press, 1997), 265.

5. Cited in Jay Dougherty, "An Introduction to Charles Bukowski," http://www.jaydougherty.com/bukowski/index/html.

6. *Charles Bukowski: Laughing with the Gods . . . Interview by Fernanda Pivano* (Northville, MI: Sun Dog Press, 2000), 39, 47. In another interview he remarks, "I have compassion for almost all the individuals of the world; at the same time, they repulse me." See *The Poet's Craft: Interviews from* The New York Quarterly, ed. William Packard (New York: Paragon House, 1987), 320.

7. Russell Harrison, *Against the American Dream: Essays on Charles Bukowski* (Santa Rosa: Black Sparrow Press, 1994), 69. "Bukowski is the only major postwar American writer who has denied the efficacy of the American Dream," he remarks (13).

8. Charles Bukowski, *Betting on the Muse: Poems and Stories* (Santa Rosa: Black Sparrow Press, 1996), 204.

9. From "The Wanderer: A Rococo Study," *The Collected Poems of William Carlos Williams, Volume I 1909–1939*, ed. A. Walton Litz and Christopher MacGowan (New York: New Directions, 1986), 28.

10. Mark Halliday, "The Arrogance of Poetry," *The Georgia Review* 57, no. 2 (Summer 2003): 214–15.

11. *Charles Bukowski: Laughing with the Gods*, 101.

12. Gay Brewer, *Charles Bukowski* (Boston: Twayne, 1997), 5. Bukowski told Sean Penn, "[Poetry has] been fake and snobbish and inbred for centuries. It's over-delicate. It's over-precious. . . . It's a con, a fake." David Stephen Calonne, *Bukowski* (London: Reaktion Books, 2012), 53.

13. For example, "a sad poem," *War All the Time: Poems 1981–1984* (Santa Rosa: Black Sparrow Press, 1984), 69. An admirer tells Bukowski, "what I like about your writing, it's easy to / understand."

14. Howard Sounes, *Charles Bukowski: Locked in the Arms of a Crazy Life* (Edinburgh: Rebel, Inc. [Canongate Books], 1998), 36. Bukowski's discomfort with the "pre-

ciousness" (as he called it) of high-culture poetry may be traced to his sense of exclusion from prestigious journals early in his career. See "the *Kenyon Review* and other matters" in *Bone Palace Ballet*, 55–56, for a retrospective poem full of lingering resentment toward "that / tower of practiced literary horror," which he read in the public library.

15. Derek Walcott, *Homage to Robert Frost* (New York: Farrar, Straus & Giroux, 1996). "A certain deadening of the ear had dated dramatic verse since the Victorians, who tried to resuscitate Elizabethan and Jacobean drama through the pentameter, prolonging a hollow, martial echo that could not render the ordinary and domestic. . . . Frost felt that in New England he was being offered an unexplored, unuttered theater, away from the leaves of libraries, in a natural setting rich with stories and characters" (100).

16. Gavin Lambert, *The Slide Area* (1959; New York: Dial Press, 1968), 25–54.

17. Charles Edward Eaton, "The Weight Lifter," *New & Selected Poems 1942–1987* (Cranbury, NJ: Associated University Presses, 1987), 176; Harold Norse, "Mr. Venice Beach," *In the Hub of the Fiery Force: Collected Poems 1934–2003* (New York: Thunder's Mouth Press, 2003), 361.

18. Howard Sounes, 223.

19. Russell Harrison, *Against the American Dream*, 35.

20. Charles Bukowski, "born again," *The Flash of Lightning Behind the Mountain*, ed. John Martin (New York: Ecco Press, 2004), 57.

21. Brewer, *Charles Bukowski*, 188. Suzanne Lummis, in an obituary, emphasized that Bukowski's most successful creation was not some significant other but "the boorish, half-endearing underdog persona" that "won him a folk hero status in the international literary underground." "Charles Bukowski, 1920–1994," *Los Angeles Times Book Review*, 10 April 1994.

22. Charles Bukowski, *The Flash of Lightning Behind the Mountain*, ed. John Martin (New York: Ecco Press, 2004), 234.

4. *Freeway*

1. Reyner Banham, *Los Angeles: The Architecture of Four Ecologies* (New York: Penguin, 1971), 23.

2. Eloise Klein Healy, "Postcard," *A Wild Surmise: New & Selected Poems & Recordings* (Pasadena: Red Hen Press, 2013), 127. "Postcard" is an elegy for the poet Lynda Hull, who died in a car crash in 1994.

3. Joan Didion, *The White Album* (New York: Simon & Schuster, 1979), 83. James D. Houston elaborates: "When the L.A. freeway system is on your side, there is absolutely nothing like it anywhere else in the world. . . . In L.A. the freeway is a form of entertainment, a form of action, a form of commitment, a form of engaging the environment on its own terms, and, if you survive, a source of infinite satisfaction." *Californians: Searching for the Golden State* (New York: Alfred A. Knopf, 1982), 199.

4. Frank Bidart, "California Plush," *Golden State* (New York: George Braziller, 1973), 11. Unlike Jarman's devotion to the left margin and uniform lineation, Bidart employs the entire field of the page with double spacing and irregular line-lengths to score the prosody for more dramatic effect.

5. In his poem of 1876, "To a Locomotive in Winter." *The Works of Walt Whitman, Volume I: The Collected Poetry,* ed. Malcolm Cowley (New York: Funk & Wagnalls, 1968), 407–8.

6. Thomas De Quincey, "The English Mail Coach," *Selected Writings of Thomas De Quincey*, ed. Philip Van Doren Stern (New York: Modern Library, 1937), 928.

7. See the discussion of Gilman's career in Franklin Walker, *A Literary History of Southern California* (Berkeley and Los Angeles: University of California Press, 1950), 173–84. For the poem "The Grapevine," with others celebrating the landscape of the region, see *The Later Poetry of Charlotte Perkins Gilman*, ed. Denise D. Knight (Newark: University of Delaware Press, 1996), 170–71.

8. Reyner Banham, 214. Likewise, Cotton Seiler in *Republic of Drivers: A Cultural History of Automobility in America* (Chicago: University of Chicago Press, 2008) argues that driving is the "crucial practice" in the development of twentieth-century subjectivity, that is, in the autonomous self-direction that mimics Whitman's assertions throughout *Leaves of Grass*.

9. Reyner Banham, 88.

10. Eloise Klein Healy, "This Darknight Speed," *A Wild Surmise: New & Selected Poems & Recordings* (Pasadena: Red Hen Press, 2013), 52–53.

11. I derive images and quotation in this paragraph from Eloise Klein Healy, "Los Angeles Is a Virgo," *A Wild Surmise*, 118–20.

12. Wanda Coleman, "On Speed," *Imagoes* (Santa Rosa: Black Sparrow Press, 1983), 40.

13. James Schevill, *The Complete American Fantasies* (Athens: Swallow Press [Ohio University Press], 1996), 224. Schevill explores the topic of auto-mobility further in the title poem of *The Buddhist Car and Other Characters* (Chicago: Swallow Press, 1973), 1–8.

14. Thomas McGrath, *Letter to an Imaginary Friend, Parts I and II* (Chicago: Swallow Press, 1970), 4.

15. Perloff's essay can be found in her collection, *Radical Artifice: Writing Poetry in the Age of Media* (Chicago: University of Chicago Press, 1991), 93–133. For Hart Crane see the opening line of "The River" in Part II, "Powhatan's Daughter," of *The Bridge*. Tony Barnstone's poem "The Sermon on Los Angeles" appears in *The Golem of Los Angeles* (Los Angeles: Red Hen Press, 2008), 80–81.

16. Ron Koertge, "The Pasadena Freeway," *Bear Flag Republic: Prose Poems and Poetics from California*, ed. Christopher Buckley and Gary Young (Santa Cruz, CA: Greenfield Review Press/Alcatraz Editions, 2008), 243. It's no surprise that male poets sometimes analogize the freeway system to a curvaceous female; more surprising are poems that

imagine a particular female as a freeway system, such as Timothy Steele's comic address in rhymed couplets to a promiscuous woman in "An L.A. Impromptu," *Sapphics Against Anger and Other Poems* (New York: Random House, 1986), 36.

17. Carol Muske-Dukes, "Little L. A. Villanelle," *An Octave Above Thunder: New and Selected Poems* (New York: Penguin Books, 1997), 162. Early poems like this one were published under the name "Carol Muske," but the poet changed her name after her marriage to David Dukes and she has requested that all of her writing now be assigned to the later name.

18. Leo Braudy, *The Hollywood Sign: Fantasy and Reality of an American Icon* (New Haven and London: Yale University Press, 2011), 2. "In a world now drowning in a sea of billboards and brands, the Hollywood sign remains the prime visual center for a famously amorphous city and industry," Braudy concludes. "The viewer doesn't pass through such icons to another, more spiritual meaning, but stays on their surface, content with the way they gesture at that deeper reality without being too specific about it" (190).

Braudy calls attention to Ed Ruscha's painting of the Hollywood sign, "Hollywood" (1968), discussed as well by Calvin Tomkins in "Ed Ruscha's L.A.," *The New Yorker*, 1 July 2013, 48-57. Ruscha's fondness for word-paintings coexists with his fantasy depictions such as "Los Angeles County Museum of Art on Fire" (1965), part of the "burning of Los Angeles" theme surveyed in the next chapter of this text.

19. Miroslav Holub, "Hemophilia/Los Angeles," *Intensive Care: Selected and New Poems*, trans. David Young and Dana Habova (Oberlin, OH: Oberlin College Press, 1996), 81. That the freeway is an accelerated trope for the conventional "road of time" or "road of life" hardly needs stating. One of the best poems of this kind exploits a generational connection across lifetimes, between father and daughter, set on the Santa Monica and Pasadena freeways. See Alicia Ostriker, "Meeting the Dead," *Drive, They Said: Poems about Americans and their Cars*, ed. Kurt Brown (Minneapolis: Milkweed Editions, 1994), 90–91.

20. Wallace Stevens, "Adagia," Part One, *Opus Posthumous: Poems / Plays / Prose*, Revised, Enlarged, and Corrected Edition, ed. Milton J. Bates (New York: Alfred A. Knopf, 1989), 188.

21. Allen Ginsberg, "These States: into L.A.," *Collected Poems 1947–1980* (New York: Harper & Row, 1984), 377.

22. Reyner Banham, 23.

23. Mary Armstrong, "Freeway Shooting," *Grand Passion: The Poets of Los Angeles and Beyond*, ed. Suzanne Lummis and Charles H. Webb (Los Angeles: Red Wind Books, 1995), 155–56.

24. Charles Bukowski, "traffic report," *Betting on the Muse: Poems and Stories* (Santa Rosa: Black Sparrow Press, 1996), 316–17. In his later years Bukowski returned more and more often to the sinister aspects of the freeway. See, for example, "like a polluted river flowing" (109–10), "Los Angeles" (224), and "straight on" (302–3) in *sifting through*

the madness for the Word, the line, the way, ed. John Martin (New York: Ecco/HarperCollins, 2003).

Frank Romero's iconic painting *Freeway Wars* (ca. 1987), widely distributed in serigraph form, depicts a car-to-car shooting on the freeway.

25. Jan Berry had the misfortune to enact the car crash he sang about. In 1966 he was paralyzed after hitting a truck during a spell of reckless driving. See the commentary on this incident, and the made-for-TV movie of it, in Greil Marcus, "Jan and Dean as Purloined Letter," *The Dustbin of History* (Cambridge: Harvard University Press, 1995), 126–32.

26. James Harms, "Gridlock," *Quarters* (Pittsburgh: Carnegie-Mellon Press, 2001), 44–45.

27. According to an e-mail of 11 March 2012 from Harms to Laurence Goldstein, the poem was intended as a pure prose poem, with no justified right margin. But it has been reprinted more than once with the right margin from its book publication intact. I have preserved that margin and lineation in my reprint of the poem.

28. *The Land of Orange Groves and Jails: Upton Sinclair's California*, ed. Lauren Coodley (Berkeley, CA: Heyday Books, 2004), 112.

29. Tom Wolfe, "There Goes (Varoom! Varoom!) That Kandy-Kolored (Thphhhhhh!) Tangerine-Flake Streamline Baby (Rahghhh!) Around the Bend (Brummmmmmmmmmmmmmmm . . . . .," *Smiling Through the Apocalypse: Esquire's History of the Sixties*, ed. Harold Hayes (New York: McCall, 1969), 561–82. As the Hayes anthology demonstrates, the rise of the New Journalism owed much to the culture of Los Angeles. See, for example, Norman Mailer, "Superman Comes to the Supermarket" (3–30), Gay Talese, "Frank Sinatra Has a Cold" (280–310), Peter Bogdanovich, "Bogie in Excelsis" (327–38), William Styron, "Mrs. Aadland's Little Girl, Beverly" (542–46), and other articles featuring short views of L.A.

30. Tony Hoagland, "Recognition, Vertigo, and Passionate Worldliness," *Poetry*, September 2010, 437–54.

31. Dana Goodyear, "Freeway," *The Oracle of Hollywood Boulevard* (New York: W. W. Norton, 2013), 32.

32. Thomas Pynchon, *Inherent Vice* (New York: Penguin Press, 2009), 71.

33. E-mail letter from Dana Goodyear to Laurence Goldstein, 17 May 2012. "The poem has been through many iterations," she writes. "It was short, it was in four long parts, it ran in 'Slake' and then I shortened it again."

34. Tony Hoagland, 440.

35. A convenient reprint is *The Norton Anthology of Contemporary Poetry*, ed. Jahan Ramazani, Richard Ellmann, and Robert O'Clair (New York: W. W. Norton, 2003), 1055.

36. Dana Gioia, "The Freeways Considered as Earth Gods," *Pity the Beautiful* (Minneapolis: Graywolf Press, 2012), 20–21.

37. Sinclair Lewis, *Dodsworth* (New York: Harcourt, Brace, 1929), 164.

38. Gioia's sacramental reading of the freeway as a worldly phenomenon steeped in grace recalls a thirty-seven-part poem by Fanny Howe, "Catholic," in which the network of converging and diverging freeways is brought into association with the writings of Thomas Aquinas about the destiny of the human soul in the fallen world, caught in the whirlwind of desire like Paolo and Francesca in Dante's *Inferno*. *The Best American Poetry 2004*, ed. Lyn Hejinian and David Lehman (New York: Scribner Poetry, 2004), 110–22.

39. Dorothy Barresi, "Motion Picture and Television Arts Home for the Aging, Woodland Hills, California," *American Fanatics* (Pittsburgh: University of Pittsburgh Press, 2010), 90.

40. Diane Wakoski, "The Orange," *Medea the Sorceress* (Santa Rosa, CA: Black Sparrow Press, 1991), 13–14. I have adopted here several changes to the poem in Wakoski's, *The Butcher's Apron: New & Selected Poems* (Santa Rosa, CA: Black Sparrow Press, 2000), 69–70.

41. David Rieff, *Los Angeles: Capital of the Third World* (New York: Simon & Schuster, 1991), 51.

42. Edward W. Barnard, "A Ballade of California," published in Charles F. Lummis's magazine *The Land of Sunshine* 3, no. 3 (August 1895): 115–16. I am grateful to Marie Jaquelin Pelzer for calling my attention to this poem.

5. *South Central*

1. Reyner Banham, "Ecology 3: The Plains of Id," *Los Angeles: The Architecture of Four Ecologies* (1971; New York: Penguin Books, 1973), 161.

2. Wanda Coleman, epigraph for "Flight of the California Condor," *Imagoes* (Santa Barbara: Black Sparrow Press, 1983), 93.

3. Elizabeth Alexander, "Stravinsky in L. A.," *Body of Life* (Los Angeles: Tia Chucha Press, 1996), 11.

4. The actual name of the builder of the Watts Towers was Sebastiano Rodia; an article in the *Los Angeles Times* mistakenly called him "Simon," a name he disliked, and it stuck. For a full biography, see American National Biography Online: Rodia, Simon.

5. Reyner Banham, *Los Angeles: The Architecture of Four Ecologies*, 72. Kevin Starr remarks that "Rodia was busy about the task of creating a somewhere, a place fixed and defined by materialized ambitions." *Material Dreams: Southern California Through the 1920s* (New York: Oxford University Press, 1990), 230.

6. Rodia's point of view, and the community's response to his construction, is reconstituted by James Ragan in his poem "The Tower (Nuestro Pueblo)": "What's the use, he thought, to mesh the mortar once / the rain had picked the cobbles clean, / what to say / when neighbors called it curious and worse / a nuisance, petty thrift, as steep as trawler masts, / as round as whales?" *The Hunger Wall* (New York: Grove Press, 1995), 85.

7. Mildred Meyer Boaz, "Musical and Poetic Analogues in T. S. Eliot's *The Waste*

Land and Igor Stravinsky's *The Rite of Spring*," *The Centennial Review* XXIV, no. 2 (Spring 1980): 218–31. The performance occurred in the summer of 1921.

8. Robert Craft, *Stravinsky: Glimpses of a Life* (London: Lime Tree, 1992), 141. A less favorable view of Stravinsky in L.A. is John Thomas's poem "Old Man Stravinsky Rehearsing with Orchestra," *L.A. Exile: A Guide to Los Angeles Writing 1932–1998*, ed. Paul Vangelisti with Evan Calbi (New York: Marsilio, 1999), 282–86.

9. Elizabeth Alexander in conversation with Laurence Goldstein, 21 April 2011, in Ann Arbor, Michigan.

10. Elizabeth Alexander, "Miami Footnote," *The Venus Hottentot* (Charlottesville: University Press of Virginia, 1990), 48. Other cities that provide settings for the poems in this volume are Philadelphia and Boston.

11. See especially the positive remarks in the Governor's Commission Report, known as the McCone Report, following the riots of 1965: "In the riot area, most streets are wide and usually quite clean; there are trees, parks and playgrounds" and so forth. Cited in David Wyatt, *Five Fires: Race, Catastrophe, and the Shaping of California* (New York: Oxford University Press, 1999), 211.

12. Michèlle T. Clinton, *High Blood/Pressure* (Los Angeles: West End Press, 1986), 2.

13. RJ Smith, *The Great Black Way: L.A. in the 1940s and the Lost African-American Renaissance* (New York: Public Affairs, 2006), 69.

14. Walter Mosley, *White Butterfly* (New York: W.W. Norton, 1992), 15.

15. Michèlle T. Clinton, 9.

16. Wanda Coleman, *Greatest Hits 1966–2003* (Columbus, OH: Pudding House, 2004), 7.

17. See Laurence Goldstein, "'Mama How Come Black Men Don't Get to Be Heroes?': Colorizing American Experience," in *The American Poet at the Movies: A Critical History* (Ann Arbor: University of Michigan Press, 1994), 201–24, and Laurence Goldstein, "City of Poems: The Lyric Voice in Los Angeles Since 1990," in Scott Timberg and Dana Gioia, ed., *The Misread City: New Literary Los Angeles* (Los Angeles: Red Hen Press, 2003), 124–42.

18. Wanda Coleman, "Where I Live," *African Sleeping Sickness* (Santa Rosa, CA: Black Sparrow Press, 1990), 21–22.

19. Audre Lord, "To the Poet Who Happens to Be Black and the Black Poet Who Happens to Be a Woman," *The Collected Poems of Audre Lord* (New York: W. W. Norton, 1997), 359.

20. Eric Partridge, *Shakespeare's Bawdy* (1948; New York: E. P. Dutton, 1960), 9. "Shakespeare may have had a dirty mind, yet he certainly had not a filthy mind." Partridge adds, "Shakespeare is never filthy: he is broad, ribald, healthily coarse, unsqueamishly mature, and unaffectedly humorous" (12).

21. Saul Bellow, *Him with His Foot in His Mouth and Other Stories* (New York: Harper & Row, 1984), 14.

22. David Wyatt, *Five Fires: Race, Catastrophe, and the Shaping of California* (Reading, MA: Addison-Wesley, 1997), 156.

23. Wanda Coleman, "The Lady in the Red Veiled Hat," *Mercurochrome: New Poems* (Santa Rosa: Black Sparrow Press, 2001), 65. For a useful commentary on the issues raised in Coleman's poems about the difficulties of being a black female poet, see Tony Magistrale, "Doing Battle with the Wolf: A Critical Introduction to Wanda Coleman's Poetry," *Black American Literature Forum* 23, no. 3 (Fall 1989): 539–54.

24. Wanda Coleman, "Clocking Dollars," *African Sleeping Sickness* (Santa Rosa: Black Sparrow Press, 1990), 218–21.

25. Joan Didion, "Los Angeles Notebook," *Slouching Towards Bethlehem* (New York: Dell, 1968), 220.

26. Jack Hirschman, "The Burning of Los Angeles," *Front Lines. Selected Poems* (San Francisco: City Lights, 2002), 23. Of the many songs by L.A. punk bands that make use of the theme, perhaps the most relevant for our purposes is Bad Religion's anthem of 2004, "Los Angeles is Burning," especially the second stanza: "When the hills of Los Angeles are burning / Palm trees are candles in the murder wind / So many lives are on the breeze / Even the stars are ill at ease / And Los Angeles is burning."

27. T. C. Boyle, *The Tortilla Curtain* (New York: Viking, 1995), 270, 274. The fire originates in a campfire started by two undocumented Mexican immigrants and blown by Santa Ana winds into the surrounding woods above Topanga Canyon. Thus it realizes the anxieties of the white homeowners in the area that their way of life, their empire, is being destroyed by aliens in their midst. "They were like the barbarians outside the gates of Rome," one main character broods, "only they were already inside" (311). As in West's novel, the fire is a trope for class and ethnic conflicts that threaten the American Way of Life.

John Hollander calls attention to three poetic texts depicting the burning of a great city: the destruction of Troy in Virgil's *Aeneid*, the Great Fire of London in John Dryden's "Annus Mirabilis," and the fires raised by the personified figure of Arson in Herman Melville's poem about the anti-conscription riots in New York in 1863, "The House-Top." Foreword, *I Speak of the City: Poems of New York*, ed. Stephen Wolf (New York: Columbia University Press, 2007), xxiii–xxv.

A compelling forerunner of the fiery apocalypse imagined for Los Angeles, or any city, is Claude McKay's sonnet of 1921, "Baptism." The speaker enters "the hottest zone" of a fiery furnace, "Transforming me into a shape of flame." "I will come back," he promises his readers, apparently ready to do battle with those who lynch and otherwise suppress the black population. The poem obviously responds to race riots in dozens of cities during the years 1919 and 1920. *Complete Poems*, ed. William J. Maxwell (Urbana: University of Illinois Press, 2004), 177.

Luis J. Rodriguez makes the general point explicit: "Fire for me has been a constant metaphor against the backdrop of inner city reality. You see, South Central Los Angeles was once home." "From These Black and Brown Streets: L.A. Revisited," *Why L.A. Happened: Implications of the '92 Los Angeles Rebellion*, ed. Haki R. Madhubuti (Chicago: Third World Press, 1993), 221.

Worth noting as well is Arna Bontemps's introduction of 1968 to a reissue of his novel of 1936, *Black Thunder* (Boston: Beacon Press, 1968), in which he remembers how his youthful experience of racial bigotry in Watts impelled him to write this novel based on Gabriel Prosser's slave revolt in Virginia in 1800. "Had the frustrations dormant in Watts at that date suddenly exploded in flame and anger, as they were eventually to do, I think they would have shaken my concentration; but I have a feeling that more readers might then have been in a mood to hear a tale of volcanic rumblings among angry blacks—and the end of patience." (ix).

28. Samuel Maio, "South Central L.A.," *The Burning of Los Angeles* (Kirksville, MO: Thomas Jefferson University Press, 1997), 53. Another fine poem about the anxiety of living near the scene of racial violence is Richard Garcia, "Open Letter to My Friends." "I am becoming a connoisseur of night sounds," he writes. "The distant chatter of automatic rifles, / the popping of a .22, a car alarm. / I can tell the difference between the whoosh / of Molotov cocktails and the rip a shotgun / makes in the air." *Grand Passion: The Poets of Los Angeles and Beyond*, ed. Suzanne Lummis and Charles H. Webb (Los Angeles: Red Wind Books, 1995), 15. See also Amy Uyematsu, "The Ten Million Flames of Los Angeles," which recalls the "burn, baby, burn" era of the city but also the purifying fire of forgiveness that followed. *Nights of Fire, Nights of Rain* (Ashland, OR: Story Line Press, 1998), 25–26. The young speaker of Lucille Clifton's poem "4/30/92 for Rodney King" is less forgiving: "mama / if we are nothing / why/ should we spare / the neighborhood." *The Vintage Book of African American Poetry*, ed. Michael S. Harper and Anthony Walton (New York: Vintage Books, 2000), 249.

29. David Wyatt, *Five Fires: Race, Catastrophe, and the Shaping of California* (Reading, MA: Addison-Wesley, 1997), 211.

30. Thomas Pynchon, "A Journey into the Mind of Watts," *The New York Times Magazine*, 12 June 1966. www.nytimes.com/books/97/05/18/reviews/pynchon-watts.html (accessed 26 June 2009). The quotation appears on page 4 of 9.

31. Robin D. G. Kelley, "kickin' reality, kickin' ballistics: gangsta rap and postindustrial los angeles," *Droppin' Science: Critical Essays on Rap Music and Hip Hop Culture*, ed. William Eric Perkins (Philadelphia: Temple University Press, 1996), 136.

32. Ice Cube, "How to Survive in South Central." I use the version provided by OHHLA Webmaster DJ Flash derived from the soundtrack to the film *Boyz N the Hood*. Permission to reprint is pending from Hal Leonard Corporation.

33. Ice-T, "Colors," *The Anthology of Rap*, ed. Adam Bradley and Andrew Dubois (New Haven: Yale University Press, 2010), 192. "The streets are my stage and terror's my show," he writes in the same song (193). Freestyle Fellowship's song "Bullies of the Block," as seen on a video full of fire imagery, makes the same claims amid the refrain "I am a Black man / I will survive." See www.youtube.com/watch?v=dacrjD_LDna. The

editors of *The Anthology of Rap* refer to such lyrics as "racial theater" (187), turning a home-place into a scene of unending and brutal conflict. Adam Kirsch, in a review of *The Anthology of Rap*, describes the rapper as "a larger-than-life figure, closer to a movie star or a comic-book hero than a 'man speaking to men.'" "How Ya Like Me Now," *Poetry*, February 2011, 419.

34. *The Anthology of Rap*, 511–12.

35. I am grateful to my students David Kinzer, Evan McGarvey, and Adam Zucker for conversations that led me to the examples in this section of the essay.

36. *The Anthology of Rap*, xxx.

37. I am drawing upon the commentary of Donald Bogle in his study *Toms, Coons, Mulattoes, Mammies, and Bucks: An Interpretive History of Blacks in American Film*. New Expanded Edition (New York: Continuum, 1989). Bogle remarks, "The great subconscious goal of the 1980s may often have been to rid American films of the late 1960s/early 1970s rebellious figures. In actuality, the movies wanted audiences to believe that such figures no longer existed, or, if they did, they could really be tamed, disposed of, or absorbed into the system" (269).

38. Harryette Mullen, "#6 Sepulveda," *Rainbow Darkness: An Anthology of African American Poetry*, ed. Keith Tuma (Oxford, OH: Miami University Press, 2003), 86. Mullen remarks, "Some of what I know about Oulipo I think I got by way of Bernadette Mayer's long list of writing experiments and exercises, which included ideas such as taking a walk for fourteen blocks and writing a line for each block. I don't know what Bernadette calls it, but I call it a pedestrian sonnet—perfect for New York poets. Here in Los Angeles, I suggest to my students that they write their lines while riding a bus, as I have done with my poem "#6 Sepulveda[.]" *The Cracks Between What We Are and What We Are Supposed to Be* (Tuscaloosa: University of Alabama Press, 2012), 46.

39. The line appears in Part 5 of "Images for Godard" in *The Will to Change* (New York: Norton, 1971), 47–49.

6. *Californios*

1. Lorna Dee Cervantes, "Poema para los Californios Muertos," *Emplumada* (Pittsburgh: University of Pittsburgh Press, 1981), 42–43. The lines can be translated, "I remember dead ancestors. I remember them in the blood, the fertile blood."

2. Curtis Zahn, "Tijuana," *Poets of the Non-Existent City: Los Angeles in the McCarthy Era*, ed. Estelle Gershgoren Novak (Albuquerque: University of New Mexico Press, 2002), 124–25. In the version of the poem printed in the text named above, some lines begin with a lowercase letter. Seeing no precedent for this usage in any of Zahn's other poems and no purpose for it in this poem, I have made the initial letter in each line uppercase, following the version in *One Ocean, One Sky: Two Poets* (Los Angeles: Pacificus Foundation, 1992), 90–91. I have tried to reconcile the two texts to form the most effective version of a poem that exists in different manuscript drafts.

3. An anthology of his writings in several genres, *The Plight of the Lesser Sawyer's Cricket* (Los Angeles: Garland-Clarke Editions, 1987), includes a thirty-one-page section of poems, including one of his best about Los Angeles, "In the City, In the City." But it does not include "Tijuana," nor an excellent poem about the Mojave Desert, "A Desert Suburbia for Admixed Minds," published in the Autumn 1961 issue of *mendicant*.

For a Latino view of Tijuana, see Xelina's poem "tía juana u glisten," *Infinite Divisions: An Anthology of Chicana Literature*, ed. Tey Diana Rebolledo and Eliana S. Rivero (Tucson and London: University of Arizona Press, 1993), 187–88. Tia Juana is imagined as a woman who has to put up with an overwhelming stream of "sick Americans" and "anglos with their elegant cars" and incessant demands.

4. Greg Hise, "Border City: Race and Social Distance in Los Angeles," *American Quarterly* 56, no. 3 (September 2004): 555.

5. Josh Kun, "Tijuana and the Borders of Race," *A Companion to Los Angeles*, ed. William Deverell and Greg Hise (Malden, MA: Wiley-Blackwell, 2010), 316.

6. David Rieff, *Los Angeles: Capital of the Third World* (New York: Simon & Schuster, 1991), 86. A study of fiction by white authors about Chicanos in Los Angeles is beyond the scope of this book, but a place to start, after some obligatory attention to *Ramona*, would be John Fante's portrait of Camilla Gomez in *Ask the Dust* (1939). The Italian-American narrator's obsession with Camilla, whose passionate primitivism has been thwarted by her residence in Los Angeles, ultimately leading to her drug addiction, madness, and abandonment of the narrator, dramatizes a radical incompatibility with an archetypal figure of Mexico itself.

7. Gustavo Pérez Firmat, *Life on the Hyphen: The Cuban-American Way* (Austin: University of Texas Press, 1994).

8. Gina Valdés, "Where You From?", *Comiendo Lumbre / Eating Fire* (Colorado Springs: Maize Press, 1986), 9.

9. Gary Soto, "Good Buy in Beverly Hills," *One Kind of Faith* (San Francisco: Chronicle Books, 2003), 47. Readers of Diana Garcia's volume of poems *When Living Was a Labor Camp* (Tucson: University of Arizona Press, 2000) will notice plentiful descriptions of the San Joaquin Valley, as well as scenes of Chicano life common to Southern California.

10. Jimmy Santiago Baca, "These Hands," *Unmasking L. A.: Third Worlds and the City*, ed. Deepak Narang Sawhney (New York: Palgrave, 2002), 69–70.

11. Richard Garcia, "Vernon," *Rancho Notorious* (Rochester, NY: BOA Editions, 2001), 29–30.

12. I depend upon the Wikipedia entry for Vernon for the information in this paragraph. The entry speaks of the presence of industrial giants in the city: "In the 1920s and 30s, heavy industries such as steel (U. S. Steel), aluminum (Alcoa), glass (Owens Corning), can-making (American Can) and automobile production (Studebaker) sprung up in the city. The 1940s and 50s added aerospace contractors (Norris Industries), box and

paper manufacturers, drug companies such as Brunswig, and food processors General Mills and Kal Kan. Giant meat packers Farmer John and Swift flourished."

13. Gina Valdés, "The Border," *Infinite Divisions: An Anthology of Chicana Literature*, 185–86. See my discussion of the border-crossing poems of Juan Delgado in *The Misread City: New Literary Los Angeles*, ed. Scott Timberg and Dana Gioia (Los Angeles: Red Hen Press, 2003), 138–39.

14. Martín Espada, "Heart of Hunger," *Albanza: New and Selected Poems 1982–2002* (New York: W. W. Norton, 2003), 30–31.

15. Simon J. Ortiz, "Under L.A. International Airport," *A Good Journey* (Tucson: Sun Tracks and The University of Arizona Press, 1977), 27.

16. Luis J. Rodríguez, "The Blast Furnace," *My Nature is Hunger: New and Selected Poems 1989–2004* (Willimantic, CT: Curbstone Press, 2005), 38.

17. Aleida Rodríguez, "My Mother's Art," *Garden of Exile* (Louisville, KY: Sarabande Books, 1999), 23.

7. Interiors

1. Gaston Bachelard, *The Poetics of Space*, trans. Marie Jolas (New York: Orion Press, 1964), 53.

2. Ibid., 13. A later theorization of the philosophy of domestic space, urban and extra-urban, is Henri Lefebvre, *The Production of Space* (1974; Hoboken, NJ: Wiley-Blackwell, 1992). I have benefited also from two socio-historical works focused on Los Angeles: Edward Soja, *Thirdspace: Journeys to Los Angeles and Other Real-and-Imagined Places* (Oxford: Basil Blackwell, 1996), and Dolores Hayden, *The Power of Place: Urban Landscape as Public History* (Cambridge: MIT Press, 1997).

3. D. J. Waldie, *Holy Land: A Suburban Memoir* (New York: St. Martin's Press, 1996), 94.

4. Victoria Chang, "Gamble House," *Circle* (Carbondale: *Crab Orchard Review* and Southern Illinois University Press, 2005), 56. Russell Charles Leong enters a quite different interior space in his long surreal poem "Enter the Year of the Dragon, 2000," in which a car ride through many districts of L.A. brings him to the Pacific Pearl Seafood Buffet in Azusa. See *Another City: Writing from Los Angeles*, ed. David L. Ulin (San Francisco: City Lights, 2001), 93–100.

5. Garrett Hongo, "The Underworld," *The River of Heaven* (New York: Alfred A. Knopf, 1988), 64–65.

6. Helene Johnson, "Bottled," *Harlem's Glory: Black Women Writing, 1900–1950*, ed. Lorraine Elena Roses and Ruth Elizabeth Randolph (Cambridge: Harvard University Press, 1996), 327–28.

7. The director David Lynch chose the Tower Theater, down the street from the Orpheum, for the scenes that conjure the spell of the past.

8. Charles Webb, "Further Decline of Western Civilization," in *The Faber Book of Movie Verse*, ed. Philip French and Ken Wlaschin (London: Faber and Faber, 1993), 137–38. "Odium" is a play on Odeon, a popular and pretentious name for often very seedy theaters in downtown districts.

9. John Fowles, "The Woman in the Reeds," *Seasonal Performances: A* Michigan Quarterly Review *Reader*, ed. Laurence Goldstein (Ann Arbor: University of Michigan Press, 1991), 234. This story appeared originally in *Michigan Quarterly Review* 4, no. 2 (Spring 1965): 131–45. Presumably because Fowles used the central event of the story, in which a girl's drowned body is discovered by a young couple punting on a river near Oxford, in his novel *Daniel Martin* (1977), he did not choose to reprint the story in any book except the anthology.

10. Allen Ginsberg, "A Supermarket in California," *Collected Poems 1947–1980* (New York: Harper & Row, 1984), 136; Denis Johnson, "The Supermarkets of Los Angeles," *The Throne of the Third Heaven of the Nations Millennium General Assembly: Poems Collected and New* (New York: HarperCollins, 1995), 69–70. Another suggestive point of reference is James Dickey's poem "The Firebombing," in which an American pilot living a kind of posthumous life of fallen glory in the suburbs of Los Angeles indulges in a nostalgic reverie about his glamorous life during World War II as he wanders through a supermarket. He contrasts the light of the cans on the shelves to the magical luminosity of the moon over Japan in his memory. See *Poems 1957–1967* (Middletown, CT: Wesleyan University Press, 1967), 181–88.

11. Quincy Troupe, "A Poem for 'Magic,'" *Transcircularities: New and Selected Poems by Quincy Troupe* (Minneapolis: Coffee House Press, 2002), 152–53. The Lakers have cultivated a Los Angeles identity, performing with cinematic showmanship. Their leader at the time of writing is Kobe Bryant, a familiar face even to citizens who disdain basketball thanks to his appearance in endorsement ads and news stories that situate him in a Hollywood milieu of media stardom.

12. David Wyatt, *The Fall into Eden: Landscape and Imagination in California* (Cambridge: Cambridge University Press, 1986), 7.

13. Salman Rushdie, *Imaginary Homelands: Essays and Criticism 1981–1991* (New York: Penguin Books, 15.

14. Robert von Hallberg, *American Poetry and Culture, 1945–1980* (Cambridge: Harvard University Press, 1985), 64.

15. Charles Gullans, "Another Local (The Charthouse)," *The Bright Universe and Other Poems* (Omaha: University of Nebraska at Omaha: Abattoir Editions, 1983), 42–43.

16. See "The Chart House" in Gullans's chapbook *Local Winds* (Florence, KY: Robert L. Barth, 1985), [unpaginated], in which he is approached by a potential companion for the night.

17. Paul Monette, *Borrowed Time: An AIDS Memoir* (San Diego: Harcourt Brace Jovanovich, 1988), 29. Monette contrasts the cottage constantly to the UCLA Medical Center where Rog spends more and more time as the narrative progresses. The cottage

takes on the aspect of a "dead and empty" (226) place when Rog is in the hospital, a hospice when he is in residence, a mausoleum as he becomes blind and approaches death. To live in the world of AIDS is to no longer inhabit a real earthly place, Monette writes, but to be "on the moon"—a phrase he repeats often.

Monette's constant attention to his garden reminds us of the claims that bountiful and beautiful nature make upon residents of Los Angeles, as elsewhere. I have written in the Introduction that Ann Stanford's attention to her house and gardens indicated a withdrawal from the cityscape; but one could make the counter-argument that the flower garden is as much of an urban site, bristling with movement, as a freeway or a sports venue or the surf at high tide. Monette certainly saw the matter in this light. The preeminent pastoral poem set in Los Angeles—more precisely, in and around Encino—is Stephen Yenser's "Vertumnal" in *The Fire in All Things* (Baton Rouge: Louisiana State University Press, 1993), 49–60.

18. Paul Monette, "The House on Kings Road," *West of Yesterday, East of Summer: New and Selected Poems (1973–1993)* (New York: St. Martin's Press, 1994), 42–45.

19. Stanley Plumly, "Elegiac," *Radiant Lyre: Essays on Lyric Poetry*, ed. David Baker and Ann Townsend (Saint Paul, MN Graywolf Press, 2007), 32.

20. Carol Muske-Dukes, "The Image," *Sparrow* (New York: Random House, 2003), 24–25.

21. John H. Johnston, *The Poet and the City: A Study in Urban Perspectives* (Athens: University of Georgia Press, 1984), 7.

8. Exteriors

1. Don DeLillo, *White Noise* (New York: Penguin Books, 1986), 66.

2. Dick Barnes, "On a Painting by David Hockney," *A World Like Fire: Selected Poems*, ed. Robert Mezey (New York: Handsel Books, 2005), 72.

3. David Trinidad, "Hockney: Blue Pool," *Dear Prudence: New and Selected Poems* (New York: Turtle Point Press, 2011), 240. In *Pop L.A.: Art and the City in the 1960s* (Berkeley: University of California Press, 2006), Cécile Whiting suggests that painters in Los Angeles faced some of the same dilemmas of representation as I am applying to poets. (Whiting does not consider poets.) The rising popularity and critical esteem of photography throughout the first half of the twentieth century, she argues, drove some postwar painters to give up figuration completely and join the ranks of the abstract expressionists situated in New York; she uses Richard Diebenkorn as an example. Then Pop Art in some of its innovative forms departed successfully from both abstraction and bourgeois verisimilitude. Finally in 1963 David Hockney arrived from England, in Whiting's tongue-in-cheek phrasing, to serve as a "knight with shining paintbrush" and "give Los Angeles an image of itself." (16). That the preeminent image Hockney offers is a swimming pool suggests how powerfully, and desperately, the general public clings to retro iconography of the 1950s.

4. Timothy Steele, "Daybreak, Benedict Canyon," *Toward the Winter Solstice* (Athens, OH: Swallow Press, 2006), 3–4. Steele provides a guide to his poetics in a conversation with Alan Fox in the journal *Rattle* 18, no. 2 (Winter 2012): 149–63.

5. That Los Angeles might be submerged in water, Atlantis-like, either because of an earthquake or because of a hurricane, is a horror summoned by Suzanne Lummis in her poem "El Niño, After Visit from Jehovah's Witness." Her imagination is filled with the imagery of endtime thanks to the visit of an evangelical Christian missionary. "He / who said he'd come / by fire next time / lied," she reasons. "L.A. West, grand homes / dislodge from the mud, / foundations split. . . . The second coming comes / drop by drop / as the sea hums and rocks . . ." *In Danger* (Berkeley: Roundhouse Press, 1999), 67.

6. David Clarke, *Water and Art* (London: Reaktion Books, 2010), 8. One of the most ambitious recent attempts in verse to establish the ubiquitous presence and manifold significance of water is Brenda Hillman's volume *Practical Water* (Middletown, CT: Wesleyan University Press, 2009). Hillman pays considerable attention to the way commercial and governmental short-sightedness imperil the survival of nourishing bodies of water in northern and southern California.

7. John Haines, "Nineteen Thirty-One," *Michigan Quarterly Review* 16, no. 3 (Summer 1977): 258. Haines identifies the date of the Long Beach earthquake as 1931 but his description lines up exactly with the season and events of the 1933 earthquake on 10 March 1933.

The Long Beach earthquake registered 6.5 on the Richter scale. It ranks as the second deadliest quake in the history of California. Long Beach marks the southernmost segment of the Newport-Inglewood Fault system. Beverly Hills is part of that system and underwent a 3.3 earthquake on 2 September 2012—mild, but evidence of movement underground that citizens of the city rightly consider ominous.

8. David L. Ulin, *The Myth of Solid Ground: Earthquakes, Prediction, and the Fault Line between Reason and Faith* (Berkeley: University of California Press, 2004), 14.

9. Marshall Everett, *Complete Story of the San Francisco Earthquake* (Chicago: Bible House, 1906), 50.

10. Burton Pike, *The Image of the City in Modern Literature* (Princeton: Princeton University Press, 1981), 8.

11. See my discussion of 9/11 literature in "The Response of American Poets to 9/11: A Provisional Report," *Michigan Quarterly Review* 48, no. 1 (Winter 2009): 40–68. For commentary on the Wells and de Seversky books, see my book *The Flying Machine and Modern Literature* (Bloomington: Indiana University Press, 1986), Chapters 4 and 9.

12. Henri Coulette, "Quake," *The Collected Poems of Henri Coulette*, ed. Donald Justice and Robert Mezey (Fayetteville: University of Arkansas Press, 1990), 248.

13. Debora Greger, "Piranesi in L.A.," *and* (Princeton: Princeton University Press, 1985), 43. That cheerful optimism is on display in Judith Taylor's poem "Los Angeles Quotidian": "Last night that almost commonplace jolt: once, fiercely, then no more. / The psychic says not to worry: when the Big One hits, I'll be in Rangoon, Hong Kong,

Tierra del Fuego, Kuala Lampur, Jakarta, lah-de-dah." *Curios* (Louisville, KY: Sarabande Books, 2000), 54.

14. Charles Harper Webb, "You Missed the Earthquake, Bill," *Reading the Water* (Evanston: Northwestern University Press, 1997), 13–14.

15. The original anthology was published by Red Wind Books, in Los Angeles. A later edition is credited solely to Webb: *Stand Up Poetry: An Expanded Anthology*, ed. Charles Harper Webb (Iowa City: University of Iowa Press, 2002). I regret not having room in this book to consider some of the artful poets appearing in Webb's anthology, such as Bill Mohr, Laurel Ann Bogen, Gerald Locklin, Manazar Gamboa, Jim Krusoe, Jack Grapes, and Holly Prado. Bob Flanagan, Harry E. Northrup, and Scott Wannberg are other poets deserving of more attention from readers and critics focused on the Los Angeles scene.

16. Charles Harper Webb, "Invocation to Allen as the Muse Euterpe," *Reading the Water* (Boston: Northeastern University Press, 1997), 59–61. The face and body of a publicity seeker named Angelyne appeared on billboards mainly in Hollywood for years, arousing many commentaries about her campaign as the essence of Hollywood's, and Los Angeles's, devotion to surfaces and glamour. An imaginative treatment of this local icon appears in Charles Baxter's novel *The Soul Thief* (New York: Pantheon Books, 2008), 175–76. The billboards, declares the protagonist, are "dedicated to totally meaningless celebrity . . . this shopworn royalty figure, this majestic ruin, this queen without identity, this ex-beauty . . . as blank and as melancholy as fading beauty itself." See also Nik Van Brunt's poem "Los Angeles": "On the 101 South, en route to Max's house / Angelyne looks slyly down from her billboard, / A voluptuous, perfect Hollywood babe. / In reality, she's older than the speed limit." *From Totems to Hip-Hop*, ed. Ishmael Reed (New York: Thunder's Mouth Press, 2003), 65.

17. Carolyn See, *Golden Days* (1987; Berkeley: University of California Press, 1996), 190.

18. Dorothy Barresi, "Some Questions We Might Ask," *The Post-Rapture Diner* (Pittsburgh: University of Pittsburgh Press, 1996), 3–6. As often in poems analyzed in *Poetry Los Angeles*, the insistent "I" reference raises questions about autobiographical aspects of the narrative. Queried on this matter, Dorothy Barresi responded, "The references are from factual experience. Naturally things get embroidered a bit, but the stories are from my personal history." E-mail letter to the author, 8 October 2013.

19. Poems about earthquakes sometimes focus on some piece of furniture that will protect the speaker from injury. In Marsha de la O's prose poem "The Northridge Earthquake," it is the wooden chest bequeathed by her mother that comforts the speaker: "Mother described that chest many times, each with its suave dangerous stranger, pockets full of sweetmeats, out there, trolling in silent concentric curves, all the strangers she ever spoke of. *They all have a trunk large enough to wedge in a child's body*." As the speaker contemplates the chest, it moves away from her, out into the world, both ship and coffin. *Bear Flag Republic: Prose Poems and Poetics from California*, ed. Christopher Buckley

and Gary Young (Santa Cruz, CA: Greenhouse Review Press/Alcatraz Editions, 2008), 142–43.

20. The tsunami and resultant radiation leakage in Japan in March 2010, sending plumes of elevated radioactivity over the West Coast of the U.S., prompted some attitudes toward catastrophe that the poets in this essay would readily recognize: "This is a part of the world where people accept—perhaps even secretly enjoy—the reality that they may be living on the edge of disaster. . . . Californians are connoisseurs of calamity, well practiced at knowing, almost reflexively, how to weigh the approach of any fresh danger. Why fixate on something 10,000 miles away when the real thing [The Big One] looms over your daily existence?" Reported from Los Angeles by Adam Nagourney, "For Hardy Californians, Another Frisson of Danger," *The New York Times*, 19 March 2011, A17.

21. The other poem about Los Angeles in this canon-making anthology is Randall Jarrell's "Thinking of the Lost World." An excerpt from Anne Carson's long poem "TV Men" documents a "Death Valley Shoot"; Donald Davie's "In California" is set somewhere between Los Angeles and Santa Barbara; Charles Wright's "Laguna Blues" describes a Pacific site some fifty miles south of Los Angeles.

22. Joy Harjo, "The Path to the Milky Way Leads Through Los Angeles," *How We Became Human: New and Selected Poems 1975–2001* (New York: W. W. Norton, 2002), 141–42. I have used the artful lineation in this reprinting, rather than the more ragged version in the Norton anthology or the version in *A Map to the Next World: Poetry and Tales* (New York: W. W. Norton, 2000), which eschews stanza breaks.

23. Laura Coltelli, *Winged Words: American Indian Writers Speak* (Lincoln: University of Nebraska Press, 1990), 63–64.

9. Conclusion

1. Williams's lines occur in the opening passage of his long poem *Paterson* (1946). Lily Briscoe presents her aesthetic judgment in *To the Lighthouse* (1927; San Diego: Harcourt Brace Jovanovich, undated), 300.

2. Walker Percy, *The Moviegoer* (New York: Noonday Press, 1961), 63 [One; Section 7]. In a prose poem titled "Coca Cola" Martha Ronk laments a postmodern tendency, including among poets, that might be termed "decertification." Los Angeles, she claims, has become too abstract, too schematic in its lines of definition (for example, in its freeway structure) to be recognizable as a modern city. Citizens have lost "the thump of contact" so essential to the process of certification. "We don't go out," she asserts. "Today it's hard to get anyone to go anywhere but the movies: dark, safe, sensual, in an abstract sort of way, like coke. I know people who used to go everywhere, now watch TV every night. There is no city left, only threat and direction signs." That the aesthetics and ethics of Williams, Woolf, and Percy have devolved into a dystopia of abstraction, a "demise of language," calls attention to the need to write and read poems more palpable, more

located, more celebratory of people, places, and things. Martha Ronk, *Displeasures of the Table* (Copenhagen and Los Angeles: Green Integer, 2001), 90–91.

3. Walter Benjamin, "Theses on the Philosophy of History," *Illuminations*, ed. Hannah Arendt (New York: Schocken Books, 1969), 255.

4. In a prose poem disguised as art criticism, Peter Plagens elaborates on the "sabers of candescence" visible in the work of Ed Ruscha: "From a Greek-like high sun, whose baking rays speed unfettered through a dark sky and glance off hostile hills and a moodless Pacific, the light infuses everything. . . . New York is (by comparison, of course) vertical, cold, dark, and therefore rude, expensive, and criminal, whereas Los Angeles is horizontal, warm, light, and therefore (relatively, of course) friendly, cheap, and safe." Peter Plagens, "Golden Days," *Modern Art and Popular Culture: Readings in High and Low*, ed. Kirk Varnedoe and Adam Gopnik (New York: Museum of Modern Art and Harry N. Abrams, 1990), 226.

Chris Burden has emerged as a major Los Angeles artist in large part thanks to his massive installation *Urban Light* (2008) abutting the Los Angeles Museum of Art on Wilshire Boulevard. *Urban Light* consists of 202 antique street lights in even rows; they are alight during the hours of darkness in the city.

Scott Saul reports on some explanations for the uncanny light in Los Angeles: "A Cal Tech scientist, noting the number of significant discoveries made by the telescopes at Southern California locales such as Mount Wilson, Mount Palomar and the Griffith [Park] Observatory, explains how the ocean-cooled air floats from the west over the coastal plain, only to be trapped under the warmer flow coming from the desert on the east—prompting a stasis in the atmosphere that allows astronomers to view the stars without distortion. Environmental engineers in L.A., meanwhile, have coined the term *airlight* to describe the effect on the naked eye of pollutant particles, which do not simply obstruct the light but also bounce it back with a kind of ferocity." "'Mirage or No Mirage': Reading Los Angeles," http://www.bostonreview.net/BR28.6/saul.html [page 4].

5. Howard N. Fox, "Many Californias 1980–2000," *Made in California: Art, Image, and Identity, 1900–2000*, ed. Stephanie Barron, Sheri Bernstein, and Ilene Susan Fort (Los Angeles: Los Angeles County Museum of Art / University of California Press, 2000), 270. Fox may be thinking of an exhibit at the Museum of Contemporary Art curated by Paul Schimmel, "Helter Skelter: LA Art in the 1990s," which Kevin Starr characterizes as follows: "In this new show . . . the work of sixteen contemporary Los Angeles artists would be presented as a nether-world of sex, violence, perversity, and alienation spread through 45,000 square feet of exhibition space." *Coast of Dreams: California on the Edge, 1990–2003* (New York: Alfred A. Knopf, 2004), 131.

6. Kevin Starr, *Coast of Dreams*, 49. In this book, as so often in the recent scholarship about the city, the implied antagonist is Reyner Banham's foundational text, *Los Angeles: The Architecture of Four Ecologies* (1971).

7. Nik De Dominic, "September, Los Angeles," *Los Angeles Review* 10 (Fall 2011): 125–26.

8. Fyodor Dostoevsky, *Notes from Underground*, translated by Constance Garnett, part vi, paragraph 1.

9. E-mail letter from Nik De Dominic to Laurence Goldstein, 16 May 2012. The superficiality of his life anesthetizes the speaker, according to this letter, and renders him a stranger in his own experience of milieu, grasping for meaning and beauty but ultimately feeling himself to be a slacker in his stance toward the spectacle of significant events, a "prepackaged walking cliché."

Kevin Starr notes in *Coast of Dreams* that "by the early 2000s, the California Slacker—young white people going nowhere and caring even less—had become a recognizable stereotype" (630).

10. David L. Ulin, *The Myth of Solid Ground: Earthquakes, Prediction, and the Fault Line Between Reason and Faith* (New York: Penguin, 2004), 22.

11. Patty Seyburn, "surf," *mechanical cluster* (Columbus: Ohio State University Press, 2002), 14.

12. Dana Gioia, "Los Angeles After the Rain," *The Gods of Winter* (Saint Paul, MN: Graywolf Press, 1991), 58.

Selected Bibliography

Afary, Kamran. *Performance and Activism: Grassroots Discourse after the Los Angeles Riots of 1992*. Lanham, MD: Lexington Books, 2009.

Alexander, Elizabeth. *Body of Life*. Los Angeles: Tia Chucha Press, 1996.

Alter, Robert. *Imagined Cities: Urban Experience and the Language of the Novel*. New Haven and London: Yale University Press, 2005.

Avila, Eric. *Popular Culture in the Age of White Flight: Fear and Fantasy in Suburban Los Angeles*. Berkeley: University of California Press, 2004.

Bachelard, Gaston. *The Poetics of Space*. New York: Orion Press, 1964.

Banham, Reyner. *Los Angeles: The Architecture of Four Ecologies*. London: Penguin Press, 1971.

Barnes, Yolanda. *When It Burned to the Ground*. Louisville, KY: Sarabande Books, 2005.

Barnstone, Tony. *The Golem of Los Angeles*. Los Angeles: Red Hen Press, 2008.

Barresi, Dorothy. *American Fanatics*. Pittsburgh: University of Pittsburgh Press, 2010.

Barresi, Dorothy. *The Post-Rapture Diner*. Pittsburgh: University of Pittsburgh Press, 1996.

Barron, Stephanie, Sheri Bernstein, and Ilene Susan Fort. *Made in California: Art, Image, and Identity, 1900–2000*. Berkeley: University of California Press / Los Angeles County Museum of Art, 2000.

Bartlett, Lee. *The Sun Is But a Morning Star: Studies in West Coast Poetry and Poetics* Albuquerque: University of New Mexico Press, 1989.

Beach, Christopher. *Poetic Culture: Contemporary American Poetry between Community and Institution*. Evanston: Northwestern University Press, 1999.

Bidart, Frank. *Golden State*. New York: Braziller, 1973.

Bradley, Adam, and Andrew Dubois. *The Anthology of Rap*. New Haven: Yale University Press, 2010.

Braudy, Leo. *The Hollywood Sign*. New Haven: Yale University Press, 2011.

Buckley, Christopher, and Gary Young. *Bear Flag Republic: Prose Poems and Poetics from California*. Santa Cruz, CA: Greenfield Review Press/Alcatraz Editions, 2008.

Buell, Lawrence. *The Environmental Imagination: Thoreau, Nature Writing, and the Formation of American Culture*. Cambridge: Harvard University Press, 1995.

Bukowski, Charles. *Bone Palace Ballet: New Poems*. Santa Rosa: Black Sparrow Press, 1997.

Bukowski, Charles. *The Days Run Away Like Wild Horses Over The Hills*. Santa Rosa: Black Sparrow Press, 1974.

Bukowski, Charles. *Love Is A Dog From Hell*. Santa Rosa: Black Sparrow Press, 1990.

Calonne, David Stephen. *Bukowski*. London: Reaktion Books, 2012.

Cervantes, Lorna Dee. *Emplumada*. Pittsburgh: University of Pittsburgh Press, 1981.

Chang, Victoria. *Circle*. Carbondale: *Crab Orchard Review* and Southern Illinois University Press, 2005.

Christopher, Nicholas, ed. *Walk on the Wild Side: Urban Poetry Since 1975*. New York: Touchstone, 1994.

Clinton, Michèlle T. *High Blood / Pressure*. Los Angeles: West End Press, 1986.

Clinton, Michèlle T., Sesshu Foster, and Naomi Quinonez. *Invocation L.A.: Urban Multicultural Poetry*. Albuquerque: West End Press, 1989.

Coleman, Wanda. *African Sleeping Sickness: Stories & Poems*. Santa Rosa: Black Sparrow Press, 1990.

Coleman, Wanda. *Ostinato Vamps*. Pittsburgh: University of Pittsburgh Press, 2003.

Cooper, Dennis. *The Dream Police: Selected Poems*. New York: Grove Press, 1995.

Coulette, Henri. *The Collected Poems of Henri Coulette*, ed. Donald Justice and Robert Mezey. Fayetteville: University of Arkansas Press, 1990.

Davis, Mike. *City of Quartz: Excavating the Future in Los Angeles*. London: Verso, 1990, 2006.

Davis, Mike. *Ecology of Fear: Los Angeles and the Imagination of Disaster.* New York: Metropolitan Books, 1998.

Debord, Guy. *The Society of the Spectacle.* Trans. Donald Nicholson Smith. New York: Zone Books, 1995.

De Dominic, Nik. "September, Los Angeles." *The Los Angeles Review* 10 (Fall 2011): 125–26.

Deverell, William, and Greg Hise. *A Companion to Los Angeles.* West Sussex, UK: Wiley-Blackwell, 2010.

Didion, Joan. *Play It As It Lays.* New York: Farrar, Straus & Giroux, 1970.

Didion, Joan. *Slouching Towards Bethlehem.* New York: Farrar, Straus & Giroux, 1968.

Didion, Joan. *The White Album.* New York: Simon & Schuster, 1979.

Everett, Marshall. *Complete Story of the San Francisco Earthquake.* Chicago: Bible House, 1906.

Fine, David. *Imagining Los Angeles: A City in Fiction.* Albuquerque: University of New Mexico Press, 2000.

Fine, David, ed. *Los Angeles in Fiction.* Albuquerque: University of New Mexico Press, 1984.

Foley, Jack. *Visions and Affiliations: A California Literary Time Line, 1940–2005.* Two volumes. Berkeley, CA: Pantograph Press, 2011.

Garcia, Richard. *Rancho Notorious.* Rochester, NY: BOA Editions, 2001.

Ginsberg, Allen. *Collected Poems 1947–1980.* New York: Harper & Row, 1984.

Gioia, Dana. *Pity the Beautiful.* Minneapolis: Graywolf Press, 2012.

Gioia, Dana. *The Gods of Winter.* Saint Paul, MN: Graywolf Press, 1991.

Gioia, Dana, Chryss Yost, and Jack Hicks, eds. *California Poetry: From the Gold Rush to the Present.* Berkeley: Heyday Books, 2004.

Goldstein, Laurence. *A Room in California.* Evanston: Northwestern University Press, 2005.

Goldstein, Laurence. *The American Poet at the Movies: A Literary History.* Ann Arbor: University of Michigan Press, 1994.

Goodyear, Dana. *The Oracle of Hollywood Boulevard.* New York: W. W. Norton, 2013.

Gullans, Charles. *The Bright Universe and Other Poems.* Omaha: Abattoir Editions, 1983.

Harjo, Joy. *How We Became Human: New and Selected Poems 1975–2001.* New York: W. W. Norton, 2002.

Harms, James. *Freeways and Aqueducts*. Pittsburgh: Carnegie Mellon University Press, 2004.

Harms, James. *The Joy Addict*. Pittsburgh: Carnegie Mellon University Press, 1998.

Harms, James. *Quarters*. Pittsburgh: Carnegie Mellon University Press, 2001.

Hass, Robert. *Time and Materials*. New York: HarperCollins, 2007.

Hayden, Dolores. *The Power of Place: Urban Landscapes as Public History*. Cambridge: MIT Press, 1995.

Healy, Eloise Klein. *A Wild Surmise: New & Selected Poems & Recordings*. Pasadena: Red Hen Press, 2013.

Hirschman, Jack. *Front Lines: Selected Poems*. San Francisco: City Lights, 2002.

Homes, A. M. *Los Angeles: People, Places, and the Castle on the Hill*. Washington, DC: National Geographic, 2002.

Hongo, Garrett. *The River of Heaven*. New York: Alfred A. Knopf, 1988.

Houston, James D. *Californians: Searching for the Golden State*. New York: Alfred A. Knopf, 1982.

James, David E., ed. *The Sons and Daughters of Los: Culture and Community in L.A.* Philadelphia: Temple University Press, 2003.

Jarman, Mark. *Bone Fires: New and Selected Poems*. Louisville, KY: Sarabande Books, 2011.

Jarrell, Randall. *The Complete Poems*. New York: Farrar, Straus & Giroux, 1969.

Johnston, John H. *The Poet and the City: A Study in Urban Perspectives*. Athens: University of Georgia Press, 1984.

Kelley, Robin D. G. "kickin' reality, kickin' ballistics: gangsta rap and postindustrial los angeles." *droppin' science: critical essays on rap music and hip hop culture*, 117–58. Philadelphia: Temple University Press, 1996.

Klein, Norman M. *The History of Forgetting: Los Angeles and the Erasure of Memory*. London: Verso, 1997.

Kotkin, Joel. *The City*. New York: Modern Library, 2005.

Lehan, Richard. *The City in Literature: An Intellectual and Cultural History*. Berkeley and Los Angeles: University of California Press, 1998.

Lindsay, Vachel. *The Art of the Moving Picture*. 2nd ed. New York: Liveright, [1915], 1970.

Lipsitz, George. *Time Passages: Collective Memory and American Popular Culture*. Minneapolis: University of Minnesota Press, 1990.

Lipton, Lawrence. *Bruno in Venice West and Other Poems*. Van Nuys: Venice West Publishers, 1976.

Lummis, Suzanne, and Charles H. Webb. *Grand Passion: The Poets of Los Angeles and Beyond*. Los Angeles: Red Wind Books, 1995.

Lummis, Suzanne. *In Danger*. Berkeley, CA: Roundhouse Press, 1999.

MacAdams, Lewis. *The River: Books One, Two, Three*. Santa Cruz, CA: Blue Press, 2007.

Maio, Samuel. *The Burning of Los Angeles*. Kirksville, MO: Thomas Jefferson University Press, 1997.

May, Kirse Granat. *Golden State, Golden Youth: The California Image in Popular Culture, 1955–1966*. Chapel Hill: University of North Carolina Press, 2001.

Maynard, John Arthur. *Venice West: The Beat Generation in Southern California*. New Brunswick and London: Rutgers University Press, 1991.

McClung, William Alexander. *Landscapes of Desire: Anglo Mythologies of Los Angeles*. Berkeley: University of California Press, 2000.

McGrath, Thomas. *Letter to an Imaginary Friend, Parts 1 & 2*. Chicago: Swallow Press, 1962, 1970.

McMichael, James. *Four Good Things*. Boston: Houghton Mifflin, 1980.

McNamara, Kevin R., ed. *The Cambridge Companion to the Literature of Los Angeles*. Cambridge: Cambridge University Press, 2010.

Michaels, Leonard, David Reid, and Raquel Scherr, eds. *West of the West: Imagining California*. San Francisco: North Point Press, 1989.

Miller, J. Hillis. *Poets of Reality: Six Twentieth Century Writers*. Cambridge: Harvard University Press, 1965.

Mitchell, W. J. T. *Landscape and Power*. Chicago: University of Chicago Press, 1994.

Mohr, Bill. *Hold-Outs: The Los Angeles Poetry Renaissance, 1948–1992*. Iowa City: University of Iowa Press, 2011.

Mohr, Bill. *"Poetry Loves Poetry": An Anthology of Los Angeles Poets*. Los Angeles: Momentum Press, 1985.

Monette, Paul. *Borrowed Time: An AIDS Memoir*. San Diego: Harcourt Brace Jovanovich, 1988.

Monette, Paul. *West of Yesterday, East of Summer: New and Selected Poems (1973–1993)*. New York: St. Martin's Press, 1994.

Mullen, Harryette. *The Cracks Between What We Are and What We Are Supposed to Be*. Tuscaloosa: University of Alabama Press, 2012.

Mosley, Walter. *White Butterfly*. New York: W. W. Norton, 1992.

Murphet, Julian. *Literature and Race in Los Angeles*. Cambridge: Cambridge University Press, 2001.

Muske-Dukes, Carol. *An Octave above Thunder: New and Selected Poems*. New York: Penguin Books, 1997.

Muske-Dukes, Carol. *Sparrow*. New York: Random House, 2003.

Novak, Estelle Gershgoren. *Poets of the Non-Existent City: Los Angeles in the McCarthy Era*. Albuquerque: University of New Mexico Press, 2002.

Orfalea, Gregory. *Angeleno Days: An Arab American Writer on Family, Place, and Politics*. Tucson: University of Arizona Press, 2009.

Orr, David. "Beach Reading." *Poetry* 190, no. 4 (July–August 2007): 313–20.

Ovnick, Merry. *Los Angeles: The End of the Rainbow*. Los Angeles: Balcony Press, 1994.

Perloff, Marjorie. *Radical Artifice: Writing Poetry in the Age of Media*. Chicago: University of Chicago Press, 1991.

Pike, Burton. *The Image of the City in Modern Literature*. Princeton: Princeton University Press, 1981.

Pleasants, Ben. *Visceral Bukowski: Inside the Sniper Landscape of L.A. Writers*. Northville, MI: Sun Dog Press, 2004.

Rayner, Richard. *A Bright and Guilty Place: Murder, Corruption, and L.A.'s Scandalous Coming of Age*. New York: Anchor Books, 2010.

Rebolledo, Tey, and Eliana S. Rivero. *Infinite Divisions: An Anthology of Chicana Literature*. Tucson and London: University of Arizona Press, 1993.

Reid, David, ed. *Sex, Death and God in L.A.* New York: Pantheon Books, 1992.

Rieff, David. *Los Angeles: Capital of the Third World*. New York: Simon & Schuster, 1991.

Rodríguez, Aleida. *Garden of Exile*. Louisville, KY: Sarabande Books, 1999.

Rodríguez, Luis J. *My Nature Is Hunger: New and Selected Poems 1989–2004*. Willimantic, CT: Curbstone Press, 2005.

Rolfe, Lionel. *Literary L. A.* Rev. ed. Los Angeles: California Classics Books, 2002.

Sawhney, Deepak Narang, ed. *Unmasking L.A.: Third Worlds and the City*. London: Palgrave, 2002.

Schevill, James. *The Complete American Fantasies*. Athens: Swallow Press/Ohio University Press, 1996.

Schnauber, Cornelius. *Hollywood Haven: Homes and Haunts of the European Emigrés and Exiles in Los Angeles*. Trans. Barbara Zeisl Schoenberg. Riverside, CA: Ariadne Press, 1992.

See, Carolyn. *Golden Days*. Berkeley: University of California Press, [1987], 1996.

Seidel, Frederick. *Poems 1959–1979*. New York: Alfred A. Knopf, 1989.

Seyburn, Patty. *mechanical cluster*. Columbus: Ohio State University Press, 2002.

Shapiro, Karl. *Selected Poems*. New York: Random House, 1968.

Sharpe, William Chapman. *Unreal Cities: Urban Figuration in Wordsworth, Baudelaire, Whitman, Eliot, and Williams*. Baltimore and London: Johns Hopkins University Press, 1990.

Sides, Josh. *L.A. City Limits: African American Los Angeles from the Great Depression to the Present*. Berkeley: University of California Press, 2003.

Sikelianos, Eleni. *The California Poem*. Minneapolis: Coffee House Press, 2004.

Simpson, Mona. *Anywhere But Here*. New York: Alfred A. Knopf, 1986.

Smith, Richard Cándida. *Utopia and Dissent: Art, Poetry and Politics in California*. Berkeley: University of California Press, 1995.

Smith, RJ. *The Great Black Way: L.A. in the 1940s and the Lost African-American Renaissance*. New York: Public Affairs, 2006.

Soja, Edward. *Thirdspace: Journeys to Los Angeles and Other Real-and-Imagined Places*. Oxford: Basil Blackwell, 1996.

Sounes, Howard. *Charles Bukowski: Locked in the Arms of a Crazy Life*. Edinburgh: Rebel, 1998.

Starr, Kevin. *Coast of Dreams*. New York: Alfred A. Knopf, 2004.

Starr, Kevin. *Golden Dreams: California in an Age of Abundance , 1950–1963*. New York: Oxford University Press, 2009.

Starr, Kevin. *Material Dreams: Southern California Through the 1920s*. New York: Oxford University Press, 1990.

Steele, Timothy. *Toward the Winter Solstice*. Athens: Swallow Press / Ohio University Press, 2006.

Stilgoe, John R. *Landscape and Images*. Charlottesville: University of Virginia Press, 2005.

St. John, David. *The Face: A Novella in Verse*. New York: HarperCollins, 2004.

Suntree. Susan. *Sacred Sites: The Secret History of Southern California*. Lincoln: University of Nebraska Press, 2010.

Theroux, Peter. *Translating L.A.: A Tour of the Rainbow City*. New York: W. W. Norton, 1994.

Thompson, William Irwin. *At the Edge of History*. New York: Harper & Row, 1971.

Timberg, Scott, and Dana Gioia. *The Misread City: New Literary Los Angeles*. Los Angeles: Red Hen Press, 2003.

Trinidad, David. *Dear Prudence: New and Selected Poems*. New York: Turtle Point Press, 2011.

Troupe, Quincey. *Transcircularities: New and Selected Poems*. Minneapolis: Coffee House Press, 2002.

Tuma, Keith. *Rainbow Darkness: An Anthology of African American Poetry*. Oxford, OH: Miami University Press, 2003.

Ulin, David L., ed. *Another City: Writing from Los Angeles*. San Francisco: City Lights, 2001.

Ulin, David L. *The Myth of Solid Ground: Earthquakes, Prediction, and the Fault Line Between Reason and Faith*. New York: Viking/Penguin, 2004.

Ulin, David L., ed. *Writing Los Angeles: A Literary Anthology*. New York: Library of America, 2002.

Uyematsu, Amy. *Nights of Fire, Nights of Rain*. Brownsville, OR: Story Line Press, 1998.

Uyematsu, Amy. *30 Miles from J-Town*. Brownsville, OR: Story Line Press, 1992.

Valdés, Gina. *Comiendo Lumbre / Easting Fire*. Colorado Springs: Maize Press, 1986.

Vangelisti, Paul, with Evan Calbi, eds. *L. A. Exile: Guide to Los Angeles Writing 1932–1998*. New York: Marsilio, 1999.

Vargas, Joao H. Costa. *Catching Hell in the City of Angels*. Minneapolis: University of Minnesota Press, 2005.

von Hallberg, Robert. *American Poetry and Culture, 1945–1980*. Cambridge: Harvard University Press, 1985.

Wakoski, Diane. *Medea the Sorceress*. Santa Rosa: Black Sparrow Press, 1991.

Walcott, Derek. *The Arkansas Testament*. New York: Farrar, Straus & Giroux, 1987.

Walker, Franklin. *A Literary History of Southern California*. Berkeley and Los Angeles: University of California Press, 1950.

Watts, Jennifer A., and Claudia Bohm-Spector, eds. *This Side of Paradise: Body and Landscape in Los Angeles Photographs*. London and New York: Merrell, 2008.

Webb, Charles Harper. *Reading the Water*. Boston: Northeastern University Press, 1997.

Webb, Charles Harper, ed. *Stand Up Poetry: An Expanded Anthology*. Iowa City: University of Iowa Press, 2002.

Weisburd, Mel. *A Life of Windows & Mirrors: Selected Poems 1948–2005*. Marina Del Rey, CA: Conflu:X Press, 2005.

West, Nathanael. *Miss Lonelyhearts & The Day of the Locust*. New York: New Directions, 1962.

Whiting, Cécile. *Pop L.A.: Art and the City in the 1960s*. Berkeley: University of California Press, 2006.

Widener, Daniel. *Black Arts West: Culture and Struggle in Postwar Los Angeles*. Durham: University of North Carolina Press, 2010.

Wilentz, Amy. *I Feel Earthquakes More Often Than They Happen: Coming to California in the Age of Schwarzenegger*. New York: Simon & Schuster, 2006.

Wojahn, David. *Mystery Train*. Pittsburgh: University of Pittsburgh Press, 1990.

Wright, Charles. *The World of the Ten Thousand Things: Poems 1980–1990*. New York: Farrar, Straus & Giroux, 1990.

Wronsky, Gail. *Dying for Beauty*. Port Townsend, WA: Copper Canyon Press, 2000.

Wyatt, David. *The Fall into Eden: Landscape and Imagination in California*. Cambridge: Cambridge University Press, 1986.

Wyatt, David. *Five Fires: Race, Catastrophe, and the Shaping of California*. Reading, MA: Addison-Wesley, 1997.

Yenser, Stephen. *Blue Guide*. Chicago: University of Chicago Press, 2006.

Zahn, Curtis, and John Brander. *One Ocean One Sky*. Los Angeles: Ars Poetica Press / Pacificus Foundation, 1992.

Acknowledgments

A study like this one depends principally on access to a vast number of books and journals published during the last seventy years—volumes of poetry above all, and criticism that comments on them. As if the writing of *Poetry Los Angeles* had been guiding my professional life since I entered UCLA as an undergraduate in 1960, and perhaps it has, I accumulated a personal collection almost sufficient to serve as a private resource for my needs in selecting poems to analyze and for models of exposition.

From 1960 to the present I have depended on the collections in great libraries to amplify my knowledge of contemporary literature and its treatment of the poetry of place. The libraries of the University of California, Los Angeles, Brown University, and the University of Michigan became the indispensable public resources for my research. I remember with special fondness the Harris Collection of American Poetry in the John Hay Library at Brown University, where I spent a plenitude of hours reading and taking notes on the works that would nourish my sense of the field and strengthen my desire to write some extended commentary deserving of attention about my city of origin. The Special Collections Library at the University of Michigan, under the able leadership of Peggy Daub, has served my needs for more than forty years.

Once I began to focus on the topic of poems about Los Angeles I relied on the advice and experience of many poets and scholars I had become acquainted with as editor for thirty-two years of *Michigan Quarterly Review*. One of these was Charles Harper Webb, with whom I exchanged views about poetry about Los Angeles, on numerous occasions. He directed me to some of the obvious places to spend time and buy *many* poetry journals and books by Los Angeles poets, such as the bookstores Papa Bach and Beyond Baroque. Through the latter institution I came into contact with many poets and some scholars who challenged me usefully as my ideas about the relation of the city to its poets, including the "carpetbaggers" who visited the city and wrote compellingly about it, took form. Estelle Gershgoren Novak contributed to my understanding of the topic as well, in conversations and by way of her excellent anthology of the *California Quarterly* and *Coastlines* poets of the 1950s. Thanks to her I was able to meet some of those poets and try out theories that advanced my understanding of local literary history in the process.

Leo Braudy has been a valued friend and an expert on the subject of Los Angeles, who over decades encouraged me to undertake this project and helped steer me toward the issues I needed to engage in order to make my opinions credible and persuasive. Carolyn See, my freshman composition instructor in 1960 and a valued friend ever since, provided irreverent commentaries on authors whom she nevertheless accounted indispensable for sustained treatment in this book, and in several cases brought me together with poets I needed to interrogate not only about their work but about the attitudes of two generations of authors fashioning texts destined for posterity's regard. I am thankful also to good friends such as William Baer, Charles Baxter, George Bornstein, Alice Fulton, Linda Gregerson, A. Van Jordan, Lawrence Joseph, Laura Kasischke, David Lehman, Helen Marlborough, Khaled Mattawa, J. Allyn Rosser, Barbara Zeisl Schoenberg, Barton St. Armand, Keith Taylor, Gillian White, and Steven Zwicker for conversation, letters, and advice on the issues arising in this study.

The Department of English, University of Michigan, has been generous in indulging my ongoing obsession with this general area of studies. I received exemplary support for my numerous courses, especially during the last ten years, on the undergraduate and graduate level: The Literature of Los Angeles, Modern Poetry and the City, Hollywood and Visual Culture, Modern Poetry, and Contemporary Poetry. I need hardly say that my students in those and other courses rank among my most essential helpers in this enterprise. They spoke and wrote passionately about many of the poems and authors I discuss in this book. I single out Nick Richie, my research assistant, for his help in identifying relevant poems, as well as libraries that could and did provide me with esoteric literary magazines and poetry volumes. I am grateful to the Department of English as well, and to the College of Literature, Arts, and Sciences at the University of Michigan, for research grants and sabbaticals that contributed to the composition and completion of this book.

Once I began work on *Poetry Los Angeles*, and especially when I completed a first draft of the manuscript, I turned to friends who were generous about reading portions or the entirety of the text. Michael Anderegg, a friend from elementary school in Culver City who matriculated along with me through levels of secondary school and university work, brought expertise from his film studies, especially, and his knowledge of the facts on the ground. Alan Wald, a scholar of the radical and popular literature of Los Angeles, laid out some alternate pathways into the topic that influenced the final manuscript significantly. Mark Halliday read a portion of the final product and suggested ways of achieving a style and tone that kept a balance between the formal and informal, the personal and the academic.

One person I had not previously met in my visits to Los Angeles, Bill Mohr, whose book on the history of communities, journals, and presses in Los Angeles, *Hold-Outs: The Los Angeles Poetry Renaissance 1948–1992*, is an indispensable complement to my own work, scrutinized my penultimate version of the manuscript in detail. A fine poet himself, he provided me with shrewd advice for a final revision based on his extraordinary knowledge of the poets and poems at issue.

I owe a special debt of gratitude to LeAnn Fields, my editor at the Press, who has helped me prepare many volumes I have written, edited, or co-edited for publication. From the very beginning, when I broached the subject of this book, she has encouraged and guided me toward the final version, always with good cheer and a knowledge of writing and publishing that is unmatched in my experience of editors. Alexa Ducsay not only formatted the manuscript but fielded numerous questions and resolved multiple quandaries as the project proceeded through the Press.

This book could not have been written without the help of my wife, Nancy Goldstein, author of a biography of Jackie Ormes published by the University of Michigan Press. She has read every word of this and early drafts of *Poetry Los Angeles*, offering innumerable suggestions almost always perfectly apt, and never flagged in her support for the project. My sons, Andrew and Jonathan, have brought their experiences in Los Angeles to bear in the form of useful questions and remarks on the poets' sometimes odd angles of regard on the city.

Grateful acknowledgment is given to the following publishers and individuals for permission to reprint the poems that appear in this book. Every attempt has been made to locate the copyright holders.

Elizabeth Alexander, "Stravinsky in L.A." from *Body of Life*. Copyright ©1996 and 2009 by Elizabeth Alexander. Permission granted by Elizabeth Alexander; Mary Armstrong, "Freeway Shooting" from *Grand Passion: The Poets of Los Angeles and Beyond*, ed. Suzanne Lummis and Charles H. Webb. Red Wind Books, 1995. Copyright © 1995. Reprinted by permission of Mary Armstrong; Jimmy Santiago Baca, "These Hands" from *Unmasking L.A.: Third Worlds and the City*, ed. Narang Sawhney. Palgrave Macmillan, 2002. Copyright © 2002. Reprinted by permission of Jimmy Santiago Baca; Dorothy Barresi, "Some Questions We Might Ask" from *The Post-Rapture Diner*. Copyright © 1996. Reprinted by permission of The University of Pittsburgh Press; Charles Bukowski, "To Hell with Robert Schumann" from *The Days Run Away Like Wild Horses Over the Hills*. Copyright © 1969 by Charles Bukowski. "beach trip" from *Love Is a Dog from Hell*. Copyright © 1977 by Charles Bukowski. "born again" from *The Flash of Lightning Behind the Mountain*. Copyright © 2004 by Ecco Press. Reprinted by permission of HarperCollins Publishers; Victoria Chang, "Gamble House" from *Circle*. *Crab Orchard Review* and Southern Illinois University Press. Copyright © 2005. Reprinted by permission of Victoria Chang; Wanda Coleman, "Los Angeles Nocturne" from *Ostinato Vamps*. Copyright © 2003. Reprinted by permission of the University of Pittsburgh Press; Wanda Coleman, "Where I Live" from *African Sleeping Sickness*. Copyright © 1990 by Black Sparrow Press. Reprinted by permission of Wanda Coleman; Nik De Dominic, "September, Los Angeles" from *The Los Angeles Review*, Volume 10 (Fall 2011). Copyright © 2011 by Nik De Dominic. Reprinted by permission of Nik De Dominic; Richard Garcia, "Vernon" from *Rancho Notorious*. Copyright © 2001 by Richard Garcia. Reprinted by permission of The Permissions Company, Inc. on behalf of BOA Editions; Dana Gioia, "The Freeways Considered as Earth Gods" from *Pity the Beautiful*. Copyright © Dana Gioia. Permission granted by The Permissions Company, Inc. on behalf of Graywolf Press; Dana Goodyear, "Freeway" from *The Oracle of Hollywood Boulevard: Poems*. Copyright © 2013 by Dana Goodyear. Used by permission of W. W. Norton & Company, Inc.; Joy Harjo, "The Path to the Milky Way Leads Through Los Angeles" from *A Map to the Next World: Poems and Tales* by Joy Harjo. Copyright © 2000 by Joy Harjo. Used by permission of W. W. Norton & Company, Inc.; James Harms, "The Dodgers, 1958" from *Freeways*

& Aqueducts. Copyright © 2004 by James Harms. "Gridlock" from *Quarters*. Copyright © 2001 by James Harms. Both reprinted with the permission of The Permissions Company, Inc., on behalf of Carnegie Mellon University Press, www.cmu.edu/universitypress; Eloise Klein Healy, "This Darknight Speed" from *A Wild Surmise: New & Selected Poems & Recordings*. Copyright © 2013 by Eloise Klein Healy. Reprinted by permission of Eloise Klein Healy; Garrett Hongo, "The Underworld" from *The River of Heaven*. Copyright © 1988 by Garrett Hongo. Permission to reprint granted by Random House, Inc.; Robert Hass, "Old Movie with the Sound Turned Off" from *Time and Materials*. Copyright © 2007 by Robert Hass. Permission granted by HarperCollins Publishers; Mark Jarman, "The Supremes" from *Bone Fires: New and Selected Poems*. Copyright © 1985 by Mark Jarman. Reprinted with the permission of The Permissions Company, Inc., on behalf of Sarabande Books, www.sarabandebooks.org; Suzanne Lummis, "Shangri-La" from *In Danger*. Copyright © 1999 by Suzanne Lummis. Reprinted by permission of Suzanne Lummis; Lewis MacAdams, "To Artesia" from *The River: Books One, Two & Three*. Copyright © 1998, 2005, 2007 by Lewis MacAdams. Reprinted by permission of Lewis MacAdams; Harryette Mullen, "#6 Sepulveda" from *Rainbow Darkness: An Anthology of African American Poetry*, ed. Keith Tuma. Copyright © 2003 by Harryette Mullen. Reprinted with permission from Harryette Mullen; Carol Muske-Dukes, "Little L.A. Villanelle" from *Red Trousseau: Poems* by Carol Muske. Copyright © 1993 by Carol Muske. Used by permission of Viking Penguin, a division of Penguin Group (USA) Inc.; "The Image," from *Sparrow* by Carol Muske-Dukes. Copyright © 2003 by Carol Muske-Dukes. Used by permission of Random House, Inc. Any third party use of this material, outside of this publication, is prohibited. Interested parties must apply directly to Random House, Inc. for permission; Aleida Rodríguez, "My Mother's Art" from *Garden of Exile*. Copyright © 1999 by Aleida Rodríguez. Reprinted with permission of The Permissions Company, Inc. on behalf of Sarabande Books, www.sarabandebooks.org; James Schevill, "Song of Aeterna 27 Over Los Angeles" from *The Complete American Fantasies*. Copyright © 1996 by James Schevill. This material is used by permission of Ohio University Press, www.ohioswallow.com; Frederick Seidel, "1968" from Poems 1959-1979. Copyright © 1980 by Frederick Seidel. Used by permission of Farrar, Straus and Giroux; Karl Shapiro, "Hollywood" from *Selected Poems*. Copyright © 1968 by Karl Shapiro. Reprinted by permission of Harold Ober Associates; Patty Seyburn, "surf" from *mechanical cluster*. Copyright © 2002. Used by permission of

The Ohio State University Press; Gary Soto, "Good Buy in Beverly Hills" from *One Kind of Faith*. Copyright © 2003 by Chronicle Books. Used with permission of Gary Soto; Timothy Steele, "Daybreak, Benedict Canyon" from *Toward the Winter Solstice*. Copyright © 2006 by Timothy Steele. This material is used by permission of Ohio University Press, www.ohioswallow.com; David Trinidad, "Hockney: Blue Pool" from *Dear Prudence: New and Selected Poems*. Copyright © Turtle Point Press, 2011. Reprinted with permission of Jonathan D. Rabinowitz; Gina Valdés, "Where You From?" from *Comiendo Lumbre / Eating Fire*. Copyright © by Maize Press. Permission granted by Gina Valdés; Diane Wakoski, "The Orange" from *Medea the Sorceress*. Copyright © 1991 by Diane Wakoski. Used by permission of David R. Godine, Publishers; Derek Walcott, "Summer Elegies, Part 2" from *The Arkansas Testament*. Copyright © 1987 by Derek Walcott. Reprinted by permission of Farrar, Straus and Giroux, LLC; Charles Harper Webb, "You Missed the Earthquake, Bill" from *Reading the Water*, Northeastern Press. Copyright © 1997 by Charles Harper Webb. Reprinted with permission by Charles Harper Webb; David Wojahn, "History Being Made: Melcher Production Studios, Los Angeles, 1968" by David Wojahn from *Mystery Train*. Copyright © 1990. Reprinted by permission of the University of Pittsburgh Press; Curtis Zahn, "Tijuana" from *Poets of the Non-Existent City*, ed. Estelle Gershgoren Novak. Copyright © 2002 by Estelle Gershgoren Novak. Reprinted by permission of James W. Breed of the Pacificus Foundation.

Index

Poetry Los Angeles braids each poem within a discourse of affinities with other literary texts, with artworks in other media, and with historical events and personalities. Not every name or theme is cited in the Index, but every effort has been made throughout the triage process to guide the reader to locations in the book pertinent to a range of likely interests. Citations from Notes include only materials with commentary